Complete Poetry of James Agee

James Agee. Photograph by Florence Homolka.

The Works of

James Agee

Volume 6

General Editor
Hugh Davis

General Editor Emeritus
Michael A. Lofaro

Complete Poetry of James Agee

Michael A. Lofaro, Editor

Jesse Graves, Associate Editor

The Works of
James Agee
Volume 6

General Editor
Hugh Davis

General Editor Emeritus
Michael A. Lofaro

The University of Tennessee Press / Knoxville

Frontispiece: James Agee by Florence Homolka. Courtesy of and © Vincent Homolka and Laurence Homolka and courtesy of Special Collections, University of Tennessee Library.

Library of Congress Cataloging-in-Publication Data

NAMES: Agee, James, 1909–1955, author. | Lofaro, Michael A., 1948– editor. | Graves, Jesse, 1973– editor.

TITLE: Complete poetry of James Agee / Michael A. Lofaro, editor ; Jesse Graves, associate editor.

DESCRIPTION: Knoxville : The University of Tennessee Press, [2024] |

SERIES: The works of James Agee ; volume 6 | Includes bibliographical references and index. |

SUMMARY: "Knoxville-born James Agee was a prolific writer, film critic, and journalist whose output garnered him a Pulitzer Prize (granted posthumously for *A Death in the Family*) and whose journalistic opus *Let Us Now Praise Famous Men* is regarded as a canonical text for both journalists and literary scholars. While Agee published one volume of poetry in 1934, no definitive collection of it has been attempted until now. Lofaro and Graves have spent years plumbing the depths of Agee's archives to put together the *Complete Poetry of James Agee* which includes an introduction, textual commentary and notes, and all of Agee's extant poetry to date" — Provided by publisher.

IDENTIFIERS: LCCN 2024034595 | ISBN 9781621909125 (cloth)

SUBJECTS: LCGFT: Poetry.

CLASSIFICATION: LCC PS3501.G35 C66 2024 | DDC 811/.52—dc23/eng/20240911

LC record available at https://lccn.loc.gov/2024034595

To Nancy D. Lofaro and
To Lisa Graves

Contents

Acknowledgments

We wish to thank the libraries of the University of Tennessee, the Ransom Humanities Research Center of the University of Texas, Harvard University, and The James Agee Trust for their permissions, which allow the use of all the Agee materials in this volume, and to thank their professional staffs for their kindness and untiring efforts on our behalf.

Michael A. Lofaro's efforts have greatly benefited from the time provided by the John C. Hodges Better English Fund of the Department of English and the financial support of the Senior Research and Creative Achievement Award of the College of Arts and Sciences, the Humanities Initiative, and the Office of Research, all of the University of Tennessee. He has likewise benefited from the encouragement and information provided by friends and colleagues over the years, of whom I here mention but a few: David Moltke-Hansen, Hugh Davis, Paul Ashdown, Paul Sprecher, Deedee Agee, and D. Strong Wyman, all either made this volume possible or far better than it would have been.

Jesse Graves would like to acknowledge the support of East Tennessee State University's Research Development Committee for a Major Research Grant to spend time at the Harvard University Special Collections and Archives, and a Small Grant to hire a graduate student assistant for summer editorial help. Jesse Graves thanks Robert Morgan, Randall Wilhelm, Thomas Alan Holmes, and Hugh Davis for offering support and guidance on this and other projects, and most especially Michael A. Lofaro for inviting him to take part in this labor of love: working on the poetry of James Agee, his hometown literary hero.

Several graduate student assistants at both the University of Tennessee and East Tennessee State University helped in the development of this book, such as Jesse Graves (who began as a research assistant long ago and is now associate editor on this volume), Joshua Robbins, Katie Burnett, Matthew P. Smith, Jessica Hall, Jonathan Hill, Adam Timbs, Samantha Campbell, and Courtney Harvey.

Any shortcomings or errors, however, are certainly our own.

Michael A. Lofaro's wife Nancy and adult children Ellen and Christopher and their respective spouses, Harry and Caitlin, have long been in the storm of Agee, but always managed to muster an enthusiasm for it. They energized me and my labors as a researcher and editor and made them truly enjoyable. Jesse Graves thanks his wife Lisa and daughter Chloe for sharing their own love of Agee's work in support of this project, and his mother, Joy Graves, who kept a copy of Agee's novel *A Death in the Family* on her bookshelf and has always encouraged all his reading and writing.

Critical Introduction

Jesse Graves

James Agee wrote with a prodigious talent[1] that led his lifelong friend and preparatory school mentor, Father James Harold Flye, to call Agee "a sovereign prince of the English language" in the opening credits of the Oscar-nominated 1980 documentary film, *Agee*.[2] As Father Flye utters this phrase, the film shifts to the word "AGEE" in red capital letters in a handwritten style over a distant view of several men shaking hands on an outdoor porch. As the camera draws nearer, one of these men turns out to be the then-sitting President of the United States, Jimmy Carter, who goes on to speak eloquently about his experiences reading James Agee's work. A viewer could have little doubt of the resonance and cultural importance of Agee and his writing after such a dramatic opening, and the film follows Agee through to the end, lingering over phases of his life and different aspects of his work. Agee's sonorous and poetic writing style is pointed out all throughout the film by almost everyone who speaks about him, though the writing of Agee's actual poetry is never once mentioned.[3] However, James Agee made his debut as the winner of the most prestigious first-book publication in American poetry, the Yale Younger Poets Prize for *Permit Me Voyage*. This fact may surprise casual readers who recognize Agee's name from his Pulitzer Prize-winning novel *A Death in the Family*, his legendarily ambitious book of journalism *Let Us Now Praise Famous Men*,[4] his Hollywood screenplays, his magazine writing, or perhaps his role as America's first widely circulated movie critic who insisted upon interpreting film as an art form. Agee's poetry may have been overshadowed by his celebrated later work, but its radiant lyricism, textured palette of interacting thought and feeling, and virtuosic formal mastery offers readers a rich and rewarding experience entirely of its own.

This volume, the *Complete Poetry of James Agee*, brings together all the published and unpublished poems and several substantial drafts of poems that Agee wrote. Agee's poetry has been available previously in two popular editions: Robert Fitzgerald's 1968 *Collected Poems* volume, published by Houghton Mifflin and totaling 179 clothbound pages; and the 2008 *James Agee: Selected Poems*, edited by Andrew Hudgins, published by The Library of America, at an even slimmer 160 clothbound pages.[5] These two volumes nearly duplicate one another and might suggest to readers that Agee was not a prolific poet or that he only worked on poetry in the early days of his writing life.[6] Neither of these assumptions is true. In fact, taking Fitzgerald's edition as the base for comparison with the present scholarly text, and excluding *Permit Me Voyage*[7] which both works print in full, the reader will here have access to approximately four times the number of Agee's poems. The "General Editorial Method" section of this work offers further information about the poems that the reader will find valuable.

Already showing remarkable promise with language as a teenager, Agee published several poems and stories in *The Phillips Exeter Monthly*, the student literary magazine at Phillips Exeter Academy in New Hampshire where Agee attended his final three years of high school. Some of the finest writing of his youth appears in these issues, including an early version of "Anne Garner" (the first name spelled here with the ending 'e' that Agee dropped in later versions of the poem) from May 1928, and "Beauvais" from May 1926. In addition to nine poems, Agee published more than two dozen short prose pieces, both fiction and essays, and several plays in that journal, including a compelling verse play, titled "Menalcas." The total number of pieces published in *The Phillips Exeter Monthly* between November 1925 and May 1928 was 38, a remarkable amount of finished work from a high school student and one of the reasons why he was admitted to Harvard University for his college studies. Agee's first two published poems, "Ebb Tide" and "In Preparation," appeared in the November 1925 issue, under the title "Verses." From the very beginning of his literary life, he was working simultaneously in multiple genres and exploring the full field of writing.

One of Agee's strongest and most memorable early works, "Ann Garner" offers a narrative poem in the manner of Robert Frost or Edwin Arlington Robinson. Written in an unobtrusive blank verse, the poem feels more natural, less stilted, than most other of his earliest poems, especially those composed in stricter traditional forms. The poem subtly moves from a straightforward Appalachian family story into a nearly mythic folktale of the mountain people Agee remembered from his childhood in East Tennessee. The title character takes on increasing symbolic resonance as the poem develops, as Ann gains healing powers after her child is stillborn and goes from being a distraught rural farm wife to an emblem of fertility and unity with nature.

> As the years passed, the people turned to Ann
> In doubt about some matter of their planting.
> For with the years, Ann seemed to grow more learned
> In all the mysteries of darkened moons,
> Of hidden wells. And always at a birth
> Silent and skilled she bent above the bed.
> Always she moved among them like a ghost,
> Her eyes as dull and fixed as two round stones. (*16*)

The loss of her child seems to give Ann a special connection to the earth, and uncanny insight into problems with crop rearing, animal husbandry, and childbirth. "Ann Garner" also marks one of Agee's earliest successes at writing a long poem, which he attempted on several occasions, and in which he explores different narrative strategies and subject materials than in his more typical shorter lyrics.

After Phillips Exeter, Agee's career at Harvard University continued his astonishing output of creative writing and his involvement with school literary magazines. Agee eventually became the editor of *The Harvard Advocate* and published 18 poems in its pages. He also published the "Class Ode," in the *Harvard Class Album* of 1932, and the Garrison Prize-winning selection for best undergraduate poetry in the *Class Album* of 1933. Agee's poems from Phillips Exeter Academy and later at Harvard University show a remarkable promise and facility with poetic forms and techniques. Many sonnets from the *Permit Me Voyage* sonnet sequence made their first appearance in *The Harvard Advocate*, including "I have been fashioned on a chain of flesh," and "Why am I here? Why do you look at me." That scholars still examine the poems Agee wrote in high school and college a century later indicates not only his eventual eminence as a writer, but also his prodigious talent and ability to conceive and execute successful poems at such an early age.

In 1933, after his graduation the previous year, Agee lived in New York in a Greenwich Village basement apartment with his first wife, Via (Olivia) Saunders. According to Laurence Bergreen in his 1984 biography, *James Agee: A Life*, Agee "skirmished with his own writing" as he came to doubt his talents and struggled to complete any of his poems and stories:

> At this delicate stage, [Archibald] MacLeish intervened with a proposition. If Agee would collect the best poems he had written over the years, MacLeish would see what he could do about getting them published. In particular, he would talk to his friend and fellow poet Stephen Vincent Benét, who headed the prestigious Yale Younger Poets series of publications. Slowly and carefully, Agee undertook the arduous task of reassessing eight years of poetry outpourings in light of their suitability for Yale.[8]

Agee listened to MacLeish's advice and submitted his manuscript to the contest, and Benét selected the *Permit Me Voyage* manuscript from 42 entries to receive the 1934 Yale Younger Poets Prize. Bergreen rightly acknowledges the importance of Agee achieving this early success at a time when his confidence in his own abilities was likely flickering and that it also establishes a recurring theme of Agee's friends intervening on his behalf to create or facilitate opportunities when he needed them most.

Mirroring his overall body of work, James Agee's poetry is broad-ranging and sometimes difficult to classify. He could veer from sublimity-seeking Romanticism to wickedly undercutting satire within the course of a few poems. Agee was a poet both of his own time, writing about the political and social issues of the day and engaged with the work of his contemporaries, and a poet of the long history of English verse, often writing in received forms and about traditional subject matters. In an unpublished draft of a preface for *Permit Me Voyage*, already conceived of in the past tense, Agee wrote about his process for creating the volume:

> Putting the ms. together in the first place was a good deal of trouble. I had done poems and verse in many kinds and lengths and tones: all put together they would not only burst the requisite limits of the volume; they would jangle more than even I could care for. I had for instance the first chunks of a long, loose, obscure, satirical, moral, dramatic-narrative, metaphysical, lyrical poem which, were I to let it loose at this time, would knock your eye out. (Which is one good reason why I shall probably not keep on with it). I had a long job called a Preface (or at moments an Introit) which most of you would have laid to Gertrude Stein's doorstep—wrongly, of course—and which was both pitifully inferior and considerably superior to most of Miss Stein's work. I had pieces of a play, and pieces of an outlandish Radio Poem which also would have set you on your ear. I also had pieces of straight journal poetry. And it shook down, in the long run, to this: when all's said and done, what I am after in the end is poetry. I will therefore put into the book such things as seem to me, for one reason or another, finished, crystallized, behind me. I shall play the thing absolutely straight, and sober. Most of these poems I no longer give a damn for, whether in manner or in matter. But I tried well as I could at the time, and here they are. And there they were.[9]

Agee refers to "John Carter" as the poem that "would knock your eye out," and already senses that he may never finish it. He recognizes also that all his poetry taken together would not cohere for a typical reader. Early on, Agee knew that his diverse interests and varied directions might not be perceived as a literary strength, but could potentially strike readers as a disorienting deficiency.

Permit Me Voyage, reproduced in full in the present volume in its original form, was greeted by lukewarm reviews, coming with its own moderate endorsement in a preface by MacLeish, who had recently won the first of his own three Pulitzer Prizes for poetry. MacLeish mentions Agee and his book (not even noting the title) only in the final paragraph of the preface, noting, "What appears is a technical apprenticeship successfully passed, a mature and in some cases a masterly control of rhythms, a vocabulary at once personal to the poet and appropriate to the intention and, above everything else, the one poetic gift which no amount of application can purchase and which no amount of ingenuity can fake—a delicate and perceptive ear" (7). An objective reader may agree that *Permit Me Voyage* feels like the work of an apprentice poet, yet still consider that MacLeish underestimates the capability and the breadth that Agee's volume of poetry displays.

The poems in *Permit Me Voyage* offer many glimpses of the writer James Agee will become in his later work. One of the most remarkable pieces in the volume is the prose-poem introduction titled "Dedication," which shows an early penchant for the lyrical prose style that would become a signature of Agee's later work, such as descriptions of the pre-dawn church rituals in *The Morning Watch*[10] and most especially the brilliant poetic meditation, "Knoxville: Summer, 1915."[11] In "Dedication," Agee employs many techniques, such as anaphora and alliteration, that are more common to poetry than to standard prose writing:

> To those who know God lives, and who defend him.
> To those who know the high estate of art, and who defend it.
> To those who apprehend the dread of the magnitude of the
> destinies, and
> of the common conduct, of human kind, above all things known
> or earthly sought: and who as their hearts are able live toward
> the glory of the beauty, and in the shadow of the fear. (6)

Agee expresses his gratitude and admiration in this high rhetorical style for nearly eight pages, a display which follows a series of short, oblique poems, titled simply "Lyrics." The contrast between the two sections immediately reveals the range of tone and subject matter of which Agee is capable. With these poems, the time has clearly come to reevaluate his amplitude as a strength rather than a weakness.

Agee's poetry has often been considered as apprentice-work, akin to the juvenilia of other writers who went on to achieve greatness in other forms. The value of Agee's poetry lies deeper, however, than the training ground it provided for his later prose fiction and hybridized nonfiction. In one regard, Agee lived the experience most writers dream of, exploring nearly every avenue of literary and popular writing, and creating memorable and lasting works of art in many of these areas. Despite mastering several literary modes and genres, some of his critics, editors, and early readers believed his writing life to be one of unfulfilled promise. One of his oldest friends, Dwight Macdonald, put this most poignantly when he said, "Although he achieved much, it was a wasted, and wasteful, life." Macdonald believed that Agee's excesses were part of the problem, since the author was "generally cultivating the worst set of work habits in Greenwich Village."[12] Such a view underestimates the immense accomplishment of Agee's creative output, which should be considered as a whole body of collected works rather than a diffuse series of mismatched efforts (See the ongoing scholarly editions in *The Works of James Agee*). At this point in time, his best-known "poetry" does not occur in his poems at all, but in passages of his intensely musical nonfiction, such as the personal reflection of "Knoxville: Summer, 1915," and "(On the Porch: 1" from the early pages of *Let Us Now Praise Famous Men*, both written as Agee transitioned his focus from lineated verse poems to lyrical prose.[13]

This volume presents many previously unpublished, and in fact previously unknown, poems and some fragments that were written through every phase of James Agee's life. A casual reader of Agee might assume that he gave up the writing of poems after the appearance of *Permit Me Voyage,* at age 25. While his publishing ambitions shifted mainly to prose fiction and journalism, at least partly directed by financial obligations, Agee continued to compose poems, sometimes in the form of such imaginative experiments as automatic writing and sometimes in regular rhyming and metrical verse. If a signature quality exists for Agee, who was memorably described as "myriad-minded"[14] by another Knoxville, Tennessee-born writer, David Madden, surely his immense range of voice (which I use here as repository for all manner of stylistic elements such as tone, diction, syntax) would rank highly on the list of contending qualities. The expansiveness implied in Madden's phrase is the characteristic most readily apparent in his ambitious long poem, "John Carter," in which Agee pursues most of the major themes that distinguish his later work: critique of economic disparity, autobiography, family relationships, religious belief and doubt, and the fusing of high and low art.

Many of the poems in the current volume were undiscovered at the time Robert Fitzgerald assembled his text for the 1968 *Collected Poems*, and a number of them he may have determined to be insufficiently complete or polished to include. Others were excluded because they did not fit the view Fitzgerald wished to present about Agee's poetry as essentially religious and formalistic. Furthermore, over half the sections of Agee's long and unfinished poem "John Carter" are published here for the first time, and the expanded poem serves as a compelling lens through which to consider the scope of Agee's ambitions, accomplishments, and failures as a poet. Into this sprawling poem, he built an extended satire of bourgeois American culture, an intricate and classic poetic form of the *ottava rima*, and other elements of design and imagination that find expression in other poems. Agee wrote poetry about the subjects that most preoccupied his better-known prose, and readers will find moving examinations of childhood and memories of family life, the pursuit and pain of romantic love, searing political indictments, considerations of other books and writers, jokes and puns about sanctimonious topics, and searching explorations of religious belief and expression.

Agee published only one section of "John Carter," as an undergraduate in *The Harvard Advocate*, under the somewhat clever but unwieldy title "Opening of a Long Poem (Maybe)." The poem appeared in the June 1932 issue, as 47 stanzas long, but not quite a third the length of its final unfinished form. When Fitzgerald reprinted the poem in his *Collected Poems*, he omitted the original title in favor of Agee's later choice. He also included some very helpful reading tools, including Agee's 1932 application for a Guggenheim fellowship based on his project for the poem (it was unsuccessful), and transcriptions of some of Agee's working notes and prose outlines for not-yet-written sections of the poem. The poem runs to more than 40 pages in the *Collected Poems*, fully a quarter of the entire volume, yet Fitzgerald approaches it reluctantly in his "Introduction" to the book, noting that, "Some of the versing in "John Carter" is impressive, but the work is abruptly and decidedly immature by comparison with Parts I and II" (meaning his sections of *Permit Me Voyage* and "Later Poems, 1933–1950").[15] In examining the full text of "John Carter," one recognizes the qualities that made his next major project, *Let Us Now Praise Famous Men*, such a successful work of art: compassion, moral indignation, empathy, questing for truth beneath façade. The poem also presents the scope of Agee's ambition as a poet and encourages readers to ask what Agee's stature might be had he engaged material more conducive to his sensibilities, such as his later trip to Alabama, and turned that into a long poem in the manner of near contemporaries, as Hart Crane had done in *The Bridge* or Federico Garciã Lorca in *Poet in New York*.[16] It is not hard to imagine a book-length poem crafted from the Alabama experience, composed in Agee's free verse form, standing as a major poetic statement of the 1930s.

Though Agee's estate and legacy generally have benefited from his well-meaning friends who edited and compiled his work, his aesthetic aims and goals have not always been so fortunate. Editorial treatment of "John Carter" concerns four different presentations of the poem previous to the current volume, covering a span of about seventy-five years: the original publication of the poem's opening pages in *The Harvard Advocate*; Robert Fitzgerald's selections for Agee's *Collected Poems*; those passages later published in *James Agee Rediscovered*; and newly uncovered manuscripts. Even on its first appearance in *The Harvard Advocate*, "John Carter" bore the stamp of editorial intervention. The poem included a note before the opening stanza that read, "In deference to our censors we have omitted stanzas 16, 24, 25, and 26." Then, the entire sixth line of stanza 2 is covered over by a large black strip. Individual words are similarly blocked-out in several following stanzas.[17] In his Guggenheim application for 1932, Agee expresses a definite commitment to amusing and entertaining his prospective readers, and the censored presentation of "John Carter" surely contributed to the poem's entertainment value (95). For the author of sometimes bawdy satire, nothing could be better for the mythos of a poem than to have mildly offensive words censored by an uptight editorial board (of which Agee himself had been Editor-in-Chief) of an Ivy League school publication.

As previously mentioned, "John Carter" is written in *ottava rima*, an eight-line stanza of iambic pentameter rhyming *abababcc*, an Italian form used by Lord Byron, a favorite of Agee's, for his epic satire *Don Juan*, and among others by W. B. Yeats in "Byzantium" and "Among School Children." The emotional content and impact of "John Carter" occasionally suffers from a constraining sense of its form, forcing the language to take on artificial inversions and "poetic" diction. However, contrast this with Agee's most remarkable accomplishments in poetry that include his "Dedication" from *Permit Me Voyage*, "Sunday: Outskirts of Knoxville, Tennessee," published in *New Masses* in 1937,[18] and the lyric fragments of certain automatic writing poems, such as "The Tindering Stars," (*422*) and "I think that in their honey cells," (*417*) first published in *James Agee Rediscovered* (208, 207). Interestingly, none of these poems conform to any set modes or measures, but operate as free verse/prose poem hybrids, and suggest what his prose fiction confirms: that Agee's highest achievements occur when working in a more fluid and unrestrained manner. The openness of the long poem presented greatly expanded possibilities at the moment of his conception and composition for "John Carter." In a letter to his confidant, Father James Harold Flye, dated November 19, 1930, Agee confesses that after some doubting, he is "from now on committed to writing with a horrible definiteness." Agee also elaborates on his ambition to forge a new approach to writing that he insisted had to take the form of "narrative poetry," but without its characteristic stiffness of atmosphere and elevated language. He says, "I've thought of inventing a sort of amphibious style—prose that would run into poetry when the occasion demanded poetic expression. . . . What I want to do is devise a poetic diction that will cover the whole range of events as perfectly and evenly as skin covers every organ, vital as well as trivial, of the human body."[19]

In *James Agee: A Life*, Lawrence Bergreen claims that Agee "drastically misconstrued his own gifts by attempting poetic satire"[20] in the "John Carter" project, but it seems rather that Agee misread his age as much as his own talent. Agee's humor is on display in "John Carter" as it rarely is in his later works, and its wickedness can be jarring. For instance, Agee wrote eight stanzas on the unpleasant aspects of babies. The narrator also keeps a running commentary going with the reader, often elaborating on his own failures as a poet and the tedium of the digressions that befuddle and entangle him. As shown in a letter to his close friend Christopher "Goofy" Gerould, Agee took a serious interest in Sinclair Lewis's work, and the way he implemented satire in his social critique in "John Carter" and other poems reflected that interest.[21] In his application for the Guggenheim Fellowship, Agee notes one characteristic of his anti-hero protagonist as representing the average American Young Man,[22] but in the depths of the Great Depression, Agee's (and his protagonist's) experience at Harvard hardly mirrored the average American Young Man of 1932. A pertinent question might be: Why was Agee so determined to write satire, particularly after such an early success as the mournful, serious, and compassionate poem, "Ann Garner," had proven to be? One looks to the age and perhaps finds some answers in the class politics of the 1930s and the unconscious waste of 1920s prosperity. Or by looking abroad at Agee's generation of British poets to find in Auden and Spender an outrage at the promise of great societies being squandered, not unlike that of Agee's work from the period, particularly in "John Carter." A contemporary reader may catch more than a feinting glimpse of Agee's acute sensitivity to the world's suffering, and an individual perspective strong enough to lay responsibility at the feet of the guilty, that would produce such later masterpieces as *Let Us Now Praise Famous Men* and *A Death in the Family*, and that would claim a secure shelf for James Agee in the permanent collection of American literature.

Likewise, Agee developed an early mastery of fixed forms in his poetry, especially with the sonnet, which can be seen in *Permit Me Voyage* as well as his publications in *Phillips Exeter Monthly* and *The Harvard Advocate*. Donald E. Stanford, in his 1974 essay, "The Poetry of James Agee: The Art of Recovery," says:

> One of the first things one notices about his poems is the marked and yet successful imitation of Tudor, Elizabethan, Jacobean, metaphysical, and Byronic styles together with a resounding rhetoric at times reminiscent of Hart Crane (from whom his title came) and Allen Tate.[23]

Stanford's assessment is a reminder of the traditional excellence of Agee's literary education, and the beneficial way it paired with his drive to engage with the poets of his own time. Stanford considers Agee's imitations of earlier styles to be an act of "recovery" of the content of his predecessors as much as their form, particularly as that content relates to love and to religious belief. Stanford might have mentioned another near contemporary, D. H. Lawrence, whom Agee acknowledges in his expansive prose poem, "Dedication," and often resembles in his poetry. The soaring rhetorical flourish of Lawrence meets the wry satire of W. H. Auden in many of Agee's early poems, over the foundation of an Audenesque formal intricacy. All the "Lyric" poems in the first section of *Permit Me Voyage* and many of the sonnets in the sixth section merge these modern influences with early styles.

Among this volume's later poems that follow *Permit Me Voyage,* his *Early Poetry,* and "John Carter," from 1933–1953, Agee's themes and styles become even more varied and expansive, including more satirical poems, poems written in dialect, and poems that look at specific places or particular literary modes, such as the pastoral or the lyric. As deeply as Agee examined the distinct importance of place in his fiction and nonfiction prose, where his descriptions of the flora and fauna of his surroundings comprise some of his most lyrical writing, he was never truly a poet of place. In a few poems, however, he did examine his relationship with his childhood home of Tennessee, a time and place explored much more fully in his longer-form fiction. In his essay, "Progress Priced too Dear: Appalachia and Appalachian Pastoral in the Work of James Agee," Michael A. Lofaro indicates that only three of Agee's poems specifically address the region. Lofaro notes:

> Over his career, Agee's treatment of Appalachia and his exploration of the possibilities of an Appalachian pastoral present the reader with an axis of conflict that ranges from an idealized agrarian past beset with the harsh realities of mountain life to a series of artificially created pastoral moments, vignettes in which desire and imagination contend with the actuality of the region's growing industrialization.[24]

Lofaro identifies only three poems, "Ann Garner," "In Memory of My Father (Campbell County, Tenn)," and "Sunday: Outskirts of Knoxville, Tennessee," as fully engaging with Agee's native East Tennessee, but these are three of the strongest poems in all his body of work.

Agee's sonnets that were not included in *Permit Me Voyage* or that were written after the publication of the book, for instance "November, 1945," show his continued investment in the form, even for subjects that would seem to warrant longer and more open structures. Agee fit the world-historical changes of 1945 into the sonnet with deftness and skill.

> November 1945
>
> Now on the world and on my life as well,
> Ancient in beauty, infant in such fear

As no time else had dreamed, nor shall dispel,
Loosen the ashes of another year.
Whether by nature's will, man's or my own,
I who by chance walked softly past a war
Shall not by any chance the world has known
Be here, and breathing, many autumns more.
Only, with all who in past worlds have died,
I had, till lately, faced my death secure,
Knowing my hunger only was denied;
All I most loved and honored would endure.
But this year, dying, struck wild as it fell,
Ending itself, me, and the world as well. (255)

The compression of the form here suits the meditative quality of the voice, the melancholy recognition that one's own life is tied up in the events of a world that cannot be controlled, or even fully understood. In so doing, Agee echoes the view of Paul Oppenheimer, who in his study *The Birth of the Modern Mind: Self, Consciousness, and the Invention of the Sonnet*, says "The sonnet seeks to catch and echo the melodies "unheard" of the human soul, to use Keats' phrase, melodies both passionate and silent, both intimate and celestial."[25] Agee locates the universal in the personal in this sonnet, within his own fear and circumstance, "I who by chance walked softly past a war," a representative of then-modern man who feels likely to be consumed in "the ashes of another year," just as is "this year, dying, struck wild as it fell." Agee also wrote the prescient cover story for *Time* magazine on the meaning of the dropping of the atomic bombs on Japan,[26] but in this quiet, personal poem, his thoughts on the impact of unleashing such destructive power could hardly be more tender and moving.

Agee's poetry can be seen as part of a wider literary continuum. Many of the most celebrated fiction writers of Agee's generation and the previous one also began their writing careers as poets. William Faulkner, Ernest Hemingway, and Thomas Wolfe all published poetry in their early writing days, and it was well-known that F. Scott Fitzgerald venerated the poems of John Keats. Their poetry was often an overly formal prelude to the "poetic" fiction that would follow. Poets slightly younger than Agee began their writing lives, and their publishing careers, writing poems every bit as formal and frequently strained as Agee's. The "Middle Generation" of American poems, Theodore Roethke, Elizabeth Bishop, John Berryman, Robert Hayden, and closest in aesthetic temperament to Agee, Robert Lowell, all moved away from tightly fixed forms and toward free verse poetry. One wonders if Agee had lived a year longer, what might he have made of Allen Ginsberg and the phenomenon of his 1956 banned poem,

"Howl." Possibly Agee would have been too much of a classicist to embrace it fully, but Ginsberg's literary and ideological idols are almost exactly the same authors Agee credits as "unpaid agitators" in his preface to *Let Us Now Praise Famous Men*, all members of the "Visionary Company"[27] of poets and thinkers that Ginsberg emulated. William Blake, D. H. Lawrence, Walt Whitman, Karl Marx, Jesus Christ, Sigmund Freud all represent the extremes Agee admired and emulated, and who as well inspired the Beat writers and the Confessional school of American poetry.

Agee came of age as a poet at a time of great change and upheaval in English language poetry. The many facets of Modernism introduced stylistic changes that were as abrupt and disorienting as any in poetry's long oral and written history. Agee was a young reader immersed in traditional English poetry, learning its forms and techniques, its modes and measures, while also witnessing those devices being radically altered or dismissed. By the time Agee published *Permit Me Voyage* in 1934, he would have experienced an immersive instruction in the continuity of fixed forms, including the sonnet which he practiced extensively; witnessed the rise of surrealism, Cubism, imagism, futurism, and many other attempts to "Make It New," as Ezra Pound would have it, in avant-garde poetry; and as well become involved with the political and proletarian poetry of the era of the Great Depression. Agee was not a passive absorber of these manifestations, but an active practitioner of many new approaches to poetry.

Despite his brilliance with traditional poetic form, Agee's openness toward, and his ambitious pursuit of, exploration and experimentation with style and genre would become a defining quality in his work. In later poems, Agee found an interest in experimentation with lineation and other spatial elements. Many of these poems utilize dramatic line breaks and irregular spacings between words in individual verse lines. For example, note the jarring effect created in the first two stanzas of "[Uneasily, Extol/ The houses at morning.]"

>   Uneasily,   Extol
> The houses at morning.
> gambrel and dormer, spanner,   audacious
>
> Hoarsely, the eye brilliant, brilliant idiot eye, the sun, the sun,
> Snoring sun,
> old man hearing a noise in the house. (*286*)

Agee recognized the powerful effect of spatial design in his poems, which came to prominence in his youth as a Modernist technique, and he responded with enthusiasm to changes in form as well as content.

In several poems that have not been collected in any previous volume, such as "The Darkened Cage" (*88*), "[A deer went down to water]" (*176*), and "Eureka" (*424*), Agee demonstrates some of the quality of voice, some style or formal manner which he pursued throughout his poetry. Many of the previously unpublished poems offer an enlarged sense of Agee's ambitions and capabilities as a poet working in the widely different traditions of English language lyric poetry. In the "Introduction" to the *Collected Poems*, Fitzgerald says that certain of Agee's poems, " . . . are in a direct line of descent from English achievements of the period between 1550 and 1640, and yet it would be foolish to consider them merely imitative; they are poems in their own right, new increments to the tradition."[28] In "The Darkened Cage," for example, Agee displays some of the sensibilities to which Fitzgerald refers through its finely-tuned iambic pentameter line, the rhymed quatrains and concluding couplet, and the courtly, old-fashioned language of a poem despairing the emptiness of romantic love in favor of religious devotion. Agee struggled with how to balance his beliefs with the paradoxes of his experience, and if the "One" in the final couplet may be interpreted as God, then this poem shows an instance of the speaker finding comfort in embracing "remembered tunes afresh." (*88*)

Agee usually did not keep careful records of when and where he wrote his poems, or any of his writing for that matter. He would occasionally add a date to his hand-written drafts, and those poems are presented chronologically, and others are included by date of publication. All others are arranged by genre or style categories under the umbrella of "Undated Poems." A number of these are brief, seemingly fragmentary or unfinished, though all included are clearly intended as poems. For example, the undated poem, "A deer went down to water," (*176*) maintains some of the formal elements of "The Darkened Cage" while modifying others. This poem employs a tighter iambic trimeter form but loosens the formality of the diction to yield a poem that is more meditative in its perspective and more pastoral in setting. Here, Agee shows the remarkable range and facility for which he is known, adapting his tone to suit the material of the poem.

One ongoing testament to the lyricism of Agee's poetry is the number of composers who have set his work, and especially his poems, to music. The most widely known example is surely Samuel Barber's composition of Agee's prose lyric "Knoxville: Summer of 1915," which has been performed and recorded by luminary vocalists Leontyne Price and Dawn Upshaw. Such acclaimed composers as Aaron Copland, Morten Lauridsen, and Thomas Pasatieri, among more than a dozen others,[29] have arranged Agee's prose and verse into art songs, choral works, opera, and other forms of music. Lauridsen has for years been America's most performed living composer, and one of his best-known works is "Sure on

This Shining Night," a 2005 setting of Agee's untitled passage from the opening poem-sequence "Lyrics" of *Permit Me Voyage.*

Sure on this shining night
Of starmade shadows round,
Kindness must watch for me
This side the ground.

The late year lies down the north.
All is healed, all is health.
High summer holds the earth.
  Hearts all whole.

Sure on this shining night I weep for wonder wandering far
  alone
Of shadows on the stars. (4)

The sonorous beauty of these lines indicates why Lauridsen selected the same section from the same poem that Samuel Barber set to music in his 1938 cycle, "Four Songs."[30]

Agee was a talented amateur pianist himself, and the influence of musical phrasing is clear in the long and alliterative lyrical lines of many of his poems, such as "[And where in the troublous groves]"

And where in troublous groves the light was twinkling hampered
  fluttering woodland, mealy marl:

Wide whited wide the palm upspread of earth upon wide whited wide
  stooped through with gentle storm prolific:
That heated stone and the heaped and the morseled planted stones
  thralled headed
  wheat,
  marching and masking, mowing, the husky field:
  And plated waterwarmth and watershine (275)

Such poems show the impressive range in Agee's voice and, in the literary styles he attempted in *Permit Me Voyage* and other early poems, reveal his affinity with Romantic poetry. Agee's work reflects his admiration for Keats' verse in "[And where in the troublous groves]" and numerous other poems unpublished in his lifetime, that are highly lyrical with an ornate sense of word choice and landscape description. Like Keats, Agee intended to master all the modes of lyric poetry, though while Keats approached these in a systematic manner, working up from the brief sonnet form toward the expansive epic, Agee appeared to be tackling these modes all at once. Brief lyrics, such as "[And where in the troublous groves]" and "In Heavy Mind" (*188*), complement his longer narrative poems and allow heightened intensity into the imagery without the need to elaborate on elements of plot or characterization. Agee possessed a formal imagination, which may strike a reader as paradoxical given the "headlong impetuosity of his Muse," as Keats wrote of his own source of inspiration.[31] Dwight Macdonald calls Agee "oceanic"[32] in reference to his all-encompassing energy and personality, but the term also applies to this abundance in his poetic style.

One of Agee's insightful political poems, "Eureka," displays an altogether different side of Agee's voice: animated, sarcastic, and biting in ways that recall his experiments in "John Carter." Known for his sweepingly poetic descriptive language, and for the depths of his empathy for the abused and uncared-for, but here Agee shows a lesser-remarked-upon gift for parody and cutting wit in "Eureka":

Eureka

Fellows by the living Jingo
Nationalism's a damn fine thing-o!
We can prop the crumbling state
By properly directing hate. (*424*)

Though this poem is undated, Agee was often prophetic in his youthful writings, and the future appears to have revealed itself to him as he ironically assesses the risk of xenophobic nationalism, one of the twentieth century's most dangerous political tendencies. "Eureka" is also characteristic of Agee's use of humor to undercut ideology or trenchant beliefs. In his political poems, Agee regularly veers between satire and rage, often creating a distinctive hybrid tone.

Taken as a full body of work, this volume of Agee's poetry reveals some key roles he would maintain through all his writing life, especially in *Let Us Now Praise Famous Men*, but also in his film reviews and journalistic writings: Agee was a radical truth-seeker, a revealer of unearned pieties, and a fighter against complacency and self-congratulation. When Agee addresses the leaders of nations at war, his anger is more straightforward and direct, less satirical. In his World War II work "[We Soldiers of all nations]," the perspective comes from a plural voice, a collective admonishment to the powerful not to use the soldiers' sacrifice as heroic decoration for stolen valor or aggrandizement of the unidentified "you" who has survived the fallen:

[We soldiers of all nations]

We soldiers of all nations who lie killed
Ask little: That you never, in our name,
Dare claim we died that man might be fulfilled.
The earth should vomit us, against that shame.

We died; is that enough? Many died well,
Of both sides; most of us died senselessly.
Ask soldiers who outlived us; they may tell
How many died to make men slaves, or free.

But never use, not as you honor sorrow,
Our murdered days to garnish your tomorrow. (253)

The poem leaves some questions open, such as who specifically is the "you" being addressed by the soldiers, but the indications are clear that politicians and military leaders are not to be trusted with the lives and legacies of regular soldiers.

Agee wrote similarly and consistently on the events and movements of his day. He was a progressive youth who grew skeptical of the totalitarian tendencies of American leftist economic populism, and of Communism generally. This kind of disaffectedness mostly manifests in political satire pieces, like "Collective Letter to the Boss" in which he skewers Hitler and Mussolini:

Dear Boss:

The little man with the big mustache
And the man with an olive in place of a head
Are making a perfectly hideous hash
Of the prospects for Peace and I wish they were dead. (206)

He also critiqued economic policy and inequality through satires and parodies. In *The Making of James Agee*, Hugh Davis considers "Agee's Proletarian Poetry of the 1930s," both in context of the historical moment and in contrast with the image of "the poet" burnished by Macdonald, McDowell (the editor of the manuscript of *A Death in the Family* after Agee's death), and Fitzgerald, who suppressed Agee's liberal political views in favor of promoting an image as a religious poet.[33] After his early death in 1955, readers new to Agee's work would have encountered more myth than man through the reflections of his friends and publishers. However, his wordplay and parodic wit provided an important and different canvas on which to draw political satires that were both biting and timely, good-natured, self-deprecating, and shrewd:

> [Parody of Cole Porter's "You're the Top"]
>
> You're the pot,
> You're the Reichstag Trial,
> You're the pot,
> You're the Roosevelt Smile,
> You're the London Economic Conference,
> You're the car-card hand
> In the soapsuds and
> State's Evidence;
> You're the gags
> In the Conning Tower,
> You're the Stags
> At a shotgun shower,
> I'm a louse some ways and there's damn few ways I'm not,
> But if—Baby—I'm the bottom,
> You're the pot. (*155*)

Agee lived and wrote before the full arrival of the Civil Rights movement and the feminist era, and before issues concerning the environment and physical disability were as thoroughly examined and considered as today. The progressivism of his time mostly concerned class differences and the production and distribution of capital and labor.[34] At times, Agee is almost adolescently amused at sexual puns, metaphors, and figures of speech, as in the poems "My It" (*251*) and "Muzzy wuvs her Buzzy,"(*505*) which he expresses in ways that are hard to categorize, and also hard to appreciate except as wordplay. A sometimes-startling contrast to his cynical parodies can be found in Agee's nearly innocent-seeming idealism, represented in many poems about generosity and kindness. One such example appears in this later poem, titled simply, "'Help'":

> "Help"
>
> "Help" means, if I am carrying wood,
> You carry it too, till we are done.
> Or you are hungry, and I've food,
> And just as gladly give you some. (*250*)

Poems like "'Help'" reveal an unspoken acknowledgement of Agee's deeply felt religious belief. Andrew Hudgins, in the insightful introduction to his 2007 volume *Selected Poems of James Agee,* considered that Agee was a "thoroughly churched boy," and that "Agee was an instinctive believer who had done his homework, and his judgment of Western Civilization paralleled T.S. Eliot's but from the political left."[35] Hudgins recognizes the convergence of Agee's religious beliefs and his political convictions, both of which were approached with intensity, passion, and an open-mindedness to questioning that lends an ambivalence to his conclusions. Agee possessed the huge capacity of mind—he certainly contained Whitman's multitudes—to consider seriously opposing points of view, or even to change his positions on matters of existential gravity.

The spiritual and religious poems Agee composed throughout his life are well-represented in *Permit Me Voyage* with "Dedication" (6) and "A Chorale," (20) but some remarkable shorter lyrics in this vein appear among his undated poems. Poems such as "[Lord of light]" (370) and "Bethlehem" (387) display a tenderness and warmth that contrast with his political poems and satires, though these surely spring from the same sources in his imagination that insist upon truth and integrity.

> Lord of light, beginner of beginnings, shaper of harmonies, light on light on light[,] behold your child.
> Who first in his morning lifts up his unsteady voice among your children, to tell of your children: and to praise his God as he may.
> Who must show forth his God in the weight and sound of words and their bearing: who must sing of truth in the false and meager voice of a child. (370)

The gentleness of these lines offers a counterpoint to the harshness of some of his political critiques and provides a hopeful sense of faith in contrast to his often-despairing view of the material culture of his age. The distinguished Southern poet, novelist, and critic Fred Chappell offers a fine assessment of this type of Agee's poetry in his essay "Every Prayer a Heartbreak: The Prayer Poems of James Agee":

> The prayer poem has a further inestimable attraction: it is both personal and impersonal at the same time. It may give voice to the most passionate of personal feeling, and it may even confess sins and beg for absolution, but it is couched in a form that religious tradition has sanctioned for such revelation.[36]

Chappell here correctly articulates something very specific about Agee's convergence of poetry and prayer that could also serve as a lens to interpreting much of his entire body of work. The largeness of such themes as the systemic deprivation and despair of rural isolation and poverty, or the ever-expanding sphere of loss surrounding the death of a parent to a young child, which is found in *Let Us Now Praise Famous Men* and *A Death in the Family* is also fully present in his poetry.[37] Agee's prayer poems give him an ideal and powerful mode for exploring his preoccupations, and the constant pull between the subjective and the objective, the ode and the elegy, the praise-song and the satirical critique that permeates all his work.

James Agee's poetry examines timeless questions of meaning and purpose with penetrating insight and enlivening virtuosity. How should one live in a world corrupted by power and greed? How does one maintain a spiritual path while tempted by physical and material opportunity? What does it mean to love others and to share one's joy and one's despair? There is much yet to be discovered in the here newly available manuscripts, but also much to be re-discovered, or recovered, in the material that has been available but overlooked for many years. In an interview in Ross Spears' documentary, Agee's widow, Mia, says, "Jim was always writing. I mean, he always, always, wrote . . . (laughing) Jim never took a day off."[38] It now seems that early readers and critics of Agee have made too much of the lack of focus in Agee's work, the mis-dispensation of his talent, or in other words, that he spread himself too thin. A natural response to first encountering *A Death in the Family* is to wish that he had written several novels in this mode which pays such close attention to the volatile inner dynamics of family life. Any reader would look forward to experiencing more of Agee's special gift for recording the intimate conversations between relatives or the stir of evening air walking home from the movies. The same could be said for his work in investigative journalism, screenwriting, and until the arrival of this volume, poetry: we simply have wanted more. One cannot help but wonder if James Agee may have continued the focused development of his poetry had circumstances not required him to turn writing into a salaried occupation. Rather than focus on what might have been, however, future readers will be rewarded by immersing themselves in all of Agee's poems on their own eloquent, funny, lofty, barbed, and at times ecstatic, terms.

NOTES

1. All Agee poems quoted appear in this volume. Parenthetical references direct the reader to the appropriate page(s) in this volume for the quoted material and any explanatory notes.

2. *Agee*, directed by Ross Spears (1978, James Agee Film Project). Note that Father Flye is quoting without acknowledgment Robert Phelps, an editor friend he introduced to Agee, who

coins the phrase in his Preface to *The Letters of James Agee to Father Flye*. James Agee, *Letters to Father Flye* (New York: George Braziller, 1962) 1.

3. James Agee, *The Collected Poems of James Agee* ed. Robert Fitzgerald (Boston: Houghton Mifflin, 1968) was the edition available to Spears.

4. James Agee, *A Death in the Family: A Restoration of the Author's Text.* ed. Michael A. Lofaro (Knoxville: UTP, 2007). James Agee, *Let Us Now Praise Famous Men: An Annotated Edition of the James Agee-Walker Evans Classic, with Supplementary Manuscripts.* ed. Hugh Davis (Knoxville: UTP, 2015).

5. James Agee, *Selected Poems.* ed. Andrew Hudgins. (New York: Library of America, 2007), xiv. See note #3 above for Fitzgerald edition.

6. Some of Agee's manuscript poetry was also made available in *James Agee Rediscovered: The Journals of* Let Us Now Praise Famous Men *and Other New Manuscripts*, ed. Michael A. Lofaro and Hugh Davis (Knoxville: UTP, 2004), but received little public view.

7. James Agee, *Permit Me Voyage* (New Haven: Yale UP, 1934).

8. Lawrence Bergreen, *James Agee: A Life* (New York: Dutton, 1984) 135.

9. *James Agee Rediscovered*, ed. Lofaro and Davis, 187–8. Subsequent refences to this work will be cited parenthetically in the text as *JAR*.

10. James Agee, *The Morning Watch. Botteghe Oscure*, 6, 1950: 339–409. The most readily available text of this work is: *The Morning Watch* (Boston: Houghton Mifflin, 1951).

11. James Agee, "Knoxville: Summer of 1915," *Partisan Review* V (August-September 1938): 22–25.

12. Dwight Macdonald, "Jim Agee: A Memoir," *Remembering James Agee*. Second Edition. ed. David Madden and Jeffrey J. Folks. (Athens and London: U of Georgia P, 1997) 178.

13. James Agee, *Let Us Now Praise Famous Men.* ed. Hugh Davis, 17.

14. David Madden, multiple instances of this phrase. For example, see his essay, "Mapping Agee's Myriad Mind: An Introductory Exhortation." *Agee Agonistes: Essays on the Life, Legend, and Works of James Agee*. ed. Michael A. Lofaro (Knoxville: UTP, 2007) 3–33.

15. *Collected Poems* ix.

16. For an extended analysis of Agee and Lorca, please see my essay "Parallel Poetics: Ways of Seeing in James Agee and Federico Garciă Lorca," in Let Us Now Praise Famous Men *at 75: Anniversary Essays*. ed. Michael A. Lofaro (Knoxville: UTP, 2017) 153–165. Hart Crane, *The Bridge* (Paris: Black Sun Press, 1930). Federico Garciă Lorca, *Poet in New York*. ed. Christopher Maurer (New York: Farrar, Straus, and Giroux, 1998). It is worth noting that the first edition of Crane's *The Bridge* included photographs by Crane's friend, and Agee's, Walker Evans. Agee also drew his title, *Permit Me Voyage*, from a line in Hart Crane's poem "Voyages."

17. James Agee, "Opening of a Long Poem, Maybe," *Harvard Advocate* CXVIII (June, 1932): 12–20.

18. James Agee, "Sunday: Outskirts of Knoxville, Tennessee," *New Masses* XXIV (September 14, 1937): 22.

19. *Letters to Father Flye* 45–50.

20. *James Agee: A Life* 101.

21. Agee writes in a letter to his friend, Christopher Gerould: "I blew myself to a copy of *Elmer Gantry*, Sinclair Lewis' latest. As you no doubt have seen, the critics give Sinclair holy hell. In large part he deserves it. It's the most unsatisfying handling of a marvelous butt for satire that I've ever seen. He loses an immense amount of satirical power by making Elmer Gantry bestial, almost grotesque, in his hypocrisy. Again, he covers much too narrow a field—only two denominations are exhaustively squeezed out—and they are too much alike—He barely mentions the Catholics, and misses infinite opportunities in the High-Church Episco-

palians. Worst of all, there's absolutely nothing said about what Organized Religion is doing to the *Church Goers*—and after all, that's rather important. So far as the book goes, even, it can't compare in subtlety of style with Babbitt or Arrowsmith. Again, there are scenes as insane and cheaply sensational as anything in the Tabloids. And yet, it's a perfectly swell book. It has a great deal of the best humor, and satire, and drama, and characterization in it that Lewis has ever done. The hell of it is that Sinclair seems to be quickly turning from dainty swordplay to robust rancidity. Instead of a rapier, he uses the broadside of a slapstick—and even at that drives nails through it.

He entered a practically unexplored field for satire, walked perhaps ten yards right toward its center, stepped in a cow-cake and beat a graceless exit. It's still a hell of a juicy subject for a novel.

I think I know one just as good, and absolutely new: School, and teachers. The hero can follow the same path as Arrowsmith—you know, country school, big city High School, Church School, high-hat ultra High-Church boarding school, and Exeter. What a lovely chance to show things up! I'm doing a little of it for the Monthly, just to get warmed up. I'm taking Knoxville High School (I attended it a year) through a year, telling of their oversexed football coach, their Faculty meetings, the R.O.T.C., the expulsion of the Unitarian heretic history prof, and the tumult when the anti-evolution bill was passed. It can be the nuts." James Agee, Letter to Christopher "Goofy" Gerould, March 14, 1927, University of Tennessee Special Collections, James Agee Manuscript Collection, MS-3824, Box 1, folder 2.

22. James Agee, "Plans for Work: October, 1937" *The Collected Short Prose of James Agee* ed. Robert Fitzgerald (Boston: Houghton Mifflin, 1968) 131.

23. Donald E. Stanford, "The Poetry of James Agee: The Art of Recovery." *The Southern Review*, Volume 10, 1974: xvi–xix.

24. Michael A. Lofaro, "Progress Priced too Dear: Appalachia and Appalachian Pastoral in the Work of James Agee." Journal of Appalachian Studies, Vol. 17, No. 1 and 2: 85–6.

25. Paul Oppenheimer, *The Birth of the Modern Mind* (New York: Oxford UP, 1989) 3. Given that Agee refers to the Atomic Bomb in the sonnet, it would have been fitting if critic Paul Oppenheimer was closely related to J. Robert Oppenheimer, widely known as "the father of the Atomic Bomb," but alas the author is not the child of the scientist or his brother.

26. James Agee, "Victory: The Peace." *Complete Journalism: Articles, Book Reviews, and Manuscripts.* ed. Paul Ashdown (Knoxville: UTP, 2013) 316; originally published: *Time.* 46 (August 20. 1945): 19–21.

27. James Agee, "Persons and Places (Unpaid Agitators)," *Let Us Now Praise Famous Men.* ed. Hugh Davis, np. Harold Bloom, *The Visionary Company* (Ithaca: Cornell UP, 1961) 465.

28. *Collected Poems* x.

29. A comprehensive list of James Agee poems set to music can be found at *The LeiderNet Archive* website: James Agee (1909–1955) | LiederNet.

30. Barber and Lauridsen selected the same passage of text from "A Description of Elysium." Barber, Samuel. "Sure on this shining night", op. 13 (*Four songs for voice and piano*) no. 3 (1938), published 1961. Lauridsen, Morten. "Sure on this shining night" [SATB chorus and piano], from Nocturnes, no. 3 (2005).

31. Keats, John, *Letters of John Keats*, ed. Robert Gittings (Oxford: Oxford UP, 1970) 244. In writing to his brother George Keats about his poem "*La Belle Dame sans Merci*," Keats considers his need for structure and order.

32. Dwight Macdonald in Ross Spears' documentary *Agee.*

33. Hugh Davis, *The Making of James Agee* (Knoxville: UTP, 2008) 27–50.

34. Agee's negative portrayals can be viewed in a more balanced light by comparing them

with the sensitivity and thoughtfulness displayed in "America! Look at your Shame" and other pieces. In Michael A. Lofaro's article on Agee and Hemingway, he says that "Agee and/or his editor [*Fortune* magazine, 1934] seemed to reflect the discriminatory attitudes of America in the 1930s, a fact far less the case in the author's later works. 'Cotton Tenants' [1936], which was the seedbed for his *Let Us Now Praise Famous Men* (1941), and 'America, Look at your Shame!,' his posthumously published piece on the Detroit race riots of 1943, progressively revealed far less stereotypical views." See "Cock and Bull Stories: Luce's *Fortune* Magazine Features Hemingway and Agee on Bloodsport," *James Agee in Context: New Literary, Visual, Cultural, and Historical Essays*, ed. Michael A. Lofaro (Knoxville: UTP, 2022), p.188. For "Cotton Tenants," see Davis, *Let Us Now Praise Famous Men*, 565–646. For an analysis of the change of focus, especially on race, between the two works, see Michael A. Lofaro, "Famous Men By the Numbers: An Analysis of Agee's Changes from "Cotton Tenants" to *Let Us Now Praise Famous Men*," in Michael A. Lofaro, ed., Let Us Now Praise Famous Men *at 75*, 245–56. "'America, Look at your Shame!': A Previously Unpublished Essay by James Agee," is edited and introduced by Michael A. Lofaro and Hugh Davis, in the *Oxford American: The Southern Magazine of Good Writing* (January/February 2003): 35–39. Also published as "James Agee, 'After the Riots,'" *Harper's* 306 (June 2003): 27–31, and in Louis Menand, ed. *The Best American Essays 2004* (Boston: Houghton Mifflin, 2004): 1–8. For more on the Detroit riots, see: Harvard Sitkoff, *Toward Freedom Land: The Long Struggle for Racial Equality in America* (Lexington: UP of Kentucky, 2010), 43–64; Alfred M. Lee and Norman D. Humphrey, *Race Riot (Detroit, 1943)* (New York: Octagon Books, 1968); and Dominic J Capeci, Jr. and Martha Wilkerson, *Layered Violence: The Detroit Rioters of 1943* (Jackson: U of Mississippi P, 1991).

35. *Selected Poems* xiv.

36. Fred Chappell, "Every Prayer a Heartbreak: The Prayer Poems of James Agee," in Lofaro, *Agee Agonistes* 173.

37. Agee's poems that address the loss of his father include, "In Memory of my Father (Cambell County, Tenn.)" (255), "[From bed as from balcony]" (218), and "[I am not well with reason and exited]" (555).

38. Mia Agee in Spears's film *Agee*.

General Editorial Method

Michael A. Lofaro

This volume contains nearly four times the number of poems by James Agee available in previous "collected" or "selected" editions. In presenting this complete scholarly edition of Agee's poetry, the goal is to provide the reader with an accurate and relatively uncluttered text. To do so, certain editorial principles are followed. All the works published before Agee's death in 1955 are assumed to represent his final version of those texts. Those that were edited from his manuscripts and published after his death, mainly in the volume *The Collected Poems of James Agee*, ed. Robert Fitzgerald (Boston: Houghton Mifflin Company, 1968) (*CP*) and in *James Agee Rediscovered: The Journals of* Let Us Now Praise Famous Men *and Other New Manuscripts*, ed. Michael A. Lofaro and Hugh Davis (Knoxville: U of Tennessee Press, 2004), pp. 208–51 (*JAR*), are re-edited from the original manuscripts for the present work.[1] If needed, the poems are annotated with descriptive notes that are indicated by superscript letters and have corresponding explanations after the conclusion of each poem. Any textual editing is indicated by numbered footnotes and is placed in the Textual Commentary and Notes, a section which serves as the penultimate part of this book. These comments and notes will likely be of most interest to textual scholars.

The arrangement of the poetry in this volume is as follows: Agee's only published book of poetry, *Permit Me Voyage* (New Haven: Yale University Press, 1934), is first; following it, in chronological order starting with his days as a student at Phillips Exeter, are his other published poems, interspersed with his dated unpublished poems, also in chronological order. Some unpublished poems do not have a specific date, but when a range of dates could be established it is noted and the poem listed chronologically by the first date in that range. The volume concludes with Agee's undated typescript and manuscript poetry organized by topic or genre. These groupings are: Lyric; Satiric and Humorous; Spiritual and Religious; Nature; Political; Philosophical; Sensual; On Poets and Poetry; Sonnets; Dialect; and Miscellaneous. Some poems are a good fit in multiple areas, but the editors have tried to select its most dominant one as its classification.

The poems in this book are preceded by a listing of all of Agee's titles (or all or part of the first line for untitled works and enclosed in square brackets) for all of the poems and reflects the same order noted above. This list includes individual mentions of those works in *Permit Me Voyage* that were grouped under a single title as a category, such as "Lyrics" and "Sonnets." These are given separate first-line titles that appear indented and in square brackets under Agee's original cumulative title. At the rear of this volume is an index of titles and bracketed first lines serving as titles of all of the poems in the volume to give the reader another way in which to access Agee's poetical canon.

Before the publication of this volume, the bulk of Agee's poetry has remained in manuscript, both handwritten and typed, with those that are handwritten requiring by far the most editorial work. The source for a poem, both those in print and in manuscript, is given following each work. Unpublished typescript poems are further identified as "[typescript]" following the source's location; unpublished handwritten works are not labeled, but still bear all pertinent source location data for their particular archive. Variant versions of poems are often mentioned or, in a few instances, recorded in the Textual Commentary and Notes, unless the variant is deemed appropriate for separate inclusion in the volume proper.

The goal throughout the process of compiling and editing this volume has been to replicate Agee's poems with the minimal alteration required for clarity and understanding. It is worth noting that Agee's handwriting is notoriously difficult to read. His script is tiny, done in pencil, almost always on inexpensive, unlined paper, and combines print and script characters. He sometimes joins words together, splits words in parts, and is irregular in capitalization and punctuation. Agee's use of the colon, for example, will seem flagrant to some readers, but is retained; this usage is characteristic of much of his prose as well. Editorial changes are made only to avoid misreading and confusion; they strive to be conservative, consistent, grounded in available evidence, and made in accord with Agee's stated or implied desires when known. All such changes are recorded in the Textual Commentary and Notes. Thankfully for the editors, his poetry is generally more readable than his prose, in which eight hundred words can occupy one side of a handwritten page.

Some of the handwritten poems have alternative words and verses. Decisions as to the final version of these works is based on many criteria, as well as Agee's method of composition in which a poem can evolve through multiple drafts in his revisions as he often works from the top of a page to the bottom. His alternatives, however, are sometimes inscribed in the margins to the right and left of the poem proper. Subsequent versions that incorporate Agee's revisions are deemed closer to his final wishes. Significant words, phrases, and verses, whether present marginally or interlinearly, that bear no indication of the author's final choice, are recorded in the Textual Commentary and Notes; normally, this edition will record his original word, phrase, or verse in a poem and place other possibilities in its textual notes. As previously mentioned, alternative verses are likewise mentioned or recorded, if deemed significant.

Page breaks that may incorrectly be read as the start of a new verse occur at the bottom of pages 20, 36, 68, 120, 244, 402, 480, 493, and 498. Those verse sections that are obviously linked by rhyme, punctuation (or lack of), etc. are not listed here.

The location(s) of each poem is commonly abbreviated and appears after the last verse of the poem. The first location noted serves as the copy text. Frequent abbreviations are:

CP *The Collected Poems of James Agee*, ed. Robert Fitzgerald. Boston: Houghton Mifflin, 1968

JAR *James Agee Rediscovered: The Journals of Let Us Now Praise Famous Men and Other New Manuscripts*, ed. Michael A. Lofaro and Hugh Davis. Knoxville: U of Tennessee Press, 2005

UTK University of Tennessee Libraries, Special Collections

Other locations are cited in full. Locations may also appear in the Textual Commentary and Notes for a poem. No location(s) is cited for the poems in Agee's *Permit Me Voyage* (1934); that work is reproduced at the start of this volume.

Please see the headnote to the Textual Commentary and Notes for more specifics of the editing policies.

The division of labor in this volume is generally as follows: Jesse Graves, a fine poet in his own right, has written the critical introduction and provided or supervised the initial draft of the texts for the majority of Agee's poems; Michael A. Lofaro was responsible for checking, reediting, and producing the final version of those poems, for transcribing and editing approximately eighty additional poems discovered after the establishment of the initial working draft, and for creating the explanatory and textual notes. Both editors, however, have contributed significantly to each other's work in all phases of the project and to the final form of the *Complete Poetry of James Agee* over a span of many years.

Those readers who would like to know more about the life of James Agee in a compact form are referred to "A James Agee Chronology" in volume 1 of The Works of James Agee: James Agee, *A Death in the Family: A Restoration of the Author's Text*, ed. Michael A. Lofaro (Knoxville: U of TN P, 2007), pp. xxix-xxxiii.

NOTE

1. Please note that for *JAR*, although the collection number is the same, sometimes the box and often the folder references for poems have often been changed due to the reorganization and recataloging by the University of Tennessee Special Collections after *JAR*'s publication.

The present volume reflects the current location of the manuscripts. The Library of America edition, *James Agee: Selected Poems* (New York: Penguin Random House, 2008) edited by Andrew Hudgins, generally replicates Fitzgerald's volume and is not noted as a source or one of the sources in the information recorded following each poem. Also, original typescript or manuscript sources for eleven poems in Fitzgerald's edition could not be located; his work serves therefore as this volume's copytext for those works and is so noted after those poems. Even though Fitzgerald included the bits of the libretto that Agee had written for Leonard Bernstein's comic operetta "Candide" (*CP*, pp. 165–79), those were never included in Lillian Hellman's text for Bernstein's work and were judged more suitable for a later volume in The Works of James Agee.

Complete Poetry of James Agee

Titles/First Lines of Poems

Permit Me Voyage (1934)

Early Poetry: Phillips Exeter and Harvard (1925–1932)

Undated Poems

LYRIC POEMS

SPIRITUAL AND RELIGIOUS POEMS

NATURE POETRY

Poems

Permit Me Voyage[1]

I. *Lyrics.*[1]

Child, should any pleasant boy
Find you lovely, many could,
Wind not up between your joy
The sly delays of maidenhood:

Spread all your beauty in his sight
And do him kindness every way,
Since soon, too soon, the wolfer night
Climbs in between, and ends fair play.

A summer noon the middle sun
Stunned me full of waking sleep
And spread me slack as stone upon
The grass in water foundered deep

There in that steep and loaded shine
Of hungriest life and crested year
To dream what plenitudes were mine
What fat futurities made near

When cold athwart these ripening plans
The shade o'erswam me like a sheet
Of draughty disappointed vans,
And lobbered[a] beak, and drawling feet.

[a] Or clabbered, as in curdled milk.

No doubt left. Enough deceiving.
Now I know you do not love.
Now you know I do not love.
Now we know we do not love.
No more doubt. No more deceiving.

Yet there is pity in us for each other
And better times are almost fresh as true.
The dog returns. And the man to his mother.
And tides. And you to me. And I to you.
And we are cowardly kind the cruellest way,
Feeling the cliff unmorsel from our heels
And knowing balance gone, we smile, and stay
A little, whirling our arms like desperate wheels.

Not met and marred with the year's whole turn of grief,[2]
But easily on the mercy of the morning
Fell this still folded leaf:

Small that never Summer spread
Demented on the dusty heat;
And sweet that never Fall
Wrung sere and tarnished red;
Safe now that never knew
Stunning Winter's bitter blue
It fell fair in the fair season:

Therefore with reason
Dress all in cheer and lightly put away
    With music and glad will
This little child that cheated the long day
    Of the long day's ill:
Who knows this breathing joy, heavy on us all,
    Never, never, never.

A Song.

I had a little child was born in the month of May.
He croaked and he crowed from early in the day.
He sang like a bird and he delighted to play
And before the night time he was gone away.

Little child, take no fright,
In that shadow where you are
The toothless glowworm grants you light.
Sure your mother's not afar.

Brave, brave, little boy,
Angels wave you round with joy.
Soon through the dark she runs to you,
Soon, soon your mother comforts you.

Description of Elysium.

There: far, friends: ours: dear dominion:

Whole health resides with peace,
Gladness and never harm,
There not time turning,
Nor fear of flower of snow

Where marbling water slides
No charm may halt of chill,
Air aisling the open acres,
And all the gracious trees

Spout up their standing fountains
Of wind-beloved green
And the blue conclaved mountains
Are grave guards

Stone and springing field
Wide one tenderness,
The unalterable hour
Smiles deathlessness:

No thing is there thinks:
Mind the witherer
Withers on the outward air:
We can not come there.

Sure on this shining night[3]
Of starmade shadows round,
Kindness must watch for me
This side the ground.

The late year lies down the north.
All is healed, all is health.

High summer holds the earth.
    Hearts all whole.

Sure on this shining night I weep for wonder wandering far
    alone
Of shadows on the stars.

Now thorn bone bare
Silenced with iron the branch's gullet:
Rattling merely on the air
Of hornleaved holly:

The stony mark where sand was by
The water of a nailèd foot:
The berry harder than the beak:
The hole beneath the dead oak root:

All now brought quiet
Through the latest throe
Quieted and ready and quiet:
Still not snow:

Still thorn bone bare
Iron in the silenced gully
Rattling only of the air
Through hornleaved holly.

The Happy Hen.[4]

(To Dr. Marie Stopes[a] et al, and to all scientific lovers)

His hottest love and most delight
The rooster knows for speed of fear
And winds her down and treads her right
And leaves her stuffed with dazzled cheer,

Rumpled allwhichways in her lint,
Who swears, shrugs, redeems her face,
And serves to mind us how a sprint
Heads swiftliest for the state of grace.

I loitered weeping with my bride for gladness
Her walking side against and both embracing
Through the brash brightening rain that now the season changes
White on the fallen air that now my fallen
the fallen girl her grave effaces.

[a] Dr. Marie Stopes (1880-1958) was an early advocate of birth control who established the first clinic for contraception in the United Kingdom in 1921.

II. Dedication.

in much humility
to God in the highest
in the trust that he despises nothing.

And in his commonwealth:

To those who in all times have sought truth and who have told it in their art or in their living, who died in honor; and chiefly to these: Christ: Dante: Mozart: Shakspere[a]: Bach: Homer: Beethoven: Swift: the fathers of Holy Scripture: Shelley: Brahms: Rembrandt: Keats: Cezanne: Gluck: Schubert: Lawrence: Van Gogh: and to an unknown sculptor of China, for his god's head.

To those of all times who have sought truth and who failed to tell it in their art or in their lives, and who now are dead.

To those who died in the high and humble knowledge of God: seers of visions; watchmen, defenders, vessels of his word; martyrs and priests and monarchs and young children and those of hurt mind; and to all saints unsainted.

To those unremembered who have died in no glory of peace, nor hope nor thought of any glory: to those who died in sorrow, and in kindness, and in bravery; to those who died in violence suddenly, and to all that saw not death upon them; to those who died awake to the work of death; to those who died in the dizziness of many years, not knowing their children for theirs; to those who died virgin, or barren; to those who died in the time of the joy of their strength; to those who took their own lives into the earth; to those who died in deadly sin.

To those who in their living time were frustrate with circumstance, and disadvantage; to those who died in the still desire of truth who never knew truth, nor much beauty, and small joy but the goodness of endurance; to all those who in all times have labored in the earth and who have wrought their time blindly, patient in the sun: and to all the dead in their generations:

And especially to Joel Tyler, and to James Agee my, brave father, and to Jessie Tyler that became Mother Mary Gabriel, faithful maidservant of the most high God, and to Emma Farrand, the wife of Joel Tyler.

May they rest.

To those who, living, are soon to die: and especially to Via my wife, and to my mother, and to my sister Emma and to David Preston her husband, and to Gladys Lamar Agee my father's mother; and to Hugh Tyler, and to Paula Tyler, and to Erskine Wright, priest.[b]

And to James Harold Flye, priest, who befriended my boyhood with the wisdom of gentleness, and to Grace his wife; to Edwin Clark Whitall, priest, patient in all his life; to Dorothy Carr; to the leniency and wisdom of four men, and to the scorn of another, who teach at Exeter Academy; to Theodore Spencer, in gratefulness; in love, to Arthur Percy Saunders and to his wife Louise and to their children; and to a dozen friends, who know their names.

To Mark Twain; to Walt Whitman; to Ring Lardner; to Hart Crane; to Abraham Lincoln; and to my land and to the squatters upon it and to their ways and words in love; and to my country in indifference.

To the guts and to the flexing heart and to the whole body of this language in much love, in grief for my dulness and in shame for my smallness and meagreness and caution. May I in time become as worthy of it as man may become of his words.

To those living and soon to die who tell truth or tell of truth, or who honorably seek to tell, or who tell the truths of others: especially to James Joyce; to Charles Spencer Chaplin; to Ivor Armstrong Richards; to Archibald MacLeish; to William Butler Yeats; to Pablo Picasso; to Albert Edward Housman; to Stephen Spender; to Roy Harris; to Albert Einstein; to Frederick Burrhus Skinner; to Walker Evans; to Diego Rivera; to Orozco[c]; to Ernest Hemingway; to Scott Fitzgerald; to Arturo Toscanini; to Yehudi Menuhin; to Irvine Frost Upham; to Robert Fitzgerald.

To those who know God lives, and who defend him.

To those who know the high estate of art, and who defend it.

To those who apprehend the dread of the magnitude of the destinies, and of the common conduct, of human kind, above all things known or earthly sought: and who as their hearts are able live toward the glory of the beauty, and in the shadow of the fear.

To those who suspect in every man, in the instant of his getting and thenceforward, how he is dignified among created creatures, how in him the world's whole harm and the world's whole good are met in the breath of God: and how in that instant he is given a mind to know and, though he be all one mechanism, freedom in his conduct before his creator.

To those who likewise suspect that hunger insatiable of the keeping and the enlargement and the knowing of being wherein he is conceived, wherein he lives, which in its appetites he may somewhat govern, and whereby he is wholly governed in all his ways.

To those who, beholding what man is, for love and for grief of what man should and may never earthly be, detest into madness man as he is and was and shall be, and all his works.

To those wiser who do not despise man in his doom, nor in the nature of his nature.

To that nature of man in earth which out of man's necessitudes, and delusions of necessitude, has wrought the societies and the nations of man, and his laws, that make a whore of justice, and his labors in the soil, and his workings of metal and stone and fibre and fire and light to his good use, and the contrivance of his ornament and entertainment, and his ways of good conduct and politeness; and his sciences; and his philosophies, and his religions, and his arts: and which interweaved these in the troubles and the nobilities of the flesh, and made them all into a structure no generation may deface, or destroy, but it will build again: so that in all the wraths of our hope and need we are compelled forward and forever newly into a same darkness of unperfect practice.

To that nature of man in earth which has wrought this time upon us.

To all pure scientists, anatomists of truth and its revealers; in scorn of their truth as truth; and in thanksgiving for their truth in its residence in truth.

To all scientists and inventors of convenience and rapidity, and ways of health: in thanksgiving for their reductions of human pain, and labor, and unhealth; and in scorn for the same: since in the right end of their busyness we would all be healthful and undesiring as animate stones.

To those men who, of all nations unhindered, to all nations faithless, make it their business to destroy concord and to incite war and to prolong it, for their profit in the commerce of armament: to those governors of nations who, in full knowledge of this, visit upon them neither punishment nor restriction nor disapproval, but are accomplices, exhorting and deceiving and compelling the men for whose good life they rule deliberately into death, and death's danger, and the shattering of flesh and spirit. Of these merchants and of these rulers may the loins thaw with a shrieking pain, and may there be slow nails in the skulls of each, and may lost winds of plague unspeakable alight like flies upon their flesh, here in this earth and by public arrangement, to the sweet entertainment of all men of good will: and in their death may the vengeance of God shock their flesh from their bones, and their bones off the air, and all that was of them be reduced to the quintessence of pain very eternal, from moment to moment more exquisite everlastingly, by a geometrical increase: unless by improbable miracle they repent themselves straightway and for good.

To those who will not see that there is a disease of cupidity, and love of the fatherland, and pride, and the good heat for valor, upon all human flesh, which builds these men their conveniences, and makes them easy of heart in murder as a grocer selling greens: and it is a disease which may hardly be cured.

To those who are sure they can cure it.

To those merchants dealers and speculators in the wealth of the earth who own this world and its frames of law and government, its channels of advertisement and converse and opinion and its colleges, and most that is of its churches, and who employ this race and feed off it: to those among these rulers and these owners, these shapers of general thought, who decry these merchants of war: that they examine curiously, and honestly into their own hearts, and see how surely and to what like extent they in themselves are blood-guilty; and how and in what manifold ways they are more subtly and terribly and vastly accountable than for life blood alone: and that they repent their very existence as the men they are, and change or quit it: or visit the just curse upon themselves.

To those who think that any, or much, or all this condition may be a little, or much, or wholly changed. And to those who think that any one man is wholly guilty.

To those who have been deluded of their dignity as men and of their good knowledge into the practise and advancement of transient matters: to those whom love, or despair, or mildness, or magnanimity, or greed; or cloudiness of mind congenital or premeditated; or the strict allegories of the scientists, have thus deluded.

And especially to those whose souls are enraged that have beheld those practised and gravely cumulated idiocies which, since this race began, have been committed of man on men, for personal avarice or for national aggrandisement, lawlessly and by sanction and process of law; idiot children of that voracity which is the living strength of all men, and which may be changed in its courses for good or ill but never one jot altered in itself; those idiocies which have ever been and ever will be and are most obscenely now strong in the distinguishment of man from man, and strong to secure man's hatred of man and his privation, and dulness and blindness to truth, and eternal condemnation to wretchedness and all disadvantage. To those who have seen or suffered this condition, and who are fooled into the hope that it may be essentially changed. And into the hope that the cleansing of this state or its demolition and the establishment of a state new forged, and all discoveries of science applied, will do any greater service to man than to level and ameliorate the agonies and the exigencies of his living, to his ease, and into the ignorance of a contentment in earth and in the stuffs of the earth: to the blinding of his heart still further toward right knowledge of himself, and to the exasperation of those real agonies unbeheld, and in no time well beheld, of his ignorance before the mask of his destiny and before his God, where no knowledge nor ease of earth may help him.

And, knowing well that in this earth society, and law, and industry are the natural and indispensable necessities of man's earthly doom, earnestly to the hope (which can not be hope) that from this overthrow and change to come shall arise a race which, knowing concord in earth's least noisome commonwealth, may likewise know humility before God.

To those who will not watch into the mere shadow of death and behold the supremacy of man's ignorance over all man's knowledge. To those who will not see that there in that shadow is truth. To those who will not watch toward it, valuing it above all things in earth and valuing all things of earth in the thought of it.

To those among the murdering class who intend, and understand, no evil. To those among the murdered who grieve that they will murder many innocent men.

To all those who labor.

To those many who are indifferent to all semblance of truth; and to those millions who fear and detest it, and whom no change of state shall change.

To those who would not tell truth merely, but clearly in the hearts of all this people: for they crown a great impossibility, for which to die, with a mean crown and impossibility, and are somewhat mistaken.

To Leopold Bloom[d], and in his mildheartedness to all mankind.

To those who would be kind, and live quietly in the joy of their peacefulness.

To those who are more evil than kind.

To those dubious of evil, and of good.

To those who too surely distinguish them.

To those who have built this time in the earth in all its ways and who dwell in it variously as they may or must: farmers and workers and wandering men and builders and clerks and legislators and priests and doctors and scientists and governors of nations and engineers and prisoners and servants and sailors and merchants and soldiers and airmen and artists: in cities amassed, and on wide water, and lonesome in the air, and dark under the earth, and laboring in the land, and in materials, and in the flesh, and in the mind, and in the heart: knowing little and less of great and little matters: enduring all things and most enduring living, each in his way of patience, who all, surely as a brook slopes into a deep cave and is lost, must die, into what destiny not one may know: to all these who live and who must die and to those whom they breed to follow them in the earth to live and endure and breed and die: to the earth itself in its loveliness, and in all this race has done to it: and to its substance, and to its children every one, quick or quiet:

And to that space and darkness of sky beyond conjecture and to the coastless coasts that curb it if any there be such and to the whirling fires and the dead stones of the sky in their progressions upon the dark:

To the Holy Catholic and Apostolic Church and to the reach of its green boughs upon the sky through Godhead into God head, and to its branches withering and withered and fallen away:

And to that which, climbing the very sap, may deathly cling and blight that tree: in hatred, in grief, in faith:

To the entire hierarchy of the natural God, of every creature lone creator, in his truth unthinkable, undimensionable, endlessness of endlessness: beseeching him that he shall preserve this people.

O God, hear us.

O God, spare us.

O God, have mercy upon us.

Not one among us has seen you, nor shall in our living time, and may never. We fumble all blind on the blind dark, even who would know you and who believe your name. Our very faith and our desire, which are our whole and only way in truth, they delude us always, and ever will, into false and previous visions, and into wrong attributions. Little as we know beyond the sill of death do we know your nature: and the best of our knowledge is but a faith, the shade and shape of a dream, and all pretense.

Nevertheless have mercy upon us O great Lord God: for as there is some mercy, and the imaginations of nobleness, even in this your creature, surely, surely there is mercy in you and honor and sweet might: and a way to hear, and a way to see, and wisdom, and careful love. Have mercy upon us therefore, O deep God of the void, spare this race in this your earth still in our free choice: who will turn to you, and again fail you, and once more turn as ever we have done. And make the eyes of our hearts, and the voice of our hearts in speech, honest and lovely within the fences of our nature, and a little clear.

[a] Agee here participates in the then current debate over the spelling of Shakespeare's last name. For more information, see David Kathman, "The Spelling and Pronunciation of Shakespeare's Name," https://shakespeareauthorship.com/name1.html.

[b] This and the preceding list name members of Agee's family

[c] José Clemente Orozco (1883-1949) was a Mexican muralist and colleague of Diégo Rivera

[d] Leopold Bloom is the fictional protagonist of James Joyce's *Ulysses* (1922)

III. Ann Garner.[1]

Like a stone set to mark a death, the bed
Leaned through the leaping darkness, gaunt and square
Against the firelight.
                    In her agony
Bent like a birch ice-laden, Ann Garner lay:
The silent woman by her in the dimness
Turned to the firelight, and said to the husband,
"She's laborin' hard; best set the plow beneath her."[a]
Hips leant between the handles of the plow,
He thrust the flame-blue share beneath the bed.
And all the anguish flowed from her taut body,
Leaving her limp and silent in the darkness.
Then from the shadows the old woman walked,
Holding on rootlike hands the stillborn child.
The father drew the sheet to veil the eyes
That sought to pierce the leaping darkness where
Against the firelight, gaunt and square, the bed
Leaned like a stone set up to mark a death.

In harsh nakedness the earth upward thrusts
Its gaunt body, through the thin shroud of snow.
Above the rim of rocks, in the east,
Like a dull band of metal bends the dawn.
In the ice-clamped earth ring the shovels
And the ice-clamped earth leaps black
Against the sky.
                    At the grave, Ann Garner
Holds the child, in a fleece close-wrapped,
Close-locked in a strong oak box.
In a strong oak box close-locked
They lower him into the frozen earth,
Lower him among the frozen roots.
The earth drums loud on the box.
Loud ring the shovels, and the wails
Of the women ring across the barren fields.
The mother stands silent by the grave.

Here, on this height of pasture, where
The wheeling sky and turning earth
Convolute, grind;
Here, at the universe's core,
Here, on infinity's blind shore
Let him lie buried.

Here earth bereft again receives
Into her open womb, her babe;
Let the womb cohere:
Let the flesh of her babe become her flesh,
Let the blood of the babe to the hidden wells
Of life drain downward.

Let him live in womb and womb of earth;
In the swelling seed of every plant
Let him live.
Let him distil on rising mists,
Let him be blown along the sky,
Let him rise through womb and womb of light;
With stars at their birth
Let him again be born.

High in the dark looms of the sky, the wind
With gentle hands wove a fine web of snow
Which from those silent fingers flowed in silence
Downward, to trail across the stony hills,
Downward, to settle over the black fields.
And now about Ann, the white-shrouded fields,
Swept outward into an oblivion
Of whiteness. On every side an even whiteness
Was all that Ann could see, save where the wind
Laid bare and dreadful some black, angled stone.
That night her husband held her in his arms,
Spoke a few broken words, and in the darkness
Waited in sorrowful silence for the weeping
That he could better bear and better comfort
Than speechless grief. But at his side she lay,
The white snows falling, falling in her soul,
Blinding her grief save where some twisted stratum

Of her soul's framework thrust up bare and black.
And thus she sat throughout the winter days,
Holding her grief within her as a woman
Carrying a child unborn cradles its presence,
And sits apart in silence, cherishing
Its unborn life in joyful solitude.
Her husband would sit in sorrow, watching her;
Watching her daily slip a little farther
From his desire, and sympathy, and love.

A few days later, answering his call,
The midwife came once more to minister
To Ann, in whom the unsuckled milk had curdled.
Down to the pond's edge the old woman led them,
Jeff with an axe and shovel. "Now start diggin',"
She said, "An' keep on diggin' till ye strike
The muck. Ye're sure to find one hereabouts."
He shoveled off the snow, and with the axe
Chopped out the ice. Kneeling, the woman peered
About, and with her fingers clawed aside
The frozen reeds. There, in the splintered ice
And twisted roots, she found a frog, frozen.
Cupping it in her hands, she blew upon it,
The white breath streaming from her twisted fingers,
Until life stirred within him. "Open yer bodice,"
She murmured. And Ann bared her aching breasts.
Then, holding by two legs the frog, she suddenly
Jerked, and the frog hung throbbing, torn asunder.
Against Ann's breasts she laid the trembling flesh.[2]

That night Ann left her husband's side, and stole
Out to the barn. Through the warm dimness surged
The lantern light, and in the light she saw
The plow. She stood a moment, very still;
Then, grasping the smooth, lantern-shining handles,
And between the handles leaning, through the chaff
Deep-sifted on the floor, she pushed the point,
Webbing the dust with strange significance.
Deep in the barn a restless hoof struck wood.
Ann left the plow, and holding high the lantern

That shed the light in dipping circles round her,
She stopped before the stall where the black bull
Stood breathing silver mist into the darkness.
The heat rolled out against her from his body
As, wondering at the gigantic power
Low-swung and latent on those wide-spread legs,
Staring, she reached out with an eager palm,
And laid it, for a moment, on his body . . .
Then, with a shudder, drew her hand away,
And ran, with the lantern sucking all the light
From the warm barn, and from the stamping cattle.

After that night Ann was more strange and silent
Even than formerly. Through the steel-blue dusk
That joined so closely night with winter night,
She would sit spinning in the chimney corner,
The white thread flowing round the polished wheel,
The white snow falling, falling in her soul . . .
The ice thinned outward from the banks; the ice
Thawed upon birches pitifully bent.
From upland pasture the cold winter sky
Lifted its weight. And yet Ann sat and spun.
Always her eyes, dull as two stones, were fixed
On the white circle streaming through the darkness.
Thus passed the dim short days; and then in silence
Drawing the sheet to veil her eyes, she lay
Upon the bed which leaned against the firelight
Like a dark stone set to mark a death.

One night Ann woke, and, ear pressed to the darkness,
Knew that the world was called again to life.
Life poured against the walls in silent torrents . . .
The walls of wood, that locked her close within them!
She sprang up, and ran out into the night,
Blind in her running. Through the hissing pines
And out upon that naked lift of pasture
Where lay her stillborn child, she came, and there
Was caught in the wash and welter of two waves
Of life. From field and forest life welled upward,

And from the sky life fell like streaming rain
And lay upon the earth in a black flood.
Over the rock-rimmed pasture heights, the stars
Poured through the sky, and earthward from the sky
Struck silver rods of starlight, in black prisms
Of night.
                    Ann stood a moment, hands upraised,
Then sank upon the grave, her body tense
Against the earth. And there she lay until
Dawn's white sun-bladed wings soared up the east.
Then standing up, beneath her feet she saw
Fields rear their arched brown backs above the mists,
Saw the wild foaming green on every tree.
She saw black cattle moving through the dawn
Up heights of pasture. Through the spreading dawn
Leaped a wild, silver wind, that circled round her,
Then gathered all its power and blew against
And through her, whipping her joy-maddened body
Into the riot and revel of its dance.

Now the blue plowshare surged in the broad fields,
The black earth, riven by the flame-like blade,
In sinuous furrows flowed behind. Ann watched
The plunging and inexorable plow,
Watched her husband guiding it, and when
The work was done, and over the quiet hills
The sky glowed greenly, stealing out alone,
Ann pressed her body to the raw, rich earth
And felt life swelling great against locked stones.
As the fields grew toward grandeur of the harvest,
Ann walked in silent joy through the tall grain
Silver and shadowy in the shifting wind,
Or stood beneath the dip of apple-boughs,
Long fingers searching out the ripening fruit
Let down in heaviness through clasp of leaves.

Now in the fields men cradled flashing scythes
Slanting in unison close to the ground.
The wheat sank ripe and rustling, and the women

Following, swept it up in golden armfuls,
Binding it on their hips.
                                        But Ann stood by,
Chained to the earth by the ripe, gold grain,
Her body towering in the gold sunlight
Above the crash of wind-bewildered grain,
Above the harvest-work of man and metal.

On windy nights the apples thundered down.
The fields grew hard and black as the cold crept
Little by little down the bitter sky.
Ann saw the trees bleed on the earth their leaves,
And saw the rose-bush cower against the trellis,
And saw the rose lock all its life and color
Within a bitter berry, tremulous
On the bare bramble, in the icy wind.
She took her child and buried him again
High on the pasture, under the cold stars,
And bent her body to the whirring wheel.
When in the high looms of the windy sky
Fine veils of snow were woven and blew out
Above the naked fields, then in her soul
Fell the white snow, the blind and soothing snow.

*   *   *   *   *   *

As the years passed, the people turned to Ann
In doubt about some matter of their planting.
For with the years, Ann seemed to grow more learned
In all the mysteries of darkened moons,
Of hidden wells. And always at a birth
Silent and skilled she bent above the bed.
Always she moved among them like a ghost,
Her eyes as dull and fixed as two round stones.
But while the people round her bent their backs
Beneath the inexorable scourge of age,
Her body gained in stature and in strength,
Becoming every spring a little richer,
More flowing in its grace. And when alone,
Her eyes were still as water beneath mist.

All through the winter days she sat alone,
Spinning the white thread round the dark wood wheel;
At night she lay sometimes beside her husband,
Silent and grey and bitter, and more often
She stole out to the barn, and gazed about her
At all the symbols of the black earth's yield—
Plow, scythe, harrow—and lay down
To sleep among them, with the stamping cattle.
In winter she was never seen outdoors,
But locked her grief within the cabin's dimness.

But on the night
When Spring and Winter overlapped great wings
High in the sky, and like two eagles fought
For dominance below, she would run out
Into the flooding winds. And after that
She scarcely lived within the cabin's walls,
But with the cattle moving up the mountain
She walked along the streaming mists of dawn,
Until beneath the sun they burned to nothingness;
Then in the swaying dimness of the forest
She lay beneath the gnarled mountain laurel
Or on the cool and calm of fallen oak leaves,
And heard the rush of wind among the leaves,
The subtle writhe and shiver of an earth
Forever tortured by the myriad roots
Sprawling in darkness downward. And at night,
When the sheep whitely streamed down the bare hills,
When darkness welled down the wide peaceful sky,
And silence mourned over the misty earth,
She rose, and from the height of naked pasture
Watched the stars slowly swing across the sky,
Or brooded above the dark, wide fields that flowed
Into the starlight, cradling the life
That blindly moved within.

Life was in death:
The world rolled black and barren in its mists,
And life was locked deep in the sheathing snows;
Then wind and sun and rain came, like a lover,

Clasping the world in fierce, caressing arms,
And on her body lying, warm and undulant;
And all life sprang to meet him.

                                        And with life
Of her own life thus given each year's rebirth,
Ann came to look upon herself as earth,
And lying strained against the earth, cried out
In joy at sweeping winds, at the warm sun,
At the black rain that plunged into the earth.
And thus, as the years passed, she lost the rhythms
That govern human life, and seemed to live
More like a tree, or like the earth itself.
The only intercourse with humankind
She held, was at a childbirth or a funeral,
Or in the spring, when all the people turned
Toward her to guide them in their planting. Then
With strange serenity she moved among them,
Handling the simple farming implements
Like sacred symbols of fertility.

As long as Ann lived, all the countryside
Was rich in produce—as long as Ann lived.

*   *   *   *   *   *

Ann never would have died within four walls,
Her body stretched beneath a fear-clutched sheet.
She never could have died, save in some great
Catastrophe of all the universe.

On a night in moon-dark, all the people stood
Silent and fearful, at the soil's first breaking.
The horses loomed against the starry sky,
And Ann, behind them, stood a minute, gazing
Across the black earth, and the shrinking snows.
Then, grasping the curved handles of the plow,
She poised the point against the earth, and pushed.
The horses started forward, and the earth
Rolled back before the darkly gleaming blade.

Then, stepping silently along the furrow,
With a wide-sweeping arm she cast out grain,
And once more stood in silence, staring out
Across the windblown fields, the windblown stars.

Next morning, all the preachers of the country
Saddled their horses, rode to every cabin,
Stood in the doorway, clenching in white knuckles
A roll of scripture, and forewarned the people
That in the darkened moon, only two nights
From then, all in the dread of God should gather
To greet, amidst fearsome falling of the stars,
The blasting of evil and the doom of earth.
And all the people swarmed down the ravines,
And crowded the frame churches, and began
Even in early dusk, to wail and sing
And pray, and hear the preacher's exhortations.

Ann lay half sinking in the fragrant needles
Fallen beneath the pines. Above her rose
The pasture, straining toward darkening sky.
Faint upon the crest she could discern
The higher grass beneath which lay her child.
The pines hissed softly in the evening breeze,
And in the clear sky, one by one, the stars
Burned through. From far below in the valley
The slow bells of returning flocks rang out.
Then darkness, like a slow wind in the sky,
Settled upon the hills—
                                        Down through the sky
A star streamed, like a golden rod that split
In half the darkness.

                                        Ann sprang to her feet
And, running to the highest crest of pasture,
Stood, staring out across the world. Another
And yet another, and again a star
Streaked downward. All the heavens seemed to slip
And swoop and shuttle, weaving a wild web
Of gold across the sky. And then, through all,

Fell a great, burning sphere, and myriad stars
Around it.—
    Sweeping above her wide black fields,
    Rending screaming air asunder,
    Into fields glowing stars
    Plunge with roll and groan of thunder.
    Down wide skies the golden plow
    Riving, cleaves a flaming furrow
    Wide for the seeds of a greater sowing.
    Whence comes the sower? Along the furrow

    Striding great upon the sky,
    Sweeping wide a flaming hand,
    He sows the universe anew,
    Advancing toward her pasture-land,
    Arms flexed above her, blotting the sky
    With body bent to the world's rim. . . .

*   *   *   *   *

Her husband found her on the heave of earth
Beneath which lay her child, in six oak boards
Tight-locked against the earth. Ann's hair was blown
Back from the hollow temples, in a way
To mould the head in savage eagerness
Which bent her body into one taut curve.

Clawing in jealousy at his swept beard,
He pondered the chisellings of lust
That so transformed in death the woman who
Had lived beside him silent as a ghost.
Then seeing that the clothes torn from her body
Were clenched in her own hands, he made all haste
To bury her before his neighbors, coming
And staring at that flared and joyful mouth,
Should nudge and whisper, and believe the thing
He knew could not be true. So, from his cabin
Returning with a shovel, he began
To dig, fearing to question the lustful mask.

He dug down through the grave where, years before,
His shovel rang out in the ice-clamped earth,
And digging, struck the box. He pried it open
And strangely gazed upon the fleece that wrapped
His child. Then, lifting in his arms his wife,
He lowered her among the broken roots,
And starting to replace the little box,
Stopped. From the fleece he clutched the crumbled bones,
And in Ann Garner's mouth he sprinkled bones,
And on Ann Garner's eyes he sprinkled bones—

Then gently laid the earth above her body,
And looked about him at the windswept dawn,
And slowly through the trees walked to his cabin.

1928.

[a] The reference is to the folk belief that placing a sharp instrument, such as a plow or axe or knife, under the bed of a woman in labor will cut the pain of childbirth.

IV. A Chorale.

Who, knowing love must die or live free-fated,
Free in your heartsearth headlong man created:
Who manly died and sealed from all perdition
Our ill condition:

Your crown not God nor your great death retains you:
As you are man so man for man ordains you:
Who reign in man's regard O much forsaken
Dear Christ awaken!

Range the blest hordes that rest in you around you:
Look down kind prince on treason to astound you:
See now sweet farmer what a wasting shadow
Takes your green meadow:

How, love of self, fact, state, and art much prizing,
Men move in manners of their own devising:
How they kill truth to find out truth more nearly
That's mortal merely:

How knowledge muffles wisdom's eye to danger:
How greed misrules: how greed's enraged avenger
Swears greed the equal prize for man's pursuing,
And your undoing:

How many ways men build up man's disaster:
How all are armaments against man's master:
How surely soon comes toward without atonement
Your disenthronement:

How cowardly those few that still exalt you
Worship their death while wildly men assault you:
How not one dares who knows what men intend you,
Die to defend you:

Though you outreign our time which is an hour,
Yet you in us have put you in our power:

What God man builds in God His truth is ended
Not well defended:

O Godsent Son of God our allsalvation,
Is faith so sickly slow to indignation
Your murderers against? Then faith betrays you:
Your friends destroy you:

Your faith who gave your heart for our safekeeping,
Your love who sweated blood while we were sleeping,
If so these waste within this generation
Death is your nation:

The time is withered of your ancient glory:
Your doing in this sweet earth a pretty story:
O noblest heart fare well through the conclusion
Of all delusion.

Great God kind God the deep fire-headed fountain
Of earth and funneled hell and hopeful mountain:
Of ghosted Gods the eversame survivor:
Of shoreless strength of peace the prime contriver:
If this your Son is now indeed debasèd
Among old effigies of Gods effacèd,
Blaze in our hearts who still in earth commend you:
Who through all desolation will defend you:
For we are blinded all and steep are swervèd
Far among many Deaths who still would be preservèd.

V. Epithalamium.

I.

Now day departs: Upreared the darkness climbs
The breathless sky, leans wide above the fields,
And snows its silence round the muttering chimes:
The night is come that bride to bridegroom yields.

The night is come, that hallows as it harms,
That in perfection clothes the flesh defaced.
Now let the mother gather in her arms
The body that to other arms must haste.

For lo: from Oeta's[a] wild and windflayed height
A star takes wing, soars up the wide arched sky.
And, from the constant fountain crest of flight,
Lowers on the marriage bed its prospering eye.

Still, with the glad impatient waiting o'er,
Weeping, with weak embrace, the mother shields
The maiden who is hers to guard no more:
The night is come, that bride to bridegroom yields.

[a] Mount Oeta (7,060 ft.) is chiefly celebrated as the scene of Heracles' death in Greek mythology. The central area of the mountain was declared a national park in 1966.

II.

Thick through the blended darkness slow-born dews distil,
Swell upon stem and stone, confuse the night.
Toward Hesperus[a] still gazing poised fond above the hill
Now wind the glad torch flames, full blown and bright.

Soft through the sleeping meadows blind with dark and dew
We move, our torches shaking off the gloom.

We maim the soundless woodland, we bear our drenched yew,
We come to the marriage bed, the waiting groom.

[a] Hesperus, subsequently also called Hesper, is the Evening Star, the planet Venus (visible during the night) in Greek mythology. He was a brother of Atlas, the father of the seven sisters known as the Hesperides, who guarded the golden apples that Hercules eventually won.

III.

Hesperus alone holds all the windworn sky,
Involves the bed in his steep, streaming light;
And dusts that ever in aloofness lie
Shudder to life, and marvel at the night.

For from the sky now falls a holy dower
Over the subtle ruin of her charms,
And the mute dusts, that swell with Hesperus' power,
Shall hold her joys and shield from all alarms.

IV.

How proud in gentle modesty she lies
And greets her lover with stately tenderness.
No wanton glance, no false coquettish sighs
Betray her love, her sober eagerness.

No smile she grants, no blushes red confuse
Her pure flesh in its white tranquillity:
Quiet on her bed amid the glancing dews,
Queenly she waits in rich humility.

V.

For that he, in whose arms you soon shall lie,
Not without guilt comes to a guiltless bride,
Still fear him not, but tender at his side
Recall his sorrow and his deep distress,
Recall his loneliness.

No boy has lived, but he has been his friend,
No maiden but has lain within his arms.
Hopeful of love fulfilled, he sought their charms,
But all the visions that his full heart cherished
In short time perished.

Through the dark depths of ocean and of sky,
Through all the world he pursued his endless quest,
And gathered every beauty to his breast:
But found no love, and sought on, unavailing,
His hope fast failing.

Now, with this night, his search is at an end.
The myriad blemished beauties you assumed,
That long were dead, late in enchantment bloomed.
Now, knowing all love and joy in you alone,
He takes you for his own.

So, wound him not with one misgiving sigh;
With his clear rapture let no sorrow blend.
Lo, holy Hesperus watches from on high,
His still fires round your lover's heart descend
And to rude passion put an end.

VI.

Now the groom joins her, and the happy lovers
Bind heart to heart with close-encircling arms.
Hesper's clear benediction round them hovers;
The night is come that hallows as it harms.

O maids, through whose translucent masks of grief
Envious gladness gleams, for all her charms
Outshine your own, nay, Beauty's, past belief,
Your night will come, that hallows as it harms.

And youths, whose loving eyes feast and delay,
Though hope is gone, and holy vows are sealed,
Put off your sorrow, woo but for a day,
And night will come, and bride to bridegroom yield.

Over the lovers and the marriage bed,
Bare to the staring sky, the chilling dew,
Now close protection and concealment spread,
Clod upon branch, soft dust and sacred yew.[a]

[a] The yew tree is sacred to the Greek goddess Hecate, who frees souls from their bodies after death.

VII.

Let no noise born of night come near their room:
No milk-eyed frog, with bubble-throated croaks,
Nor screaking bat, whose wings hook through the gloom,
Nor mournful owl, whose lost and dreary yell
The monstrous deities of the dark invokes.

Let no foul mist that cold above them trails
Settle upon them, smothering wrap them round.
But venom that the sweltering marsh exhales
Loose-coiled and prowling, let the wind confound
And in the dry blast let its damp be drowned.

Let them lie safe: from every evil spell
That witches chant to sour true lovers' joys,
From the lank spirits night recalls from hell,
From ghost that gibbers, and from ghoul that wails,
From all malevolence the night employs.

It stands not in our narrow realm of power
To ward off aught that ever joy has marred,
But put off fear, for from this blessed hour
The stars, the sky, and all the earth, stand guard.

Root clenches root, dust into hard earth blends;
With bolts of stone the door's forever barred;
Across the wounded hill the long grass mends;
Around the lovers all the earth stands guard.

The twelve thongs of the wind[a] shall lash and shred
The mists to air, shall soften, and retard,

And droop a rainy curtain round the bed:
Over the lovers all the sky stands guard.

Hesperus marshals all his myriad throng:
Down the deep night they gaze, with fond regard
And fateful, who shall shield them from all wrong:
Over the lovers all the stars stand guard.

[a] This is a reference to passages in the Book of Enoch, an ancient Hebrew apocalyptic religious text, later removed from standard Jewish Biblical Texts, except for that of the Beta Israel (Ethiopian Jews). It exists in various translations. For one example see https://www.sacred-texts.com/bib/boe/boe079.htm.

VIII.

'Tis time that we, who loved her through the day,
Whom Hesperus is urgent to bereave,
No longer should their rightful joys delay,
But fondly and forever take our leave.

Even now in tenderness the lovers pause,
And, for a moment, all is blind as night,
All, save their love, that, the next moment, draws
Them on to realms of measureless delight.

Knotted in secrecy, the sacred zone
From every harm the unharmed virgin shields:
One may unloose the knot, and one alone:
The night is come, and bride to bridegroom yields.

Close in her kindly and untroubled arms,
He sets the zone aside, with gentle haste:
The night is come, that hallows as it harms,
And she assumes perfection, who was chaste.

Flesh and bright flesh he draws from off his bride:
Dust holds her wedding garment with the zone.
He who sets carnal nakedness aside
Knows the blank final bareness of the bone.

Now all is ready, now the happy bride
Lies unclothed as her lover, and on love
That long frustration and the zone denied,
Hesperus streams his sanction from above.

Now she yields all: her body to his own,
Her steadfast loving gaze, her mouth to his kiss—
All beauty and all love has never known
The ragged shadow of their radiant bliss.

Their love burns wilder, and the steady brand
Flares into furious and holy lust.
Their substance shivers and runs down like sand
Into the dust, and is one with the dust.

IX.

For that the flesh arises like a wall
Between two souls, all love has known distress.
But they have conquered sorrow, conquered all
That clouded love: are one in nothingness.

Such nothingness remains, and yet is gone,
Looks upon all, and yet is void of sight,
Quickens the roots of every flowering dawn,
Coils in the core of every ripening night:

It breathes from steady water, is the pain
Of bursting seeds, the agony of earth
Shuddering out its life; streams down in rain
That causes and alleviates all birth:

X.

When spring returns:—with every spring to come,
When the black worldseed buds and is full blown,
When all is singing that was frozen dumb,
Behold her children, whom no man has known!

When the long hill-grass hisses and interlaces,
When the tree stands aloof that split the stone,
When the leaves greenly stream in the wind-mad places,
Behold her children whom no man has known!

She who lies at the bottom of the night,
She who was flesh ere flesh revealed the bone
And bone relaxed to dust is deathless light:
And such her children whom no man has known!

XI.

But still we stand, and they are scarce abed.
Scarce has their long and joyful night begun.
Now at their door the last yew branches spread
And hasten home; for night is nearly done.

Unformed and grey, heavy with lingering night,
Soft in its solitude stoops every tree.
All is submerged and blurred in fragile light
As at the bottom of a moonled sea.

Dispread among the hills, bemused and wan
Lie the night tarnished half awakened fields.
The stars shrink back on white oblivion:
The dim sky loosens, and the long night yields.

Over the rim of mountains in the east
The daybreak, that through all the hours of night
Welled steady from the nadir, now, released,
Floods all the earth and sky with glassy light.

Wind flaws the shifting grandeur of the grain,
Pours through the green confusion of the leaves.
The mists become as air, our torches wane:
And once more Hesperus his dark hill perceives.

His strong and bright protection is as naught:
O'er lovers whom no darkness would dismay

O'er all enchantment that the night has wrought,
Merciless storms the overwhelming day.

XII.

Quiet, forever free from all alarms,
They lie where light is strengthless to descend.
The night is come, that hallows as it harms:
The night is come that day may never end.

1930.

VI. Sonnets.

I.[1]

So it begins. Adam is in his earth
Tempted, and fallen, and his doom made sure
O, in the very instant of his birth:
Whose deathly nature must all things endure.
The hungers of his flesh, and mind, and heart,
That governed him when he was in the womb,
These ravenings[a] multiply in every part:
And shall release him only to the tomb.
Meantime he works the earth, and builds up nations,
And trades, and wars, and learns, and worships chance,
And looks to God, and weaves the generations
Which shall his many hungerings advance
When he is sunken dead among his sins.
Adam is in this earth. So it begins.

[a] Ravenous urges; extremely hungry and hunting for prey.

II.[1]

Our doom is in our being. We began
In hunger eager more than ache of hell:
And in that hunger became each a man
Ravened with hunger death alone may spell:
And in that hunger live, as lived the dead,
Who sought, as now we seek, in the same ways,
Nobly, and hatefully, what angel's-bread[a]
Might ever stand us out these short few days.
So is this race in this wild hour confounded:
And though you rectify the big distress,
And kill all outward wrong where wrong abounded,
Your hunger cannot make this hunger less
Which breeds all wrath and right, and shall not die
In earth, and finds some hope upon the sky.

[a] This is a reference to Psalms 78: 24–25 (KJV). "And had rained down manna upon them to eat, and had given them of the corn of heaven. Man did eat angels' food: he sent them meat to the full."

III.

The wide earth's orchard of your time of knowing,
Shine of the springtime pleasures into bloom
And branchèd throes of health: but soon the snowing
And tender foretaste of your afterdoom,
Of fallen blossoming air persuades the air
In hardier practises: and soon dilate
Fruits and the air together that shall bear
Earthward the heavied boughs and to their fate:
Wrung of the wealth and wonder they unfurled
By that same air: which air the sun deranges
To slope the living season from the world
And charge the world with snow that all estranges.
Watch well this sun, and air, and orchard green:
None stay these changes every man has seen.

IV.[1]

I have been fashioned on a chain of flesh
Whose backward length is broken on the dust:
Frail though the dust and small as the dew's mesh
The morning mars, it holds me to a trust:
My flesh that was, long as this flesh knew life,
Strove, and was valiant, still strove, and was naught:
Now it is mine to wage their valiant strife
And failing seek still what they ever sought.
I have been given strength they never wore.
I have been given hope they never knew.
And they were brave, who can be brave no more.
And they that live are kind as they are few.
'Tis mine to touch with deathlessness their clay:
And I shall fail, and join those I betray.

V.[1]

Strengthless they stand assembled in the shadow,
Blind to all strife and all to sorrow blind
Who reared the tower, who scored the April meadow:
Sheltered, they overshade my strengthless mind.
Those hands that gave their kind ungentle power
To summer's travail, autumn did not spare:
That mind which knew the clear, the intact hour,
Now is disparted on a changeful air.

The hands that ached to help are pithless bone
(Mind, mind, the harsh pain and the unalloyed:
What fruit you bear, that must you bear alone!)
The broken helmet nods around its void:
So I disclothe me of this shadow's blight;
And stand the axis of swift noon, sure night.

VI.

Season of change the sun for distaff bearing
In your right hand and in the left large rains
And writhen winds and noiselessly forth faring
The earth abroad, and streaming wide your skeins,
When in unfathomed fairness you have clothed
The sea with quiet, the land with painless wealth,
Turn you to those who changelessly have loathed
All and their kind, and grant them peace and health:
The proud stone-parting ardor of the tree,
The glee of ice relaxed against new earth,
Joy of the lamb and lust of bloom-struck bee
Grant to the sick, stiff, spiteful, like fresh birth.
Let this new time no natural wheel derange:
Be ever changeless, thus: season of change.

VII.[1]

What dynasties of destinies undreamed
And truth to halt the heart does man descry
There, that so rarely has his heart beteemed
His eye to frankly watch into an eye?
The earliest marvelings only of the heart
Estranged of blindness of its living care
And from beholding Being held athwart
By narrowest shade, so deeply make him dare.
What truth we glimpse that each see other so
That stills our blood with horror of delight
Which once alone with other each may know:
Who swiftly changed recoil from that dread sight:
And how, if that were told, would change this day:
All human kind has seen, and none can say.

VIII.[1]

What curious thing is love that you and I
Hold it impervious to all distress
And insolent in gladness set it high
Above all other joy and goodliness?
Ignorance and unkindness, aspiration,
The weary flesh, the mind's inconstancy,
Even now conspire its sure disintegration:
Be mindful, love, of love's mortality.
Be mindful that all love is as the grass
And all the goodliness of love the flower
Of grass, for lo, its little day shall pass
And withering and decay define its hour.
All that we hold most lovely, and most cherish
And most are proud in, all shall surely perish.

IX.[1]

Why am I here? Why do you look at me
Triumphantly and lovingly and long?
When were we captured? When shall I be free
From your delight and this delicious wrong?
Not by your will I trust, nor by my own
I swear, nor any close device of reason
Are we engulfed by thicker walls than stone,
Mismated victims of unfounded treason.
Forbear, forbear to look at me with joy.
I would not do you hurt who will no harm,
But that sure smile I surely shall destroy—
Its covert meaning and its patent charm.
Awakened to our love's surprising hell,
Your dream struck sleep befits it hardly well.

X.

Wring me no more nor force from me that vow
Which lovers love to hear for reassurance;
Rest faithful in firm silence, which is now
Frail but sole bulwark for our love's endurance.
However mad, it is my heart's belief
That he who lies of love trumpets instruction
For anger and terror, scorn and doubt and grief
Swiftly to marshal toward our sure destruction.
Since, though we know naught else, we know love true,
When from the strict course which love's truth affirms
The sick brain swerves, to guiltless hearts accrue
Love's penalties and unpalliable terms.
If you love truly, speak the vow for me:
My lips can ill afford the blasphemy.

XI.[1]

For love departed, lover, cease to mourn.
Of flesh conceived, love fed upon our flesh
And of our agony and joy was born;
Whence often we have wept: weep not afresh.
How love grew strong and lovelier than we
Was all our joy, is for our solace still:
Woe though it was that wreck of strength to see
Thaw down and die, it was not by our will.
Our will? who sleepless and with anguished care
Plied every heartful balm and thoughtful cure,
Due rite of lust and precondemned prayer:
All which despite our love might not endure:
Because this forewrought evil has prevailed
Shall we mourn love and say that we have failed?

XII.[1]

Is love then royal on some holy height?
Thence does he judge us, thence dispense his grace?
There strike apart the darkness and the light
And shroud in light his sight-destroying face?
What are his laws? By what high-dealt decrees
Do lovers snared by all the laws of earth
Transcend the pain and cruelty and lost ease
That globes our globe, and soar to heavenward birth?
I have known love as lowly, full of lust,
Bent on contriving Godhead from the flesh,
Wrought of desire and waning through mistrust,
Starved in the sinuately[a] carnal mesh.
Is there indeed a God who can redeem
The love we know as a dawn-tinctured dream?

[a] Wavy, winding, bent in and out.

XIII.[1]

Sorrowful or angry, hold it no way remiss
That, with the last gasp of love's healthless breath
(More cruelly stopped than with our latest kiss)
I would dissuade you from my imminent death.
The heart knows love exanimate of reason,
And your love thus beyond all reason dead;
The astounded brain, incredulous of treason,
Still must defy what heartful hope has fled.
Though the deliberate autumn air bereaves
With curious raveling all the rich-wrought earth,
The stringent winter through some idiot leaves
Outbrave defeat until the new leaves' birth:
When only (should that dubious spring renew)
Dying to live, I'll know my heart was true.

XIV.

Not of good will my mother's flesh was wrought,
Whose parents sowed in joy, and garnered care:
The sullen harvest sudden winter brought
Upon their time, outlasting their despair.
Deep of a young girl's April strength his own
My father's drank, and draughted her to age:
Who in his strength met death and was outdone
Of high and hopeless dreams, and grief, and rage.

Poor wrath and rich humility, these met,
Married, and sorrowing in a barren bed
Their flesh embraced in pity did beget
Flesh that must soon secure their fleshlihead:
But knows not when, on whom cannot descry,
And least of all could vaunt conjecture why.

XV.

But that all these, so hopeful of their day,
Highsouled in joy and hungry for the fight,
Loved all too well such loving to betray,
And linked in love declined into the night
Whose dusk is flesh, whose dark is family,
Whose midnight is despair full-wrought from love;
Despair of strength and the soul's entity;
Opposed to noon by this thick world's remove.

And since I burn so wrathfully with joy,
And love also, as kindly as did they,
And so would fight, and so would not destroy
Night-hearted love that shows so proud a day:
I'll choose the course my fathers chose before.
And, with their shadows, pray my son does more.

XVI.

How all a hurrying year was negligence,
Each meeting other as the casual merely,
In aimless fondness and the year's expense
Of much not seen and nothing sought sincerely:
Knowing such little truth, so lightly wearing
The small regrets of ill-established friends,
And our unmeasured liking meanly sharing,
And wanting yet evading all amends:

How, for all fear, that thing which dignifies
Our selves in each above those affable
So used its strength once that our helpless eyes
Killed and restored us in thc fact in full:
How these things were, stuns and outstands my thought,
Now we are joined in all we scarcely sought.

XVII.[1]

I nothing saw in you that was not common
In some degree to any other friend,
Nothing that any amiable woman
Might not possess or by her wit pretend:
Only that we were straggling in our speech,
Uneasy in our liking, much as though
There dwelt such content in the heart of each
As needs must speak, but how it did not know:
True, this seemed strange to me, as well it might,
And did to you, yet neither had the art
To guess the truth and certify the sight
To the perceptions of the powerless heart:
Which now our selves so powerfully convince,
All the world else is idiocy since.

XVIII.

The way the cleansouled mirror of a soul
Dreams in the darkened flesh and smoky breath
That only takes and tells the image whole
When all obstruction's wiped away by death:
So with our hearts that sleeping long have dreamed
Imaginations of celestial love.
Their flaws in each the other has redeemed
(True lovers such obscurities remove).
And now, but slowly, see our hearts awake.
The eyes unshut, the living sight shine clear;
How still each heart reluctant lies to take
The image of its image: though so near
We lie, that surely both our hearts perceive
Identities they scarcely yet believe.

XIX.[1]

Those former loves wherein our lives have run
Seeing them shining, following them far,
Were but a hot deflection of the sun,
The operation of a migrant star.
In that wrong time when still a shape of earth
Severed us far and stood our sight between,
Those loves were effigies of love whose worth
Was all our wandering nothing to have seen:
So toward those steep projections on our sky
We toiled though partners to their falsity
Who faintly in that falseness could descry
What now stands forth too marvelous to see:
Who one time loved in them the truth concealed:
And now must leave them in the truth revealed.

XX.[1]

Now stands our love on that still verge of day
Where darkness loiters leaf to leaf releasing
Lone tree to silvering tree: then slopes away
Before the morning's deep-drawn strength increasing
Till the sweet land lies burnished in the dawn:
But sleeping still: nor stirs a thread of grass:
Large on the low hill and the spangled lawn
The pureleaved air dwells passionless as glass:
So stands our love new found and unaroused,
Appareled in all peace and innocence,
In all lost shadows of love past still drowsed
Against foreknowledge of such immanence
As now, with earth outshone and earth's wide air,
Shows each to other as this morning fair.

XXI.

Who but sniffs substance gorges it, my soul,
Smothers digestion with stuffed appetite.
Disorders work in him and he is whole
One swill of dreams that all ways wreak him spite.
As arsenic can make a plant seem fresh
So are these hoisted dreams that are the flesh
A health not his and false and neverlasting
But loved once known which blinds with change and wasting.
So by my birth are you: wherefore this wry,
This raw corrective that alone outwrings
These doubly deathful healths: so though we die
Yet so die not one coward but two kings.
So should we live, why then God lives also.
That was His Will which then will be our Woe.

XXII.

When beyond noise of logic I shall know
And in that knowledge swear my knowledge bound
In all things constant, never more to show
Its head in any transience it has found:
When pride of knowledge, frames of government,
The wrath of justice gagged and greed in power,
Sure good, and certain ill, and high minds bent
On destiny sink deathward as this hour:
When deep beyond surmise the driven shade
Of this our earth and mind my mind confirms,
Essence and fact of all things that are made,
Nature in love in death are shown the terms:
When, through this lens, I've seen all things in one,
Then, nor before, I truly have begun.

XXIII.

This little time the breath and bulk of being
Are met in me: who from the eldest shade
Of all undreamt am raised forth into seeing
As I may see, the state of all things made:
In sense and dream and death to make my heart
Wise.in the loveliness and natural health
Of all, and God, upon the void a part:
Likewise to celebrate this commonwealth:
Believing nothing, and believing all,
In love, in detestation, but most
In naught to sing of all: to recall
What wisdom was before I was this ghost:
Such songs I shall not make nor truths shall know:
And once more mindless into truth shall go.

XXIV.

Sure fortitude must disabuse my mind
Of all enlargements in unfounded hope
That I perceive whom fear of self made blind
My destiny constrained in my own scope.
All memory of magnificence of sound,
All grandeur and finality of word,
All nobleness some alien pain has found
That lives here painless, let them be interred.
Those men I worship and would stand among
In death well gained and reverently would greet,
Those immense souls have peopled mine too long,
And blown it broad with hope that was deceit:
And my poor soul, if aught it would create,
Must fast of thesc, and feed on its own fate.

XXV.

My sovereign souls, God grant my sometime brothers,
I must desert your ways now if I can.
I followed hard but now forsake all others,
And stand in hope to make myself a man.
This mouth that blabbed so loud with foreign song
I'll shut awhile, or gargle if I sing.
Have patience, let me too, though it be long
Or never, till my throat shall truly ring.

These are confusing times and dazed with fate:
Fear, easy faith, or wrath's on every voice:
Those toward the truth with brain are blind or hate:
The heart is cloven on a hidden choice:
In which respect I still shall follow you.
And, when I fail, know where the fault is due.

VII. *Permit Me Voyage.*[1]

From the Third Voyage of Hart Crane

Take these who will as may be: I
Am careless now of what they fail:
My heart and mind discharted lie
And surely as the nervèd nail

Appoints all quarters on the north
So now it designates him forth
My sovereign God my princely soul
Whereon my flesh is priestly stole:

Whence forth shall my heart and mind
To God through soul entirely bow,
Therein such strong increase to find
In truth as is my fate to know:

Small though that be great God I know
I know in this gigantic day
What God is ruined and I know
How labors with Godhead this day:

How from the porches of our sky
The crested glory is declined:
And hear with what translated cry
The stridden soul is overshined:

And how this world of wildness through
True poets shall walk who herald you:
Of whom God grant me of your grace
To be, that shall preserve this race.

Permit me voyage, Love, into your hands.

Early Poetry: Phillips Exeter and Harvard, 1925–1932

Verses

Ebb Tide

He's gone, he's dead; he's carried away my soul
To empty space where stars sink sighing past.

And now—my life to live, a gaunt, sad life . . . .
My life—it's like a little shallow pool
Left in the hollowed rock by ebbing tide;
A pool which slowly turns to bitter salt . . . .

My life . . . a tepid, slowly dwindling pool,
To join—once more—the vastness of the sea.

In Preparation

Strip off these glittering baubles—robe in white.
Kneel! On the bare floor of thy wretched cell,
Blind in the wan chill light of Advent's moon,
Weave thou the Carpet of thy Penitence!

The Phillips Exeter Monthly, November 1925, p. 27[1]

Pygmalion[a1]

World, my beloved world, scarce can I bear
The rending and transcendent joy that flows
High in my heart! Gone the dire loneliness
Of countless aeons past, when here I sat,
One Solitude pervading solitude,
Watching my ordered wilderness of space
Sweep past in still and solemn pageantry—
Watching the ordered swerving of the stars,
The rolling constellations, and the bright
Swoop of screaming comets—When I heard
The swishing of the stars across the sky,
The smothered sighs of burring nebulae;
The hollow and reverberating crash
Of universe convolute. That day
Sorrowful midst my lifeless wilderness,
There surged into my brain a glorious dream
Of thee, my World, as still thou art tonight.

Down through the sweeping, billowing veils of Space
I thrust my gentle and gigantic hands.
Heavy and damp in the warm, curving palms
Lay thou, unborn, but flaming in my mind.
In a slow fever of delight I worked,
Worked, tireless, through the rain of centuries.
Under the subtle smoothing of my hands,
The strong eternal soothing of my palms,
I moulded out a warm rotundity,
Plastic, and sheathed in one unbroken sea;
And pressed the sea with unrelenting palms
Until it sank deep in the followed earth.
Then, with the roll of land that damply rose
Out of the girdling water, I began:
Here, with the pressure of my thumb, I scooped
A socket for one blue and bitter jewel—[2]
That lake, which elevates its glaring plane

To flash the mirrored sunlight in my face.
Down to the seas I dragged my fingertips,
And water sprang beneath them, and flows still.
From the moist earth I pinched thy little hills;
After the passage of my pressing palms
Brown prairies hinged the rivers and the rocks—
And mountain peaks I chiseled from the rocks,
And girdled them about with rolling mist . . .

Thou, multiplicit[3] glory of my dream,
Lay in perfection, lifeless in my palms.
Stooping, I laid my fact upon thy seas;
Thrice round thy surface swept my wreathing breath.
Then burst from out thee Life. I let it swarm
Into the warm and shallow seas. From then
Till now, and through eternity, I Am;
Watching that life unfolding and diffused—
Watching it scramble o'er thy splendid frame
And try but vainly to remold my dream.

O world, what joy is mine thou canst not know!—
To know thy beauty, formless, millionformed!
To hear the breathing of the sea at night,
The sagging of the wearied, sleeping hills,
The stifled whispers of o'erlapping leaves—
To hear the breathless silence when the tide
Slinks through the darkness, outward from the shore!
To lose myself in that bell-haunted fog
That stalks among the drenched and spiky pines
And broods above the terrified flat sea!
To see night spread her silent wings and flee
Headlong the clarion assault of dawn—
The swoop of glistening steams down to the sea,
The unperturbéd surge of misty plains,
Their verdure breaking high on mountain-sides . . .

To see thy beauty parched and crackling,
Thirsty and caked with summer dust; to hear

One raucous groan of color, dying out
As one leaf swirls; o'erlaps a fading leaf
And drains thy life-blood back into thy breast . . [.]
To see thy beauty sprawled and stark in death,
The staring of the grey and glazéd seas—
To gently shroud thee in my silent snows
And brood above thee, holding in my heart
The calm sure solace of the spring to come . . .

Not in the memory of a million springs
Is there the joy of watching, through this night,
Spring, crouching noiselessly upon the hills.
I see thee shrink, thou tattered shroud of snow,
Discovering the body of my world,
Naked, and palpitant with new-found life.
I press my face into thy hot, sweet earth,
And hear the steady singing of the sap
And feel the prickling grass against my cheeks—
Trees! Thy red buds unfolding stickily,
Tumbling joyous hills and shouting brooks,
Full throated rivers, pounding, shattering seas,
Seaweed, strangling the rusty rocks—
Mist-hidden mountains, cold and haggard crags—
Upward ye fling your arms—Upward ye hurl
Your voices in gigantic jubilance!
O world, too beautiful thou art today!
Be not afraid—I cannot but caress
The rondure of that hill—cannot but clasp
Thy teeming plains against my breast . . [.]
                                        Fear not,
Belovéd earth; if I must strain thee close
'Tis to alleviate the agony
Of such a passion as I never knew
Could—Closer I must press thee, though I hear
The crumbling of thy framework, though thy seas,
Forced from their sockets, shiver into space;
In opalescent globes they slowly[4] sink,
Weaving their trails of light among the stars—

The stars that swing in grand processional
Ever, and ever on.

Here in my hand,
I hold the bruised and broken form of Earth.

UTK MS 3824 Box 7, Folder 5 [four pages of typescript; 1925–1928(?)][5]

[a] In Greek mythology, Pygmalion is the legendary king of Cyprus who sculpts a female figure of ivory that he loves and is brought to life for him by Aphrodite. In a more general sense, a Pygmalion is someone who falls in love with his own creation. *Pygmalion* is also a title of a famous play by George Bernard Shaw (1913).

The Poets' Valediction

We, with our eyes impaled of fire,
We, with our hearts suffused of flame,
Our lips made lurid with desire
And our hearts hooded dark with shame.

Once, in a young and evil hour
Ran foul of beauty on the air,
And since that time are in her power
To her delight and our despair.

Whence forth through all her weird ways
And devious incarnations, we
Have sought, whom guileless things amaze
With labyrinthine falsity,

That essence which is beauty's life
Clothed in a myriad disguise
Which keenest thought nor shrewdest knife
Most swiftly urged may never surprise.

When we were nearest her deceit
And she imperiled[1] of her power,
With windy grass she bound our feet,
Or in a bright malignant shower

Involved our passage, and when these
Delusions served but to refresh,
In new dissemblance of dis-ease
She wove herself a gown of flesh

Wherein she strolled athwart our way
Young, and irrationally wise,
And swift accomplished our dismay
With furious and gentle eyes.

Some time as thoughtless as the air,
Remorseless and regardless quite

Of lost and further seeking, there
By love deceived and love's delight

We lingered in the simple joy
And operation of our lust:
Which that sweet texture did destroy
And sharply raveled[2] toward the dust

Then rose the mind in his despair
To kind obscene philosophy.
Impervious to such repair
Love died of unsimplicity.

Half sure of finding, surer of
Solaceous[a] ease if she were sped,
Rifling all various looms of love
We set corruption on each thread.

She was dissolved out of flesh
And was departed out of love,
And urged no summer wind to thresh
Music from no harmonious grove,

But from all bygone semblances
Which now were vulnerable of proof,
And every proof the heart assays
And soon destroys, she held aloof.

All these old seemings were become
Our property, who exercised
Our wit and knowledge of their sum
And that familiar sum despised.

Out of that wealth which we despise
We fashioned various hymns, to be
Sung in her worship, which, being lies,
Fractions of false totality,

As well we knew, whenever sung
Did but contaminate her name.

Men's praise and her own silence flung
Our hearts athwart, the midnight's shame.

In self despisal and despair
Alone and unobserved, each
Knelt, and addressed to her a prayer
In broken undeviséd speech:

And saw the hills resolve to their
Essential and primeval fire,
The shaken seas on air, the air
Athwart ethereal space expire,

While through demolishment and smoke
And all creation set awry,
Loud the ambiguous thunder spoke,
Articulate along the sky

The lightnings wrote what none might read,
The imperious patterened stars revolved
Their influence round the changing seed:
Despite which seed and stars dissolved:

The mad oracular din was quelled,
All elemental stuffs unjointed,
And all molecular mists dispelled,
And all sure substance disappointed:

And down that spaceless disarray
Where now we waited undistressed,
Where night concentralized with day,
Beauty her Self made manifest.

Of that high Presence who shall prate
Who from the black disanimate flame
And quiet whence all things emanate
Declared her multiplicit name?

Silent we knelt, and silent she
With never a need for any word

Proclaimed those verities which we
May find no speech for, who have heard.

While still we knelt, from out that space
Of holy nothingness, exhaled
All things to their appointed place
And we to earth, whom speech has failed

Truly to make what we perceive
Identical with what we see:
All guileless things which now deceive
With labyrinthine verity.

To the old quest we've fallen heir
Once more, and to the ancient pain
And sick desire, who could not bear
For long the sight without the stain;

Wherefore, with eye impaled of fire
And with our flesh suffused of flame,
Our lips made lurid by desire
Our hearts destroyed by hooded shame,

Silent henceforth, we march toward
That silence which is beauty's soul:
Be our oblivious reward
That some man tell of beauty whole.

UTK MS 1500 Box 1, Folder 11 [1925–32[b]; three typed pages]

[a] Perhaps Agee's coinage meaning full of solace, or a double meaning joining it to salacious, or a misspelling of salacious.

[b] The date range is determined by the fact that this poem was turned in as a class assignment. The instructor ("T.") liked it a good deal.

China

A junk with sails of gilded reed
Rides high the shimmering flood;
Above the willows hangs the moon,
A scarlet drop of blood.

Water splashes, crystal-clear,
In a fount of polished jade;
A jeweled hand lies on its brim,
And a sleeve of green brocade.

The maid has lustrous, narrow eyes,
And a waist like a roll of silk;
A poppy bleeds in her bound black hair,
And her throat is pale as milk.

Her fingers brush the taut lute strings.
As she sings a strange, sad song;
Each rich note fades in the fragrant dark
With the vibrance of a gong.

Huge carven gates of olivine[a]
Swing silently a-jar.
Drums throb; the chants of Buddha's priests
Is wafted from afar . . . .

Phillips Exeter Monthly, January, 1926, p. 79

[a] Olivine is the name of a group of rock-forming minerals that are typically found in igneous rocks such as basalt and peridotite; they are usually green in color.

La Fille aux Cheveux de Lin

In the bleak land of Burgundy she lives,
Sits singing silent songs in a high tower,
Weaving the while a brave bright tapestry,
Smiling her changeless smile, her calm, strange smile,
Gazing at nothing—at infinity—
Her blue eyes narrow, mystic, like the smile.
Quietly she sits and weaves her tapestry.
Upon her bosom falls her fragrant hair,
Shining 'gainst flaming satin and her jewels—
A wealth of pale flax, rippling to the reeds.

Phillips Exeter Monthly, January, 1926, p. 68

Beauvais[a]

I see the musty vastness of Beauvais.
In twilight, when the Vespers had been sung,
I stood in solitude; above me hung
Torn sheds of incense, wreathing, holy mist.
Then through the windows shone the dying sun.
It smote the pearly smoke, and turned it gold;
Across the mournful gray of dusky walls
It lay in splashes varying in tint
From clear blood-red to iridescent blue,
So that the crumbling stones above my head
Seemed transformed, for an instant, into jewels.
The lofty vaulting soared, suspended, then—
Useless the columns at whose base I stood!
Then sank the sun, and stole away the jewels,
And there was left
Only a crumbling shell of what had been
The ancient glory of a bygone age.
Across the lofty transept flew a bird,
Dipping in frightened circles in the dusk,
His spirit chilled in the vast fragrant quiet . . . .

Phillips Exeter Monthly, May, 1926, p. 177

[a] Beauvais is a city and commune in northern France that is located approximately 75 kilometers north of Paris.

Widow

The children are asleep, and now I sit
Stringing flaky pop-corn, bit by bit;
Polishing the apples till they shine—
Hark! "Annie, won't you *ever* stop your whine?
Yes, Santy Claus is comin'—go to bed,
Dear"—(God, how memories pound through my head)!
And now the tinsel, and the fragile balls—
Bubbles of flashing fire among the twigs.
One drops, bursts, lies in splinters at my feet:
Brakes shriek and scrape and grind in the dark street;
The radiator bangs and the Big Ben
Alarm clock buzzes . . . "Gentlemen,
May nothing you dismay"—the carolers.
"Dismay, you blabbering idiots"—here, stop!
I've got to take things quietly, I can't
Go raving crazy now, dear God, I shan't!
More tinsel now, to decorate the tree—
There, I step back a little bit to see
The finished job. My, how they'll love all that!
(They'll dance and squeal and howl and blab and blat
And make my day a hell)—But they don't know;
They can't see what I see now—*all* I see;
The coffin lowered in the sifting snow
Only this afternoon—and now to go
Through Christmas, keeping up a silly sham
Just to make those kids upstairs forget—
Forget the thing they never understood! . . .
That branch is thick—it spoils the symmetry.
I'll get the hatchet now, and lop it off . . .
How sharp and bright it is; how cold the blade!
I draw my thumb along the edge; and think
What it could do! Oh, God forgive me that!
I can't do it—the children sleep upstairs,
And I must cook the goose, dole out their shares,
And stay with them, at least till after that. . . .
And stay . . . with them . . . till. . The blue night is flat
Against the window panes; it stares at me

And seems to lick their lips! The back-stairs creak. . . .
I cannot stand it more; with stifled shriek
I creep to our old bedroom. I undress
And lie . . . and wait a comforting caress . . .
And your hard arms . . . and find but . . . emptiness.

The Phillips Exeter Monthly, May, 1926, p. 180[1]

Class Poem

I
Before us yawns the dark abyss,
Which we must seek to span;
Behind us lie four years of bliss
Which we must pause to scan.

II
In those four years our lives were shaped
As never, quite, before.
For we from childhood had escaped,
And saw the priceless store.

III
Of Knowledge, precious longed-for state,
So thirsted for of old.
For *Knowledge* is the pearly gate
Through which is glimpsed the Goal!

IV
Four years of joy, and sorrows, too —
Four years of work—of play.
And now at last the cloudless blue
Of Graduation Day.

V
Four years of youthful loves and quarrels,
Of finding our Soul Mate.
And now, together, boys and girls,
We stand before the Gate!

VI
For now approaches fast the time
Of saying fond good-bye.
So let us join in "Auld Lang Syne"
With many a parting sigh.

Phillips Exeter Monthly, November, 1926, p. 50[1]

The June Ball[1]

Up through the twisted strata of my brain
Surges a deep still pool, that mirrors plain
The happiest of my memories today.

Then, as the riffled surface grows more clear,
Retrospect sharpens, and upon my ear
There beats the music of that memory:

Cymbals shout with shattering laughter,
Brasses bark and horn-bells gleam.
A blatting saxophone sprawls a tune;
The music swoops like a swollen stream.

Swept by a sparkling wind we dance,
Shuttling over the shining floor,
The air seems bright with a tingling dust
And the music swells to a rhythmic roar.

The floor beneath us bulges high;
Faint feet shuffle, miles below.
Pastel streamers weave a misty web;
Waterspouts of music upward flow.

What matter all the lifeless days that pass,
To one who sees, as in a silvered glass
Your subtle shimmering magic, that June night!

PEAN [The annual yearbook of Phillips Exeter Academy] 1927, p. 204

Water

I

Suave shadows smear across the saffron swirl
Of water, filmed with iridescent oil.
A ghoulish fish with phosphorescent eyes
Lurks in the clammy ooze among the weeds.

II

Out of the bellowing blue
Swoops a grand gale,
Churning the open sea
Into insurgent mounds—
Gone just as suddenly;
Chaos its trail.

The Phillips Exeter Monthly, February 1927, p. 96[1]

Orbs Terrae

Earth, thou art turning, turning endlessly,
A ripening fruit upon Time's laden bough.

Swollen with ripeness, strange and poisonous fruit,
Who dared to pluck thee?
    Cooled and shriveling now,
Drained to thy wine by greedy parasites,
How short must be your time before you drop
Silently and unnoted, into Space?

Phillips Exeter Monthly, May, 1927, p. 188[1]

[When I was ten-and-seven]

When I was ten-and-seven
 I thought I'd never seen
A sadder child than I myself
 Going on sixteen.

When I was one year older,
 I pondered once again
How few the weeks behind me
 Since I'd possessed a brain.

Now, ten months older, knowing
 That neither pride nor pelf[a]
Will be mine—yet I'll never
 Catch upon myself!

UTK MS 3824 Box 7, Folder 1 [1928–1929][1]

[a] "pelf" is one's wealth.

Suggestion to D. P.

You who loll and languish
On unflagging Love Forsaken:
Ponder once the anguish
Of the one who was mistaken.

UTK MS 3824 Box 7, Folder 1 [1928–1929][1]

[Stripped of bark and raw][a]

Stripped of bark and raw. the Rood above Him leans; square-flung arms
The murderers and their dark spite. are spanned with its
In torture up steep Golgotha. toils the living God,
Scoffed by those He dies for. scarred by their lashes.
Now ends His journey: of Jews the Lord
He stands as His People strike,. strip Him, revile Him.
When the long nails stab,. starlike His palms
Spread in His agony,. splayed from the iron core.
Bare unto Heaven,. broken and twisted,
Helpless His flesh. hugs close the wood.
They that piled hammers . now plunge the cross
Into a strait pit . stricken from the stone.
As it shakes like a grounded prow. sheltered from storm,
The body sags. and a shiver of triumph
Grates among the watchers. And the granite's roots
Vaults quiet over Hell's realm. quake with foreboding.
From light to darkened light. level o'er the earth's round
Arch the thunder's wings. and woe leans on the mountains:
Furious the pinions. their fledged points
Laced across the Light-spring. locking o'er the sun.

UTK MS 2474 Box 1, Folder 1of 3 [typescript; 1928–1932]

[a] Agee's intentionally irregular (and multiple) punctuation and spacing are maintained. The reverse of the page bears the handwritten identifier "J. R. Agee / English 16"; Agee received a grade of "B+."

[The year twins on him]

The year twins on him and fulfils his worth:
We too, of many motions in one mind.
No more anatomize our present dearth
But think of one who did the task consigned—
A century past he drank his first brave breath.
The undeviant, the rich and deep in heart
Who knew his height and toiled it into death.
Humble and honorable in his art.

UTK MS 1500 Box 1, Folder 5 [1928–32[1]]

To Lydia

Horace, Bk. I, Ode xxv

With violence diminished they rattle thy windows
Fast-joined—all the youths in their wantonness eager;
No more do they rob you of rest, and the door
    That often and silently

Swung on its hinges with ready complaisance,
Now lovingly lies in the sill's close embrace.
Now, seldom and seldom again do you hear:
    "O Lydia, Lydia,

"Now are you sleeping the long night through
While I perish, who love you?" Nay, now comes the time
When, forsaken and aged, down dimness of alleys,
    Of alleys deserted—

You wander and wail of the insults of rakes
Who beset you—While moon-maddened winds leaping down
From the Thracian[a] highlands hold revel and riot;
    Then that furious lust,

That desire which with frenzy is prone to beflood
The dams of strong horses, shall rage in your vitals,
Shall foam round your ulcerous liver. Ah, Lydia,
    Not tearless ye mark it,

That Youth in its sprightliness sooner rejoices
In sap-singing myrtle and dusky-leaved ivy:
But dry leaves a-clatter in cold winds of Death,
    Youth offers to Winter.

The Harvard Advocate, April 1929, p. 33[1]

[a] Today, Thracian is a geographical term used in reference to Greece, Turkey, and Bulgaria. In ancient times, the area was composed of large swathes of land between southern Russia, Serbia and western Turkey.

Hymn to Diana

Horace IV: xxiii

O guardian chaste of mountains and of grove,
Thrice called upon, thou heedst the cries of maidens
In labour and dost ease their wombs of death.
Goddess Thrice-blessed,

Thine be this pine that slants above my villa,
To which, as each year leads the appointed day,
Glad will I offer blood of a boar that pondered
Sidelong swift onslaught.

Letter to Dwight Macdonald, May 10, 1929[1]
Yale University Library, Manuscripts and Archives
Dwight Macdonald papers, MS 730, Box 5, Folder 64

Apotheosis

Lovers, make your kisses light,
    Weak, your embrace;
Keep passion cool and slight,
    A mask, your face:

Else (take heed) the sweet flesh slips
    Down from the dull
Dead bones, and lover's eager lips
    Kiss but a skull.

The Harvard Advocate, June 1929, p. 21[1]

[The storm bows[a] black on Stratham]

The storm bows black on Stratham[b],
    And strong through elm and ash,
Lashing the leaves to silver,
    Low winds thrash.

From nought to life awakened
    My puzzled soul is rent
By storms that know no ceasing,
    Nor ever will relent

Till I bow black on Stratham
    And strong through elm and ash,
Lashing the leaves to silver
    With the winds thrash.

Letter to Christopher "Goofy" Gerould, September 12, 1929[1]

UTK MS 3824, Box 1, Folder 4

[a] Curves; alternatively, though less likely, a misspelling of "blows."
[b] Perhaps Stratham, NH, a town located four miles from Phillips Exeter, Agee's alma mater.

The Rendezvous[a]

The Morn of Resurrection[1]
Globes world and skull with jubilance of sound:
Perfect, my soul and flesh
Resolve from living sky and deathly ground.

Ah, true to our appointment
You join me, that together we may rise
To love's eternity!
But tell me—what has saddened, so, your eyes?

"Only that you, who love me,
Have waited 'long in vain new love to share:
Beneath the blazing God
That cloudy love has burned to clearest air."

Be sad no more; forget me
As now I can you; lose in God your soul:
Me, love's thin fever
Could not beguile from death's white ruinous coal!

Letter to Dwight Macdonald, undated [December 1929][2]
Yale University Library, Manuscripts and Archives
Dwight Macdonald papers, MS 730, box 5, Folder 64

[a] In the letter, Agee calls this poem "a malformed bastard of Donne and Hardy."

Jan 1[a]

Now flowers are guttering[b] fallow,
and now the year is gone.
With thoughts serenely shallow
I face the hopeless dawn.

Catullus 86

My life, my Lesbia[c], it is your hope
That this one love shall ever be our joy.
O high Gods, grant fulfillment of her wish,
Grant that the wish come truly from her heart:
Grant that our love, freed of the doors of lust,
Endure this brief hour arched above the dust.
([Composed] This fall)

From Catullus

Aye, Quintia[d] is fair of face;
Her body, schooled in every grace,
Is lithe and white and deftly wrought
Into a fine and dazzling feast.
Yet Quintia's but a lovely beast.
For Quintia's beauty is a shell—
A banquet served with n'er a fault—
And n'er the merest grain of salt.
In all that masterpiece of flesh,
Naught can the hungry soul refresh.
Of women, Lesbia's loveliest:
Perfect in brain as well as heart.

Ditto

If aught can pierce the deafness of the tomb,
I know our grief, O Calvus[e], must bring joy.
Vainly, we seek to summon friendships lost,
And mourn anew the lovers that are dust . . .
Surely Quintilia[f] grieves her death as naught
Beside the perfect solace of your love.

Letter to Christopher "Goofy" Gerould, undated [December 1929]

UTK MS 3824, Box 1, Folder 4

[a] All four poems are from the same letter.

[b] Dying or nearly dead; a guttering candle, for example, is one that is flickering and about to go out.

[c] Lesbia was the literary pseudonym used to stand in for the person of his lover by the Roman poet Gaius Valerius Catullus (c. 84–c. 54 BC).

[d] Catallus sees Quintia's beauty as lacking the grace/"salt" (perhaps intellect or charm or humor) that Lesbia has. Agee's translation follows this comparison.

[e] Gaius Licinius Macer Calvus (82 BC–c. 47 BC), a contemporary of Catallus, was an orator and poet of ancient Rome.

[f] Quintilia lived during the 1st century AD. An Ancient Roman stage performer, she was a famed beauty during the reign of Caligula.

[My love is like a red, red rose]

My love is like a red, red rose
    No longer; in its stead
A symbolic dreamland throws
    Its web above my bed.

And now my love's a curving reed
    Besides a silver brink[a];
And one by one, the while I plead,
    My teeth fall in the drink.

Or once again, my love's a room
    Dim-lit and silken-soft;
Which means I want her (I presume)
    Beside me in the loft.

UTK MS 3824 Box 7, Folder 1 [c. 1929][1]

[a] A "brink" is a bank, often of a river.

The Shadow

The moon from shred to sickle grows,
Greatens to a monstrous tear,
Fattens almost overnight
Into a drunk o'erladen sphere:

Loses its rotundity,
Madly greets approaching doom;
Sickle dwindles into shred,
Shred melts grateful into gloom.

So, for a space, the Shadow will relent,
Befooling us with slow yet sure consent:
And, in due time, once more it will return,
Coolly to blot out what once more must burn.

The Harvard Advocate, February 1930, p. 17[1]

A Lover's Dialogue

"O, let me set to this new wick,
Dry, and athirst for light, love's name.
So, we may watch the slow descent
Of wax ascend in steady flame.

For thus, virginity grows small;
Thus fails the firm and gallant flesh:
But, surely as it burns to naught
The soul arises, hot and fresh."

"No, I shall keep the wick unsinged:
The taper, white and whole and cool,
Shall never dwindle uselessly.
I shall preserve all."

"Ah, sad fool,
You think a selfish beauty lasts;
Or, to bestow it whole were shame.
Hear: A sure death encases it
In one bright tube of instant flame!"

The Harvard Advocate, February 1930, p. 29

Lullaby[1]

Hush, little wanton, do not weep,
But on this white and swelling breast
Where once a lover scorned to rest,
Lean now your little head, and sleep.
        Hush-a-bye, my little one,
        For your sorrow's scarce begun.

Now stem these plenteous welling tears
That veil in random silver lace
The soft round of your infant face,
For tender flesh such weeping sears.
        Hush-a-bye, my little one,
        For your sorrow's scarce begun.

Aye, weeping sears such tender flesh,
And wrinkles to one subtle scar
The loveliness that naught must mar:
Fair maidens hold their lads, and fresh.
        Hush-a-bye, my little one,
        For your sorrow's scarce begun.

When youth shall crack this infant mold,
And swell this chest to poised bubbles,
Then's the time to watch for troubles.
Let flesh but wanton, heart stay cold,
        And hush-a-bye, my little one,
        For their sorrow's scarce begun.

Then's the time to float each tress,
Baited for myriad hapless swains.
Laugh at each lad who guileless drains
The venom brimming loveliness.
        Hush-a-bye, my little one,
        For their sorrow's scarce begun.

Let flesh wanton, heart stay cold,
And watch the subtle poison brew;

Watch every stile[a] grow rank with rue[b]
O'er those the crossroads could not hold.
Watch the wide fields cloud o'er with mold,
And watch the lads hang, duel, and plunge
Till all the sea's one carrion sponge;
Let flesh but wanton, heart stay cold.
Then may you weep, my little one,
For their sorrows all are done.

UTK MS 2474 Box 1, Folder 1 of 3 [typescript: March 5th, 1930][2]

[a] A stile is a structure which allows people passage through or over a fence, wall or hedgerow and prevents farm animals from escaping.

[b] A species of Ruta (Ruta graveolens) grown as an ornamental plant and herb. A double-meaning (regret) may also be intended.

[The sun, that lay beneath our bed][1]

The sun, that late beneath our bed
The day over India had led
While we lay in the tower of night,
Shatters the eastern wall with light.

Now let us rise, nor longer sport,
Though day be long, and the night short;
But seek the flowers that filled our dreams
Where light along the woodland streams.

For lo! All silver strides the morn
Over heaving hill and whiteblown thorn.
O lover, lag no longer, pray,
For all the world's alive with May.

Tarry no longer. Let us chase
Sunlight and shadow as they race.
Nor tarry the long day to rue;
Night and our joys will soon renew.

And a night comes when we shall lie
While suns rise, and days flutter by
Pursuing nights, by nights close-prest:
But naught can rouse us from our rest.

Then centuries shall fall like rain
Athwart the swell of yonder plain,
And the light that storms this windy glade
Our dark room never shall invade.

So, lover, lag no longer, pray,
While still the world's alive with May.

UTK MS 2474 Box 1, Folder 1 of 3, [typescript; March 5th, 1930][2]

Good Friday

High in Dodona's[a] swaying groves,
High in the grey, the glimmering oaks,
Dodona's cauldrons, convolute,
Groan on the wind strange prophecies.

Among the whispering laurel roves
Great Pan,[b] and on the tall sky, smokes
Of Delphi write; and now are mute
The graded reeds of Pan: he sees

Across the grey, the glimmering seas,
A leafless tree take barren root
On Golgotha;[c] he hears the strokes
Of iron on iron, and his own hooves

The iron strikes through. Against two trees
Are driven his outstretched hands. Strange fruit
Hangs in the grey, the glimmering oaks,
Hangs in Dodona's swaying groves.

The Harvard Advocate, April 1930, p. 25

[a] Located in Epirus in northwestern Greece, Dodona was the oldest Hellenic oracle, perhaps dating to the second millennium BC, according to Herodotus. Homer describes Dodona as an oracle of Zeus.

[b] Pan, perhaps one of the oldest of the Greek Gods, is associated with nature, wooded areas and pasturelands, from which his name is derived. The bottom half of his body was like a goat, with the top half of his body like a man, but with horns. He ruled over shepherds, hunters, and rustic music and was often in the company of the wood nymphs and other deities of the forest.

[c] Also known as Calvary, Golgotha (meaning skull), was the site outside the walls of Jerusalem where Jesus was crucified.

Résumé

A year ago we wandered
The empty uplands wide,
Or in a leafy hollow
Mid wind-bewildered flowers
Forgot the turning hours:
Nor mused on what might follow,
But far too glad for thought
Strolled homeward silent, side by side
Through veering sunlit showers.

Today, alone I wander
The empty uplands bare,
And, where the earth is hollowed
I strew the flowers that wane
To thwart autumnal pain:
Nor muse on all that followed,
But sorrowful past all thought
Stroll nowhere, anywhere,
Through the tall, sunless rain.

The Harvard Advocate, June 1930, p. 22

Sonnet

Death never swoops us round with sudden black.
No Gothic grin greets our affrighted groans.
Our flesh alone cries out, upon his rack,
Of snapping cartilage and splintering bones.
Secret and happy as a summer dawn
Blooms and releases its reluctant light
Full blown along the dusk, our souls are drawn
Beneath the vast and unrelenting night.

Even now, a serpent swells my living skull:
Its thirsty tongue, struck barbèd through my brain,
Sucks all the cherished beauty dry and dull
As dust: and faint and failing is the pain.
I murdered joy, that your love might abide:
A precious skeleton lies at my side.

The Harvard Advocate, Commencement, June 1930, p. 19

[Loves flame-fresh]

Loves flame-fresh, and lovers whose love wanes—
All who seek comfort here, or idle pleasure
In heart-blown lovers' ecstasies, that stains
Of sorrow never spoiled, cease with this measure.
These pages cannot please your wit, nor heal
A withering concord with an oily charm:
But rather, in matter they reveal,
May do your love some dark heart-shattering harm.

For, frail as love in love's true name can stand,
Of myriad doubts and monstrous ill compounded,
And scanted joy, in pitying lust's command
Valiant mine fights, and soon shall be confounded.
Such love enchronicled if still you'd read
From hooded lies to clarity may lead.

Letter to John Brooks Wheelwright, undated [summer 1930][1]
Brown University Library, John Wheelwright papers, Ms-79–1-TEMP

Dear Mr. Wheelwright[a]—

Was that my correspondent muse has failed
Those two long weeks—nay, not so much, not two—
But nearly two,—and still I have not mailed
Reply nor fresh nor stale, that was your due.
But nine malignéd and laborious hours—
The nine wan Muses of negation, stand
Circling my brain, and breathe their deadly powers
And witherings o'er that fat and genial land.
And all the goodly produce, that in May
Was green profusion on a wealthy loam—
Friendship and Courtesy until today
Their death-struck stalks sprawled crowned[1] from their anandrous morinda[b][.][2]
If these[3] slant members fail their clear intent:
After nine hours of work, my mind was spent,
For pride would not permit reply in prose
To verse that merited a twice-golden Rose,
Nor would a mind that wept for kindly sleep
Emit a single half-poetic peep.

Today, all's different; the sky
Has condescended silver rain
Athwart my dry and hopeless brain,
Athwart my work; and thwarted work—
But all those plants that curled and sick
Straggled the land that fed them woe—
Those happy plants, they stand tip-toe
Upon their roots—and into the high
And streaming storm, their quondam mean
Mute heads, shout triumphant green.

And then those green and happy maps
My glad soul strides, still in a daze,
But well aware that work has naught
To splay the seeds of fruitful thought.
And then—to change the metaphor,

And slay from memory fields and[4] rain,—
My soul hold converse with my brain[.]

UTK MS 3824 Box 7, Folder 4, undated [1930?][5]

[a] See also "[Loves flame-fresh]" sent to John Wheelwright.

[b] "Anandrous" means destitute of stamens, as in certain female flowers; "morinda" is a genus of flowering plants in the madder family, Rubiaceae. Morinda citrifolia is commonly called Indian mulberry. It bears lumpy, potatoe-shaped fruit. For more information and pictures, see https://www.nybg.org/bsci/res/MORINDA.HTML.

Most beloved:
within whose peace would God I lay[a]]

What errand I am on in this my father's country you know well, and its meaning to me, and more conceive some idea what frustration I have run; enough I was half dead, and ready to die—I might never tell you. Know it now then I have found what I sought after into heart breaking, in such fulness, such a breaking-open of wonder beyond utmost hope,

This is insane I know, I know I trust you will forgive me, I shall not be ashamed, I will learn at least not to be ashamed, I will come of age that much anyhow, I will dare that much—

Where you lie, my hand is beneath your head: I meditate upon you a regard no less tender nor less full of worship than on these most pitiful who lie near me sleeping

May God be ever upon your life and on us all, and may there one day be wisdom and justice, health, peace, joy, unanimous as air:
Yet almost, in bitterest anger, let there never be, since these shall never know it:
no not the lightest, littlest taste

(as so pled Lazarus starved in fire) but most each poor ruined, cheated plant be damaged down drained into the endless usual history of the earth with other millions

Two billion, by the latest count
Nor *any* cure:
Not one a man may trust not fearing himself a traitor:
Nor even surely trust the health of cure:

(Hold us, hold us, there *are ways*: a man may
know whom he loves and whom he trusts

I know of what brotherhood we are: their nobility
In the air: they are wheat in all the earth.

I am not worthy:

I do not fear any scorn on earth.[)]

UTK MS 2730 Box 8, Folder 15 [c. 1930; photocopy]

[a] This piece begins in letter form and then evolves into poetry.

Description of Elysium[a] (With Reservations)

There is a pleasant land
 That has forgotten woe
Where time has lost command
 Nor flowers fear the snow,

Where silky waters stream
 That nevermore shall freeze,
And jewelled meadows gleam,
 And all the gracious trees

Spout up their standing fountains
 Of wind-beloved green,
And the blue conclaved mountains
 Are grave guards and serene;

There brook and stone and flower
 Are one wide tenderness,
And they and a changeless hour
 Are touched with deathlessness:

Dear lover, lived we there
 Forever from tomorrow,
That loveliness we'd share
 We'd murder with our sorrow.

The Harvard Advocate, March 1931, p.18

[a] Elysium or the Elysian Fields or the Isles of the Blessed is an evolving ancient Greek religious and philosophical conception of a heavenly afterlife.

The Truce

When, in such anguish of our love
As naught can temper or remove,
We lie beyond the hope of speech
And breathe our sorrow each to each,
One passion stands within my breast
Annihilating all the rest:
Lip and hand and flesh and bone
Are one large pity; pity alone
Is all my body can devise,
And pity gazes through my eyes.

Pitying, I seek your own,
And there, as still as any stone,
Pure as water wrung from flame,
Dwells a pity much the same.
While we look, those pities swell
Wide from double-sourced hell;
Deep and wide within that pool
Shines the pity of a fool;
Closer pressing, gazing, we
Know the idiot pity we.

So we look, and so love passes:
Take two flat quicksilvered glasses,
Press each to each the mirroring planes,
You naught can see, but much remains:
Bound in those flat and fragile walls
Stretch two bright and spaceless halls;
Beyond the glass, beyond the dull
Sponge of brain and box of skull
That straight and empty hall extends
And binds infinity's curved ends.

So much can our love attain,
Just so much, and that with pain;
Though we die to change the score,

Just so much, and nothing more.
Pity need not be the passion,
Though it be our private fashion:
Any single joy or grief
Turns the trick that cracks belief;
And the body's left behind
Whispering to the abandoned mind:

"So they look, and so Time passes
Withering o'er the glorious grasses:
Time shall ravel us asunder:
Mind's delight and body's wonder
And our shrewd-contrivéd lust,
Time shall wither into dust.
Where two pities stand displayed,
Shade shall mirror endless shade,
And they that have themselves forgot
Shall find no joy where self is not."

And the quiet mind makes reply:
"Many a time, before they die,
They shall hear our[1] mutterings
And return to earthly things:
Try once more each sly device
We invent; none shall suffice.
Since much joy, but much more sorrow
Stands before their sunless morrow,
Vex not their unperplexity;
It cannot last as long as we."

The Harvard Advocate, May 1931, pp. 58–59[2]

Resolution

This fire that lances me about,
This thunderous benumbing doubt,
This ocean-rooted sheer of rain
That brims the dark with smothering pain—

This wrack of murderous storm shall melt
Clean from the sky, and on the sky
The long-arrangéd stars have spelt
A fate no storm can set awry.

The Harvard Advocate, May 1931, p. 77[1]

The Darkened Cage

I looked on love, and love was meaningless,
No meaning more had music to my ear,
Nor knowledge, other than my mind's distress,
Nor beauty's self to me other than fear:

Nothing had power to move me or to wrest
Speech from my lips, who stood irresolute,
Knowing the measured perturbation in my breast
Of one who lived, but was bestunned and mute.

Then One twitched off that shroud of flesh,
And my heart sang remembered tunes afresh.

UTK MS 2730 Box 5 Folder 12 [typescript; June 11, 1931][1]

A Poem of Poets

The harsh and profitable seasons pass
Bestowing each their own inestimable burdens,
Love its peculiar joy, love's end its proper grief,
Beauty its image, wisdom sought, its pain:
The mind so richly dowered, all withered are its guerdons[a];
Bloodless and sere[b] and joyless, whose hour of green was brief,
They whisper deathly riddles to confused and dying grass:
Soon shall the mind be thoughtless, soon shall the autumn leaf
No more be bright memorial to the ancestral rain.

The mind is stunned, the tongue may find no word,
Nor in themselves may either find ever any thought
Beneath the awful instant of each high visitation,
Beneath the blinding and celestial fire,
Fit to do thankful honor to Him the fire Who wrought:
Wherefore with gilded praises and with false lamentation
We sing into the darkening sky too tardily to be heard,
Who soon shall be brought low to earth and that humiliation
Which gluts the oak with pride and burns the poppy with desire.

All seasons pass, once more they swerve above,
Once more the mind is granted the living fire to breathe,
Once more of green and holy and far-gathered leaves we fashion
Straitly implied with brief domestic flowers,
Pride, artifice, despair, our wild half-hallowed wreath:
To crown the mind with fame, and God with earth-bound passion,
Flaw truth with beauty, make a holy whore of sickened love:
Once more, and now forever, impends that immolation
Whence we shall rise to damn still other poets with half-blind power.

The Harvard Advocate, October 1931, p. 37

[a] "Guerdons" are rewards.
[b] "Sere" means dry or withered.

A Parable of Doors (and of their construction)

All things of life I term as many doors:
Entrance to each or all, that man may win
Who neither questions, nor no more implores
But that with mindless ease he be let in.

Such men are myriad and the doors swing wide
And smoothly they swarm through, who care not why,
Initiate to those mysteries most denied
Those who most seek them: such a man am I.

I would expound those truths unalterably
Flayed to strict harmonies no mind has sung.
Mindful that truths are founded axially,
By too much mind all hinges I have sprung:

For it was thus: I lunged the brutal mind
Shoulder to hinge post, since the truth stood there;
Which neither yielded nor have I repined,
But lunge and batter and am in despair.

I cramped all gates of love forever shut,
All beauty is for ever wrecked for me,
And God all spiked with brain, and there is but
One door, whose certitude the others flee.

That door is death: and though my chief assault
And shrewdest labor I've assembled there,
Dark hinges no conjecture may default
Soon shall devolve me on a doorless air.

The Harvard Advocate, Christmas 1931, p. 31; *CP*, pp. 135–36

The Passionate Poet to His Love

Come live with me and be my love
Provided you think little of
Such stodge encumbrances as friends
Who keep their means for their own ends;

Granted we mutually agree
That yours was never a mother's knee,
Or, if the spiteful slime should bud,
Will nip the foetus while it's mud;

Provided you can smoothly be
Wife, mother or nonentity
As metamorphic moods require;
Provided, also, you admire

Nor ever dare to criticize
Each syllable that I devise,
And shall apprise me (though I know it)
Of my majority as a poet,

And, like four angels each with sword
Will guard the Inception of the Word —
If such persuasions aught can move,
Then live with me and be my love.

The Harvard Advocate, February 1932, p. 21

Class Ode [1932]

Now the winter is past and the storms of our youth:
    We who gather to part in our power,
Long acquainted with dreams, seal our sight to the truth,
    Who shall labor to live for an hour:
Now the snows are withdrawn and the fields young in bloom,
    All that lives strains in strength toward the light,
And the comrades who halted in doubt and in gloom,
    Depart drunk o'er the down-trampled night.

Ay, the sun rides the zenith and sunk under the earth
    Huddle midnight and winter and death,
But the smothering darkness that paled at our birth
    Shall return to reprieve us of breath:
And the oak shall be stripped, the bright furrow lie bare,
    The man wane, the tall shadow destroy;
We shall waste on that vast and invincible air
    And our valour be naught, and this joy.

When the slow wheel shall turn, and our course shall be run,
    In the breath that the brave season brings,
Fallen flesh shall upwield from each husk to the sun
    The wild strength of all sorrowless springs:
And all wisdom we wring from our pain and desire
    On this field between devil and God,
Shall resolve to a white and unquenchable fire
    That shall cleanse the dark clay we have trod.

Harvard Class Album, 1932, p. 204; *CP*, pp. 140–41

[How, through a hurried and oblivious year][a]

How, through a hurried and oblivious year,
Knowing each other as the casual do,
Shouting from distances, however near
We were, with neither shout nor thinking true:
Knowing so little truth and little caring,
Save some regret that being so good friends,
Despite such liking were but sparsely sharing,
And would for this make glad and quick amends:
How this could be, that I perceived in you
Little that other dozens did not hold,
Nor even might discern you of the few
To whom some secrets of the heart are told:
How this could be outweighs and stuns my thought,
Since now we're joined in what we scarcely sought.

Letter to Via Saunders, August 24, 1932[1]
Princeton University Library Special Collections
Manuscripts Division, James Agee Letters, Box 1, Folder 1

[a] This is a Shakespearean sonnet.

As You Came From the Holy Land[1a]

As you came through the far land
  Many speak well of,
Saw you there, anywhere,
  My own true love?

You would know her, if you had,
  By her quiet eyes, and bright smile,
By her small breast and her soft step,
  By her wit without guile.

How shall I know your true love
  From another one,
Who saw many like her you speak
  When I was there, who are gone?[2]

All dwellers in that far land,
  Their eyes are quiet, and bright their smile;
Their flesh is small and their step soft,
  And they have neither wit nor guile.

And are they never cruel,
  Never harsh nor unkind?
Do they never clench the hand
  Nor strike with the mind?

Nor hurt with the sullen glance
  And the bitter tongue?
And do they never know distress
  Who are lovers, and young?

Do they not contract the brow
  In silent rage?
Nor ever forget and hate
  And falter in age?

O, they are free from all these things[3],
The dwellers in that strifeless land,
They speak and think no evil there
Nor deal it with the heart or hand:
Their brows are smooth as ivory,
Their tongues are sweet as morning air,
Their hands are quiet as carven wood,
And neither anger nor despair

Shall move them more: young lovers lie
Freed from all malice and regret:
The aged hate no longer there
And no more falter and forget—

O, God himself made such a land!
To that sweet land I'd hasten now
Did I but know her surely there—
But cannot know: and know not how

To make my journey to that place:
    Tell me, that I may see it soon:
Shall I obey the landward sun
    Or seaward errors of the moon?

To get there soonest: do not budge:
    Unbuckle with a knife
The slippery harness of the blood:
    And thus race free of life.

And if your true love dwells not
    In that far land you seek,
She will come, soon enough,
    Next year, or next week:

All your search will be done,
    And all your despair:
You shall embrace in solid stone,
    You shall kiss in shining air:

You shall be nor two, nor one, but none:
        But none:
And neither of you shall care.

UTK MS 1500 Box 1, Folder 1 [typescript carbon; 1932][4]

[a] Although offering no direct quotation the poem appears to be a dialog.

John Carter (1932–193?)

[Introduction to John Carter]

Plans for Study[a]
[Submitted with Agee's application for a 1933 Guggenheim Fellowship]

I would perhaps finish a long short story called "Let Us Now Praise Famous Men," and revise and write other short stories I have in mind. I would perhaps develop a sonnet sequence, and would probably write miscellaneous and fortuitous poems. I would hope, of course, to come nearer the solution of various problems which have preoccupied me in both mediums.

But I am uncertain how much I would do of the work suggested above: for I would chiefly concentrate on a long narrative poem, tentatively called *John Carter.*

This poem is to be written in ottava rima, somewhat in the manner of *Don Juan*. It should have great diversity and flexibility of diction, but should be more organized than *Don Juan*. Predominantly it is satirical and comic: fundamentally serious and moral; and ultimately metaphysical.

It is to be the life-story of one John Carter, who humanly speaking is the typical American Young Man: spiritually speaking, he is an orthodox Roman Catholic devil, God-given to the world, a New Messiah of Evil. His human personality is so completely extraverted and so childishly sensitive and intuitive that he is a perfect mirror of whatever surroundings he finds himself in. He uses his diabolic powers never supernaturally, always humanly: in other words, moved from place to place throughout America, he destroys whom he pleases according to that person's idioms of thought and conduct. This formula should give (a) a clear reflection of any aspects of custom and fad and conduct and (b) an index for them in terms of pure evil.

In other words, with far more luck than I shall probably have, the poem could be a complete appraisal of contemporary civilization, and a study of the Problem of Evil in relation to civilization and in relation to universal human conduct.

Should this poem be successful, its contribution to art would be more considerable than I have a right to expect. I can therefore only set down some of the things I hope to do with it:

1. To make a poem varied enough in subject matter and in manner, in length and character of episodes and personal comment, to be widely read by every sort of person.

2. To keep the general tone amusing enough to hold this popular interest: yet to enforce consideration of serious and didactic passages.

3. In the long run, to make the reader perceive, and persuade him to accept, a moral and religious intention at least as strong as the various artistic and comic and general emotional intentions.

4. Thereby, if possible, to establish a widespread popular awareness of the prevailing validity of religious faith and of religious and artistic morality as opposed to "scientific morality."

5. To suggest that it is as possible now as it ever was to write major poetry and to write it in verse rather than in prose. (This, I believe, the poem might demonstrate whether or not it should turn out to be in itself a "major" poem.)

6. To give the language of poetry the peculiar sort of variety and vitality it has generally lacked since the Elizabethans.

7. To use the American Language as a sort of cement for all other dictions: to make it valid in all kinds of poetry.

8. To help establish a proper sort of pride in American civilization: to reduce our intellectual and spiritual humility and dependence.

9. To bring back into poetry a sense of dramatic and narrative (as well as lyrical) vigor and resourcefulness which now, for the most part, is found at its best only in prose.

10. In short, to help to change (if it can be changed) the prevalent negative state of mind into a positive state: and to present as many and as strong matters as possible for the positive mind to advance upon.

I hope this program will be understood as not bumptious. It states in part not what I shall do, but what I wish I could do, and what could be done with such a poem, granted the right poet.

I began this poem last February, wrote and published about forty stanzas in *The Harvard Advocate*[1], wrote some more this summer, and have at present about a thousand lines.

I have really no idea how long it might be. My plan is to divide it into three long parts, each of which would certainly fill a volume. Volume One will be devoted to statements of intention and to the conception, birth, baptism, infancy, behavioristic early education, grade-school education, religious and sexual education, adolescence, first love, prep-school education, Harvard matriculation, and self-discovery of John Carter. It will be the shortest of the three; and it is the first volume I want to get to work on immediately.[b] I should hope to finish this volume within two years. Of course to complete the whole poem, if I should keep at work on it, would take an indefinite number of years;

and since there are other things I hope to write, I have no invulnerable confidence in ever finishing it.[2]

UTK MS 2730 Box 8, Folder 12 [before November 1, 1932 (the application's due date); typescript photocopy]

[a] While not a part of the poem, this edition follows Fitzgerald's *CP* in thinking that Agee's "Plans" do shed light on his early intent. Fitzgerald gives his introduction from Agee's 1933 Guggenheim application the title "*A Project for a Poem in Byronics,* John Carter." There is no such title in the application; it only the required a "Concise statement of project" on its first page. Fitzgerald omits the first two paragraphs above.[3] Agee did not receive a fellowship.

[b] Agee changed his planned structure for the poem numerous times (given his many prose summary projections) and much of what he notes as the contents for what he then called "Volume One" was not completed.

John Carter[1]

Like Byron, I'll begin at the beginning.
Unlike that better bard, my lad's a new one,
Expert in charm, supremely so in sinning,
Nevertheless he differs from Don Juan
In ways enough to set your brain to spinning.
For how he differs, read the books ensuing:
For this time's being and this Being's place
Are both beginning and in medias res.

In medias New York State stands the Homestead;
In medias that, in medias modest gloom,
Is a large room: in medias that, a bed:
In medias which a man and wife consume
The night with pleasure: for they're three weeks wed,
And the bride's trained at last: in medias whom
George Carter labors lovingly: deception
Is not my aim: you're in at the conception.

A present fad, especially in sex,
Flatters the reader's fond imagination.
All right as art, it has its ill effects,
I find, in causing curious agitation
Miles wide the subject: Reader then suspects
Author of plans to undermine the nation—
All cleanmindedness; and maybe takes his pleasure
No more in reading, but in legislature.

I know a type the governors of whose eyebrow
Are most unstable, and whose inner cheek
Pockets his tongue, while "This is pretty sly now,"
He neighs, and gives your elbow a smart tweak.
I'd dearly like to know the reason why, now:
I use my tongue to taste and kiss and speak,
And never use my eyebrow, even to ogle;
And *my* verb for his action is, "to groogle."[a]

"*Groogle*: to love subversive wit and wary;
    To draw the mouth down; lecherously to leer;
To be a slob and something of a fairy;
    To snout out filth in every word you hear.
Synonymous with pseudo-literary."
    I think our word has onomatopoeia:
Anyway, Webster'd thus anatomize it:
    I coin, define, with all my heart despise it.

Let subtleties rejoice within their due.
    I find no subtlety in new-ploughed earth,
Whether that earth be meadowland or you,
    But honest beauty and fit cause for mirth.
Both at their best are far between and few,
    But sweetest in conspiracy toward birth,
Whether the pair be nomad, noble, citizen,
Or the young Carters ready to beget a son.

However that may be, they knew a joy
    As strong as the arched sea, as common, too;
Knew pain, mirth, beauty—what could ever destroy
    That speechless fire of liking twixt the two?
Naught, at this hour; the elements of their boy
    Knit, and enwrought their cloudless love, and knew
All evil and scorn straightway, but they two wept
Their utmost joy, quietly embraced, and slept.

Even as they slept beneath the unslumbering dawn
    There was a stirring, and the spiteful slime
Sucked livelihood from her most kindly brawn,
    Huddled its core, began the gradual climb
Whence ageless life forth from the dust slow drawn
    Flowered into grass, beast, man: abiding time,
Our hero framed his black chill clarity
From his first hour with blood of charity.

Warning: I've given my boy his proper start;
    He's on the fire; we'll all have months to wait.
And if the last two stanzas please you not
    As too obliquely stated, obfuscate,

Abstruse, or what not, blame it not on art.
    You'll find abundant justice, soon or late,
Whether you're priest, pimp, matron, child or spinster,
If they seem strained, or even a trifle sinister.

Meanwhile, the young wife slumbers in the arms
    Of her young husband, and he slumbers, too;
The incipient contriver of dark harms
    Slumbers (I guess) where harm cannot pursue;
All prospects please but one. That one alarms
    Me plenty: namely, reader, slumber you?
For now we face the hideous jaws of Lull.
I'll do my damnedest not to make them dull.

Of course for you, reader, the problem's easy:
    I must write on; it don't have to be read.
Some poets' alchemic bellows are so wheezy
    They turn the best of gold to their own lead.
God spare me that: my first aim is to please ye
    If this part fails, why take a look ahead.
You'll find large portions (this I swear to you)
Will please most anyone, I don't care who.

For my intention's to diversify
    My subject matter and my manner too:
I'll use all styles from Lardner[b] to blank verse if I
    Can make the grade, which should please you and you
And even you, in turn. And my own 'erse[c], if I
    Fail, I shall duly kiss, and up to you
I leave that wager, choice, and member also:
Lots like to "take the literary pulse," so.

Now that demands another parenthetic
    Remark or two; I'll cut it fairly short.
If that last stanza seem a bit splenetic,
    It's just because it makes me fairly snort
To see the anemic, phthisic[d] and emetic[e]
    Verdicts doled out in Literary Court.
There's too much sugary simpering civility:
When a book's rotten, roar it down as guilty!

Critics, you overrate our sensitivity.
    We'll take it, *we'll* receive it on our chins,
Except those lads who, through your own proclivity
    For stuffy talk upholstered with glazed chintz
Are frail, though sweet; and if you're wrong, we'll give it ye
    Back where it came; the sharpest penman wins.
Besides, I think good tooth for tooth invective
Far more effective than a Mild Corrective.

Observe the hallmark case of Leonard Dash.
  Sad as a schoolchild, pained in adolescence,
    His frail deistic dreams went all to smash
      With worrying sick about the Actual Presence;
    First Mumsy, then Our Lady was his mash;
Myrrh was his mouthwash, frankincense his essence:
And he bothered more than any sane youth ought to
Whether 'twas nice to wear lace on his cotta[f].

He had a secret vice, as you and I did,
    But being shy, indulged it rather more;
And when he'd made his penance and had tidied
    Himself, and lay and heard his roommate snore,
And felt that granulation of the eyelid,
    The brain grow corky and the gums get sore,
He prayed to God to save him from that doom
The Rector's said was sure to happen to 'm.[2]

Meanwhile, he tried Tom Jones[g] and couldn't keep on,
    But did like Poe and Bierce and Baudelaire[h],
De Musset[i] and La Forgue[j], nor went to sleep on
    De Quincy[k] and the Book of Common Prayer,
And Celtic Crepuscules[l], nor counted sheep on
    A lot of things that needed country air.
(Some of these things are more than pretty good:
The trouble was this Artist's attitude.)

His literary likings, then, were Gallic[m].
    He also liked black candles and Debussy[n],
Old prints and Wagner[o], heavily metallic
    Brocades. His best friend's name was Hubert Pusey.

They learned all holy cults sprang from the phallic,
  And ecstasized o'er every iterant pussy,
And read translations from the Ancient Persian,
And did lots more things which are my aversion.

You see the trouble was, he needed Girls:
  For while it's fine to give one's God His due,
And thrilling fun to gather up those pearls
  Spurned by one's rough schoolmates, but good as new,
To watch that wonder which the dawn unfurls
  Exclusively to one (or maybe two),
One horrid urge can drive one to despair
Who wastes one's flagrance on the desert air.

It flurried Leonard frightfully at times.
  At nights, he thought of one thing and another,
Of sweet-fleshed maidens bred in palmier climes,
  Also of Jesus, Hubert, and his mother.
So finally, when he'd hoarded enough dimes,
  He snuk to Boston . . . Well, I guess I'll smother
That little incident (which nearly threw him):
A friend has come, I want to read this to him.

The friend has gone, and so have twenty days;
  So have several stanzas, and my manuscript.
So have my wits. My mind is in a maze.
  All energy and all high hope have slipped
Smoothly away. And thus the poet oft pays:
  Imagination's subtle skein is snipped
When by weak will or strong against his liking
He shelves too long his too young undertaking.

By all I love, I'll make no alibis!
  Blame my own mind or curse the circumstance:
It matters little where the trouble lies
  Or by what slant collusion of brute chance
I could, and can not now; for I despise
  More than I pity that egregious nance[p]
Who gilds with tears the wasted morning-glory:
Therefore, for good or ill, on with my story.

There were no red plush draperies round the bed,
　　There were no silver mirrors on the ceiling,
No dizzying reek of musk involved his head,
　　No candle flames assayed the dusk's unsealing,
No stifled streams of hidden music bled
　　Their muted loveliness round love's revealing:
All lavender lore that Leonard had devoured
Defaulted him the night he was deflowered.

Her purple locks were silvering through the dye,
　　Each royal breast was like a splotchéd melon,
Her teeth were caulked with gold: I'll not deny
　　Hers was an epiderm to gaze, not smell, on:
Her guts were bunchy and each marble thigh
　　Was like an o'erlain pillow: and a felon
Glowed on one knuckle of one square-nailed hand:
She smacked his withers[q] and said, "Ain't love grand?"[2]

Squelching his bitter nausea he replied
　　That yes it was, and fumbled his cravat[r]:
Ruth cast her dress and kicked her mules[s] aside:
　　He turned his back: gulped: glanced at his hat:
Stepped from his trousers with a desperate pride
　　(Ruth smoked and watched him sidelong as she sat)
Sank shuddering on the bed he would abuse:
(And Ruth undid the laces of his shoes).[2]

True lust will triumph over indigestion:
　　(God moves in a mysterious way, I hear,
But here and now I think we'd really best shun
　　Such thoughts, and say biology is queer)
So Leonard, when he'd understood her question,
　　Put his five dollars on the chiffonier[t],
Porous-Knits on the floor and self upon
The whore: and in two shakes the job was done.[2]

Just how this influenced Leonard's later Work
　　Or why I told or what it did to him
I can't quite know: I blush to say, I shirk
　　These chores which keep the Artist's soul in trim.

But here's the point: I'll leave it in its murk,
    You may extract it, if so runs your whim,
Artists will understand, for it's in style:
The Frailest Plants take root in what's most vile.

Artists who can't refer to such a night,
    Like Artists who affect complete monogamy,
May rest assured their genius is but slight,
    Unless, indeed, they find a touch of sodomy
More fits their fancy—but a leaden blight
    Sickens my spirit way down deep inside o' me:
The poor pure Minors—for the work's so poor all
Of those who choke their souls with staying moral!

Well, back to Leonard. Things were very strained,
    He found, when he divulged to Hubert Pusey
His wonders and his horrors and regained
    Some sort of balance (having thought it Juicy
One moment, Sin the next); Hubert was pained
    Beyond all words, he stammered, "I accuse"; he
Rushed from the room, wept out his shock and fear,
And three weeks thence contracted gonorrhea.

I'm rather sick of Leonard; so are you.
    And so, although there's much more to be said,
I think I'll chuck him one more verse or two
    (It's more than he deserves) and so to bed.
Such lads as he, alas, are more than few,
    And more than few of them, now be it said,
Hover their spark, as he did too, and fan it
And, even as Leonard, publish "Gold from Granite."

Or some such title. What a nice slim book!
    Those grim grey covers stamped with slender gold.
You've seen the dedication? Give a look:
    "This young book TO MY MOTHER, never old."
How charming, and see here, the printer took
    Such pains to choose a type precise and cold,
Biting yet delicate, but none would do,
So a young German flute[u] designed a new.

Some of the poems have six lines to a page!
 They promise easy reading for weak eyes.
Can poets achieve nobility of rage,
 Be witty, sensuous, passionate and wise,
When soul's subjected to this stringent gauge,
 And mind reigns at the juncture of the thighs?
Poems, like the sea, might lunge and weave and flow.
Are these poems oceanic? Jesus, no!

Or do they even approach the mathematical?
 Sinews and guts demand a skeleton,
And it's a matter highly problematical
 Whether elastic flesh or rigorous bone
Is most important. This remark is what I call
 Something which poets had better leave alone,
Remembering, though, that naked bone is death,
And boneless flesh is soon unpleasant breath.

But these have neither bones nor face nor bowels,
 And they are neither fish nor flesh, but foul:
Squeamishly juggled consonants and vowels
 Raise the Soul's Paean to a placid howl—
Oh, scores such bland and well-upholstered owls
 Squat in their stumps and make believe to prowl
Wide through that blind and noisome realm of night
Which they term Life, being short or nil of sight.

Some might be richly leaved and lordly trunked, if
 They could work out a good excuse for life:
One Neo-Arthurian scales the dread subjunctive
 Gathering samphire[v] with a neat desk-knife;
One farmer's verse in splendor might be dunked, if
 His hired man, farmer, or the farmer's wife
Shut up their dismal dialectic squawking
For even five lines, and let *him* do the talking.

One Californian's vision is gigantic
 In images alone; his line's too long;
His people start at scratch and end in frantic
 Rape of wild beasts or brothers, which is wrong,

I'm told, who never tried it, and romantic
Beyond the scope of measured sin and song:
Great tragic poems have less unleashed ferocity,
More rhythm and much more temperate reciprocity.

One, of a great but singular ability,
Contrived expert symbolic bellyaches,
Toiled thence to higher, drier debility;
Now, Anglo-Tory-o-Classico, he shakes
(Solemnly slow, with infinite gentility)
Stark cypress and jewelled pomegranate, and makes
From drifted talismans and ripe archaics,
Rich, rigid, undecipherable mosaics.

By this time it is nearly seven-thirty.
My poem thus far is heavily digression,
Some critical, some moral, some just dirty
(If so you think) some riding my profession
(If such I have); if anyone feels hurt, he
May find cross-irritants in the procession
Of stanzas which ensue, for there he'll see
(If I'm in luck) himself, and you, and me.

For we're Americans, for which we may
As well thank God, since that's our pleasant doom.
It just ain't done, forever or today
By taking thought to backslide to the womb
And thence emerge, to everyone's dismay,
In other times or as a gaudier bloom,
As Negro, nabob[w], Greek or Jacobite[x],
Elizabethan or New Muscovite.

Homer and Plato and the dirt are one,
Shakespeare and Swift inform the deathstruck flower;
The wild black breadth of Russia's but begun[y]
To rear its green illimitable power;
Our Western Zero shrewdly chokes our sun:
Yet, in this brief and steeply shadowed hour
Ere flesh deserts and earth adopts the bone
There's more to do than sit and make sweet moan.

The piebald earth revolves and still the rain
　Silverly stoops on tower and field and hill;
Still man is man and still the man-wrought pain
　Is studious to hurt and waste and kill;
Still there is loveliness and love of gain
　And love and love of hate and therefore still
The farmer knows a newness in each seed
Nor need the poet deplore a gorgeless reed.

Murder and stealth and raw-eyed revelry,
　Popular noises, mineral-hearted light,
Flawed lust and pure and sweet inanity
　Of general sleep: these breed beneath the night:
Such is the stifled turmoil of a sea
　Flattened by fog of steep and stormless height:
Thus for the comedy of this our age
Behold the wide, dark and unpeopled stage.

This breadth of earth is crumpled into stone
　On east and west, and broad on either hand
Two seas are spread, and on the east alone
　The daybreak leans and soon will find the land:
The gleaming looms of gloomy brine are grown
　Sure in the light, and now discovered stand
Islands and toiling ships and the long shore
Fire-born, sea-suckled now and evermore.

Over one badge of city on broad ground
　A breathing silver brightens and is day:
The dark falls westward and a subtle sound
　Climbs with the clear surf's everlasting sway:
Immortal morning, furiously crowned,
　Walks shod with music on her earthly way:
Music of bird in branch and scythe on wheat,
Of startled engines and a million feet.

But of the wide realm of the joyous field
　With beast and farmer bustling in the grain
And of this grimed but sweetly glistering shield
　With early citizens hustling to their pain—

Of all this land which mildly lies revealed
    To busyness that soon enough shall wane,
Of Asia reeling upward toward the dawn,
No more: Return to our Heroic Spawn.

A man and woman, young, and freshly wed
    And tenderly in love, lie sleeping here.
Awake, they're kind, not greatly grown to head,
    Steady, perhaps, but not too damned severe,
Intelligent, attractive and well-fed,
    Eager for all good things, but not too clear
What those may be: with this much for a starter,
Reader, I give you George and Helen Carter.[3]

The Harvard Advocate (June 1932), 12–20

[Here Fitzgerald inserts a now unlocated "Author's working note" and three handwritten verses not a part of the typescript (*CP*, pp. 94–95). That note begins by stating "You try to make as good a thing as possible of this sunrise section, probably considerably expanded: at any rate trying to get the whole continent spread out beneath the light—and suggestion of astral influence on America—stars slanting light toward us and moving toward us: and with Asia rolling from under night into day: i.e., that America is somewhere near a balance in civilization, a monopoly on day, she'll never have again: then narrow down to the father & mother (incipient) asleep and proceed. . . ." There are two sections of the poem which can credibly be characterized as sunrise sections and these are included next under the heading "Sunrise," though the first is not included by Fitzgerald. The second of these sections is in the Fitzgerald version of the poem, but is placed after those verses that he uses from *The Harvard Advocate* (see Textual Note 3). Three other verses included by Fitzgerald after the "Author's working note" and labeled "[*Three unplaced stanzas, probably for Books I or II*]" are kept in the same relative position (after the inclusion of the "Sunrise" sections), but are preceded by five additional handwritten verses not in *CP* (UTK MS 1500 Box 1, Folder 7) that seem appropriate.

After these two short "Sunrise" sections the poem returns to Fitzgerald's ordering, because a note by Agee at this point in the typescript reads: "In the next book, the love of John Carter's parents; John's lineage; his birth. In the next, his baptism. All material from here on leads up to his baptism, which is not yet written."[4] The following handwritten verses (UTK MS 1500 Box 1, Folder 7) are here inserted because they are likely a part of "the love of John Carter's parents" mentioned as the beginning of a second hypothetical section. They are given the title "The Love of John Carter's Parents." The "Five Additional Handwritten Verses" and the "*Three unplaced stanzas*" thus serve as a kind of introduction to this next part of the typescript, since this "introduction's" last line reads "Each lover his humanity resumes."

The poem ends with a section the editors have named "[Toward His Baptism]," following Agee's note.]

[Sunrise][5]

Greetings, kind gentlemen; good evening, all.
    Let's take the present, as the case may be.
What's the world up to? What is on the ball?
    Who wreck in bondage? and what man is free?
What stroll down what inestimable Mall
    To what good end, or bad, or just to tea
Takes the weird planet now? Precisely why
Does Haven do its Heaven in the eye?

Round five tonight, our Seaboard sun was low:
    Now Denver drifts the dark: now in Spokane
The belts are slackening and the shadows grow:
    Now noon treads the bright islands: now Japan
In morning loud and strong through China blow
    Youthful and broadening airs that erstwhile ran
The land's great warp of Russia where day break
Wrests the new race up that the dark shall take.

The fenced-off nations, leagued beneath the night,
    For all their hate, are past their midnight now:
They flow toward morning whose allianced height
    Takes England next: and all the voided brow
And dreamless of this earth is under sight
    Of deepest heaven's dark that shall allow
Sparse while at best for honesty to move us
Before its changing eye wreaks light above us.

Our midnight stands: stone horns of Labrador
    Slice past his scatheless thighs, and broad Quebec
Her steeples but a thistle-burr, no more,
    Rustling his walking leg: sky's steady deck
This continent, this America, meadow floor
    Cluttered with brittling turfs against that trek
Of city stoneblade grasses in a Fall
That will turn midnight's winter winter's all.[6]

UTK MS 1500 Box 1, Folder 11 [and draft]; UTK MS 1500 Box 10, Folder 1 [draft]

Now the wide-bellied ocean sunward drawn
    Swollen with light against full morning moves
Flexing its glad and multitudinous brawn:
    While steeply from the carved Atlantic coves
Flare the wild gulls who slivering catch the dawn
    On wind-hooked pinions and in flashing droves
Shift and dissolve in swivelling flight and squeal
Stooping toward waves to strike with glittering heel.

Levelled to earth the broad loud-chattering blade
    Drops the gold barley backward from its stance;
And where the clamorous roiling knives invade
    Grasshoppers spangle up in desperate dance
Showering aslant to patter disarrayed
    Into the unhurt grain and unknown chance,
While still the blade whirrs forward and around,
Narrowing the green sphere of their scatheless ground.

Just so the light's unvanquishable blade,
    Whetted to darkness on its eastward edge
From dew-shot turf and reed and songless glade
    As lately from bald isle and seaward ledge
Upwields the birds from out the deafened shade,
    And that keen height of purest air they fledge
With wings splayed wide and wide the thrilling gorge:
Blind, toward the unapproachable high forge.

Oh, blind they scale that brightest air and keen,
    Free up the uncieled[z] porches of the day,
Beyond the shadow of the night's cruel screen,
    Beyond the solitude of birds of prey
And, as a crested fountain stands serene,
    So stand the birds above the earth's dismay:
Who, as the dawn glides past, once more decline
Into the green world and the steep dayshine.[7]

UTK MS 1500 Box 1, Folder 6

[The Love of John Carter's Parents]

["Five Additional Handwritten Verses"]

Nothing on earth could disalign that smile,
    Surprise that exquisite omniscient taste:
Anguish at large? They knew it all the while;
    Men die for causes? That's a common waste.
The suicide . . . Did it, we trust, in style.
    Starvation, greed, dishonor, good outfaced—
Spiked with existence, broiled between black and white
The race roils deathward: sniff, and simper: 'Quite.'

You Chaps disgrace the sperm whence you were hatched,
    Meaning, you aren't worth much. I take you up
Because you're known to the vulgar as[8] 'detached.'
    So is a weak flea on a lively pup:
DeFachment[aa] and such terms are misattached
    Oftener than not: the rich and gleaming cup
Serves fifth[-]rate nectar to some tenth-rate mouths
Just now, who in good time shall know their drouths[bb].

That's off the point. But this, I hope, is it.
    Many have launched their hearts and found no mark,
Some honorably, others like you a bit.
    I, dumb and green and most ways in the dark,
Leaning much on opinionated wit,
    In time must muff my bite and tune my bar.
To lubricate a universal joint
Takes smooth grease: that begins to be the point:

Things I love deathly: things I dearly hate:
    Manners: materials: passions: words: the race:
Brothed in this ignorance I must toil to state
    In terms indigenous as this my face;
Trying meantime, backstage, to integrate
    The brain, Medusa's crept scalp: to displace

Private observance with a lens brought clear
Of those locked flaws the person who is here.

Should, by God's grace, that lens be found entire,
    Fair of distraction, bubble, feather, hue,
Alien to strictured frost and rumpling fire,
    Full gauged for comprehending all things true:
Of faith, fear, judgement, sorrow, love, desire,
    No heartmost breath shall mask its heart with blue:
Then on the blind heart of the regal sun
Trained in God's strength it truly has begun.

UTK MS 1500 Box 1, Folder 7 [two pages]

[Unplaced Stanzas]

Lord Jesus, how presumptuously we shroud
    Thy mirror clean of immortality
With breath of mortal longing and harsh cloud
    Of tears, who seek to tell what can but be!
Lord God of Love who Love on us bestowed
    Pure beyond death and poured all full of Thee,
Forgive our soilings and our faults reprieve
Who meanly such high goodliness receive.

When Christ upon The Cross's rigor died
    For love of man, few words of love spoke He,
But with his corpse and five wounds red and wide
    Such loving showed to all men who would see:
All who have loved and all who have denied
    This Lord of love, they still know this to be:
When most they love they weep nor reckon why
'Twere Paradise on earth for love to die.

When that was finished which outsoars all thought,
    Wherein all sense and all emotion dies,
And they are all the race who compass naught,
    And being void of mind are more than wise,

Then slowly from their nothingness was wrought
　　Their entity that full love deifies:
Much as a slow-born flower broadly blooms,
Each lover his humanity resumes.[9]

UTK MS 1500 Box 1, Folder 7 [one page]

Of that high love and strenuous intent
　　Of flesh on archéd flesh, and how full well
Each cherished other; and what deep content[10]
　　Were essences that death alone might quell:
How kind for either other sought content;
　　How measureless their love, I cannot tell,
And would not sully with my trivial tongue
What all have known who lovers were and young.

You lovers who lie young and free from care
　　And the lost earth and hungering each for each
Find God, now bear me witness when I swear
　　How high above all certitude of speech
This glory's throned; and knowing your despair,
　　Dumb, and unsouled, your patience I beseech,
And more—your aidant[cc] pity, who assay
Humbly to tell what lovers cannot say.

Bear witness first how often you have lain
　　So deep in joy and from all ill so high
That holy joy knew holiness of pain
　　So sharp[11] it was all blessedness to die,
Since[12] that the high-borne soul and heart and brain
　　Could make no noise above a broken cry
That wished a world of words and paradise
Of music, but that these could not suffice.

They knew what all who loved have ever known,
　　They knew it with their fresh unstaléd sight,
How wide the dark that cradled them alone,
　　The quietness of their flesh now full and light,

Eyes sharp with love; and how their faces shone
    With matter more than lifted morning bright:
How they being silent in the night and bare,
To yield the other joy was all their care.

[“]My loveliest dear, what pleasure had been mine
    To have known you green and clumsy and afraid!
To have known your croaking and the secret shine
    Of earliest man-hair sober into shade,
And watch your watchfulness of every sign
    That slowly wrought you to this man full-made:
To have breathed your thoughts and to your loneliness
And ardent blindness brought one such caress.”

To have lain with you at night without your knowing:
    Within your unfulfilled flesh to have lain;
That would be joy, to feel the forthward blowing
    Of breasts beneath their skin, the skin's new grain,
Smaller and smoother, and your clear eyes glowing
    With far surmisal of unfathomed pain:
O, I've lain thus with you and held you dear
Long before either knew the other here.[13]

Later, when you have met them socially
    And seen their little world and littler ways
(Don't get me wrong. They're nice as you and we,
    That's just the point) you'll know this bed-time phase
For what it's worth. And then you may agree
    With wise old uncle Rufus[dd], when he says
Out race is near its wisest and its best
Wholly in love and prostrate and undressed.

Meanwhile, take my word for it and meanwhile,
    There's too much talk of later. Now this poem
Aims to be epic, and the epic style
    Requires a red-hot take-off, just to show em.
The poet can take and dish it with a smile.
    After the battle or the brutal storm[14]
A princess helps our hero: just a peach,
She lets him make an after-dinner speech.[15]

If I could see this straight, and say it straight,
    And if you listened to it, and dared to hear,
I think there might be no more cause for hate,
    No wrong, no wrath, no worth, no peace, no fear,
I think that in the unthinkable estate
    Of being, which my words would bring quite near,
Our knowledge might end knowledge and all care,
And we be less than air, along with air.

Or, if we knew, and cared, that we would know
    The old time anguish of our breath as light,
And all our passions as an anxious show
    Staged to divert us from a melting sight;
And how like fish we swam the dark sea low
    Who dreamt of heavens like our drowned night,
And flailed our fins, and spoke with bubbling words
That now were soaring shining throated birds.

UTK MS 1500 Box 1, Folder 7 [five pages]

[Here the text returns to the typescript]

[Toward His Baptism]

In days defunct, when everyone feared God,
    A child born blue or badly undersized,
His soul flashed heavenward, and tender sod
    Cradled the flesh, and Satan was misprised.
A babe had scarcely wit enough to nod
    When darkness struck him, ere he was baptized:
Yes, ere the midwife spanked his bottom twice
He was made son and heir to Paradise.

Not so with child of George and Helen Carter.
    The wonder was, he was baptized at all.

Like many babes of parents even smarter,
　　John had developed quite a splendid crawl
(Much like that used in wild Australian water)
　　Ere he was cleansed of his First Parents' Fall[ee].
(Only he wasn't: why, you'll shortly hear.
So stick around. It's really pretty queer.)

Now shall I tell you of their quaint religion?
　　I'd almost rather not: but they believed
The Holy Ghost a gaseous sort of pigeon,
　　The Son of God was not, they thought, conceived
By ornitheological miscegen-
　　Ation, but maybe lawful, maybe thieved
By night, and needed no celestial urging
To trot about and call His ma a virgin.

He was a charming fellow, though a Jew.
　　All MAN, no god: a credit to our race.
Kindly to quadrupeds and floozies too,
　　He thawed to butter when a baby face
Peeked up and squeaked, "Ooh, Mister Gods, goo-goo,"
　　And preached and wandered round from place to place
Barefoot and poor, while tony sheenies[ff] sneered,
And Jesus raised a carroty forked beard.

Meanwhile, he gathered in the twelve apostles,
　　All fishermen, plain simple-hearted folk.
They ate bad figs and rarely slept at hostels
　　(Though scarce among the thirteen owned a cloak).
Four of these men could write and wrote the Gospels,
　　Quite fine in parts, but blown so full of hoke [hokum]
Their meaning was disturbing and uncertain,
Till God gave man a sunrise called Bruce Barton[gg].

This little man I'd like to say more of:
　　His business is Humanizing God.
Quite a tough task, unless you're hand in glove
　　With something more than mind, and even then odd,
I think, to reassure illicit love
　　Of Christ's okay—but think what a wad

You hook, although you know Christ never said it.
As for this Barton's work, I've never read it.

But they used to read his little gems at Chapel
(This was at Exeter[hh], a splendid school.)
They thought it well that cleanlimbed youth should grapple
Realities: Christ probably used the stool,
Even as you and—you: and Eva's "apple,"
Which couldn't have grown except in climates cool,
Was likelier a banana. But suppose
We label it "The Fruit Nobody Knows."

That fruit part goes for Barton, I might add,
And so I do. "What *Can* a Man Believe?"
"Well, to be frank, of course, it's very sad
But must be said: I really can't conceive":
But think a method[16] something worse than mad
That through pure textured light presumes to weave
The rotten hemp of Practical Idealism[ii]:
More foul than mad, more Godless far than schism.

"Jesus made easy for Big Business men."
"They laughed when I knelt down, but when I prayed. . .
"Ever tried God?" "Naw, what about him?" "Then,
Just ask the man who owns one!" "Tired, dismayed?
Our Modern Science sickens seven in ten."
["]Don't be a weakling, join the Sky Parade[jj]"
"Jesus is all for Progress: Man, don't doubt!"
"The Man Nobody—" "Sorry, all sold out."

For solid comfort, I advise you all
To drop these shaky matters of Belief.
Get hep to Barton's God: He comes at call,
He doesn't know a tycoon from a thief
And loves them both, and also loves baseball
And Ethyline[kk] and sidecars[ll]: to be brief,
He loves His neighbor as He loves Himself,
So long as that can net a little pelf.

I want a god less Paraclete than Pal.
One Who can understand that certain itch
That leads a man to cheat and chase a gal:
Impress a bitch by being a sonofabitch.
And pour le sport[mm] He'll wear (for sport He shall)
Suspensories from Abercrombie & Fitch—
These for diurnal: for nocturnal feats,
New toothbrushes and Lady Pepperel[17] Sheets.[18]

This man performs great service to Jehovah
By making it as easy to have faith
As 'tis for pigs to swill the intact clovah.
He makes mirages damp enough to bathe.
Fat earthly hens first laid the Cosmic Ova.
Sour dough's the matrix of the Holy Wraith[nn].
Everything's tangible as nose on face:
Therefrom partaking more of snot than Grace.

Suppose, my friends, our God a silken purse
(For silk we value as we God revere).
Doesn't our God come off a shade the worse
When we are reassured He's a sow's ear?
Himself assumed the primal eldest curse
Of human flesh, but somehow burnt it clear
With Godhead: but by Bruce's exorcism
He becomes skunk, our worship Narcissism.

Trick mirrors never yet true faith have shown:
If you believe you do without such help.
And if you don't, for God's sake and your own
Don't compromise as does this timorous whelp:
Thereby the sea of glassy light is grown
Sponged to the brink with sprawled and bubbling kelp:
No soul but drowns in such a slippery brew:
Be honest, if you must, and worship YOU.[19]

I'd like to know his scheme of Paradise:
I may be wrong but trust his face would fall
To find God like *him*, *every bit* as nice:
Bluff, hearty, bellowing "This is Liberty Hall[oo];

You'll have a private bath!" He'd not go twice,
    I fear, and wish he'd never gone at all,
To spend a weekend of eternity
With such a host as he himself must be.

He'd find the Son of God dressed to the nines,
    Full of sharp rye and post-collegiate slang:
And Mary juggling with the dinner wines,
    Making the Party Go Off With A Bang:
The Holy Ghost a shadow behind blinds,
    Mad with unmentionable sturm und drang[pp]—
And he'd buy a lodge in hell, if he could get it,
And weekend there and call it Hatetoquitit.

I fear that I could never understand this
    Vision of heaven: (I wish someone would muzzle him)
But this I know: it's not as good as Dante's:
    I even doubt it's equal to the Moslem,
Where squads of Asian mamas minus panties
    Loll round and smirk beseeching you to nuzzle 'em—
Why bother to *invent* a Paradise?
Give God a break: He'll make it plenty nice.

I'm not an expert in theology,
    And wouldn't use such knowledge if I could.
I hereby register apology
    But claim that naïve faith is just as good.
If you can't swallow the Doxology[qq],
    Aquinas[rr] will be quite repellent food—
O for an epithet for our friend Bar-
Ton . . . self-made God? . . [.] or . . [.] "You Are That You Are."

That ought to hold him; let him think that out.
    He'll take it as a compliment, but I,
Thinking meanwhile, discern a bald Boy Scout
    Who builds himself a tissue-paper sky
And peoples it with creatures of his doubt:
    Which sick, pseudo-celestial I-spy
Were sad enough if private; as it is,
Public and overprinted:— Judas' kiss.

Rather more treacherous than Judas, though—
    More shameful and more pitiful by far.
This Judas profits by his pleasant show
    Of chumminess with Jesus: but the scar
Trenches Bruce deeper: who can never know
    The sin he does that heavenly mouth to mar:
He rests assured he's doing naught but good,
And never dreams that Jesus Christ is screwed.

In all this violent and gratuitous verse
    I hold no enmity with him alone.
He's little better and God knows no worse
    Than other thousand who, cheap concord sown,
Reap their complacent cash: A sky-broad curse
    Hovers them all, will take them flesh from bone
Who, in a world too adept now in doubt,
Kill faith and show it with its entrails out.

But we were talking of the Carters, eh?
    Back to our Theme, by all and every means!
We must remember, reader dear, that they
    Had had a Break with God in their late teens—
Not bad, of course—the merest mild dismay,
    Which such as Bruce patched up with rehashed scenes
From our Lord's life and so on, and our thesis
Is thus their vulcanized idea of Jesus.

Well: Jesus, once or twice, performed—a miracle.
    They needn't bother us; they're made quite clear:
He had it in His Hat: The Age Empirical
    Credits what it can see and maul and hear—
Mother-fixations—let's not be satirical:
    Fraud though He was, He really was a dear,
And caught five thousand converts, maybe six,
Purely by sleight of hand and parlor[20] tricks.

He changed twelve tubs of water into wine
    (We can do that with grapes and Fleischmann's Yeast):
He seaward drove the devil-bloated swine
    (The hog's a skittish and pig-headed beast):

And just to prove He really *was* Divine
He gave five thousand ravenous Jews a feast
Out of a lunch would barely smudge a bib.
We can't explain this, it's a dirty fib.

He gaily trod the wildly bounding wave
(Locked seas are thick as bouillon cubes with salt):
He raised up Lazarus laughing from the grave
(He was just playing possum in the vault):
He told [a] twisted and bed-ridden knave
He was disparted from his body's fault:
The knave leaped up and hauled his bed away
(Faith healers do the same job to this day).[21]

[Agee's note: "And so on, perhaps, about the life of Jesus, and their ideas of sin & judgement, getting around ultimately to:"]

St. Wilfred's is the nicest church in Rome[ss],
And barring the new A. C. and the new
Rotunda Palace with the marble dome,
It is the newest prettiest building, too.
Rome's a fine city, so that's going some,
But when some rich Episcopostate Jew,
Twelve vestrymen and one smart architect
Conspire, that cause is sire to an effect.

The Jew was named Edwin McKim Fairfax.
His father'd prospered with Jim Dandy Shoes.
Louis his name. His brother's name was Max.
And Louis married Eleanora Hughes.
And Judah waned as Fortune gan[tt] to wax.
Were I a Jew I'd make polite excuse
(I think) nor lean toward those who take their hats off
In church, but cleave to gander-lard and Matzoth.

However, Edwin found it inexpedient
To do as I might do but maybe wouldn't,
And with that scant Brittanical ingredient
Leavened his lump (Rhodes loafers[uu] do but shouldn't),

Agreed the setting sun should never see de ent
    Of any land once Albion[vv] put her foot in't,
And signed a check against the Holy Rood:
And Wilfred[ww] rose where Wilfred Burnt had stood.

Well, let it pass. When all is done and said,
    He's welcome to his wants for what they're worth,
And if to have fat Gentiles call you Ned
    Gives you a sense of heritage of earth,
And if your curious fortune's better sped
    Far from the ways and wild lands of your birth,
And your dark rue is made a little glad
In such devices—follow up the fad.

But all the same I think that I'd fight shy,
    Had I such heritage, of such decoy:
Since, among such to be a damned good guy,
    By the same token you're a damned good goy[xx],
And at such times as Nordics heave a sigh,
    You can't relax into a heartfelt oy—
You see, for Jews I'm booster more than knocker,[22]
But think such sighs less kosher than they're cocker.

The architect— . . [.] Well, *he* was English too.
    Not *really* English, if you must be legal,
But quite as English as the aforesaid Jew,
    With slim long legs and eyes just like an eagle,
And in his country home, South Sussex Mew,
    He had four silver salvers[yy] and a beagle,
Nine briars and daily quarts of parboiled tea
With scones, gay chatter, and a wife named Squee.

Maybe you think that for the sake of rhyme
    I made that name up on the moment's spur.
Well, you are wrong. I knew it all the time.
    But if you want me to do right by her,
Her name was Gwladys and for half a dime
    I'd tell you—I will free, slur or no slur:
Her nickname wasn't that me verse is flimsy,
True though that be—but just her husband's whimsy.

For he, like better blooded Englishmen
    In business matters quite quite *quite* astute,
Was never quite so happy, boys, as when
    He sat at tea and swung his little boot
And chirped and chittered and then chirped again
    And really was unconscionably cute,
With heah two lumps and theah a spot of jam
And yon five pet names and an epigram.

He stood about on one leg, like a crane,
    Dimpling the deep rug with a varnished toe,
And smirked like one caught in puerperal pain[zz],
    And laughed hee-hee or guffawed hohoho,
And when his turn for epigrams again
    Swung round, why in his right coat pocket, so,
He snugged four fingers—heavens, *not* his *thumb*!
Preening, and thinking "Martial, here I come!"

When it was necessary for any reason
    His taste in dress stood locally alone.
For though he had beneath just BVD's on,
    His trousers soared at least to the wish bone.
He knew the weaves and shades of every season
    And carried his six foot two and his twelve stone
As gracefully as any Harlem nigger.
But all in all, he cut a finer figger.

And ducky English slang: for breakfast, brekkers,
    Or funking that, we'll snatch a spot of brunch
Or just a wee snort of our choicest liquors—
    You like yours neat as I remember, deuntch[aaa]?
Those who aren't preggers[bbb] find the medics wreckers
    (That last's a shade farfetched, I have a hunch)
Frightful congratters—(Little to my liking
I find this slang. It is, in fact, sick-making.)

They did have fearful fun though, all that set—
    Sinjun and Squee and Babs and Bloke and Sue,
Miggie and Doakes and Mops (the Madcap Pet),
    Norman and Jennifer, Steward (whom they called "Stew"—

Quite apt, poor dear, he was just too-too-*too*—)
    Hell, for the sake of rhyme we'll call it wet.
They stopped with tootootoo; you guessed the rest:
If they'd gone dumb on *goo* I'd think it best.

But back to Sinjun (Lathrop Thorpe's the rest):
    I want to use a cute set such as this
When John's developed to a full-blown pest—
    (John is my hero, and that child, y-wis[ccc],
Even now for christening should be getting dressed?
    No, now he's being dredged up from his piss—
For on the loftiest rung of Nature's ladder
Alone, are babes so casual with the bladder.)

I know it's not a vicious act of will, as
    I once was sure it was. And yet I think
Polyps and gogs[ddd] and infants of gorillas,
    Though lowlier bred and quite fond[23] of drink,
Never release the constant sinuous rill as
    Prodigiously as babes, twixt wink and wink,
Babes of our own, the sapient, human, species—
To say naught of their shining morning faeces.

And that's not all. I hate to be unkind,
    But babies almost make me void my meal.
Spouting from both ends, thoroughly unrefined,
    With bottoms damp as any champion keel,
Sponge-skulled, clam-handed, red, bald, rubber-spined,
    Cold-snouted and pap-gutted—well, I feel
I've said enough about the Gift of Sex.
You can look up their other worse defects.

And I'd suggest you start in with the lung:
    (Lungs, to be strict) You'll find them made of leather,
And even more redundant than the bung[eee],
    And worst of all when both tune up together:
Yells crud the blood more slab than their own dung—
    Oh, all in all they're pretty stormy weather,
These belches, squalls and stinking damps in flood
That equivate[fff] the high noon of the blood.

And yet, you know, in spite of all I say,
    Somehow, I think, although I may be wrong,
That if I had more luck and got more pay[24],
    And thus got married (may I, God, ere long!)
Or even bred him tumbling in the hay,
    I'd change my mind and possibly my song:
If I could have my own exclusive baby,
Maybe I'd like him rather more than maybe.

But I'll be damned (I hate to be so callous)
    Be damned, I say, if I'd say "ah-ah-BOO![")]
Or be its diaper-boy and dreat bid pal, as
    I've seen so many men so often do.
They look like Irish comics at the Palace,
    And not like me and not, I hope, like you:
And so I think I'd find it sort of nauseous
To hear he had my nose and was just gorgeous.

He hasn't got my nose, the little wart,
    And if he has he'd better turn it loose,
For I've heard, by dependable report,
    It has identified me with the Jews:
My nose is mine, and I'll not cut it short
    To share with Baby: no! Bring on your noose!
Come Rack! Come Rope! Come put me on the spot!
My nose is mine. I'll keep it till I rot.

That goes for eyes, I might as well say now,
    Rather than leave a corner free for doubt,
And ears and hair and lip and tooth and brow—
    All things, in brief, which will go up the spout
When I go ditching—These I disallow
    (And even in my will, that clause is out)
My wife, my child, or you, on any terms.
They're signed up as the future diet of worms.

This really doesn't quite make sense, you know.
    I guess perhaps I'm not myself tonight.
I really should have gone out to a show.
    Or maybe should have sat down and got tight.

Or smoked a muggles[ggg]. Or sniffed up some snow[hhh].
    Or sliced my crotch out, in pure girlish spite.
Or blown my skull clean of its clouded yolk:
Which would relieve but grieve a lot of folk.

And since that act would do more harm than good,
    And make me and my room even more a mess;
Since, too, I'm not quite celibate in mood,
    And never cared for drugs, I must confess;
And since I'm lately tired of being stewed[iii],
    And since there are no decent shows, I guess
Although perhaps I'm not myself tonight
And can't make sense, I'll stick around and write.

And that, my dears, is what is sometimes known
    Among us Boys as Peeks Behind the Scenes.
And I shan't blame you if I hear a groan,
    Or comment of the sort inspired by beans.
And if conceivably I can atone
    I'll set to work to do it by every means.
Perhaps just now I'd make the best impression
If I fought clear of all this damned digression.

I haven't got the trick, as Byron had it,
    Of working up the story to a point
Where he could pause: and if he then got mad, it
    Was not a fly but more oil in the oint-
Ment; if instead he took time to be sad, it
    Was o. k. all around, though out of joint—
(Of all the words to rhyme, these are the worst—
Another quatrain and I would have burst.)

I nearly did, over this past weekend.
    I melted like an effigy of wax.
Perhaps somebody thawed one, to that end.
    I had one of those miserable attacks
While I was visiting a Princeton friend
    Upon the intestinal and gastric tracts—
Christ, not the friend, the malady, I mean,
So that I had bad cramps and turned pale green.

However, pardon me if I digress—
    I said I'd stop it and I swear I will.
Before I do I'd like to make a guess:
    It's a wet albatross, a bitter pill
(To coin a phrase) but still I must confess
    I think a poet is from the Holy Hill
Most far removed, with least to say, when so
He gabs of number one. I ought to know.

So now let's get to St. John Lathrop Thorpe:
  What manner of man he was, and why and how
He draughted neath the patronage of—orp!
    Not such a stalwart rhyme—well, too late now—
Of Wilfred, Anglic Angel, he whose corp-
    Se is now so well disparticled[jjj]: his brow
Now lost, his beard in eight and ninety shrines:
And fourteen parishes claim his fourteen spines.

The Saint had two and twenty hundred teeth,
    Nine were of glass and two obsidian,
One was of burning gold and held beneath
    The sword of Govan that was Gideon[kkk]:
And each year English Girlhood makes a wreath
    And traipses round (but keeps her middy on)
Squealing for Wilfred and the blithesome May,
And does a loud rambunctious Shepherd's Hay[lll].

They don't go in for festivals by halves,
    I'll vouch you that, above all if it's pagan,
These non-conformist girls with formless calves.
    And when the Old Roman sets the blood a-ragin',
Up shoots the trade in liniment and salves,
    And there's a glorious potpourri of Dagon,
Thoth, Iacchus, Deirdre and the Owl-Eyed Ox,
Ahriman, Jesus, Calvin and John Knox[mmm].

When Wilfred stood just knee-high to my leg,
    He made a vow and started there and then
Never, no matter *who* might kneel and beg,
    To look upon the opposite of men:

Females, in short: but once he boiled an egg
    And opened it, and found therein a hen,
So young, forsooth, he scantly told the sex:
Yet therewithal he sorely gan him vex.

He smeared himself with all that made him loath,
    Gums of the civet, asafoetida[nnn],
Ordure of beast and bird, he got them both,
    And both with these and else his flesh did mar,
And stewed himself also in his own broth,
    That those who saw not knew him from afar
And[25] cried out "Mercy on us, Holy Man!"
And when he close approached them, they ran.

Each daybreak found him barefoot at the Mass,
    Crouched at a prie-Dieu[ooo] driven full of nails.
He never walked upon the gracious grass,
    But trod the rude rocks and the angled shales.
He never looked and seldom made a pass
    At anyone save some adoring males,
But got five bastards, which is quite enough
To make him patron saint of blind-man's-buff.

Hell, there I go again! This architect—
    St. John the name, his last all rhyme exceeds—
In orange tie and grey tab shirt bedecked
    And hat and breast-kerchief and bearded tweeds,
Stood on the spot where Wilfred first[26] was wrecked,
    Among the charred bricks, clay and Jimpson-weeds,
And munched his wee moustache and drummed his toe
(Of pebbled leather) and then said "Oh-HO!"

So the church was St. John Lathrop Thorpe's idea
    Of what the firm of Hepwaite and McGhee
Would think Ralph Adams Cram[ppp] would make appear
    If he set out upon a royal spree
And tossed in everything, or pretty near,
    That such a church for such a sum should be
In such a town for such denomination:
It was, in short, a nobby edification.

First of all, it was Gothic, be at rest.
    Ripe Angl-Ameri-Gothic. In effect
(As the French say, of Goths the eternal best—
    I'd smile if all the Anglic ones were wrecked)
This lovely church was nothing if not correct.
    It *was* correct, I'll grant it that, but lest
You think I think that worth a wooden farthing,
Aside from this chalked up to less than nothing.

Like all true English Gothic, it was Staunch.
    That first of all: and it was likewise Sturdy.
Both of which words unseat my last week's lunch.
    A masterpiece, a gem, a downright birdie!
Can't you just see it now, eh reader, cawn'tche[qqq]?
    My diction here is getting rather curdy,
To put it chastely, so I'll now describe
The object of this little diatribe.

So let's shove right off with the Oxford Chimes.
    The cheese is more fromage, the more Oxonian[27],
When in the wide belts of all earthly climes
    Daily you'll hear (or ask someone to tune you in,
If you can stand it) ninety and six times
    Those clabbered bells. They sounded pretty tony in
St. Wilfred's, too, with their Bang, Bung, Beng, Bong:
But sound still better Back Where They Belong.

But maybe the Oxonian Chimes delight[28] you.
    Well, you're a good man. Buck up. Carry on.
If you like bells, get someone to invite you
    (I'm sick tonight) to hear the carillon.
And if you'll get inextricably tight, you
    May live it through and down and think it fun,
But I advise you now, to make quite sure,
Pocket a brace of earmuffs and a skewer.

St. Wilfred's like all better ones, were Russian,
    And grossed the Five Year Plan[rrr] a gaudy price.
The Soviet must have smirked to make hard cush[sss] in
    With riddance of the people's opiate vice:

And as for me, I'd like to hook my tush in
The next tone-deafened love that thinks they're nice—
These bells, this bellyache, this rosy cancer
Of sound—but that demands another stanza.

The trouble is, there's something in a bell
That hates to hold a tone. It makes the spine
Shimmer with pain, to hear the clapper tell
The dark iron tone and hear the iron decline,
To hear it grumble and complain like hell
And grongle wangle muffle mooch or whine
According to its size, and then devote
Its energies to keeping off the note.

Religious trombones or the steel guitar
Used to cajole the suave Hawaiian hips,
The sobbing of a sixth-rate movie star,
A torch-song moaned through slabbering negroid lips,
Musical saws and all else that can mar
And does, with all chromatic starts and slips,
The clear sharp note—all these are pure as ice
Beside all bells of carillon device.

This apotheosis of all Jews-Harps[ttt],
This slathering tangle of cacophony,
Careened embroglio of flats and sharps
With every flat and sharp sprained off the key:
This, caged in Wilfred's chastely chiseled scarps,
Flutters and pranks and trills in deafening glee,
Like a canary hatched in Brobdignag[uuu],
With guts of granite and a gorge of slag.

As such, in such a high (and gilded) cage
(Nor bird nor bells I can but must endure)
There'd be a way to quell that pretty rage:
In dark star-strangling round about immure
This spinster's pet: Lord God on high, engage
The looms of blackness[29], weave us out a cure:
Swathe the stone cage with blindness shawled in the hell:
Smother with sleep this puking Philomel[vvv].[30]

The tower was tall, but in the best of taste.
  That is to say, that tendency to soar,
To squirt toward heaven furiously laced
  A foam of stone that scorns an earthly shore,
Was here discouraged: quietly, firmly chaste,
  Chary of ornament, this tower bore
Its four-square Arrow-Collar[www] eminence
Politely and with ice-cold common sense.

About its upper reaches the tower sported
  Two kinds of gargoyles, one a humpbacked hound
And one a crosseyed eagle, both imported
  Designs, and archaeologically sound,
But scarcely like the monsters which cavorted
  And still cavort, above the mote[xxx]-crawled ground
In Gothic lands where monster-minds were bold:
For these were multiplied from a tame mold.

So gargoyle A and gargoyle B leered down
  As if they begged a handout or a dime,
Slightly malicious, with a bothered frown,
  And so did gargoyle A-prime and B-prime
And the four understudies, o'er that town
  And their dark backward and abysm of time:
And each, the weather[31] favoring, sourly slung
Rain-water down from a grooved copper tongue.

The tower and all that blocky church was cool,
  Spat-colored[yyy] stone, perfectly joined and sleek,
Scored with the breath of every rapid tool
  That shaved and manicured it in a week.
The speed they put it up with was just crool,
  And I must say, the job was pretty chic
Compared to those cockeyed asymmetries[32]
Which peasants labored up for centuries.

The door was quaintly arched with statuary
  Quite primitive, but in the nicest way:
Each saintly face resembled the same fairy—
  All smirked archaically, that is to say:

They arched their necks together, and their very
Slim hands and lissome legs were quite o. k.:
They must have been. They were the dying embers
Of Byzantine: sculped after Chartres[zzz] members.

There was a Crucifixion in relief:
A tall slim Christ with laminated tresses,
Ribs like a rat-trap, belly like a leaf,
And several other stylized distresses.
And ladies lolled about in stylized grief,
Looking like people asked to make three guesses—
All, in its era rather more than snappy,
But faked at present, rather less than sappy.

Before we step inside, examine, please,
This nice announcement sign of wood and felt,
You can see many thousands more of these
In office buildings and the quick-lunch belt,
But this one proffers neither Kuhns[aaaa] nor cheese,
And it is nicely spaced, correctly spelt,
And says the sermon (he who runs may scan)
Is "Jesus Christ, the Perfect Gentleman."

So now we know what we can hope to find
Within: an atmosphere that *breathes* of culture—
Not militant but thoroughly refined,
And so this curious air of cool sepulture
Cannot surprise though it benumb the mind,
Nor can that polished and accomplished vulture
Paul Inchbald Whitaker, M.A., D.D.,
Take you aback: but now, just let him be.

First, let this whetted blast envelop you,
Quell all your nerves and still all earthly thought,
Don't roll your eyes or stagger or say phew:
Think rather what this lovely church has aught!
Such invitation to such worship—who
Can resist this? for know, this air is wrought
More subtly than they knew: it is the breath
Chilled by the furbished ribs of Godless death.

Now that you've drawn a bracing lungful, glance
About: just get the spirit of the place.
Note how the tall fish-belly-white expanse
Of slickened stone tones up that gelid Grace
Which[33] knifes the nostrils and assoils the pants
With sanctity: and how extremely naice
The windows are: the suave conglomeration
Of oysters that died young of strangulation.[34]

Also the altar, crested by this cross
Of fat bare gold distilled[35] with amethyst
All in the memory of Emily Foss:
No memory else; the Body is not missed:
Christ is deleted to a total loss:
X marks the spot where Death and Jesus kissed,
And whence the killed victorious Christ descended
The blank cross simpers "Least said soonest mended."[36]

The blenched and naked altar marbles glare
Beneath their four-inch pudor[bbbb] of pale lace,
And lilies stark and bone-white candles flare
Or rule this nudeness upward into space:
The silver ewers all in phalanx stare
The image roundly back; and all that place
Of holiness and Godly love and wrath
Needs only spigots[37] to invite a bath.

To right of which (thank heaven) they've found room
You see, for country quite as well as God.
A little touch of Glory in the gloom,
Gift of the Goldstar champion Mrs. Dodd[cccc]
And other Goldstar motherbirds, for whom
Forty-four doughboys[dddd] sought the Land of Nod:
And so this fringed gold and tricolored silk
Even now draws tears and beefs up mothers'-milk.

UTK MS 1500 Box 1, Folder 6 [Here ends
the typescript material of this folder]

O wives who have and maids who are to wield
    From out your flesh a flesh more young in might
That they like these may fall upon the field
    Shouting for God and dying in His Right,
Be not aghast; by these Stripes ye are healed;
    Your glory is, to breed stars for the night:
(So Whitaker declaimed, or defecated,
Just as you wish, when this he dedicated).

Still farther to the right, the lectern gleams,
    A great bronze bird, wings lifted in elation:
Hence not the eagle but the Doctor screams
    The smoky angers of a vanished nation:
And up the polished lapidary streams
    That smoothly modulated ululation,
To shiver and collide and keep you guessin'
Long after he has ended the first lesson.

The eagle looks familiar? Good for you.
    You guessed it; there's a lot in what you say.
Where did you see it? When and how? And who
    Brought it in here and how'd it get that way?
Well, you'd die laughing if you only knew;
    As Bible-bearer here it's quite o. k.
The fact is, friend, you've seen it—not to vex
You more, on every silver dollar Mex.

UTK MS 1500 Box 1, Folder 7 [one page]

[Summary of materials used: UTK MS 2730 Box 8, Folder 12; UTK MS 1500 Box 1, Folders 6 [typescript] and 7 [handwritten manuscripts, drafts of typescripts and unique materials]; "Opening of a Long Poem (Maybe)," *The Harvard Advocate*, June 1932, pp. 12–20 [a censored version with 47 stanzas total: four stanzas are omitted as are words and phrases in others; the last stanza (47) is an temporary conclusion to this section of the poem (later given the title "John Carter"); its last line is "Anyway, this (to date) is all I've got."]; *CP*, 79–122; UTK MS 1500 Box 1, Folder 5 [partial draft]; 1932–1936.]

[a] Agee's apparent coinage today has several meanings and often with similar sexual overtones. He may have sought to combine "grin" and "ogle" in creating the word.

[b] Ringgold William "Ring" Lardner (1885–1933) was an American sports columnist and very popular satirical short story writer of the time who enjoyed poking fun at marriage, theater, sports, and other highly regarded institutions.

[c] A dialect spelling of "arse" or ass.

[d] A wasting illness of the lungs, such as asthma or tuberculosis.

[e] An agent that induces vomiting.

[f] A short garment resembling a surplice, that is typically worn by Catholic priests and servers.

[g] The main character of *The History of Tom Jones, a Foundling* (1749), by Henry Fielding (1707–1754), is one of the earliest of English novels. This comic, picaresque tale was famous for its bawdy scenes.

[h] Edgar Allan Poe (1809–1849), Ambrose Bierce (1842–1914?), and Charles Baudelaire (1821–1867) were writers famous for exploring the dark side of humanity.

[i] Alfred Louis Charles de Musset-Pathay (1810–1857) was a French dramatist, poet, and novelist.

[j] Jules Laforgue (1860–1887) was a Franco-Uruguayan poet and one of the early proponents of free verse.

[k] Thomas Penson De Quincey (1785–1859) was an English writer, essayist, and literary critic, best known for his autobiographical *Confessions of an English Opium-Eater* (1821).

[l] A crepuscule is twilight or dusk; celtic refers to the Celts or their languages, such as Irish, Scottish Gaelic, Welsh, Breton, Manx, and Cornish, all part of one language family.

[m] French.

[n] Claude Debussy (1862–1918) was a French composer who was very influential in the late 19th and early 20th centuries. His music was in part regarded as a reaction against Wagner and an earlier German musical tradition.

[o] Wilhelm Richard Wagner (1813–1883) was a German Romantic composer, theatre director, and conductor chiefly known for his operas, especially the cycle "Der Ring des Nibelungen" ("The Ring of the Nibelung").

[p] In Britain, nance is an offensive slang term for an effeminate male.

[q] The withers are the highest part of a horse's back, lying at the base of the neck above the shoulders.

[r] A cravat is a neckband, the forerunner of the modern necktie and bow tie.

[s] A mule is a closed-toe, backless, slip-on shoe.

[t] A chest of drawers or dresser, often with a mirror on its top.

[u] A fool, a foolish person; also slang for a penis, as in "skin flute."

[v] Samphire is a name given to a number of succulent salt-tolerant plants (halophytes) that tend to be associated with water bodies. In England its leaves were gathered early in the year and pickled or eaten in salads with oil and vinegar. The poet referred to in the first line of the next verse is possibly Robinson Jeffers (1887–1962).

[w] A wealthy person; or more particularly, a person who returned to Europe having made a conspicuous fortune in India; or possibly, a Muslim government official under the Mogul empire.

[x] A supporter, mainly highland Scottish Catholics, of the deposed King James II and his descendants who claimed the British throne after the Revolution of 1688.

[y] The rise of Communism in the Soviet Union under Stalin began with his rise to power in 1927.

[z] An unfinished surface.

[aa] In the military, a specially organized separate unit usually smaller than a platoon.

[bb] Scottish dialect for "droughts" or "thirsts."

[cc] Helpful.

[dd] James Agee's middle name was Rufus.

[ee] Baptism cleanses the soul of Adam and Eve's original sin of disobedience.

[ff] The phrase "tony sheenies" is a derogatory reference to wealthy or fashionable Jewish people.

[gg] Bruce F. Barton (1886–1967) was an American business executive and Republican Congressman from New York (1937–1940), and the most famous advertising man of his day, mainly due to his best-selling book. *The Man Nobody Knows* (1925). Agee satirizes the book, as well as "Eva's 'apple,'" when he suggests two verses later that the latter be called "The Fruit Nobody Knows."

[hh] Phillips Exeter Academy is a highly selective, private school for students in grades 9 through 12. One of the oldest secondary schools in the United States, Agee attended it from 1925 to 1928, when he graduated and enrolled at Harvard University.

[ii] Practical idealism is a term first used by John Dewey in 1917 to describe a philosophy he espoused that holds that implementing ideals of virtue or good is an ethical imperative.

[jj] Agee may be referring to ascension into heaven or to "The Sky Parade," an aviation movie drama based on the earlier radio series "The Air Adventures of Jimmie Allen." The film was released on April 17, 1936, by Paramount Pictures.

[kk] Ethyline is a hydrocarbon with many uses. For example, in medicine it is used as an anesthetic and it is also used in the extraction of rubber and as a gas in cutting and welding. What Agee wishes to refer to in this instance is ambiguous.

[ll] Again an ambiguous reference. Agee could mean a cocktail or one-wheeled attachment to the side of a motorcycle, scooter, or bicycle, making a three-wheeled vehicle and room for an additional person.

[mm] "pour le sport" means "for the sport." "Paraclete," is the Holy Spirit/Ghost.

[nn] "Holy Wraith" likens God to a wraith, a ghostlike image or apparition of someone, that often appears shortly before or after death.

[oo] "Liberty Hall" may be a generic reference on Agee's part (there are numerous Liberty Halls), but may also refer to the land surrounding the Liberty Tree in Boston, Massachusetts, given that he was a Harvard graduate.

[pp] "Sturm und Drang" was a pre-Romantic movement in German literature and music that occurred between the late 1760s and early 1780s that was characterized by emotional unrest and a rejection of neoclassical literary norms.

[qq] The Doxology refers to an oral expression of praise and glorification of God.

[rr] St. Thomas Aquinas (1225–1274) was an Dominican friar, philosopher, Catholic priest, Doctor of the Church, and an immensely influential philosopher, theologian, and jurist in the tradition of scholasticism.

[ss] As near as the editors can determine, Agee's St. Wilfred's, its architect and his family, are fictional.

[tt] began

[uu] Rhodes is a then current brand of footwear. Agee may also have meant the upscale shoe manufacturer Erich Rohde GmbH, a German company founded in 1862.

[vv] The earliest name for England.

[ww] Wilfred is an alternate spelling for St. Wilfrid (originally Wilfirth) (c. 633–709 / 710), an English bishop highly recognized for his staunch advocacy for the papacy. Agee may or may

not have intended this reference; likely not, if he was continuing the fictional portrayal. St. Wilfrid was not burnt; a successor bishop had the same name.

[xx] A Jewish name for a non-Jewish person.

[yy] Salvers are serving trays, generally silver, that are used for formal occasions.

[zz] The pain resulting from when a mother's reproductive organs return to their original nonpregnant condition, usually about six weeks after childbirth.

[aaa] "deuntch" is a dialect rendering for "don't you (cha)."

[bbb] British slang for pregnant.

[ccc] Archaic word for certainly, from the Old and Middle English.

[ddd] English dialect for bogs or quagmires.

[eee] A stopper, but Agee's reference, given the previous statements, likely means the slang word for an anus.

[fff] Agee's coinage likely meaning to moderate.

[ggg] Marijuana cigarettes.

[hhh] Slang for cocaine.

[iii] Slang for drunk.

[jjj] Parts of St. Wilfred's body have evidently become holy relics in the ensuing lines.

[kkk] The sword of Govan is likely a Pictish short sword, if a 9th century stone carving found on a sarcophagus at Govan, in Glasgow, Scotland, is correct; Gideon and his 300 warriors, much like the 300 Spartans at Thermopylae, have become symbolic of a small elite force that won victory over their enemy against overwhelming numerical odds. Agee seems to link the two ideas together.

[lll] "Shepard's Hay" is a popular English folk tune which was played at Morris dances.

[mmm] Following up on May Day and pagan celebrations, and before he moves to Christianity by mentioning Jesus, and the protestant leaders John Calvin and John Knox, Agee brings in the following: Dagon is a West Semitic god of crop fertility, worshiped throughout the ancient Middle East; Thoth is the Egyptian god of equilibrium, writing, magic, wisdom, and the moon; Iacchus, the son of Dionysus and Aura, is a minor Greek God of the ritual cry of the Eleusinian Mysteries, which were initiations held every year for the cult of Demeter and Persephone; Deirdre, best known as "Deirdre of the Sorrows," is the foremost tragic heroine in Irish legend and her story formed part of the pre-Christian Ulster Cycle of stories; the Owl-Eyed Ox could not be identified; Ahriman is a Persian (Iranian) demon, God's adversary in the Zoroastrian religion and the ruler of chaos and darkness.

[nnn] Both the civet and asafoetida (asafetida) are references to "Odure" (odor) that Wilfred applied to his body. A civet is a mammal marked the distinctive musky scent used in perfumes; asafoetida is an herb with a pungent smell and sometimes called "stinking gum" and "devil's dung."

[ooo] A prie-dieu is a type of individual prayer desk that usually has sloping shelf for books or hands, and a kneeler.

[ppp] Ralph Adams Cram (1863–1942), a Boston architect and writer, was the foremost Gothic revival architect in the United States in his day and designed many churches.

[qqq] "cawn'tche" is a dialect rendering of "can't you (ya)."

[rrr] The Five Year Plan was instituted by Joseph Stalin in the late 1920s as part of the ideology of the Communist Party for development of the Soviet economy.

[sss] A contraction for "cushion," cush is slang for money, especially when reserved for some special use.

[ttt] A Jew's harp, also known as a jaw harp and by many other names, is an inexpensive

lamellophone instrument, consisting of a flexible, vibrating metal or bamboo tongue or reed attached to a frame and is usually played pressed against the teeth.

[uuu] Brobdingnag is a fictional land occupied by giants in Jonathan Swift's novel *Gulliver's Travels* (1726). While a captive there, Gulliver fears that, if a woman of his race was captured, they would be bred and their children "kept in cages, like tame canary-birds, ..."

[vvv] A figure in Greek mythology who is frequently invoked as a symbol in literary and artistic works; also, in poetry, a name for a nightingale.

[www] Arrow Collars were detachable shirt collars manufactured by Cluett Peabody & Company of Troy, New York; they were mass-produced from 1907 to 1931, and featured the dapper Arrow Collar Man. The fictional Arrow collar man became an icon and by 1920 was receiving fan mail.

[xxx] A mite or a tiny piece of a substance.

[yyy] Spats, a shortening of spatterdashes, are a type of overshoe footwear accessory for outdoor wear, covering the instep and the ankle. Now available in many colors, in the 1930s the classic spat for men tended to be light-colored as a contrast to their shoes.

[zzz] Agee is referring to the numerous statues in the Cathedral of Our Lady of Chartres in France.

[aaaa] Unknown. Possibly Agee refers to the slang term meaning "well done" or "attaboy." It might also be a different off-topic reference to Fritz Julius Kuhn (1896–1951), a German Nazi activist who served as elected leader of the German American Bund before World War II. A naturalized United States citizen in 1934, his citizenship was cancelled in 1943, and he was deported in 1945.

[bbbb] A sense of modesty.

[cccc] Mrs. Alice Gresham Dodd was the first Goldstar Mother. Her obituary, stating her age as 67, in the New York Times (2/27/1927) cites the February 20, 1927 story from Evansville, Indiana. Her son, James Bethel Gresham, was the first soldier to die in WWI. The Gold Star was meant to honor a United States Armed Forces member who died while engaged in action against an enemy recognized by the Secretary of Defense, making this supreme sacrifice. It was meant to underscore the pride of the family in this sacrifice, rather than the sense of personal loss which would be represented by mourning symbols.

[dddd] There were over 53,000 American combat fatalities in WWI. Agee may refer to a particular battle in mentioning 44. While H. L. Mencken claimed that the term "doughboys" began with the Continental Army in the Revolutionary War, the nickname is most linked to the troops of General John Pershing's American Expeditionary Forces on the Western Front in World War I.

Later Poems: 1933–1953

[Womblight on the wombat][a]

Womblight on the wombat
Women on the wane
Men who pause for menopause
    And cheap tin trays

Womblight on the wombat
Wombmen, wane, the womb blight,
Men who pause for menopause
    And cheap tin trays.

UTK MS 3824 Box 6, Folder 34 [August 20, 1933][1]

[a] Agee dates his nonsense verses "Aug 20 1933."

[O question not, nor force from me that vow][a1]

O question not, nor force from me that vow
Which scantly lends the sick heart reassurance;
Rest faithful in firm silence, which is now
Frail but sole bulwark for love's endurance.
However mad, it is my heart's belief
That he who lies of love trumpets instruction
For anger and terror, scorn & doubt & grief
Swiftly to marshal[2] toward our sure destruction.
Since, though we know naught else, we know love true,
When from the strict course which love's truth affirms
The sick brain swerves, to guiltless hearts accrue
Loves penalties and unpalliable[b] terms.
If you love truly, speak the vow for me:
For from my lips it now were blasphemy.

UTK MS 3824 Box 7, Folder 4 [1933][3]

[a] Agee dates the sonnet "(Spring 33)" in the upper right-hand corner of the page.
[b] Agee's term, possibly meaning unpalatable and also unbending.

Sonnet

Now it is competent, our common heart
And we two fragments found to fit entire
And we two whom the long night held apart
Meet in the high wealth of the morning's fire:
With all predictions cancelled in the fact
And our rich insufficience satisfied.
I meditate those things our life has lacked:
Some things our love must ever be denied.
I am most envious of those careless years
When full of care we knew each other not
And green false love, false happiness, false tears,
Ripened this whole heart, which must wholly rot;
The dreamful heart that woke toward prime of day
Dreams now of dawn and darkly wastes away.

CP, p. 143 [1933]

Johannes Brahms: May [7], 1833[a1]

The year turns round him and fulfils his worth:
We too, of many motions in one mind,
No more anatomize our present dearth
But think of one who did the task consigned.
This century past he drank his first brave breath,
The undeviant, the rich and deep of heart.
Who marked his height and toiled it unto death,
Humble and honorable in his art.
No slyness his, no roaring at the air;
Splendor of honest sound was all his use:
From which intent no envy nor despair
Nor ease of life compacted might seduce.
And we, to all we and the world disclaim
Swear new, single allegiance by his Name.

UTK MS 1500 Box 1, Folder 12 [c. 1933];
CP, pp. 144–45; *JAR*, pp. 228–29 (drafts).

[a] The date is that of Brahms' birth. See also "A Poem for Brahms' Death-Bed."

[Sugah-foot, set on mah knee][a1]

Sugah-foot, set on mah knee
    Ah wants to ax you sumpn
What is dis stuff de Regionalis'
    An Nationalis' is dumpin'?

Hit smell so quair I cann't make aout
    Rightly, honey, was it
Food fo de privy-chickens, gal,
    Aw foe de tuhkey buzzahd.

Dey shaouts fer Nawf dey shaouts fer Saouf
    Dey shaouts fer Ees un Wes
Haow all de othah places may be good
    But dey's de bes':

An' dem as outgrows his neighbahhood
    Sets up a laoudah scream
Abaout de hull dang countryside
    An' de American Dream.

What was dat dreamin', sweetie-pie?
    Dey ain't no one will set
N' let on was it skeery, sweet,
    Or jist de ole fashion wet.

Who dreamp it fo dat mattah, chile,
    An what he doin naow?
Whatevah hit was hit must abeen
    No Injun, but a waow.

Dis Engle feller, naow, he looks
    A powful nice young man:
Folks tell me haow he's jist a flash
    In D. J. Adam's pan.[b]

But I wouldn' take nobody's word
    Fer nufn, not no mo,
Not sence dey give de Plitzah Prize
    To Striblin's book, de Sto'.[c]

UTK MS 1500 Box 1, Folder 14 [c. 1933]; *CP*, pp. 147–48[2]

[a] As with all of Agee's dense dialect poems, this one is best read aloud as an aid to understanding.

[b] The identity of Engle and Adam could not be established. Adam may be a critic; he was not a member of the Pulitzer Prize Board (1932–1933).

[c] T. S. Stribling (1881–1965), won a Pulitzer Prize in 1933 for his novel *The Store*, the second book in his "The Vaiden Trilogy" that focused on the South.

[Ah calls awn ivah Dimacrayut (typed version; see manuscript version below for help with dialect; reading the poem aloud is also helpful in this regard)]

Ah calls awn ivah Dimacrayut dats shonuf Dimacrattic
To rally raoun n clean dem vaarmints outen ouah Nation's attic.
Ah calls awn ivah fahmuh dat aint got no adjucation
Tmake *me* Pres Dent soah cnclean de hull dadbuhn nation.

Ah calls on ivah thenkn mayun datlaks mah briyut riyud gallusses[a]
Tsiyun manayun tda What Haouse dat sets daown awn hahd uhned callusses:
Nahcalls awn ivah dipaty, Klu Kluxah n ix-Sojah
Tkeep deyum niggahs in day place tllah gits beck tJojah[b].

UTK MS 3824 Box 7, Folder 1 [typescript; c. 1933]

[a] Bright red galluses (suspenders).
[b] to Georgia

[Ah calls awn ivah dimocrat (manuscript version)][1]

Ah calls awn ivah dimocrat dat's sho nuf dimocratic
    To rally raoun en smoke dem varmints outen aouh nation's attic:
Ah calls awn ivah fahmuh dat ain't got no adjucation
    To git a *Prez-Dent* dat can *plaow un*dah dis hu*ll dadbuhned nation.*

Ah calls awn ivah thenkn mayun dat liaks mah briaght reyud galluses[a]
    To sind a mayun to da Whiat Haouse dat sets daown awn handuhned
    calluses:
An ah calls awn ivah dipaty, Ku Kluxah an ex-sojuh
    To keep dem niggahs in dey place till ah gits back to Jojuh[b].

UTK MS 1500 Box 1, Folder 14 [c. 1933]

[a] Bright red galluses (suspenders).
[b] Georgia

[Theme and Variations]

Night stands up the East:
Day lies down the West:
Lax in his fur, the beast
The bird with brow in breast

Yields each the addled hope
That stood him sunward guide:
Cold on the shadow's scope
The dew distends its tide:

And all is strifeless quite:
All free, from all affray:
And down the West falls night:
And up the East stands day.

1.
Whole to the hollow shadow
Commend your heavy brow,
All pomp of day put from you
And deep through darkness bow.

The margin withers of the morning dew:
Weighed clear, the lands that loved this keep of shade
Now mount the noon beneath and meet for you
The terms wherein the round lands are betrayed.

The same, the deep-dealt law that you debased
Into this bourne of death where you are whole
Now lifts refreshed to lower these lands defaced:
All withered is the early dew.

Some high delirious meadow
Delivers the late letter of your mutual vow:
Peace, peace, be healed, all wholesomeness become you:
Your night is on you now.

2.
The whistlers slick and chortlers
The free, the smart of song,
The deft on wing in the wild white day
Throng muttering shrugged and asleep nor stray
The green boughs deep among:

Safe from the shadowing high-ways
The latest wing is home:
The eagerest wing that was abroad
Is idle now and the wing outlawed:
The happiest throat is dumb.

Beneath the king-armed buzzard
The air stands damp and blind;
And hunched in tenting cumbrous wing
He sleeps who leaned in a deathward ring
His downright hand behind.

3.
They that led the long loam open,
They that mouthed the meadow short,
They that scruffed the wry roots' sweetness,
Beasts of this laborious sort;

Sour-brained mule and horse meek-headed,
Grim-butted cow and daft-eyed sheep,
Gristly hog and their gay children
All have shut them safe in sleep.

Quiet, the jaws on bruised kernel,
Coffined quiet, the mauléd cud:
Safe also the soft, the young ones:
Shy the doomsday takes their blood,

4.
Where now the lizard and the rinded snake
That skipped and slurred their lengths and lusted in the heat?
Where the small bugs that on the water break
Their rapid dances and each other eat?

The lithe-tongued butterfly where now is he,
That chanced his bright wings on the unequal air?
Where the mean hornet and the sweet-groined bee?
Now they are under night how may these bloodless fare?

The reptile's eye is blue: the thready fly
Stands on the skin of water; he is well;
The tongue is furled, and the fair dust not flawed, and the wings, shut high:
The stout bee dozes in his paper cell:

UTK MS 1500 Box 1, Folder 21 [typescript, three pages; c. 1933][1]

Outcast Earth[1]

Locked from the poring air he lies, lives in your love
Who travel from the earth's outposts and file, silently, past him;
In red stone tabernacled, and in your breasts, in honor.
And there are others,
Imprisoned, dead, now busy, now not yet born
Whose lives shall bring this race first taste of living,
Whose memory shall resist the air;
Whose names, whose eyes and gestures,
Shall live like alphabets in the lives of this people.

UTK MS 1500 Box 1, Folder 15 [1933–1939?]

[Nine miles from Selma]

Nine miles from Selma, down a red dirt road,
Still sucking shreds of fatback from his teeth,
He slows, along the dark pines, listening.
The man comes up and sure enough it's Cabe.
You got your nickel? Yeah, I got my nickel,
I told Sam Cass and Jube's a comin too.
What's all this leadn up to, boy? Shet up.
Come on along. You'll find what quick enough.[1]

UTK MS 1500 Box 1, Folder 15 [1933–1939?]

[No candle for the bindle[a]]

No candle for the bindle
In any window on all this world.

From chimney stones all down the valley hickory smoke stands up out of the barnyard dew. A gobbling dog, gobbling his suet and his growlings, breaks into bark and the long steel pike, the long steel pike, the long steel pike, uh, winding: into the land of: thy dreams.

Go into your gandy dance[b] big boy. This town don't like your kind.

No candle for the bindle
In any window on this world.

Drown this gay cat with cream.
Give this little prushun[c] a great big jocker[d].
Let the yarddick sap the bakehead[e] by mistake.
And a warm jungle by a stiff gradient[f], O Lord.
And dream of girls that know how to pull the sap out of you.
Spare us, likewise, the mission fight-talk: oh, spare us the CCC[g].
For Jesus sake, amen.

From all the easy windows of this earth
No candle peers for bindle.[1]

UTK MS 1500 Box 1, Folder 15 [1933–39?]

[a] A bindle is the bag, sack, or device for carrying your possessions that was often used by American hobos, particularly in the Great Depression.

[b] A "gandy dancer" is a slang term used for early railroad workers or "section hands" in the United States, who laid and maintained railroad tracks.

[c] Prussian

[d] A jocker is slang for a man who perceives himself as straight and is the aggressor in a relationship between two men, especially in prison.

[e] Three slang terms comprise this line. The "yarddick" is the railroad yard's detective; to "sap" is to hit; and the "bakehead" is the fireman on the locomotive.

[f] A prime place for a hobo "jungle" or camp is next to a steep grade, or "stiff gradient," of the railroad line. The train slowed and facilitated a hobo's jumping on or off.

[g] The Civilian Conservation Corps was a part of Roosevelt's New Deal designed to help lift the United States out of the Great Depression. Established in 1933, it employed single men between the ages of 18 and 25 in work programs to improve America's public lands, forests, and parks.

[The little guy was waiting at the door][1]

The little guy was waiting at the door.
The gun's stirred gently in the evening breeze.
Good evening, madam, I'm Sir Samuel Hoare[a].
This doberman is unfair to organized fleas.
But that made General[2] Johnson[b] plenty sore.
Damn Jake the Barber[c]. Screw the Duc du Guise[d].
What are we, men or malmsers[e], I required.
The hood lit up and said: my lad, you're fired.

His foot is in the door, but not for long.
The early guns bloom silence, beneath our wings.
Live pure, speak truth, buy low, sell high, right wrong.
Their yeastless Christs absorbed, the last five Kings[f]
File the bare yard and die. We need a song.
Where are the woodwinds? Bear[3] down on the strings
And now I'm using the cross-country tube.
Milk below, farmer's daughter: heads up, rube.[4]

The gunflowers wither: a city crumbles there.
Suck in your guts there, bitterling[g], wipe that smile.
Banquet the gonads, doctor, shoe the gray mare.
Frowning, he walked to meet the falling tide.
Cut out your heart, old pal, and do your share.
Lake Tana[h] feeds the fanspread of the Nile.
Good evening, madam, I'm Sir Samuel Hoare.
Boss-mistah, sah, dey aint gonna *be* no core.

Keep us kind shepherd; blessed are the meek.
Her wambling[i] child beside, unsteadily the wrung doe
Churches herself in shadow at the cold creek.
He knows because his mother told him so.
This world's a yo-yo. Let the carnival freak
Visit his parents in the winter. Oh,
Give us one word, or two, right down the groove.
On that smooth[5] tongue whose music hell can move.

UTK MS 1500 Box 1, Folder 15 [1933–39?; two pages][6]

[a] Sir Samuel John Gurney Hoare (1880–1959) was a British politician most of his adult life. Perhaps most famous for authoring the Government of India Act 1935, which granted provincial-level self-government to India, here Agee likely refers to his appeasement stand that same year in regard to Mussolini's annexation of Ethiopia (then Abyssinia), under the Hoare-Laval Pact with the French Prime Minister, which was so unpopular it led to his resignation as British Foreign Secretary.

[b] The particular "General Johnson" to whom Agee refers is unclear.

[c] "Jake the Barber" was an alias of John Factor (1892—1984). Born Iakov Faktorowicz, he was a swindler first in Great Britain and then in the United States where he became a Prohibition-era gangster affiliated with the Chicago Outfit.

[d] The house of Guise was a French noble family, many of whom took this title. Agee likely refers to Prince Jean, Duke of Guise (1874—1940) who, despite the French Revolution, still claimed the throne of France.

[e] Drinkers of "malmser," a wine; i. e. not "manly" men.

[f] Agee likely refers to the Last Five Kings of Judah who reigned for forty years, while all the while Jeremiah warned of impending destruction. His words unheeded, Judah fell and the people entered Babylonian captivity. See also 2 Chronicles 34–36, Jeremiah 22, 2 Kings 24.

[g] A bitterling is a small European carp-like fish two to three inches in length of little value. This lack of value and its size, as well as its being noted for its unusual manner of breeding, indicates that Agee means to emphasize both its insignificance and sexuality.

[h] The source of the Nile, Lake Tana is the largest lake in Ethiopia.

[i] Perhaps a dialect rendering of "cure."

[j] To wamble is to move unsteadily.

[There is pepper to stop the most intelligent bloodhound]

There is pepper to stop the most intelligent bloodhound.
The soul concedes in a swamp: breathes through a straw.
Vestigial organs may yet assert supremacy
Over (even) the compounded eye.[1]

UTK MS 1500 Box 1, Folder 11 [1934[2]]

STRAIGHT[1]

How we scan, on coastal air, development of clouds.
But they, exhausted on mountains, overmarching us,
Tease with dry shadow. The whole light is tin.
Tin the expensive taste of water.
Corn is aborted inches under earth. Corn, started,
Stalls in the sun, rattles, in no wind.

Sun burns a hallow in our air: and, draughted
The whole side of the earth, winds strip us clean
Five hundred miles of skin laid east to the bone.

Horses in Ohio swell like toadstools, die of the dust.
In Washington, typewriters urging crop reduction are stalled with it.
New Yorkers rub their eyes, sympathize;
New England gulls out climb each other avoiding it.

Here in our streets at noon,
Headlights jab two feet and are blunted.
Cows follow dry channels: buzzards stoop to conquer.

UTK MS 1500 Box 1, Folder 11 [1934]

[Parody of Cole Porter's "You're the Top"[a]]

You're the pot,
You're the Reichstag Trial[b],
You're the pot,
You're the Roosevelt Smile,
You're the London Economic Conference[c],
You're the car-card[d] hand
In the soapsuds and
State's Evidence;
You're the gags
In the Conning Tower[e],
You're the Stags[f]
At a shotgun shower,
I'm a louse some ways and there's damn few ways I'm not,
But if—Baby—I'm the bottom,
You're the pot.

You're the pot
You're the Scottsboro Jury[g],
You're the pot,
You're a homo's fury,
You're the hanker of Shankar[h] to do the Lindy-Loop[i],
You're tutti-frutti
You're Joe Venutti[j]
You're Betty Boop[k];
You're the aches
After Pluto Water[l],
You're the breaks
In a song by Porter,
I'm a rolling stone and I broke a bone that shot,
But if—Baby—I stall in Flushing[m],
You're the pot.

You're the pot,
You're the Brothers Powys[n],
You're the pot,
You're Lipstick Lois[o],

You're a color jag in Fortune Magazine,
You're a suit by Brooks
And a tour by Cook's
And the Phaerie Queane:
You're the pearl
In an August oyster,
You're the swirl
Of an Esquire roister[p],
I find Knickerbocky, Cholly[q], frightfully jolly, What?
But if—Baby—I'm the Sitz-Bath[r],
You're the pot.

You're the pot,
You're the skin on salmon,
You're the pot,
You're Percy Hammond[s],
You're a stickler for les ticklers of La France[t],
You're a silver wig
You're the Third Little Pig
You're a Ballet-Daunce:
You're a breeze
From the Jersey Meadows,
You're a wheeze
From the words of Beddoes[u],
I'm a wag in the can and a Crime-Club Fan, a scut[v]—
But if—Baby—I'm a square one,
You're the pot.

You're the pot,
You're a News-Week cover,
You're the pot,
You're the Perfect Lover,
You're the once-a-day—Hey-Hey—for Shredded Wheat,
You're caviar,
You're Harry's Bar[w]
You're Cream of Feet[x]:
You're the Drews,
You're the Abbe Dimnet[y],
You're the flooz,
Ie of Walker, Jimnet[z],

I'm a fool for Guy Lombardo[aa], Bilin' Hot—
But if--Baby—I'm the Bell-Ans[bb],
You're the pot.

You're the pot,
You're the great Jane Austen,
You're the post,
You're the Best in Boston
You're the goim[cc] that inspired a poem by E. Millay[dd],
You're black lace undies
You're Wall Street Sundays
You're Massanet[ee]:
You're a Find
In a play by Barry[ff],
You're the Kind
That your Dad Would Marry,
I'm a headleigh[gg] and a rather deadlegh sot,
But if—Baby—I'm a wetsmack[hh],
You're the pot.

You're the pot,
You're the Roerich Banner[ii],
You're the pot,
You're a silk bandanner,
You're the fan-clad mare on the floor of the Par-adise[jj],
You're Kit Cornell[kk],
You're *Peter Bell*[ll],
You're Clara Tice[mm]:
You're the spats
On a charming fellow,
You're the cats
In a rube bordello,
Now I may see the Cosmos wrong-end to or not:
But if—Baby—I'm De Sitter,
You're the pot.

UTK MS 3824 Box 7, Folder 4 [typescript[1]; two pages; 1934?][2]

[a] "You're the Top" is a Cole Porter song from the hit 1934 musical "Anything Goes." It is a dialogue song about a man and a woman who take turns complimenting each other; its great

popularity engendered many parodies, including these attempts by Agee. The meaning of some of Agee's references, for various reasons, could not be ascertained.

[b] The trial resulted from the Reichstag fire on February 27, 1933, four weeks after Adolf Hitler was sworn in as Chancellor of Germany. An unemployed Dutch construction worker named Marinus van der Lubbe set fire to the German parliament building, causing serious damage. The Nazis blamed the Communists for the fire and used it as an excuse to seize emergency powers and crush all opposition.

[c] The London Economic Conference was attended by representatives of 66 nations from June 12 to July 27, 1933. Cordell Hull represented the United States. Its purpose was to win agreement on measures to fight the Great Depression, revive international trade, and stabilize currency exchange rates, but failed after President Franklin D. Roosevelt denounced currency stabilization in early July. He had removed the country from the gold standard in April.

[d] A small cardboard advertising placard or other display usually in or on streetcars and buses.

[e] A raised structure on the deck of a submarine used at the time for navigation and attack direction.

[f] Single males.

[g] The trial of the Scottsboro Boys was a notorious example of racism. They were nine African-American teenagers, ages 12 to 19, accused in Alabama in 1931 of raping two white women. The first jury was all white. After numerous trials and appeals, several reaching the Supreme Court, charges were finally dropped for four of the nine defendants. The others' sentences ranged from 75 years to death.

[h] Likely Uday Shankar (1900–1977), an Indian dancer and choreographer. He was famous for his fusion of European theatrical techniques and Indian classical dance, folk, and tribal dance, popular in India, Europe, and the United States in 1920s and 1930s.

[i] The Lindy, or Lindy Hop, was a dance that was a fusion of jazz, tap, breakaway, and the Charleston. It is frequently described as a jazz dance and is a member of the swing dance family. Born in the African-American communities in Harlem, New York City, in 1928, it was very popular from the 1930s to the early 1940s.

[j] Giuseppe "Joe" Venuti (1903–1978) was considered the father of jazz violin in 1920s and early 1930s.

[k] The popular cartoon character Betty Boop began as both a parody and a symbol of female sexuality. Created by Max Fleischer, with help from animators, she appeared in the Talkartoon and Betty Boop film series starting in 1930.

[l] Pluto Water was a strong laxative water product popular in the early 20th century.

[m] Wordplay denoting Flushing, NY, and the act of flushing a commode or "pot."

[n] Charles Powys's eleven children formed one of the most remarkable literary families of the twentieth century. The most famous of the brothers were Llewelyn Powys (1884–1939), a British essayist, novelist and younger brother of novelists John Cowper Powys (1872–1963) and Theodore Francis Powys (1875–1953).

[o] Lois Bancroft Long (1901–1974) was an American writer for *The New Yorker* from 1925 to 1970. Regarded by some as the founder of fashion criticism, she was known under the pseudonym "Lipstick" and as a flamboyant flapper.

[p] To roister is to behave wildly.

[q] The first to use the byline of Cholly Knickerbocker was John W. Keller, in a column for the *New York Recorder* in 1891, but he brought the character with him to *New York American* in 1902. The pseudonym, which combined Washington Irving's character Diedrich Knickerbocker with a play on how upper-class New Yorkers supposedly pronounced "Charlie,"

continued in use by a series of society and gossip columnists, especially those who wrote for the *American* and its successor, the *New York Journal-American.*

[r] A sitz bath, or hip bath, is used to relieve discomfort and pain in the lower part of the body, for example, due to hemorrhoids. A basin or device designed to fit in a toilet bowl can also be used.

[s] Percy Hammond (1873–1936) was a journalist and theater critic for the *Chicago Tribune* and the *New York Herald Tribune.*

[t] An allusion to the type of condom known as a "French Tickler" that was believed to enhance a woman's sexual pleasure because of its ribbed construction.

[u] Perhaps Thomas Lovell Beddoes (1803–1849) who was an English poet, dramatist and physician.

[v] Scut is a slang term for a worthless person.

[w] Founded in 1931, Harry's Bar in Venice became the place where writers, painters, artists, aristocrats, kings and queens would meet. It was a favorite of Ernest Hemingway's.

[x] A play on "Cream of Wheat," a brand of farina, a type of breakfast porridge mix and an alternative to oatmeal.

[y] Ernest Dimnet (1856–1954) was a French priest, writer, lecturer, and best known for *The Art of Thinking*, a popular book during the 1930s.

[z] Gentleman Jimmy (actually James John) Walker (1881–1946), also known as Beau James, was the flamboyant mayor of New York City from 1926 to 1932. At the instigation of Governor Franklin D. Roosevelt, he resigned on September 1, 1932, because of a corruption scandal.

[aa] Alberto "Guy" Lombardo (1902–1977) was a well-known Canadian-American bandleader who formed the Royal Canadians in 1924. They billed themselves as creating "the sweetest music this side of Heaven." He became a staple of New York City's New Year's Eve celebrations for many years.

[bb] A pharmaceutical company noted for its remedy for indigestion.

[cc] A Hebrew word denoting a gentile or non-Jew.

[dd] Edna St. Vincent Millay (1892–1950) was a popular poet of the time.

[ee] Perhaps Agee meant "Massenet." Jules Émile Frédéric Massenet (1842–1912) was a French composer best known for his operas.

[ff] Agee likely meant "Barrie." Sir James Matthew Barrie was a Scottish novelist and playwright, most famous as the creator of Peter Pan.

[gg] A play on Headley or Hadley. The name means "heather meadow" and was one sometimes given to fictional characters who were artificial and pretentious.

[hh] The sound a man's testicles makes when slapping against his partner during sex.

[ii] A banner of peace symbolizing the Roerich Pact. This pact is the pan-American treaty dedicated to the protection of artistic and scientific institutions and historical monuments. It was signed on April 15, 1935, and was the first such international treaty.

[jj] Agee may refer her to Smalls, a famous nightclub in Harlem, New York City. At the time of the Harlem Renaissance, Smalls Paradise was the only one of the Harlem clubs owned by an African-American and integrated. It was known for its dancing and roller-skating waiters who sometimes sang as part of the shows as well. It never closed at the normal time of 3 or 4 a.m. and offered a breakfast dance with a full floor show at 6 a.m. In the first half of the 1930s some of the featured artists included Bill "Bojangles" Robinson, Fats Waller, and a young Billie Holiday.

[kk] Katharine Cornell (1893–1974) was a wide-ranging actress, writer, producer, and theater-owner. Regarded as one of the great actresses of the American theatre, her most famous role was that of English poet Elizabeth Barrett Browning in the 1931 Broadway production of *The Barretts of Wimpole Street.*

[ll] The reference is perhaps to *Peter Bell: A Tale in Verse*, a long narrative poem by William Wordsworth, written in 1798, but not published until 1819. Peter is a potter, a commoner and a sinner, who is downcast by his experiences, but by the end of the poem is saved and emerges as a better man.

[mm] Clara Tice (1888–1973) was an American avant-garde illustrator and artist and a significant part of the art scene in New York City. She was known as "The Queen of Greenwich Village" because of her provocative art and bohemian appearance.

[Good evening]

Good evening, God be with my great unseen
Audience. How are you? And you? And you?
I hope you're useful cogs in the great machine.
And know your way around and what to do
And why you're where you are and how you lean
Daily more deeply toward the deathly new
Incredible futurities of God
That flower upon the nether side of sod.[1]

UTK MS 3824 Box 6, Folder 36 [c. 1934]

[Possible Comic Address to the Readers of *Permit Me Voyage*]

Well, folks, here comes another nice slim book,
My first and not the best and not the worst
Of hundreds of its kind: wherefor[a] I took
Some pains to train my indiscriminate thirst
On truth and nothing but: so give a look,
Doubt, if I've clicked, and dance to find me cursed
And tell the worst you feel and please don't fake it:
I dish this out because I want to take it.[1]

UTK MS 3824 Box 6, Folder 36 [c. 1934]

[a] An older, outdated spelling of "wherefore."

[Four Bits of Doggerel]

One Cucky[a] night Maid Marion[b]
By stirring to the core
A man who lived on carrion
Became a gilt-edged whore.

She knew the nicest boys in town,
She took them in her stride
Quite often as a bridesmaid
But never as a bride.

Mr. Agee Regrets[c]

Sorry not to keep our date.
Fact is, I have (I hate to boast)
A Rendezvous, old fellow, with
The Nation's[d] host from coast to coast.

The lady lives on Midol[e1]
And who's[2] the heel to stop her
If she cut her troubles right in two
And dropped them down the hopper.[3]

UTK MS 1500 Box 1, Folder 12 [1934, or after]

[a] "Cuck" is a slang term for a cuckold.

[b] Likely Marion Davies, whose original name was Marion Cecilia Douras (1897—1961), an American actor who was more famous for her 34-year affair with publishing giant William Randolph Hearst.

[c] This title may be Agee's parody of the popular song, "Miss Otis Regrets," a song about the hanging of a society woman after she murders her unfaithful lover. It was composed by Cole Porter in 1934, hence the approximate date given to these pieces by the editors.

[d] Agee is likely referring to the editor of the magazine, *The Nation*, founded in 1865 by Henry Villard. His son, Oswald G. Villard, inherited it in 1900 and remade it into a current affairs publication. Villard welcomed the New Deal and supported the nationalization of industries. Villard sold the magazine in 1935, but nearly all thy editors from Villard through the 1970s were evaluated for "subversive" activities.

[e] Midol is a brand name of Naproxen; it is used to relieve aches, pains, and menstrual cramps.

[Now on the stunned floor of darkness]

Now on the stunned floor of darkness
Grateful in their element,
Lovers poets and dreams awakening
Wrangle, shine, and learn content.

Windlassing their chiming[1] buckets
Heavily on the unspeaking mouth
Out of wells of worlds forgotten
Dreams allay the daylight drouth.[a]

Strolling stone and taciturn pavement,
Swift behind the spearing light,
Sorrowfully poets deliver
Resolutions of the night.

Lovers eating love of either
With insatiable hand
Lie like starfish of the seafloor
Through this wild and wicked land.

UTK MS 2730 Box 5 Folder 32 [1935][2]; *CP*, p. 152

[a] Scottish dialect for "drought" or "thirst."

[A low pit and sink of shade]

A low pit and sink of shade
And funneled dark I find me made:
Long has lapsed my laden sight
Sourceward down that floorless night:
Down the echoing skull's delusion
And the hooded soul's confusion,
Down my marrow into earth
Searching out my nether worth.
Deeper than my breath can follow
Silence falls beneath me hollow.
Naught of all I'd die to do
May I do, who find naught true
That's truly mine: I find me made
A cistern full of standing shade.[1]

UTK MS 1500 Box 1, Folder 12 [1935][2]; *CP*, pp. 56–57; *JAR*, p. 228;

[Him we killed and laid alone]

Him we killed and laid alone
Is not sleeping in the stone.
Stopt in spices, shelved in stone,
He is not sleeping in that cell.
Death paid and living earned he walks
The spirals of our present hell.
Steep on whose terrific street
Shines the calmness of his feet.
Sulphurous around him glare
The maledictions of despair.
He looks out in that sad land
Those of whom that land was made
And for whose love his life was paid.
And granting each a cloven hand
Forth from the ruined realm of shade
Before God's light as I believe
Leads out Adam, leads out Eve.

CP, p. 56 [1935]

A Poem for Brahms' Death-Bed

Fulfilled, the long, the well-wrought life,
Accomplished, the undeviant years:
The man who took his work to wife
Dies in high grief of childish tears:

Still with the Death-Tears on his eyes,
New beauty starts about his brow:
Humbly astounded, he descries
Those lordly ones his comrades now:

One grandly gay, serenely strong:
One who walks shining in his grace:
One gross-cheeked in huge natural song:
And one with stunned translated face:

These catch in theirs his own wide hand,
They hail him brother: (and the large air
Burns with the music of that land,
The sovereign music that is there).

CP, pp. 144–45 [1935]

[The sunflowers wither]

The sunflowers wither: a city crumbles there.
Pull in your guts there, bitterling[a], wipe that smile.
Buck up those gonads, doctor, shoe the gray mare.[b]
Frowning, he walked and met the falling tile.
Cut out your heart old pal, and do your share.
Lake Tana feeds the fan spread of the Nile.
Good evening, madam, I'm Sir Samuel Hoare.[c]
Boss-mistah, sah, dey ain't gonna *be* no core.[d1]

UTK MS 2730 Box 5 Folder 32 [1935?]

[a] A bitterling is a small European carp-like fish two to three inches in length of little value. This lack of value and its size, as well as its being noted for its unusual manner of breeding, indicates that Agee means to emphasize both its insignificance and sexuality. This line introduces what may be references to a military induction physical and then the political problems leading to World War II. See note c below.

[b] "shoe the gray mare" is part of a children's song. It strengthens Agee's previous mockery and can be found online in this 1914 *Kindergarten Primary Magazine*, vol. 26: https://books.google.com.

[c] Sir Samuel John Gurney Hoare (1880–1959) was a British politician most of his adult life. Perhaps most famous for authoring the Government of India Act 1935, which granted provincial-level self-government to India. Here Agee likely refers to his appeasement stand that same year in regard to Mussolini's annexation of Ethopia (then Abyssinnia), under the Hoare–Laval Pact with the French Prime Minister, which was so unpopular it led to his resignation as British Foreign Secretary.

[d] This line in dialect likely relates to the subsequent prose passage Agee writes (on the same sheet immediately after the poem) on the "Tampa flogging," of November 30, 1935, in which the police arrested six "Modern Democrats" of whom four were Socialists. After their release, three were taken by a vigilantes, whipped, tarred and feathered. The use of dialect seems meant to link their treatment with that of African-Americans. The word "core" is clear in the manuscript and appears to be intended as a dialect rendering for "cure" or "care" and provides a better rhyme with "Hoare" in the couplet than either of those words. See Textual note 1 for the passage and more information.

Hymn of Faith[1]

Mumsy told me not to play with all those rougher girls and boys
And that is why I sleep today with a girl in smelly corduroys:
And if only Mumsy had kept mum about the brighter side of God,
Perhaps I wouldn[']t have left him on the seamier side of the sod.

Mumsy you were so genteel
That you made your boy a heel:
Sonnyboy must now reclaim
From the sewerpipe of his shame
Any little thing he can
To reassure him he's a man:
One of those slick wooden dimes
That are the breastworks of the times
Though personally he would hate to
Try it out on that potato
Known still to reactionaries
And a few misguided fairies[a]
Of the older[-]fashioned kind
As the human heart and mind.

So, Mumsy, I go round and round the streets and the hired halls
Shouting by mouth and placard The Dialectic[b] is The Balls[c]:
Taking at every chance my ideological temperature,
Hoping to God it's normal but keeping-my-mouth-wide-open-to-Make Sure.[2]

I still like William Shakespeare but I see just where he lacks,
I'm the staunchest of admirers of Miss Clara Weatherwax[d]:
I'm sometimes in my heart of hearts think Granville[e] comes a cropper:
But I manage to forget with Forsythe. Limbach, Gold, and Gropper[f].

I'm a Friend of the New Masses, I'm a Friend of the New China,
I'm a Friend of the New Spirit that's Alive in Carolina:
I'm a Friend of everything on earth from shit to sasparooly[g]
Except, of course, the bosses, you[h], J. Christus, and Yours Truly.

UTK MS 3824 Box 7, Folder 2 [c. 1935; typescript; two pages][3]; *CP*, pp. 145–46

[a] A pejorative term for male homosexuals.

[b] An argument based on reason between two or more people holding different points of view about a particular subject and seeking to establish the truth.

[c] A slang, vulgar term (also referencing testicles) of approbation.

[d] Clara (Weatherwax) Strang published *Marching! Marching!* in 1935. It is generally categorized as proletarian literature.

[e] Likely Granville Hicks (1901–82). He was a leading critic in the Proletarian movement of the 1930s, a novelist, and a frequent contributor to and literary editor for the *New Masses* magazine that Agee mentions in the first line of the next verse. The magazine was associated with the Communist party. Hicks joined the Communist Party in 1934 and became one of the party's chief cultural spokesmen.

[f] Robert Forsythe and Michael Gold were contributing editors and authors for *New Masses*; Russell T. Limbach was an editor and illustrator; and William Gropper was an illustrator.

[g] Sarsaparilla is a soft drink much like root beer in taste.

[h] "you" refers to the "Mumsy" in the poem.

Theories of Flight[a]

How from that birdless heights the air
Plaited upon the miles of wheat.
But there were flattened faces where
Glass dammed away the hungering street.

Kansas and Crimea were
The mileages we overstood.
Moscow and Chicago were
The cities where they did no good.

Here, the starving is for hate.
There, to serve the first good State.
In either place, for lack of bread,
You'd weigh as light: you're just as dead.

UTK MS 1500 box 1, Folder 17 [1935–36; typescript][1]; *JAR*, p. 212

[a] The typescript is headed at the top right of the page as "James Agee / Anna Maria / Florida." This dates the poem between November 1935 and May 1936.

[Has life so meagre frontage on the sun]

Has life so meagre frontage on the sun
As we descry by jewel and number?[1]
Were there not angels in our towns
Before trains ran on schedule?
Why else the locust shell? Why else
In the large heaven such flowering of milk?
No suckling mouth but ours?
Why else, that breaks disengaging from the bark, this locust shell.[2]

UTK MS 1500 Box 1, Folder 15 [1935–36[3]]

To Harvard University.

Schools, oh, shoals of kind young men
Erroneous on the earth as rains,
Lounge in the lukewarm colleges,
Their mothers nursing at their brains:

The empty water lying through
Their jaws and through the empty gills;
Purchasing acquaintance to
The will-less ways, the wayless wills:

Upon those sweet incurious snouts
The water splits without a stir:
And clearly closes on the doubt
That such mild creatures ever were.

UTK MS 2730 Box 5, Folder 31[1935–36; typescript][1]

Lines for the Near Future.

Night is broken between hands above the cities:
Night leaves the plains, slides under mountains.
Morning looks through the wave above the cities:
The wave walks over: the bare morning stands.

The wave bursts on all continents: the speaking light spreads:
All is searched out: turns in continual day.

Wheat: frees out its roots and marches on the wind
With wheels, buildings, on the enormous street.

Fences go down with flags. All colors greet.
The mined dome sinks. Steeples breathe out their bats.
Their little laws their gods and their little guns
Fritter and faint:
While through the unavoidable membrane of blood
Millions on millions in our level wrath
Pour to the building of the lawless peace.

Friends: blood brothers:

Our strength is the whole earth's, yet we have more.

Millions in graves stand up and shout in us:
Billions in groins are furious for joy:
The earth's whole angry past compels us forward:
The earth's whole fate of future drafts us forward:
We labor in the hand of destiny:
We shape that destiny in our racial hands.

UTK MS 3824 Box 7, Folder 1 [1935–36; typescript and drafts][1]

Rhymes on a Self-Evident Theme[a]

'. . . and I look to the resurrection of the dead, and the life of the world to come.'—The Nicean Creed.

I look forward to that day
When human work is human play;
When all the Men with all the Hoes
Cut sirloins from the Morgan nose[a].

If you would raise that pleasant time
Work in the spirit of the following rhyme:
The man who weaves the future's wreath
Socks the present in the teeth.

If you haven't learned it, learn
Discontent with what you earn:
You'll get more only if you get tough
And more than you'll get's not half enough.

Learn to mistrust the sort of God
Who promises a Land of Nod[b]
To those who ruin out their day
Meekly in their own decay.

Such a god can only be
A talking doll on Swindler's knee[c]:
The church of such a god, remember,
Is nothing but a lethal chamber.

Learn the truth of present law:
It is a snaggletoothed crosscut saw
Swapped back and forth continually
By greed and fear: and we're the tree.

It is a narrow-wefted[d] sieve[1]
That screens off every urge to live:

Through which the guilty lifeless lapse
While anger and purpose rot in traps.

Learn the bloody fact of State,
The great fence with the narrow gate
Through which the splintered brotherhood
Is marched to meet itself in blood.

And learn the happy size of truth:
The human race is in his youth:
New power of metal earth and light
Are huge around him and his right.

He is not split hand against hand
By accidents of flesh and land
But is one man, whose farm's the earth.
And he is learning what he's worth.

What he's worth and what to do;
And the human race is you.
The earth turns in a morning air:
Wake your lungs and drink your share:

And, as along the wind's design
Wheat and the forest leaves align,
Stream in that strength of history
Which makes man what is man's to be:

Learning, above all, how the right
Is only forged of those who fight:
Who, more than leaves, have privilege
To lend that air their shaping edge

And who, their foot inside the door
Must urge it open more and more,
Dreaming no pity, nor self-merit,
Nor of the great house they inherit.

UTK MS 2730 Box 5, Folder 25 [typescript; 1935–36][2]

[a] "the Morgan nose" refers to robber-baron J. P. Morgan the financier. His large, bulbous, red nose was due to a disease called rhinophyma, which can result from rosacea.

[b] The "Land of Nod" is mentioned in the Book of Genesis. It is located "east of Eden" and is where Cain was exiled by God after murdering his brother Abel.

[c] This line may refer back to J. P. Morgan, casting him as a master manipulator / ventriloquist who controls "god" (likely money).

[d] Warp and weft are the two basic components used in weaving to turn thread or yarn into fabric. The weft is drawn through the warp and inserted over-and-under it to create a web.

[A deer went down to water][1]

A deer went down to water.
And we walked under night.
She stood there with her daughter.
And night was over us all.

She lifted from the leafmold
Into the wetted air
Her listening snout and heard us
Because we were right there.

There by that talking water
Before her knees were sprung
The bullet spread inside her.
Her mouth spilled out her tongue.

Her child is in the oakwoods.
We saw it : it was gone.
It gasps in the far oakwoods.
Her child is hoof and bone.

And therefore was some sorrow
For salt for that red steak.
Therefore, long since, in dead of nights,
I find I am awake.

UTK MS 2730 Box 5 Folder 32 [1935–36; typescript][2]

[Four wisdoms round my bed][1]

Four wisdoms round my bed,
Ironed sentinels at my head,
Darwin, Einstein, Freud and Marx
Guard the bed that I lie on.

Jesus, Dostoevsky[2], Blake,
In that shadow where you watch
Bide your peace, abide that hour
When the dreadful morn shall break.

And should one watch who can't forgive
Our insolences while we live:
Surely he must, seeing our shy
Puzzled faces as we die.

UTK MS 2730 Box 5 Folder 32 [1935–36][3]

A Mother, to the Child in Her[1]

Most of us million millions, child, have had nothing but life
itself, nothing to hand on but hard life itself.

(Lie easy, drink me up: I'm not afraid for you.)

Yet since we walked on two legs and were human, women have laid
down with men for love: millions of mothers and millions, all
gone now, have cherished their strength into their poor creatures,
and hopefully delivered them into hell.

They have them nothing but hard life itself :[2]

(Lie easy, drink me up :)

And faded like seeded crops into the earth.

Food starved those little children : those twisted and sprained
their spirits : that found any glimpse of the sun at all.

Ignorance and deception polluted them : near the very sources
of their lives.

And slavery took their bodies : and their lives.

(Lie easy : I'm not afraid for you.)

They delivered them into the crazy hands of hell : and into the
cold white smile of ruin : Great mouths ground them in : teachers
cleansed them of claws, taught the cramped wings close to the
body, the head its sleepy meekness : Justice and God stood by
with napkins : [3] provided the special dismembering silver : the
great gut shat them drained into the earth.

I would not guess what those poor mothers hoped. I would not guess
why those poor fathers fed them. Children, their futures known,
would have withered in wombs.

Lie easy, drink me up : I'm not afraid for you. Drink my life up
and let me live in you : let all that race continue and find
meaning.

For now, how any Queen must envy me : how every King your father's
crown the sun. Child I am proud serene and glad : and you're more
fortunate than ever a prince : who inherit the knowledge, the
danger, the friendship, the winning, and the world.

How should I fear for you : how ever pity your hard time : stand
up and laugh in me : drink up : drink my life dry and let
me work in,
let me march on in you so long as human joy shall last.

UTK MS 3824 Box 7, Folder 1 [1935–36; typescript;
three pages of drafts, one typewritten]

[From bed as from a balcony][a]

From bed as from a balcony: how like leaves are my Dominion round an apple.
The whole work is spun; the power shut, the belts
Slade[b] on the slowed wheels still. In the whole factory floor,
From all that iron, only the final whicker[c].
Rain runs on like a broom.
Grandmother saw it grow. And grandmother: she sleeps in her short coffin.
Grandmother can not know.
Father is folded under. God's own thunder
Floats as a word not rumored round his skull.
Now are we all null.

Son, you are old with waiting.

Our fleet relaxes and the Suez Gate.
The young captain will take what care he can.
Trouble is everywhere. You shan't lift your foot
But what the edge may open where it falls.
Best watch the East.
Trouble is big and sure from the thin island:
Yet care perhaps shall fend it.

As for the worst: man; man, from the first,
We most of all, have mined our fall[1] beneath us.
Best disregard it. Oh, best hang to the slanted sill
With face untroubled through the fingers yield.
Warm in that good regard which still is with us
For all the ash drinks up: outwait the wind.

Son, dear graying son:
Your hand, where:
I think you are the last. Edward[d].
Edward, do well: good night.

Mary[e]:
Mary: do not delay too long.

England, my England:
O spreaded Empire:
O my good millions, my watching faces, my deluded, my simple and my poor,
Flowers still requiring of a dwindled sun,
Learn better: find your own. And yet meanwhile,
Remembering England and a dying man
Who did as he was born,

Many of his millions, weeping, accompanied by brass horns, sing,
    God save our Gracious King,
    God save the King!

UTK MS 3824 Box 6, Folder 35 [two pages; first dated "Jan 20 1936"]

[a] Agee wrote the poem and dated it the same day as the death of Great Britain's King George V (1865–1936). He reigned from May 6, 1910 until his death.

[b] A dialect term for a small valley; in this use, "slack" is likely a comparable word.

[c] A soft breathy whinny, normally of a horse.

[d] Edward VIII (1894–1972) succeeded his father George V on January 20, 1936, but abdicated on December 11, 1936 to marry Wallace Simpson. Edward then became the Duke of Windsor. He married Simpson in France on June 3, 1937, after her second divorce became final.

[e] Mary (1897–1965) was another of George V's children. She was Princess Royal and Countess of Harewood and was also the aunt of Queen Elizabeth II.

[Happy that type of poet]

Happy that type of poet
Whose Muse is so adroit
She can bring it in thin as the point of a pin
Or spread it out flat like a quoit[a].

Here, Muse, are planes and dynamos
And here are roses dipt in wine,
Sugarlumps, candy, fancy clothes—
Aw, Muse, *please* be my Valentine.[1]

UTK MS 1500 Box 1, Folder 12 [April 1936][2]

[a] A ring made of metal, rope, or rubber thrown in a game to encircle or land as near as possible to an upright peg.

Night on America.[1]

Here rest a hundred million ruined souls
Of their indignities: who through the day
Wanting the knowledge of a healthy food
Wolfed the peculiar poisons of our air:
Gaining and hating, fearing and simulating,
Strangling each other in the name of breath—
These are good people: how must they thrive on death
And why insist allegiance to despair.
O might their dreams tonight like water from deep wells
Wash them awake and wiser to their living,
Then might the lovely earth be planted toward her joy
Little in killing and in glad forgiving.
Or better might they learn: which many can not:
The love[2] of Jesus and the mind[3] of Marx.

UTK MS 2730 Box 5 Folder 32 [April 1936][4]

[Three Verses, Serious and Ribald][1]

Speak in the several weathers of the mind
Love and hate do not cohabit but one—as the sun
Burls in the ribbling air

Hold your water and I'll hold my own.

The meek shall inherit the earth
In eye, ear, nose and throat,
For exactly what that's worth.[2]

Not that it makes any difference,
You're large, and I am small.
Still, for my satisfaction,
I now say, fuck you all.

UTK MS 3824 Box 6, Folder 36 [April 1936][3]; *Modern American Poetry: A Critical Anthology*, Louis Untermeyer, ed., 5th revised ed. (New York: Harcourt, Brace and Company, 1936), p. 635; *CP*, p. 58 (for first two verses).

Hommage Á Briffault[a]

(Tune: Moonlight and Roses)[b]

Forsythe[c] and hindsight
Are helping *Europa* a lot:
Half-asses reviewers
Are overflowing your pot:

Laura Jean Libby[d]
Topped off with a jigger of Freud
Served with chilled horse-turds
Rates yours truly's boid.[e]

Humorous Leftists find The Dance[1]
Grounds for going off in their Leftist pants
As for me I think a fart
In a typhoon stands a better chance of art.

UTK MS 2730 Box 7, Folder 23 (1936)[2] [typescript photocopy; April 1936]

[a] Agee seems to here refer to Robert S. Briffault (1873–1948), a physician in New Zealand who joined the British Army in 1915. Briffault gave up medicine shortly after the war and became a social anthropologist and, later in life, a novelist. Two of his novels bear the title "Europa": *Europa: A Novel of the Days of Ignorance* (1935) and *Europa in Limbo* (1937). He also became famous for what was called Briffault's Law which states that the female, not the male, determines all the conditions of the animal family.

[b] The tune for the song "Moonlight and Roses" was originally composed by Edwin H. Lemare as Andantino in D-flat, Op. 83, No. 2, in 1888 and is one of his few well-known original compositions. American songwriters Ben Black and Charles N. Daniels, using the pseudonym Neil Moret, added words to the melody, without permission, in 1921, and it became a hit.

[c] "Robert Forsythe" was the pseudonym of Kyle Crichton (1896–1960) who wrote numerous articles for the Communist publications the *Daily Worker* and *New Masses* during the 1930s.

[d] Laura Jean Libbey (1862–1924) was an author of sensational dime novel romances for women who, over her career, wrote eight-two novels.

[e] Given the tone of the poem, Agee appears to use what became the stereotypical New York / Brooklyn pronunciation of "bird" to indicate an off-color insult, that of an extended middle finger, i. e. giving someone the "boid." The other meaning of "boid," that of a member of the boidae family of snakes, seems less likely.

A Song

Give over, give over,
Whose grievance ever yet delayed the sun?
White flowers the dew, the summer's work is over
And your kind love, your lover
Is no man now, and now's another one.
Give over, give over:
What profits an arraignment of the sun.

transition, 24, June 1936, p. 7[1]; *CP*, p. 58.

Lyric

Demure morning morning margin   glows cold   flows foaled:
Fouled is flown   float float   easily earth before   demurely:

Chanced gems   leaves their harbors
Sparkle above leaves   whom light lifted

Drilling in their curly throats   severally   sweet ordinate phrases
                    Smooth ancestral phrases:

Teaching: touching: sinuous disunison.

Drinking: drafting: each of all   serenest pleasure.

Bring   floral earth   your breast before her,
Afford your breast before the morning.

Demurely,   the early margin:

Fouled is fallen   flower   flower   fearless earth before: serenely:

transition, 24, June 1936, p. 7[1] ; *JAR*,
pp. 213–14 (drafts); *CP*, p. 153.

In Heavy Mind

In heavy mind I strayed the field
The chilly damp and devious air
The restiveness the rags of snow
The mulled and matted blackness where

The summer overthroned with leaves
Had shown its cloudy loveliest
And I had lain along the shade
In tears that fully undistressed

Me among men upon the earth
In flowering sky of every doubt
But only so much natural joy
Might flare the flesh,   thaw the wick out:[1]

But now was logy with the weight of brain
Flat in the eyes and of my love most low,
Hate toward,   and clambering thought   and failure sure,
And life a lean long while, the starving slow

When,   not to see, some precious bird
Mad whistling from a bramble tree:
And all my will was not enough
To hold the heavens out of me.

Modern American Poetry: A Critical Anthology,
ed. Louis Untermeyer, 5th ed., (New York: Harcourt,
Brace and Company, 1936), p. 635[2]

Song with Words

When Eve first saw the glittering day
    Watch by the wan world side,
She learned her worst and down she lay
    In the streaming land and cried.

When Adam saw the mastering night
    First board the world's wan lifted breast
He climbed his bride with all his might
    And sank to gentlest rest.

And night took both and day brought high
The children who must likewise die.

And all our grief and all our joy
To time's deep end shall time destroy.

And weave us one, and waive us under:
Where is neither faith nor wonder.

Modern American Poetry: A Critical Anthology,
Louis Untermeyer, ed., 5th revised ed. (New York:
Harcourt, Brace and Company, 1936), p. 635[1]

Two Songs on the Economy of Abundance

Temperance Note: and Weather Prophecy

Watch well The Poor in this late hour
Before the wretched wonder stop:
Who march among a thundershower
And never touch a drop.

Red Sea

How long this way, that every where
We make our march the water stands
Apart and all our wine is air
And all our ease the emptied sands?

Modern American Poetry: A Critical Anthology, Louis Untermeyer, ed., 5th revised ed. (New York: Harcourt, Brace and Company, 1936), p. 635[1]; *CP*, p. 58.

[Now I Lay Me Down Beside]

Now I lay me down beside
My friend, my girl, my love, my bride.
And where you bless another bed
My hand sustains your lovely head.

Though we spend this night apart,
By an illimitable art
Separation, quite undressed,
Yields me your look, your laugh, your breast.

O should our thoughts lie down to sleep
I pray the Lord our love to keep.
If love should die before we wake
I pray the Lord our love to take.

UTK MS 2730 Box 5 Folder 32 [typescript; 1936][1]; *CP*, p. 152.

[Dear Irvine (an incomplete verse letter)]

Dear Irvine: This to advise you in advance
That you're at liberty to kick my ass
To sprain your ankle, next time there's a chance,
And that had best be soon; but let that pass.
You must know why; the easiest passing glance
At these few lines has put me in my class
(If not at the head of it) as the sort of fairy
Reduced to writing poems epistolary.

The point, as usual, being, to get said
Things you lack brains and guts enough to lay
Clean on the strict and calm Procrustean bed
Of art, and yet must get out of the way
If they aren't to clot and swell to break your head
And put your brains on more complete display
Than can grant health to them or help to you[a]

Draft of Letter to Irvine Upham[b], undated [1936]
UTK MS 3824, Box 1, Folder 12

[a] The draft lacks the final line of this verse and likely more verses.

[b] Upham is a friend of Agee's and listed by him as one of the "unpaid agitators" in *Let Us Now Praise Famous Men*, p. [xvi]. Upham is also mentioned by Agee in a September 20, 1950 letter to Father Flye. See *Letters of James Agee to Father Flye*, p. 182.

[Sweet anodyne[a]]

Sweet anodyne.
My anodyne.
Better than women, song, or wine.
There's no escape
For man or ape
Quite like hewing closely to
The Party Line
    The Par Ty Line.[1]

UTK MS 1500 Box 1, Folder 11 [1936][2]; *JAR*, p. 217.

[a] This satiric poem / song uses the tune of "(You're the Flower of My Heart,) Sweet Adeline," a barbershop quartet standard. Published in 1903, its lyrics were written by Richard H. Gerard and set to music written in 1896 by Harry W. Armstrong. An "anodyne" is something that numbs or relieves pain.

[Intelligence that freezes love]

Intelligence that freezes love
Commits a murder on the heart:
Love that consumes intelligence
A murder on the mind:

They are the same, as collaborative as the river and the earth,
That shape each other level.[1]

UTK MS 2730 Box 5 Folder 32 [1936?]

[Night overmasters us]

Night overmasters us:[1]
Now the steep and chiming coasts
Alaskan lose the final light:
Greenland and Bermuda still
Sleep in the watches of the stars:
And like two leaves upon a lake
From ice to ice along the sphere
Float the Americas in the damp
Complete renewal of the night.[2]

UTK MS 1500 Box 1, Folder 12 [1936?]; *JAR*, p. 230.

[Don't talk to me of those]

Don't talk to me of those who will see it:
I'm angry enough & glad though for them:
Call to mind rather, those who will not:
The eternal scab: with whom America is peculiarly rich;
The middleclass: tremendous organism of the midclass,
Pat in the tissues of the brain and soul who go down
    with their tasteless wives and their smooth children
The capitalists themselves:
    Kill them you must but killing them
    Keep what pity in your mind you can:

Cracking the skull of a Georgia vigilante:
    pity him.

Pity is not slop: it is HARD FACT. Much harder act than any of yours.[1]

UTK MS 2730 Box 5 Folder 32 [1936?]

Fight-Talk

Pal, have bosses bled you so
There's no blood left nor place to go?

You find it hard to get a job
Since that cold night you tried to rob?

You're ousted by the rectal grab
Since you were dope enough to scab?

Your father died when that last dram
Of Sterno[a] broke the diaphragm?

Your mother lies and[1] eats her lip?
Her wailing gives your wife the pip[b]?

Your wife is more than half-seas over
With another shoat and no more clover?

Your oldest son is on the bum?
The Amateurs have slupped[c] him numb?

Your daughter walks the easy street
And gathers and dispenses gleet[d]?

Your little children sit around and cry
And cry and cry and cry and cry?

Your priest brings round the Peace of God;
Advises you to carry a hod[e]?

The lights are doused? the gas is dead?
You've hocked the chair and extra bed?

The landlord's issued final warning
Against eight-thirty Monday morning?

Pal, have the bosses bled you so
You've no blood left nor place to go?

O heavens and its angels no!
By Roosevelt's smile it is not so!

Such talk's the ugliest sort of lie,
And all the world is apple pie.

Stand firm, my boy, resist the passes
Launched by the readers of New Masses[f].

O plug against the Syren song
Of the cuckling priest[g] and hooey long[h].

Remember too that Hammy Fish[i]
Is victim of a Freudian wish.

The man who ever stops and thinks
Relieves his mind of all such kinks.

So stop a sec and realize:
The men who run this show are wise,

The cards are right, the deal is new,
The aces are for me and you.

They're killing off the extra hogs
To keep clean writing in the logs.

They're cutting down on planting wheat
Lest anyone should overeat;

Or if not to keep the hand-from-mouth,
Then, maybe, hand-in hand with drouth[j].

And plowing under extra cotton
To prove the tenant's not forgotten.

Giving us sleep by burning coffee.
Handing out hot horseshit and toffee.

Selling the auto workers out.
Being photographed among a Boy Scout.

(Probably the only Miner
(Whoever sat in the President's diner)[k].

And wrangling over Bonus Bills[l]
And other mild cathartic pills.

Now, gleaming Capitalist Dome,
Farewell, and coming nearer home,

Behold how love outsmarts belief:
We've signed you up for Home Relief[m]:

Don't be afraid: pull in your feelers:
Ward heelers have become ward-healers.

We've broken up the old machine
And now we run our city clean.

Though we tax our people to the bone
We'll take care of our very own:

We've found the solution, we consider it a wow:
It Works: and this is how:

Nobody's any excuse to get sore,
For every dollar is accounted for:

Of every million we are fed
Half of it goes for overhead,

Another half for office space,
Another half to make a place

For Mister Mugwump's Nephew's Wife[n]
Who's grown a trifle tired of life

And still another half to keep
Investigators half asleep,

And still another half to buy
Cars that will match our Chairman's tie,

And still another to make chauffeurs
Out of incipient corner loafers,

And more to lubricate the game
That brings us more whence that much came:

Oh, money charitably invested,
Rest assured, is well digested.

There's precious little wasted and
That falls afoul a needy hand:

Twenty-odd a week for me
And food and rent and fare for thee.

I'm overworked and yet fear not
You'll find me Johnny-on-the-Spot

Or vice-versa, quick as one
Can get three dozen families done:

Very soon now, never fear,
By Monday week or month or year

Attention will come your way:
And *that will* be a Gala Day:

Always oatmeal in the pot,
Always cocoa, piping hot,

Irish potatoes by the peck,[2]
A nice cut off the horses neck

Starchily erected soup,
Split beans to hand you all the poop,

And each fortnight a plug of soap
To keep up appearances, and hope,

And milk for baby, blue as blue,
And broth for me, and gas for you,

A quarter's-worth at very worst,
Enough to bloat you till you burst:

And everything that gave you fright
From that time on will be all right:

And that's the way the world is run.
Ain't we, or ain't we not, got fun[o]?

So pledge allegiance once again
To Franklin and his merry men.

And demonstrations three times three
In praise of Franklin's Mother's Knee.

And ululations nine-times-nining,
Find in each swine the pearly lining.

No matter how many lives are sperled[p]
God's in his heaven to hell with the world[q].[3]

UTK MS 1500 Box 1, Folder 12 [3 pages; c. 1936][4]; *JAR*, pp. 233–39.

[a] Sterno, a brand of canned cooking fuel, can be drunk for a cheap high: usually by someone considered down and out. It sometimes could cause blindness. It also releases a high level of carbon monoxide when burned.

[b] To "get the pip" means to become irritated or annoyed.

[c] To "slup" is to swallow hastily or carelessly.

[d] "Gleet" refers to a non-specific venereal disease.

[e] A "hod" is a builder's V-shaped open container on a pole, used for carrying building materials, often by an unskilled or beginning laborer.

[f] *New Masses* was a Communist journal founded in 1926.

[g] "Cuck" is a slang term for a cuckold, but used in conjunction with "priest," likely refers to Father Charles E. Coughlin's actions that were, to Agee's mind, against the beliefs and practices of his religion. For more on Coughlin, see "[Major Douglas]," note c.

[h] The reference is to populist demagogue Huey P. Long (1893–1935), former governor of Louisiana (1928–1932), who was elected to the Senate in 1932 and attacked the New Deal as doing too little to redistribute wealth. Agee's narrator is ironically calling on victims of the depression to resist the "Syren song" of New Deal opponents from both the right and left.

[i] Hamilton Fish (1888–1991), Republican congressman from New York, was a vigorous anti-Communist and opponent of Roosevelt—he thought the New Deal even more insidious than Communism because the former disguised its true intentions. His father, Hamilton Fish, also a U.S. congressman, was assistant secretary of the treasury under Theodore Roosevelt, and his grandfather, Ulysses S. Grant's secretary of state, was the subject of a 932-page Pulitzer Prize–winning biography by Allan Nevis, *Hamilton Fish: The Inside History of the Grant Administration*, in 1936.

[j] Scottish dialect for "drought" or "thirst."

[k] Here Agee puns on minor; that is, Boy Scouts are the only "miners" Roosevelt will have in the White House.

[l] In 1924 Congress voted to pay World War I veterans a bonus adjusted for length of service over a twenty-year period. During the depths of the Great Depression, however, many former soldiers found themselves in dire financial straits and demanded immediate cash payment, marching to Washington and camping out in a shanty town just outside the city limits. In 1932 the House of Representatives passed the Veterans' Bonus Bill, but the Senate defeated it. With the support of populist figures such as Huey Long and Father Coughlin, the Bonus Bill was revived in 1936 and passed over President Franklin Roosevelt's veto.

[m] The New York City Home Relief Bureau accounted for about 5 percent of the total federal welfare benefits distributed by the Works Progress Administration in 1935.

[n] The Mugwumps were Republican reformers who deserted the party during the 1884 presidential election due to scandals involving candidate James G. Blaine. That a Mugwump's distant relative is the beneficiary of political patronage is indicative of the level of corruption in the political status quo.

[o] The line is an ironic allusion to the "Roaring Twenties'" popular song "Ain't We Got Fun" (1921), music by Richard Whiting and lyrics by Gus Kahn and Raymond B. Egan.

[p] A possible meaning for "sperled" is to be caught in a net. This may be one of Agee's self-created words. A sperling is a smelt, or young herring, that is frequently caught in large quantities using a net.

[q] The line parodies the famous "God's in his heaven— / All's right with the world!" (from Act I: Morning) of Robert Browning's "Pippa Passes," a verse drama. It was published in 1841 as the first volume of his *Bells and Pomegranates* series.

Minority Report.

In fun with our wives,
Our donations to drives,
Our political lives,
We diverge from the Norm:
But we read the right books
And we know the right folks
And we go to the Acme[a]
    To keep ourselves warm.[1]

UTK MS 1500 Box 1, Folder 12 [c. 1936][2]; *JAR*, p. 239.

[a] Possibly the Union Square Theatre built in 1870 as a variety theater that became a movie house, then the Bijou Dream Theatre in 1908, and finally, in 1921, the Acme Theatre. It closed in 1936 following a period of years screening Russian films. Its location, 50 E. 14th Street, New York, NY, meant that Agee was likely familiar with it.

[Madam, is baby's evening stool]

Madam, is baby's evening stool
As smooth (if not as sweet[1]) as silk?
Tell me, do his affections cool
At mention of his mother's milk?

(Lady, does your baby tipple
At the O K Feller Nipple[a]?)

Do you find his love grown cold?
Do you miss that ole sensation?
Maybe baby's grown too old
For mother's favorite fixation.

Let our agent drop around.
He'll fix everything up fine.
Baby gains a half a pound,
You drink whiskey, beer and wine.

He'll supply that old sensation,
You will never know the diff,
Let him have just one demonstration,
Absolutely free from syph[b],

Meanwhile see what he's brought Junior!
All to keep his snookums quiet!
A slight extra fee brings youn yr[c]
Husband too the Oyster Diet:

Wait'll baby, (little love):
See's it! Why his little lips'l
Fit our product like a glove:
The (Guess what) O Kay Feller Nipple.

Baby's happier at the puss,
Baby's tougher at the stern:

And without a bit of fuss,
While our agent earns, you learn.[2]

(Lady, does your baby tipple
At the O K Feller nipple?)

(How bout it, lady?)

UTK MS 1500 Box 1, Folder 12 [c. 1936][3]; *JAR*, pp. 240–41.

[a] Likely a play upon "Rockefeller's Nipple," i.e, capitalism as an ironic source of food for those not as wealthy as Rockefeller, as opposed to various economic reforms. See also note "i" in "Collective Letter to the Boss."

[b] A contraction of "syphilis," a venereal disease.

[c] A contraction for "you and your."

Collective Letter to the Boss

Dear Boss:
The little man with the big mustache[a]
And the man with an olive in place of a head[b]
Are making a perfectly hideous hash
Of the prospects for Peace and I wish they were dead.

But that goes too far for the man with the jaw[c]
Like a pickerel winning a merit-badge:
And the man with the moss all over his maw
Whose wife (named Mary) should be named Madge[d]:

And it goes for the man with the ranch-and-whore
And the gold and the long clothesline of sheets[e]:
And the priest with the champion fan-mail score[f]
And the man with the mug like a row of teats[g]:

And the man with the teeth and the Commodore's hat
And the glasses and the cruiser quarrel[h]:
And the snakeyed man as small as a slat
And men by the hundred thousand barrel[i]:[1]

And every man in fact who owns
And turns the screws to own some more
And malts our blood and vats our bones
Compels our blood and[2] bones to war.

New Paragraph:
Since, sir, that whole machine is set
Beyond your wish to ever change,
Beyond your power should even yet
The wish by chance your mind derange:

Since, in a word, you force our hand:
Since, in a word, it must be war:
Align[3] your men and guns and be
Advised: you are the enemy:

All human rage in every land
Rares[j] up to wreck you from the floor.

UTK MS 1500 Box 1, Folder 12 [c. 1936][4]; *JAR*, pp. 241–43.

[a] Adolph Hitler (1889–1945), Nazi dictator of Germany, rose to power in 1933.

[b] Benito Mussolini (1883–1943), Fascist dictator of Italy from 1922 to 1943.

[c] Franklin D. Roosevelt (1945), Democratic president of the United States from 1932 to 1945.

[d] King George V of England (1865–1936), whose wife was Mary of Teck (later Queen Mary), favored a policy of appeasement towards Hitler, which his successor continued.

[e] William Randolph Hearst (1863–1951), media magnate and isolationist, owned a 240,000-acre ranch in San Simeon, California, and was married to the much younger Marion Davies, a chorus girl whom he attempted to make a star. The "long clothesline of sheets" refers to his publishing empire, which at its peak numbered twenty-eight newspapers and eighteen magazines.

[f] Father Charles E. Coughlin. See "[Major Douglas]," note c.

[g] Unknown.

[h] Possibly a reference to Admiral William H. Standley (1872–1963), U.S. Chief of Naval Operations and one of the negotiators of the London Naval Treaty in March 1936. The treaty, signed by the United States, Great Britain, and France but rejected by Italy and Japan, set limits on armaments and tonnage of warships, including a six-year ban on building heavy cruisers. Completely ineffective, it was one of the stepping stones toward World War II.

[i] John D. Rockefeller (1839–1937), founder of Standard Oil, and the richest American of his time. His inflation-adjusted worth circa 1913 was over $400 billion dollars.

[j] Colloquial for to rear or get up, usually in reference to a four-legged animal, quickly standing up on its hind legs.

Rapid Transit

Squealing under city stone
    The millions on the millions run,
Every one a life alone,
    Every life a soul undone:

There all the poisons of the heart
    Branch and abound like whirling brooks
And there through every helpless art
    Like spoiled meats on a butcher's hooks

Pour forth upon their frightful kind
    The faces of each ruined child:
The wrecked demeanors of the mind
    That now is tamed, and once was wild.

Forum and Century, February 1937, p. 115[1]

Sun Our Father

Sun our father while I slept
    You lifted like a field of corn
The smiling and the peaceful strength
    Of those that are the race new born:

The infant future waked in you
    Once more, and at the world's rich breast
Drank the day's courage and lay down
    In fearless and refreshing rest:

And while the russian[a] field you raised
    Dreams in the star-flung shadow's keep
You wake these backward lands to work:
    Good work to do before we sleep.

Forum and Century, February 1937, p. 1161

[a] Agee may be referring to the field as "russet-like" by using the word "russian."

Sunday: Outskirts of Knoxville, Tennessee

There, in the earliest and chary spring, the dogwood flowers.

Unharnessed in the friendly sunday air
By the red brambles, on the river bluffs,
Clerks and their choices pair.

Thrive by, not near, masked all away by shrub and juniper
The ford v eight, racing the chevrolet.

They cannot trouble her:

Her breasts, helped open from the afforded lace,
Lie like a peaceful lake;
And on his mouth she breaks her gentleness:

Oh, wave them awake!

They are not of the birds. Such innocence
Brings us whole to break us only.
Theirs are not happy words.

We that are human cannot hope.
Our tenderest joys oblige us most.
No chain so cuts the bone; and sweetest silk most shrewdly strangles.

How this must end, that now please love were ended,
In kitchen, bedfights, silences, women's pages,
Sickness of heart before goldlettered doors,
Stale flesh, hard collars, agony in antiseptic corridors,
Spankings, remonstrances, fishing trips, orange juice,
Policies, incapacities, a chevrolet,
Scorn of their children, kind contempt exchanged,
Recalls, tears, second honeymoons, pity,
Shouted corrections of missed syllables,
Hot water bags, gallstones, falls down stairs,
Stammerings, soft foods, confusion of personalities,

Oldfashioned christmases, suspicious of theft,
Arrangements with morticians taken care of by sons in law.
Small rooms beneath the gables of brick bungalows,
The tumbler smashed, the glance between daughter and husband,
The empty body in the lonely bed
And, in the empty concrete porch, blown ash
Grandchildren wandering the betraying sun

Now, on the winsome crumbling shelves of the horror
God show, God blind these children!

The New Masses, September 14, 1937, p. 22[1]; *CP*, pp. 65–66.

Lyrics

1.[1]

Remember limber thunder in the deaf: the metal tasting air:

Cities like silly medals lay: wind:
Flashed the whole forest pale:

Spasm and blindness blenched and the bunched cloud
Delivered his blue columns.

Remembering thunder: deliberating in the shadow cold: the fuse air:

The paltry metals on that pitiful breast: the wind
Violating the pale forest crest:

Twittering blaze, the hunched cloud
Voided, and slept aloof, the miles
Restored into the sun, the clean sun
    Sheened in his scope:

Remembering unlimbering thunder in the deafness and the tinder air:

The pinned and pendant cities: in the woods
A whole year's generations struck one white:

Collaborative, and determinate thunder:

2.

Soft heaven shuts: at length the latest
Plaintiff is silenced and the ample south
Absorbs him unlamenting:

Here, moreover, subdued, the seed
Meditates and shall publish the usual flower:

And he, restored, bounding on bloodied twig,
Schemes out his spiritual music.[a]

[a] See also the variant entitled "[Heaven shuts]."

3.

His subtle throat is broken on the air;
    (Reproachfulness, outbreast the wind)
That pointed eye, narrow hands, the fluted bone
    Lie with the forest fall.

Yet with the year, shall, with the wrinkling leaves,
    The frail shell break, the fragile monster breathe, and,
Falling, wing find air: and talk to god
    Much like his grandfather in his time.

4.

Tonight sweet heart I think in graves of the wild earth forgotten,
Straws of old harvest whom the sun ignores,
Bones, and their bran, congratulate.

I do not think they pity us.
They pity less than they are glad.

All that was ardent and which now is air:
Warms round our wrestling here.

5.

Heal, hardy air, harm in earth.
And yield these lungs the while to breathe
It takes to whisper out that worth
Whose cloudy forehead you enwreathe.

6.

Not for your ease or pleasing was the air
Mild, a while past, and loving with the earth.

What for the seethe of health up breadth of summer
I cannot know; but doubtless not for us.

Cruelest[1] and dingiest of the squatters we
Who wring and craft and tease this earth apart.
From the huge kindness of their kingdom's edge
The citizens peer seldom but to hide.

However, there are harms about the heart
We never dealt us, but can only serve.
Serve them then as we must, to further harm,
And help what can; and mean time let who will
Lift on this glimmered dark his joy, his small surmise, while,
Serious and unregarding, with stiff hands, the heavens
    Rust and unwreathe the world.

7.

Squared behind intellectual hedges:
Bloodhounds and rifles arrayed to guard:
Be sure: subtly, how cheated faith avenges.

Make the mind only a little too hard:
Suspect too fearfully the irrational:
Your feet will break through tunnels under your yard.
You will unseated by an unforeseen international.

Have you surely added it up to the right amount?
Shall florid history never split your pot?
Have you taken the animals thoroughly into account?
Are you sure you still dream of yourself or not?

8.

Your end's to end forever
    War's wrath, the rotted laws.
But man in his last anger
    Shall kill for larger cause.

9.

Tears are the touchers of that secret earth
No alien rains attend; be therefore tears;
Grieve, and your holy land affords you mirth;
Pity brings wrens of the most batflight fears.

10. *A Nursery Rhyme.*

Glimmer, glimmer, universe
Whom storms of mysteries immerse:
Nebulae not grieved for Zion,
The blown seeds of a dandelion:

How I wonder by what rules
Beyond the touch of local fools
In the anarchic spring unborn
Whose front lawn you shall adorn.

What immeasurable child
Shall your burning have beguiled
Before another picks you dry
And puffs your promise down the sky.

In what city shall that be
And in what strange vicinity.
(Hark my friend, we've had our day,
School is out, they're on their way.)

Gods snub each other on our back stairs
The ancient time contemned as snares.
Our galaxy, so runs the hope,
Is mirror for a telescope.

Curved brightness is a beveled jewel
Examining minute renewal.
All things undreamt, one atom's core.
One spark of sand, its endless shore.

There thrive fish the dark sea down
Unsuspicious of our town.
We each are lumps in a same leaven
And Friday's print amazes heaven.

11.

Education of the Prince.

He must strike down his father's cedar shadow:
Sever his mother's terrible and sorrowing mouth:
Abandon, under their stone labels in the charted meadow
His tired friends, and start the journey south.

Follow the man on the hill with the fire on his back:
Outbrave the monstrous lady of the woods:
Speak dialects, snap twigs deceptively, destroy his name:
He must make the dark journey under the hollow sea.

Partisan Review, December 1937, pp. 40–43; *CP*, pp. 60–65.

In Memory of my Father[a]
(Campbell County, Tenn.)[1]

allegretto

Bluely, bluely, styles from stone chimneys crippling smoke of
hickory larch and cedar wood of ash[2] of the white oak. The quell
night blues above. The quell night blues : branchwaters,
the black woods, begin to talk.   The blue night blacks above.
Lamps: bloom in their glasses and the stars: splinter and glister
glass. Warmth: slops[3] from the pigsty. In the barn pale hay,
tusseled in teeth, darkness, a blunt hoof.   The black night
blinds above. Tell me was ever love. so gentle in the hand.
so tender in the eye.was ever love:more lovely to the loved. The
secret water smiles upon herself; the blue cedar: stands in his
stone of smoke. Mile on mile in mountain folded valley fallen
valley lies.   Eyes fixed on silence small owls preach forlorn,
forlorn: the metal thrill of frog and cricket thousands in the
weltered grass: swinging his chain the whippoorwill; the whippoorwill the answering chain: deep chested from his bowstring
a big frog bolts response : swinging his grieving chain : cry,
lonesome preacher; choir, shrill creatures of enamored dew;
amorous water, parley, elapse; slow stars, display your edges;
effortless air, love in the neat leaves the neat leaves: gentle colony
in your green harbor throes of a common dream: throes in the
leaves, and quiet : sweet tended field, now meditate your children
: child, in your smokesweet quilt, joy in your dreams: and father,
mother : whose rude hands rest you mutual of the flesh : rest in
your kind flesh well.

And thou most tender earth:
Lift through this love thy creatures on the light.

transition, 27, 1937, p. 7; *CP*, pp. 59–60; UTK MS 2730 Box 5, Folder 31.

[a] Agee's father, Hugh James Agee, was born in Campbell County, TN, born in 1878. He passed away on May 18, 1916, at the age of 38, in a car accident as he traveled from his parents' home back to Knoxville in his new Model T Ford. James Agee memorialized him in his Pulitzer Prize-winning autobiographical novel, *A Death in the Family*. For both Agee's intended version of the novel and also the one that received the Pulitzer Prize, see Michael A. Lofaro, ed., A

Death in the Family: *A Restoration of the Author's Text* (Knoxville: U of Tennessee P, 2007). For further information on Agee's father, please see Paul F. Brown, "A Well-Known Postman: James Agee's Father Before *A Death in the Family*," in Michael A. Lofaro, ed., *James Agee in Context: New Literary, Visual, Cultural, and Historical Essays* (Knoxville: U of Tennessee P, 2022). See also Brown's *Rufus: James Agee in Tennessee* (Knoxville: U of Tennessee P, 2018).

[God's scorn each other on our back stairs]

God's scorn each other on our back stairs
That ancient time escaped in snares:
Our galaxy, so runs the hope
Is mirror for a telescope.

Curved brightness is a beveled jewel
Examining minute renewal:
And all undreamed one atom's core:
A spark of sand's its endless shore.[1]

UTK MS 1500 Box 1, Folder 11 [1937]

[Length of stars shall not outlast us]

Length of stars shall not outlast us.
We have no more need of Things.
God is our child no less than father.
Our bodies are two learnéd wings.

They that were blunt beasts and lonely
Learn new usages. They bear
One princely aboriginal creature
Fearless in unfamiliar air.

Wings, cruising unpredicted sky,
Acquaint unsolved equivalents.
Steep beneath the bellowing sty
Faints out of our farthest sense.

UTK MS 3824 Box 7, Folder 2 [1937][1]

[Hold.Hold.One dies first.][1]

Hold.Hold.One dies first. One Must.
Lucky for this at least:
These faults that all but wrench me out of life
These fears and flaws
Attach[2] me young.Hold : Hold.
What worse may be comes surely soon.
We strengthen of our weakness.Hold.
Still should I breathe with all the worst upon me,
One must tire first.
Still, still should I live,
Not crack, and all be sucked away
No.Hold.Hold.Still Hold.
Then time, health, one left no harm can harm.
So bravery still and thankful, that so young.

Thus while the infant starfish clasped, the young clam thanked the Lord.

Letter to James Johnson Sweeney, undated [1937]
Harvard University, Houghton Library,
Papers of the magazine *transition,* MS Am 2068, Box 1

[In Tokyo]

In Tokyo, in a student's uncle's room,
Lamp shines on their cool lenses. A boy stands,
Outlines in Cornell slang, French, Japanese,
Progress on hillside farms; the next month's work.
Feet seem to loiter on the stairs[1]; go on.
As I was saying, the boy says, and he says it.

UTK MS 1500 Box 1, Folder 15 [1937?[2]]

[Night, over Youngstown]

Night, over Youngstown[a], is a red, brown bruise.
Angling their pulps[b] to catch the twenty watts
In little cabins besides every gate,
Their rifles handy, men loll, seem to wait.
Along the ten-foot and barbed-wire-topped fences,
Two hundred yards apart, for twenty a week,
Ulstered[c] and holstered, others stroll the dark:
And jerk hands to their chests: and the shift changes.[1]

UTK MS 1500 Box 1, Folder 15 [1937?]

[a] The poem may refer to the time in 1916 when Youngstown Sheet and Tube plant rioted during a strike over working conditions, which resulted in most of the town's business district being burned to the ground. The strike was quelled by the arrival of National Guard troops. In 1937, Youngstown Sheet and Tube again played a prominent role, along with other steel companies' workers, in a strike that ended in violence.

[b] Pulps are works of pulp fiction, often containing racy, action-based stories published in cheaply printed magazines on inexpensive (pulp) paper mainly in the United States.

[c] An "Ulster" is a working daytime overcoat, with a cape and sleeves.

[He swings off the five-seventeen]

He swings off the five-seventeen; two hours late.
Cigarette[1] lights shift, down the platform.
Being late, he takes a taxi: turns some corners:
Gets out: they get out from the cab behind.
He walks: their feet are nearer: and he slows,
And lights a cigarette: they watch windows:
He shrugs, beneath his coat, looks up a diner
And eats slowly. They line up down the counter.

UTK MS 1500 Box 1, Folder 15 [1937?[2]]

[Child, a prince in prison lay]

Child, a prince in prison lay,
I had everything my way.
But I gave that prince the key
And he ran out & ruined me.

Treat me as you think is just,
Not as you surmise you must.
Once your murderer is free,
Turn from him, and hunt down me.

Never dream you've cause to fear
Judgement Day: your case is clear
Beside the shade & scope of shame
That stands against your Judge's name.
Though the whole sky should not chore
The ruins round that are your score,
You have accusations two:
God must answer you for you.

However, there is kindness here,
Cheap as air, & no less dear.
Learn its ways; use it well:
Kindness can draw the teeth of hell.

Only kindness ever can
Straighten the crippled feet of man.
And surely shall in time suffice
To pardon even Paradise.[1]

UTK MS 2730 Box 5 Folder 32 [c. 1937]

Poems Spoken to a Child

[1]

Child, a prince in prison lay.
I had pretty much my way.
But I gave that prince the key,
And he ran out and ruined me.

Treat me as you think is just,
Not as you surmise you must.
If you find your freedom good
Keep it jailed up in your blood.

If you find it hard to take
Hand it on for its own sake.
Once your murderer is free
Turn from him, and hunt down me.

2

Never think you need to fear
Judgement Day. Your case is clear
Before the size and shade of shame
That stands against your judge's name.

Though the whole sky shall not shore
The ruins in that are your score,
You have an accusation too:
God must answer you for you.

3

However, there is kindness here
Cheap as air, and not less dear.
Learn its ways, Use it well.
Kindness can draw the teeth of hell.

Only kindness ever can
Straighten the crippled fact of man.
And surely shall in time suffice
To pardon even paradise.[1]

UTK MS 3824 Box 7, Folder 2 [typescript; two pages; c. 1937]

[The kings and queens we sometimes are][1]

The kings and queens we sometimes are
We cannot always hope to be;
Yet may we set our humbler lives
To do them service faithfully:

We may at least in honor hold
The throne-room and the ritual clear.
We may at worst die at the gate
Rather than serve a prince less dear:

O at the worst we surely can
Take care lest merchants, prelates, whores,
Farmers, machinists, demagogues
Democratize beyond those doors.

UTK MS 2730 Box 5 Folder 32 [c. 1937]

Child, oh, child[1]

Was it for this that I was spread
So broad with pride I laughed in pride?
Or stared into your soul and saw,
Living, all that has ever died?

He leaned his strength, my weakness I
Raised; we met on such a kiss.
All is decline before and since;
Was all our tenderness for this?

Was it for this, so suddenly
Those dazzling pangs that all but took
The heart, those royal signals which
Shone in your voice, your walk, your look?[2]

UTK MS 3824, Box 7, Folder 2 [c. 1937]

[Child, a child was latched in jail]

Child, a child was latched in jail,
I ran loose and had my way,
But I gave that child the Key
And he ran out and ruined me.

Never think you need to fear
Judgement Day: your case is clear
Before the size and shade of shame
That stands against your Judge's name.

Though the whole sky shall not shore
The ruins in that are your score,
You have one arraignment too:
God must answer you for you.

However, there is kindness here
Cheap as air, and not less dear.
Learn its ways, and use it well,
Kindness can draw the teeth of hell.

Only kindness ever can
Straighten the crippled fact of man.
And surely shall in time suffice
To pardon even paradise.[1]

UTK MS 1500 Box 1, Folder 11 [c. 1937]

Millions Are Learning How[1]

From now on kill America out of your mind.
America is dead these hundred years.
You've better work to do, and things to find:
    Waste neither time nor tears.

See, rather, all the millions and all the land
Mutually shapen as a child of love.
As individual as a hand.
    And to be thought highly of.

The wrinkling mountains stay: the master stream
Still soils the Gulf a hundred amber miles:
A people as a creature in a dream
    Not yet awakened, smiles.

Those poisons which were low along the air
Like mists, like mists are lifting. Even now
Thousands are breathing health in, here and there:
    Millions are learning how.

Common Sense,[2] January 1938, p. 26[3]; *CP*, p. 155 (but see note 1).

Summer Evening

Bandstands every tuesday evening
Bring us to the drawling square:
Braid, glad horn, blunt drum, commend us
Each another, shed of care.

Locusts with enthusiasm
Celebrate the spended day:
In the dappling shadowed porchswing
Love finds out the usual way.

Children are composed this season.
There is hope among us yet.
Hope can cut the roots of reason:
And the sorrowful man forget.

Harper's Magazine, January 1938, p.209; *CP*, pp. 154–55;
UTK MS 2730 Box 5, Folder 31 [typescript]

Dixie Doodle[a1]

In the region of the Tee/Vee/Aye[2];
Of the cedars and the sick red clay;
We've discovered a solution
Neither hearstian[b] nor rooshian[c]
In the embers of a burnt-out day.

When the world swings back to sense
(But the world is *so* damned dense)
An indisputably aryan
Jeffersonian Agrarian[d]
Will be sittin on the Ole Rail Fence:

Swaying lightly with a hot cawn bun,
Quoting Flaccus[e] and the late Jawn Donne[f],
He will keep the annual figures
Safe away from the eyes of niggers,
And back his Culture up with whip and gun.

And every single solitary region[g]
And we'll each frame our millennium
In a native-hewn proscenium
Unbedunged by any non-indigenous pigeon.

Partisan Review (February 1938), p. 8[3]; *CP*, p.146

[a] Agee also wrote an article on the TVA (Tennessee Valley Authority) for *Fortune* (October, 1933) and published *Permit me Voyage* in 1934. That volume has no poems on one of the New Deal's great experiments.

[b] William Randolph Hearst (1863–1951), was a media magnate and isolationist.

[c] Russian.

[d] Jeffersonian agrarianism included the belief that the American economy would be best served if it continued its focus on agriculture rather than business and industry. Its ideal citizen was the independent and self-sufficient yeoman farmer.

[e] "Flaccus" was perhaps a nickname, probably of Marcus Fulvius Flaccus. He was a Roman consul in 264 BC, not the later Roman senator of the same name.

[f] John Donne (1572–1631), the famous English metaphysical poet of the seventeenth century.

[g] There is an additional line in UTK MS 3824 Box 7, Folder 2, after this one. It reads: "Will cultivate its own religion" and its inclusion presents this last verse in the same 5-line stanza format as the preceding ones.

[Under me the root has sharpened]

Under me the root has sharpened.
I must tilt my eyes to find
The scar in the bark. Smoother, wider.
What was the message, it signed?

In all that I can see or hear
No motion new. The bird is still.
The ants seep in the ground. The woods,
Each leaf awake, wait until

The unwanted has moved past, unwakened.
A dead twig sparks. And he—
That heavy stride, bone forehead, o those
Ruined eyes: can that be me?

Brown trunk, gray; the holy gloom,
Silence of pure spring-water. Not
Leaves, lights, fragrances,
Can reach, restore, can heal[1] me where I rot.

In all that unmoving unwavering realm,
That held breath, for his grief
Signaling[2], in its own soul's temblor[a]
Moved, works one leaf.

Trembling, it talks. And stopped with fear,
I watch (he watches), and my heart
Stirs, shakes, shudders, at throat and eyelid.
(His hand). I have taken my life apart.[3]

UTK MS 3824, Box 7, Folder 2 [1938]

[a] To quake or shake, as in an earthquake.

[What do you carry into this woodland][1]

What do you carry,[2] into this woodland
Which makes it all one denial, one frown?
What have you brought, from the unshadowed
Region, that you would here lay down?[3]

Lay down, be cleansed of, silently,
Here, where the patient mold drinks in
Like ants, leaves, rains, the years,
To kill and bury immortal sin.

Never hope it. None can help you.
Where you search, comfort veils,
Cryptic as a negro. Every
Prayer's a heartbreak. Desire fails.[4]

UTK MS 3824, Box 7, Folder 2 [1938]; *CP*, p. 67 (but see note 1).

[As in a woodland rarely]

As in a woodland rarely,
Still to the ear, the eye,
Signals in its own soul's temblor
One leaf works, talks, so I:

Just[1] so, in my devastation,
Rarely, the trembling[2] soul
Takes me, tells at[3] my throat and eyelid.
The legend whole.

Only, how long since wind
Made a wooden sea, since a tear
Sprang like a seed, since the leaf knew
I am not there to hear.

UTK MS 3824, Box 7, Folder 2 [1938]; *CP*, p. 67
(but see note 1 of "[What do you carry into this woodland].").

The Sick Snook.[a]

Those who frequent the undershadow of wharves.

A big sick snook like a log, under the wharf; I watched him
 through the trap;
Hung on the water, four feet down; and he swam slowly.
Splotched with brown, the slick gray body: some eating growth?

Runin : collision with a shark. Escaped.

He swam alone,[1] scarcely employing the film that fledged his tail,
 his flat eyes flat, while children, people, watched.
He did not watch. A shark had lounged and struck him. We felt he
 was not fit to eat.[2]

I dropped fat bait a yard before his snout and he stood towards it:
And inch supplanting inch, lay past it, whisping his flank : stern,
 noble, sorrowing, an old priest teased;

Cherishing that private horror : which like a worm was fastened
 upon his brain.

UTK MS 3824, Box 7, Folder 2 [typescript; 1938–1939][3]

[a] A snook is an excellent food fish; the common snook is fished commercially and foreign-caught fish are sold in the US.

[Only that though so eager in their day]

Only that though so eager in their day,
Whetted with joy and valiant for the fight,
They loved too well such loving to betray,
And linked in love declined into the night:
Whose dusk is flesh, whose dark is family,
Whose midnight is despair full wrought from love –
Despair of strength and the soul's entity,
Opposed to noon by the thick world's remove.
And since I burn so wrathfully with joy
And love also, as kindly as did they,
And so would fight yet so would not destroy
Night-hearted love, that show so proud a day:
I'll choose the course my fathers chose before
And, with their shadows, pray my son does more.

UTK MS 2730 Box 5 Folder 32 [typescript; after 1940?][1]

[Poor naked wretches]

Poor naked wretches, wheresoe'er you are,
That bide the pelting of this pitiless storm,
How shall your houseless heads and unfed sides,
Your loop'd and window'd raggedness, defend you
From seasons such as these? O! I have ta'en
Too little care of this! Take physick, pomp;
Expose thyself to feel what wretches feel,
That thou may'st shake the superflux[a] to them,
And show the heavens more just.

James Agee and Walker Evans, *Let Us Now Praise Famous Men*
(Boston: Houghton Mifflin Co., 1941, p. [xii][1]

[a] A superabundance, superfluity.

(To Walker Evans.[1]

Against time and the damages of the brain[a]
Sharpen and calibrate. Not yet in full,
Yet in some arbitrated part
Order the façade of the listless summer.

Spies, moving delicately among the enemy,
The younger sons, the fools,
Set somewhat aside the dialects and the stained skins of feigned madness,
Ambiguously signal, baffle, the eluded sentinel.

Edgar, weeping for pity, to the shelf of that sick bluff,
Bring your blind father, and describe a little;
Behold him, part wakened, fallen among the field flowers shallow
But undisclosed, withdraw.

Not yet that naked hour when armed,
Disguise flung flat, squarely we challenge the fiend.
Still, comrade, the running of beasts and the ruining heaven
Still captive the old wild king.

James Agee and Walker Evans, *Let Us Now Praise Famous Men*
(Boston: Houghton Mifflin Co., 1941, p. [5][2]

[a] The poem refers to Shakespeare's *King Lear* throughout.

[I walked into a wasted place][1]

I walked into a wasted place,
And laid my head against a stone.
I heard its humming and the stars
Appeared. I was alone.

I was alone and in such hope
(The cooling stone, the pointed stars)
I cried the name of God; proud tears
Sprang. (The sharp stars.)

I challenged Him that he should send
The cruelest[2] champion of his choice,
All ire, and raving wings, I prayed,
In my angry voice.

And sleeping, opened like a bride
To all the dream would surely bring.
And fought (or such as I recall)
My wounded King,

A city, and a wife and son,
Ten thousand masks of fear and law,
And faceless creatures of the depths:
And woke, in awe.

The stars were tired. The stone slept.
Colors hinted themselves. I knew.
The Angel had stood near, and gone.
Gently, the night turned blue.

UTK MS 2730 Box 5 Folder 32
(Agee dates this poem "16 Nov. 1945"); *CP*, 159–60.

Dear Father

Dear Father:

Monday evening, fairly late—
Too late for serious work, not late enough,
Quite yet, to lay the insomniac's nightly bait
For sleep, with cards, trash-reading, all such stuff
Beside which I, the crafty victim, wait
Hours, while sleep sniffs and snarls its mild rebuff—
I wonder whether I can manage better
To pass time than by writing a verse-letter.

I'll probably manage worse; but there's one stanza
Anyhow; and another on the way.
With help enough from lazy Sancho Panza,
Don Quixote may, somehow, get through the day.
Failing all else, that improvised cadenza
Lord Byron patented, wherewith to say
In bland digression everything that came
Into his head, may sit in on the game.

For my main trouble, as I can foresee
Already, is, and will be, even more,
That though I'd like this verse attempt to be
Expressive both of prophets and the law
(Maine's accent rhymes it) why, I lack the key
Even to unlock wit's and poetry's door.
Or briefly, though the impulse is O.K.,
I haven't, really, a damned thing to say.

The things most seriously on my mind
Oh, war; free speech; my soul; atomic fission;
Whether the egg first saw the world behind
The chicken, or before; towards what perdition
Lapses all good and ill in humankind;
And other aspects moot to our condition—
Are much too hard to tackle at my best,
Far worse when all I'm trying to do is rest.

Then too, I've always felt that poetry,
Or even verse, if saying anything
(*Not* its essential business, but for me,
At present, easier anyhow than to sing),
Should say it tersely as the verb "to be,"
In language worthy of the kind of king
Kings seldom are, or ever were,—to say
Nothing of most who take their place today.

But there, you see, in spite of these convictions,
Already, now, with several stanzas done,
They are composed wholly of derelictions
From sense and duty; why, they aren't even fun.
But patience! If my personal prediction's
Halfway correct, your best bet is to shun
What follows, even more sharply than what's past;
For heavy seas begin to hide the mast.

Well—to our muttons; which are jumping fences
Well out of earshot, if not out of sight.
This week, as you remember well, commences
My thirty-seventh year.[a] I'm neither tight
Nor quite exactly sober. My defenses
Shaky and breached, yet hold. Eternal might
Enlarges to engulf my little world.
Soon, soon, my bugle bleats; my flag is furled.

All autumn long, through the magnificent slope
Of all the smoky year towards dissolution,
Much more than Nature—man's fate, and man's hope—
Have, in that avalanche, been in full collusion
Caught, shaped, and colored, even, on a scope
Grand as man's very being; a diminution
As huge to witness, and as full of grief,
As if each star were but a falling leaf,

CP, pp. 157–59 [November 25–26,1945]

[a] Agee birthday is November 27. In 1945, Sunday was November 25.

On the Word Asleep[1]

Asleep, perfected, you would never believe
Harm, of a one of them. That stirring hand,
That leg, might clasp, might be thrown[2] across
An enemy, as gently as a wife.
How God must grieve,
Watching in all this shadow land,
The flinching vigil candles of this countless loss,
In night's nave, each a life:
Who groans, smiles, murmurs, quiets; then on the horn
Transpierced, assembles upward, and reborn,
By all that skill and bravery crowns him with,
Works, while he wakes, to put himself to death.

UTK MS 2730 Box 5, Folder 23[3] [1945]; *CP*, p.156.

On the Word Kingdom[1]

In that kingdom, no one cries.
No one doubts, for no one lies.
No son ever dreads his mother,
Nor no brother envies brother.

Families, there, like shady[2] trees,
Spring and shelter, and the bees
Groan among the cloudy flowers:
Angels, each a soul devours.

There, continually, the smile
Of the heart that knows no guile.
There, untroubled, people greet
Death like an old friend in the street.

UTK MS 2730 Box 5, Folder 23[3] [1945]

[Happy the Huntsman]

Happy the huntsman, his dog and his gun,
Away in the woodland before the red sun.

And happy at noon by the frost-quieted creek,
Shunned by the strong while he eats of the weak.

But happiest at evening when the red sun
Goes to bed before he does, and hunting is done.[1]

UTK MS 2730 Box 5, Folder 23 [1945]

[Creep, walk, trot, sprint]

Creep, walk trot, sprint,
Fly, swim, hop, tunnel, dive:
However we choose to get around
We'll never get out alive.[1]

UTK MS 2730 Box 5, Folder 23 [1945]

[The moon once lived]

The moon once lived just down the street
And angrily ran off
The thousandth time its mother earth
Scolded it for its cough.

It ran to tell its father,
Who, no matter what happened, smiled.
But the sun was away, and hard at work,
Unluckily for the child.

And so he stuck, out in the sky,
Too angry to come home,
To[o] small to find his father
Under the sky's huge dome

And you may see on most clear nights
And sometimes in the day
How lovesomely he turns his face
Forever, our way.

He shines, because his father smiles;
Bur he is sorry too.
And hides his face behind his coat
And then looks out anear.

No matter when you see his face
His sorrow's never off.
And always, if you watch him close,
You'll see, but not hear him cough.[1]

UTK MS 2730 Box 5, Folder 23 [1945]

[A hungry man]

A hungry man ran up the stairs,
A well-fed man walked down.
He walked to the cigar-store,
Then he walked all over town.

He walked and walked and walked till he
Was hungry as a bear.
And when he walked back home at six,
Supper was waiting there.

A hungry man ran up the stairs
And when he was well fed,
He smoked two pipes and five cigars
And fell upon his bed.[1]

UTK MS 2730 Box 5, Folder 23 [1945]

[When the ogre came home]

When the ogre came home from the Feast of the Dead,
He saw that a black flea was eating his bread,
And he roared in his rage and he rolled in his glee
When he thought of the beating he'd give to that flea.

"Bend over!" he bellowed, "and turn your pants down!
I will spank you my friend from your toe to your crown.
But most I will spank where I know it will hurt
On the bare skin right under the tail of your shirt."

"O you think so," the flea said. "I will not bend over[2]
You think you're so big but I will not uncover
My bottom for you or for anyone else.
And I doubt if you'll beat me with hairbrush or belts.

For if as you think you are going to beat me
Why catch me first. If you do you can eat me."
"You fresh little flea I will swallow you whole.
But first I will beat till you burn like a coal"

He beat him with carrots[,] he beat him with feathers
He beat him with grants[a] and the twelve stormy weathers[b]
And with every whack he did harm to his house,
His wife and his children, but never the louse.

For the louse, or the flea, as his other name is,
Was quick on his feet as a bottle of fizz,
And every time that a blow fell to slay,
He jumped in good time to get out of the way.

He jumped on the ogre's favorite rose
He jumped in his beard and he jumped up his nose,
And wherever he jumped there the ogre hit next
And broke it until he was thoroughly vexed.

Then the flea jumped into the ogre's brain
And tickled him into such terrible pain
That he beat his own head into splinters and pulp
Which the flea ate at leisure in ten thousand gulps.[1]

UTK MS 2730 Box 5, Folder 23 [1945]

[a] To "beat him with grants" means that the ogre would beat the flea as much as it merited, evidently quite a bit, given what the ogre thought of the flea's audacity.

[b] This may be Agee's very oblique reference to the second verse of the famous 1933 torch song "Stormy Weather" written by Harold Arlen and Ted Koehler. It reads

> Oh, yeah
> Life is bad
> Gloom and misery everywhere
> Stormy weather, stormy weather
> And I just can get my poor self together
> Oh, I'm weary all of the time
> The time, so weary all of the time

Ethel Waters performed the song first at the Cotton Club in Harlem in 1933 and recorded it the same year. Agee was more likely familiar with the rendition by Leana Horne in the 1943 movie musical "Stormy Weather." It featured other notable African-American stars such as Bill "Bojangles" Robinson, Cab Calloway, Katherine Dunham, Fats Waller, the Nicholas Brothers, Ada Brown, and Dooley Wilson.

Alternatively, but still an oblique reference, Agee might be making a pun about the "withers," the ridge between the shoulder blades of an animal, typically a quadruped. Or he might simply be making a nonsense addition to his humorous poem.

"Help"

"Help" means, if I am carrying wood,
You carry it too, till we are done.
Or you are hungry, and I've food,
And just as gladly give you some.

It is not help if I beg you,
Or if you pay me for the meal.
It is not help unless we do
Each other good just as we feel.

If I help you, and you help me,
We will not need to beg or pay.
If everyone did this, you'd see
Only friends' faces every day.[1]

UTK MS 2730 Box 5, Folder 23 [1945]

[My It]

My It has ruined every chance,
Just as I've had, to learn to dance.
And when I eat too much roast pork,
My It puts poison on the fork.

It was my It, not I, that chose,
In company, to pick my nose.
And usually, when I shit,
It is not me, it is my It.

Or when I try to coax the Muse,
My It is hoody[a] with the booze.
Or, if that ruse by chance should fail,
Teases me with thoughts of tail.

When, in my declining hours,
I ask you kindly to omit flowers,
And breathe my last, hold on a bit:
Don't bury me; cremate my It.[1]

UTK MS 2730 Box 5, Folder 23 [1945]

[a] "hoody" is a slang term for the physical reaction to sexual arousal in some woman wherein the prepuce of clitoris (hood) pulls back. The male counterpart of this term in slang would be a "woody" or erection.

[O my poor country I have so much hated]

O my poor country I have so much hated,
How can I hate you now your doom is near?
How still revile a soul so desolated,
Or hold your hideous sickness else but dear?
Ruthless in force but not so ruthless quite
To use it wholly in the last thin chance
History affords, against eternal night;
Kindly, but so roared round by circumstance
Of greed, self-love, self-righteousness, the shattered
World groans its anguished last against your ear,
And you are merely petulant and flattered;
Incurable through pity, love, guilt, fear:
A dying grandmother, babbling of a ball:
Take her just so, Death; let her enjoy it all.[1]

UTK MS 2730 Box 5 Folder 32 [1945]; *CP* p.157.[2]

[We soldiers of all nations]

We soldiers of all nations who lie killed
Ask little: That you never, in our name,
Dare claim we died that man might be fulfilled.
The earth should vomit us, against that shame.

We died; is that enough? Many died well,
Of both sides; most of us died senselessly.
Ask soldiers who outlived us; they may tell
How many died to make men slaves, or free.

We died. None knew, few tried to guess, just why.
No one knows now, on either side the grave.
If you insist you know, by all means try,
That being your trade, to make the knowledge save.

But never use, not as you honor sorrow,
Our murdered days to garnish your tomorrow.

UTK MS 2730 Box 5 Folder 32 [1945]; *CP*, pp. 160–61.[1]

[Now on the world]

Now on the world and on my life as well,
Ancient in beauty, infant in such fear
As no time else has known, nor shall dispel,
Loosen the ashes of another year.
Whether by nature's will or by my own,
I, who by chance walked softly past a war,
Shall not by any chance the world has known
Be here, and breathing, many autumns more.
Only, with all who in the past have died,
I had, till lately, faced my death secure,
Knowing my hunger only was denied,
Knowing that all I loved was to endure.
But this year, dying, struck wild as it fell,
Ending itself, me, and the world as well.

UTK MS 2730 Box 5 Folder 32 [1945]; *CP*, p. 68.[1]

November 1945

Now on the world and on my life as well,
Ancient in beauty, infant in such fear
As no time else had dreamed, nor shall dispel,
Loosen the ashes of another year.
Whether by nature's will, man's or my own,
I who by chance walked softly past a war
Shall not by any chance the world has known
Be here, and breathing, many autumns more.
Only, with all who in past worlds have died,
I had, till lately, faced my death secure,
Knowing my hunger only was denied;
All I most loved and honored would endure.
But this year, dying, struck wild as it fell,
Ending itself, me, and the world as well.

UTK MS 2730 Box 6, Folder 16 [typescript photocopy; likely 1945][1]

Christmas 1945

Once more, as in the ancient morning,
The slow beasts, the fierce new-born cry;
And, in the heart the dreadful warning:
    Is it I?

All each heart holds of love, resolves
Once more, today, in angry grief,
Enduring courage; and dissolves
    In unbelief.

The Magi's gifts are subtle bribes:
The shepherds worship clock and wage:
In rattling arms, roared diatribes,
    Wakes the new Age.

And even now, at the town gate,
Welcomed by many, fought by few,
The clangor grows, of Herod's hate
    In the morning's blue.

And, in the straw, they hear; and stay.
All that is brave and innocent,
All that is love, reborn today,
    Is its time spent?

Where shall He flee, whose force is naught?
Where lies that Egypt which sufficed
Of old, now that each man is wrought
    Herod, and Christ?[1]

UTK MS 2730 Box 5, Folder 11 [typescript; likely 1945]; *CP*, pp. 161–62.

[This being so][1]

This being so, and thirty and five years
So nearly vanished, and so little used;
All delights turned as trivial as all tears,
All meanings altered and all hopes refused;
By[2] what means shall I, in what little while
Abides my being, on such narrowed span
As will and world allow, find out that trial
Of strength wherethrough, well fought, I die a man?
O long, long, idle in tribulation,
Grown fat in all I did because I must,
I dreamed at least I knew my own salvation:
Now I begin to wake, and it is dust.
Where is the Angel in whose rage alone
Wrestling, I live? The night is nearly gone.

UTK MS 2730 Box 6, Folder 16 [typescript photocopy; 1945?][3]

So you want to write?
Come on in, the water's fine.

This is the hard, almost impossible thing:
        To begin.
Even before that, to be sure you want to begin
        Or even try
The slow, defective stagger toward something
        Which may never
Provide you satisfaction or even a place
        To rest your head.

A set of blinders painted with pleasant scenes
        Would be nice,
Or a bell that would ring of its own accord
        To clear the head,
Or better that anything else at all, someone
        To tell you you're right.
But of course such devices are absurd:
        They wouldn't work.

So get a move on, skip the self-hypnotic stall
        Of dabbling the big toe.
Get used to the idea of being your own hope
        And your own reason
For you own activity. See? The water is icy
        Only at first.
Keep swimming hard. Now, doesn't it feel good?

UTK MS 2730 Box 5, Folder 3 [typescript; June 1947[1]]

Dialogues on a Sleepless[1] Night.

Authority speaks: "Why can't you be sweet
About duties; stop trying to fight?
We're only telling you for your own good
And because we know we're right.
Why don't you uncurl your fists and start
Trying the easy way?
As you know, we speak from Experience,
Forever and a day."
"I don't know," mutters the Child at bay.

"I'm Rational Thought," intones a voice,
"You're simply blind to insist there's choice
Or any hope for such as you,
Who repeat that is wrong but this is true.
Look, I can balance a plate and spin it—
You're getting dizzier every minute.
Can you hear me? lie flatter into the bed
Let the fever ease and the darkness spread.
In a moment deep music will come, do you hear it?"
"Very nice, but no thank you," says the Spirit.

The smooth grey Brain leans forward now
With a firm sweet look on its noble brow.
"You must give up soon before it's too late;
Your wish is impossible—learn your fate
Like every sensible human being.
Start compromise now, your days are fleeing.
You'll find life very pleasant indeed
If you'll learn that part of the grass is the weed,
But if you keep on the way you're going
Wanting love for your answer but always knowing
It may never come, then you'll split apart."
"Then I'll just have to split," replies the Heart.

UTK MS 2730 Box5, Folder 31 [1947; typescript][2]

[Just this: from now on, to go on foot]

Just this: from now on, to go on foot,
Knowing what I have ridden, and deprived.
From now on, knowing what it is I put
To death; and, what it is, to have survived.
Wondering, while I can, if it be true
Water that bleeds[1] here, or the spring's last tears:
And what, if anything, might be to do
To remedy the ruins of these years:
And knowing, knowing hopelessly, that I
May labor all I please and[2]
May yet raise[3] water though the world be dry,
But[4] never find a mouth to take his place.
For by my blind will now my only one
Lies dead and buried here. From now on.

UTK 2730 Box 5 Folder 32 [1947]; *CP*, p. 163.[5]

[O I begin to know][1]

O I begin to know: neither could live
Long, and the other gone; it lay with me
Once I had broken him, with me, to give
Each, or refuse, his need. O now I see.
Only by flying could he know his thirst.
Only by drinking of her could he fly.
Only his absence filled her. But, not nursed,
After a time, the aching breast goes dry.
And all that while I bent his bleeding mouth away,
It was not only he who slowly died;
The starving water shrank into the clay.
She became barren, who was once his bride.
And I, who parted them, for this return:
What then of me? In what hell[2] shall I burn?

UTK MS 2730 Box 5 Folder 32 [1947]; *CP*, p. 163.[3]

[In the Street][a]

The streets of the poor
quarters of great cities are,
above all, a theater, and
a battleground.

There, unaware and
unnoticed, every human
being is a poet, a masker,
a warrior, a dancer: and
in his innocent artistry
he projects, against the
turmoil of the street, an
image of human existence.

UTK MS 3824 Box 6, Folder 35 [1948; typescript[1]]

[a] This is Agee's introduction to "In the Street," a short silent film by Helen Levitt, Janice Loeb, and James Agee. It may also be considered poetic prose rather than a poem.

A Lullaby

Sleep, child, lie quiet, let be:
Now like a still wind, a great tree,
Night upon this city moves
Like leaves, our hungers and our loves.
    Sleep, rest easy, while you may.
    Soon it is day.

And elsewhere likewise love is stirred;
Elsewhere the speechless song is heard:
Wherever children sleep or wake,
Souls are lifted, hearts break.
    Sleep, be careless while you can.
    Soon you are man.

And everywhere good men contrive
Good reasons not to be alive.
And even should they build their best
No man could bear tell you the rest.
    Sleep child, for your parents' sake.
    Soon you must wake.

From *100 Modern Poems*, ed. Selden Rodman.
New York: Pelligrini & Cudahy [1949], pp. 120–21[1]; CP p.70.

Exiit Diluculo[a]

Exiit diluculo
rustica puella
cum grege, cum baculo,
cum lana novella.

Sunt in grege parvulo
ovis et asella,
vitula cum vitulo,
caper et capella.

Cons pexit in cespite
scolarem sedere:
quid to facis, domine,
veni mecum ludere.

[Agee's translation][1]

In the smallest light of day,
    Country Girl came walking;
Wool and spindle strung for play,
    All her young ones talking.

In her little herd she brought
    Lamb, and baby donkey,
Bull-calf, and the calf half-wrought,
    Kid, and the kid manqué.[b]

Then found an Intellectual
    Waking in the pasture;
And said, "Can't we be sexual?
    Mister, at least I asked you."

UTK MS 2730 Box 5, Folder 15 [carbon typescript; 1949 or 1950][2]; *CP*, p. 76.

[a] Agee and his poker buddy, Willy (no last name or date given in his return letter), exchanged translations of this song which appeared in the illustrated medieval manuscript entitled *Carmina Burana*. The thirteenth-century document contained 254 texts many of which are mostly bawdy and satirical.

[b] The "kid manqué" refers to the "calf half-wrought" of the previously line, to reinforce its failure to live up to expectations.

Two Sonnets from a Dream[a]

I

Who was that boy, ranging the ruined hill,
Spine humbled to the horse's huge, light ghost,
Who would not lay the burden down until
He found the place he knew would please it most:
Then opened the rude ground, and tenderly,
But without tears, buried the old, great frame,
Masking the grave with leaves, that none might see;
And, standing up, first saw the eyes of shame?

O it was I; no doubt but it was I.
Nor doubt, I fear, what ghost I put away.
But how I killed my carrier, or why,
I cannot fathom; far less could I say
Where one might seek, who cared to prove such things,
The lost, betrayed, mangled, magnificent wings.

II

I bore my bearer on a wasted mountain,
His weight being nothing, though the form stayed whole
(But for the wings); Yes, it was to that fountain
Where first I saw him drink, I took his soul:
So cloyed with clay, so stifled full of stone,
I hardly forced it open for his rest,
Where once a liquid more alive had grown
Than ever cherished in a mother's breast.
By what cause, right, or means, ever should I
Grieve? The immortal Spring itself is dead.
Tearless I laid my killed soul to the dry
Root of his nurture. Yet the poor place bred
Just damp enough to lift up leaves in time
To mark the grave, heal the wound, and hide the crime.

Bottegbe Oscure, V, 1950, pp. 336–37[1] ; also in *CP* (dated 1947), pp. 68–69.

[a] Bellerophon (or Bellerophontes) was the typescript title (see note 1). Bellerophon, the son of Poseidon, is the Corinthian hero of Greek mythology who famously battled and killed the fantastical Chimera monster (a fearsome fire-breathing mix of lion, goat, and snake) upon the winged horse Pegasus, that was a gift from his father. Bellerophon likewise famously fought and defeated the warlike Solymoi, the Amazons, and Carian pirates. The overly proud hero then flew into the sky on Pegasus to try to join the gods on Mount Olympus. Because of his hubris, Zeus sent a gadfly to bite Pegasus and Bellerophon fell to the ground and was killed. For a full account, see https://www.worldhistory.org/Bellerophon/#:~:text=Bellerophon%20(aka%20Bellerophontes)%20is%20the,lion%2C%20goat%2C%20and%20snake.

Agee's two sonnets seem to continue the story from Pegasus's point of view. Fitzgerald (*CP*) and *Bottegbe Oscure* do not mention Agee's original title in his typescript.

Variations, Free Fantasy and Fugue

On a Theme of Night and Day

Theme: The night slopes up the east:
The day glides down the west:
Lax in his fur, the beast,
The bird with brown in breast,

Yields each the addled hope
That stood him sunward guide:
Through all the shadow's scope
The dew distends its tide:

And all is strifeless quite:
All free from all affray:
And down the west falls night:
And up the east fares day:

Variation 1:
Whole to the hollow shadow
Commend your heavy brow:
All pride of day put from you
And deep through darkness bow:

The margin withers of the morning dew:
Weighted clear, the lands that loved this keep[a] of shade
Now mount the noon beneath and meet for you
The terms wherein the round lands are betrayed:

The same, the deep dealt law that you debased
Into this bourne[b] of death that makes you whole
Lifts up refreshed and lowers these lands defaced:
All withered is the early dew:

Some high delirious meadow
Delivers the late letter of your vow:
Peace: peace: be healed: all wholesomeness become you:
    Your night is on you now:

2: They that led the long loam open
They that mouthed the meadow short
They that scruffed the wry roots' sweetness:
    Beasts of this laborious sort:

Sour-brained mule the horse meek-headed:
Grim-butted cow and daft-eyed sheep:
Gristly hog and their gay children
    All have shut them safe in sleep:

Light the jaw on bruiséd kernel,
Coffined quiet the mauléd cud:
Quiet also the soft, the young ones:
    Shy the doomsday mounts their blood:

3: The whistlers slick and chortlers,
The free, the smart of song,
The deft on wing in the white wide day
Now throng and mutter and sleep nor stray
    The green boughs deep among:

Safe from the clouded highways
The latest wing is home:
The eagerest wing that voyaged abroad
Is idle now and the wing outlawed:
    The happiest throat is dumb:

Below the proud-armed buzzard
The air stands damp and blind:
And hunched in tenting cumbrous wing
He sleeps that leaned in a deathward ring
    His downright hand behind:

4: Where now the lizard and the rinded[c] snake
That skipped and poured their lengths and lusted in the heat?
Where the slim bugs that on the water break
Their rapid dances and each other eat?

The lithe-tongued butterfly, where now is he
That gave his proud wings to the unequal air?
Where the mean hornet and the sweet-groined bee?
Now they are under night how do these bloodless fare?

The reptile's eye is blue: the thready fly
Stands on the skin of water and is well:
The tongue is furled, the bright dust is safe and the wings shut high
The stout bee drowses in his paper cell:

UTK MS 2730 Box 5, Folder 27 [signed on each page of a two-page typescript; 1953 or earlier[1]]

[a] A "keep" is a fortified tower built within castles during the Middle Ages as the last defensive position against invaders.

[b] A "bourne" (or bourn) is a limit or boundary; also a destination or goal.

[c] "rinded" means stripped of its outer covering; in this case, shedding its skin.

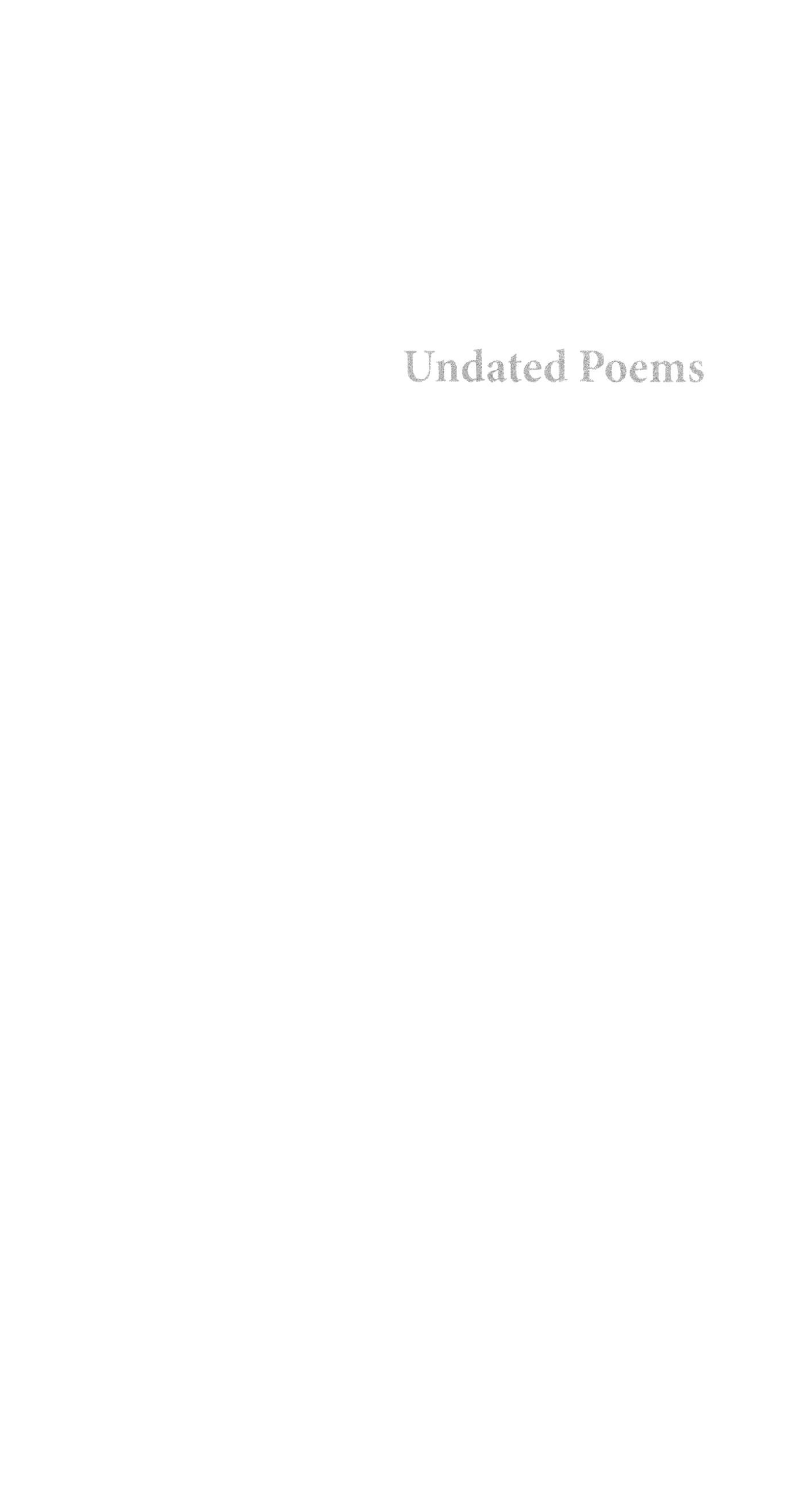

Undated Poems

Lyric Poems

[Which I, who know best]

Which I, who[1] know best
And cannot quite detest,
Nor send without regret,
Nor ever more forget.

And would not have her meet
Her slaughter in the sheet.
But bow to history
Eye to eye with me.

So will she understand
Mercy of my hand,
And right and right shall part
And heart shall crack[2] with heart.

And one at least shall die
Knowing all reasons why.
And one at least remain
Whose freedom cost him pain[.]

I thank you very much.
Mercy is hindrance still.
When men have won goodwill,
You will have use of such.

UTK MS 2730 Box 5 Folder 32

[A fugue]

A fugue
Commencing in a cord
Of which the tones
Are indecisions.
Repeated make a theme
Of which the meaning
Lies only in the overtones.

UTK MS 2730 Box 5 Folder 32 [typescript]

[A sound tied with twine to a tree]

A sound tied with twine to a tree
In a lover's knot asserting
A design: What cords can bind
The clouds' roaring in the sea?

UTK MS 2730 Box 5 Folder 32 [typescript]

[For now no least remembering]

For now no least remembering[1]
Of light survives in all this world.
Silent heaves the dreamless hill;
In silence is the hill flower furled:

And in that field where sun and wheat
Confronted lions, roared gold to gold,
Now blesses the wounded[2] brow

Now light's utmost remembering
Fails in the sunflower's loosened foot[.]

UTK MS 2730 Box 5 Folder 32

[And where in the troublous groves][1]

And where in troublous groves[2] the light was twinkling hampered
            fluttering woodland, mealy marl:

Wide whited wide   the palm upspread of earth upon wide whited wide
            stooped through with gentle storm prolific:
That heated stone and the heaped and the morseled planted stones thralled
headed wheat,
            marching and masking, mowing, the husky field:
And plated waterwarmth and watershine:
(In middle water water underlifted overlifting collects
below the doffḗd day the shorenoise
                        bowling toward),
And flexed in earth strenuously the throttling scarves of roots:
            bridled all rooted things upstanding.

The lifted bloom compelled to the whole day:

The baldwing folded on the rusty[3] bark,
He feels, feels the dark:

Rolled over rolling, rolls: (grows):
Now shines his seeing forehead that kept the undertwigs and swampish
glooms; he stirs:
And was upon the earth: and was what ways on water where:
And where:

And where the hoisted shadow was of the hill above the fields;
            The[4] winking the breathing, firefly shine[s]:
Latest light on shadowing beshadowed hill beshadowed:
Last, O latest light:
Manifold infolded declineth on loosening root the hill flower tallowy,
unhaltered:

Small, starvéd from the farther hill:
One hooky hand ahold: spread, spread the lanky cord
Slur, dim[5] air, the green fur:

And humping looms upon the shoal his barm[a] back breadth glistening:

And from the farthest awn of sky now fainting, falls, fallen from the faint, frail,
falterable, sky freshening brightful stars:[b]

UTK MS 2730 Box 5 Folder 32[6]

[a] "barm" is an archaic term for the froth on fermenting malt liquor.
[b] See also "[Starred from the sky]" as a possibly related poem.

[As women once from childbed]

As women once from childbed
Got up to make them clean
Before their God, so ever
Young parents may be[1] seen.

Churching themselves of evils
Newborn, and brought along,
Crying, sleeping, suckling,
Which shall outlive their wrong.

UTK MS 2730 Box 5 Folder 32

[Bowled over blade shade]

Bowled over blade shade under all her creatures
Fallen, fainted, folded in the black shade under
Wrung down, wrought down in deep earth shade her children
Fallen all fallen her sweet children fallen:

All gathereth under shade; folded and fallen low in fealty rest, rest: O, loftily quiet,[1] no harm:
Slow through starshine peace and starcharm lowly following fallen all:[2]

Wide whited wide the palm up staid of earth upon wide whited wide
stooped through with gentle storm prolific

That heated stone and the heaped and the marveled planted stone, thralled headed wheat,
marching, mashing and mowing, the husky field

And plated water warmth, watershine?

In middlewater water underlifted overlifting calls up tumultuous below doffed day, balked on strength, bulk on balk leaning :

Flexed in earth the throttling scarves, roots, and brailed all rooted tribes up standing,
The unwilling bloom compelled to the whole day:
Rolled over rolling, rolls, grows:[3]
The baldwing reefed on rusty bark
He feels, feels the dark:

Leaning larging lathering loose the shore noise bowling towards:
Now shines his seeing forehead who clung the under twig and swampish gloom, he stirs:

UTK MS 2730 Box 5 Folder 32

[Down by the swamp]

Down by the swamp at the midnight hour
Sits an old black granny with the houdoo power
She can houdoo you low she can houdoo you high
She can houdoo you to wither like a leaf and die.[1]

UTK MS 2730 Box 5 Folder 32

[If I should tell you what you know]

If I should tell you what you know
Weighs on my tongue that I'll not say
We'd not so much as falsely smile
And even less than cruelly play.

So smile at me as now I smile
And once again as times before
Pity and grief and feel of flesh
May fool us into love once more.

UTK MS 2730 Box 5 Folder 32 [typescript]

[Sad heart stray backward through the lifted shadow]

Sad heart stray backward through the lifted shadow,
Glean the lost plantations of their heavy gear
Those things we knew when we and they were green and careless,
That now are ripe and rich, that now are past and dear.

CP, pp. 139

[No room: hard weather]

No room: hard weather:
Two in the careless dark
Who nurse numbed love alive
Wince against the wall together.

Let the deaf storm drive:
Forget the glowing room: hark:
Curse neither world nor weather,
Time shall build you time together
And an easy bed
And a safe room
Big as the dark.

UTK MS 2730 Box 5 Folder 32 [typescript][1]; *CP*, pp. 139–40

[Peace, peace, poor nightingale]

Peace, peace, poor nightingale,
  Your grievance rest,
While my own grieving song
  Pours from my breast.

It's sullen[1] winter's end
  And patient[2] man,
Heart springing, knots out friend,
  Catch as catch can.

Bring soon, soon, little wife,
  Peace where I lie;
Come, loveliest, come, my life,
  For soon I die.[3]

UTK MS 2730 Box 5 Folder 32

[The sun, that late below our bed]

The sun, that late below our bed
O'er India the day had led,
While we lay in the tower of night
Shatters the eastern wall with light.

Now let us rise, no longer sport,
Tho day be long, and night be short,
But seek the flowers that filled our dreams,
Where light along the woodland streams.

For lo! All silve[r] strides the worm
O'er heaving hill and white-blown thorn.
O lover, lay no longer, pray,
When all the world's alive with May—

Tarry no longer. Let us chase
Sunlight and shadow as they race;
Nor tarry the long day to rue:
Night and our joys will both renew.

And a night comes when we shall lie
While suns rise and days flitter by
Pursuing nights, by nights hot-priest:
And naught can rouse us from our nest.

Then centuries shall fall like rain
Athwart the swell of yonder plain;
The light that storms this windy glade
Our dark room never shall invade.

So, lover, lay no longer, pray,
While still the world's alive with May.

UTK MS 2730 Box 5 Folder 32

[These were kind people and they loved to love][1]

These were kind people and they loved to love.
They lived like mister Hand and Mrs Glove
A while; then slipped to playing father-mother;
And then at length meant nothing to eachother.[2]

They made their efforts and it did no good:
They never found eachother in the mood.
They scouted hopefully in other beds:
And brought home wiser glands and sadder heads.

They read those manuals of ideal marriage
Which no man in his sense would disparage:
But all it gave them was a fit of glooms;
And after that they slept in separate[3] rooms.

They played the records of their courting days,
Perused old programs of forgotten plays,
Drove in those stars and byways where they'd lusted
And shyly their first nudities entrusted;[4]

Grieved in those nightspots where their knees had played,
And found, in fine, that corpses, once decayed,
Can neither laugh, dance, nor take nourishment.
Also that money spent is money spent.

Also that lightning never strikes us twice.
Likewise that winter ice is winter ice.
And failed, in fact, to find a single flaw
In Thermodynamism's Second Law.[a]

Here lies, indeed, a pitiable couple.
Once he was insolent, and she was supple,
And they learned in each other's company
Some little bit of what it means to be.
They never meant each other any harm:
And now they serve to keep each other warm.

UTK MS 2730 Box 5 Folder 32 [typescript][5]

[a] The second law of thermodynamics is basically that heat always flows spontaneously from hotter to colder regions of matter.

[Those untouched eyes which just begin]

Those untouched eyes which just begin,
    Seeing, to bloom,
Must look on things, no staying it,
    Which flower and root consume.

Those hands, which hardly grasp as yet,
    Nor yet know how to reach,[1]
Time will instruct, no staying it,
    To work, love, guard, beseech.

That body, so naïve and strong,
    Bright seed of God.
It shall become, no staying it,
    A burst, exhausted pod.

Our eyes, our hands, our bodies
    Let us [i]n praise
And use in honor while we may
    For nothing stays.[2]

UTK MS 2730 Box 5 Folder 32

[Uneasily, Extol the houses at morning][1]

  Uneasily,   Extol
The houses at morning.
gambrel and dormer, spanner,   audacious

Hoarsely, the eye brilliant, brilliant idiot eye, the sun, the sun,
Snoring sun,
old man hearing a noise in the house.

The sun made brandished lions of wheat.[2]
Wheat, lion, sun.
Disturb.
He has fallen under the hill into the sun.

UTK MS 2730 Box 5 Folder 32

[Walking is putting one foot forward]

Walking is putting one foot forward,
And leaning on it and bringing the other
Forward, and leaning on it and bringing
The other forward, and leaning on it
And bringing the other forward and,

Walking is dangling one leg forward
Right from the hip, then standing on it,
And dangling the other forward
Right from the hip end standing on it[.][1]

UTK MS 2730 Box 5 Folder 32

[Hate falsehoods as diseases][a]

Hate falsehoods as diseases,
And burn them out: but never
Their victims:
No matter how convinced they are,
Smug, cruel in them, murdering,
Blocking the breath of the world.
And sure their disease is their choice and
Invention, hate them no more than their
Dupes and their victims: and indicate,
Near as you can, towards the truth:
But clear yourself of the like disease
Of hatred and scorn.

UTK MS 2730 Box 5, Folder 32

[a] See also "[O true though little poets]."

[With what patience and what fortitude]

With what patience and what fortitude, they do not even know.
Nor do I know their names, these cleanly made little homes

Is there within the heart one song,
Even one, within the deadened heart

Steep on the night their voices touched me,
Never with words, but yet with meaning,

Let there be an end to weeping.

And all their ____ ____ ____.[a]

How shall he sing whose soul whose soul these long years is deafened?

UTK MS 2730 Box 5 Folder 32

[a] Here Agee indicates that he will later insert 2 iambic feet followed by one anapestic foot.

[Random strengths arranged us here]

Random strengths arranged us here
    That shall not likely meet again:
Our living, thought and death's a wind
    Flashing in a field of grain.

How though close wept we exquisitely sieve
    Random experiences.
Yet subtle fish must slip us and outlive
    Our narrowed verse.

Therefore though happy in the leaping haul
    Meshed perception,
What soul would dare read rules to govern all
    From such deception.[1]

UTK MS 2730 Box 5 Folder 32

[Rain unlicensed of the court]

Rain unlicensed of the court lays down her peace and pity
Round farm and stream and railroad yard and round the sad stone city.
Children ramble the pure walks, douse in gargling gutters:
Butterflies with blasted wings are trembling who must die:
All the birds are brashening[a], every water mutters:
And all the land is innocent before the innocent sky.
Rain unlicensed of the court lies down in peace and pity
Round wide stream, fatal butterfly, and on the mild stone city.

UTK MS 1500 Box 1, Folder 12[1]

[a] "Brashening" is being rudely or unpleasantly confident and aggressive.

[Ten years ago, when I was full of hope]

Ten years ago, when I was full of hope,
And words ran out like children in the gutter,
My iambs frolicked like the antelope,
And only sense was carried home on a shutter
I gave myself my head, and enough rope
To hang myself in more than I could utter
Those days are gone, and I am still around,
Still talking less sense with still more sound

I would do more if I were not so lazy.
I would do less if I were not so sad.
I would do nothing if I were not crazy
I would do still less if I were not mad
As matters stand, I am a little hazy,
Staring at a few sheets of yellow pad,
Feeling the heartsick world turn on its kind
In the loose furies of a broken mind.

It is devouring itself. It is gnawing its hand.
It is beating its brains out in a looking glass
It shrieks self-hate, grows self love. I stand
Suspicious, wishing to know; and they like grass,
Are blown, like flame. Of that terrific band
I am not one. Outrageous brave, they pass
I wait, will be made one by force, and doubt
Even those ways by which I might stay out.

Those ways of principle, and those of fear,
Those of true sickness urged, those of pure guile,
Those of advantage, talent, training, mere
Luck, which is the likeliest, make me smile,
As the French used to say, yellow. Those dear
And much in need, in heart or hunger, I'll
Be held by hardest, if my guess is right
Unless the sky should make itself one light.

And that I do not see. The century,
So-designated, of the common man,
Has brought him, chiefly, eyes enough to see
That he must kill his neighbor if he can,
If not, then die himself. This seems to me
To heap Newcastle's coals[a] on the frying pan,
Leaving in golden climates luckier slaves,
Those whose liberations are their graves.

That millions who are mild are burst upon
In bestial hypnosis, and in rape
Do as they must; or that the princely sun
Himself, cannot more justly bring of age
A world's broad season, then that men should run
Mothlike in smothering millions to engage
Death's all-else: blinding, all-informing flare,
Seems, like a lost[1] sperm, neither here nor there.[2]

UTK MS 2730 Box 5 Folder 32

[a] The idiomatic British phrase that exists in several forms to which Agee refers is "to bring coals to Newcastle." It means to take something to a place where it is not needed because a large amount of it is already there. He may be also thinking of the phrase "out of the frying pan and into the fire."

[One favor if you will]

One favor if you will:
When in our strength we kill
Let me, and no man other
Bring murder to my mother.

It shall be as it ought.
She could not so be taught,
But skips our good for God,
And therefore owes us[1] blood.

Yet to this poor obstruction
I owe my life by suction,
And know a better reason
Why I should close her season.

How there is goodness there
And excellence to spare
Then all our wrath more strong
And greater than her wrong.

UTK MS 2730 Box 5 Folder 32

[Marx, I agree.]

Marx, I agree. Einstein, I partly follow.
Keep your seats please boys, I'm everybody's friend.
And still I find it hollow, hollow, hollow,
And only wish tonight it might end.

Rivers inscribe their trees: the listing earth
Retires, restores, its halves upon the sun:
Continually I hear the shouts of birth,
The sighs of death, and I wish that I were done.

All things amaze me and the time seems great
With joy and wisdom scarcely yet descried.
The chains and emblems of the ghastly State
Rust off: the race, the earth, are groom and bride.

Here where the heart inherits nobler themes
Than hope or kindness ever bred before.
Yet I must drown beneath a depth of dreams
And never hope for any breathing more.

Hunt in the thickets the magnificent danger:
Steer in the marvels of all strength unborn:
I can not though I beat myself with anger,
Nor though I cut my bowels with eating scorn.

All that I care to live for is to show
These as they seem. To see, and not to say;
I do; and can't; is more than I can go.
Then God, God, why, why, do I stay?[1]

UTK MS 2730 Box 6, Folder 16 [typescript photocopy]

[Can you write silly][1]

Can you write silly and ticklish, glad poems.
As the ticklish weakness in the hams when climbing ropes,
A column of gnats in gentling air: mantling air, mantling pool.
Flail his cold forehead through the hungry dark.

UTK MS 3824 Box 7, Folder 4[2]

[Yet even slaves]

Yet even slaves lie down and love.
A little while along this bed
Hunger is nothing and proud hate
Spills wholly from the lowered head.

Though soon we must stand up from love
And mercy and all love put by,
Belt our starved guts with wrath, and kill,
We are not sorry we have met.

UTK MS 1500 Box 1, Folder 11 [typescript]; *JAR*, p. 212.

[Seriously, if that's your vanity]

Seriously, if that's your vanity, but remember:

We all that work such grievance are less than children
dancing the lengths out of elaborate games
on a warmed threshold, in a safe dooryard:

whom shadows scare; whom the bearing evening
brings in for bed; and whom the dark undresses.

Not twenty have been more. Though more will be,
and all the race be sometime more than grown,

This summer shall not swing again
its largeness on the land:
This summer's leaves you shall not know
from this disheveled hand.[a]

UTK MS 1500 Box 1, Folder 11 [typescript;
handwritten draft in folder 12]; *JAR*, p. 213.

[a] See also "[God, God, there is not largeness in the air]."

[Somewhat less indiscriminately]

Somewhat less indiscriminately
Pour love and gratitude around
For parents to lick up like cats
And for the ravenous ground:

daughters your fathers planted you
    only to deflower you:
sons your mothers cooked you up
    only to devour you:

patterned after Stephen's sow
    who breakfast's on her farrow.[a]
Who is not Ireland but the earth
    our birthplace and our barrow.[1]

UTK MS 1500 Box 1, Folder 11[2]; *JAR*, p. 222.

[a] In James Joyce's *A Portrait of the Artist as a Young Man,* Stephen Dedalus calls Ireland "the old sow that eats her farrow."

[Father, mother]

Father, mother, whom the pleasure
cheated even while it taught,
Now your child repents at leisure
what your hasty trading brought.[1]

UTK MS 1500 Box 1, Folder 11; *JAR*, p. 222.

[Ideas, cripplings, qualify the sun]

Ideas, cripplings, qualify the sun.
Crippling into hills (or mountains)
The crippled earth
Crippling smoke.

Life, every leaf, is qualified:
The squealing axles of the mind.
Intention round his squealing axle glows[1].
Dilations in the stars.

In the gray field, minute disturbances.
IMPLODE. IMPLOSIVE.
flowers requiring of the sun.
oblige me, Lord.
small flowers wink in the wind.
wind makes a winking in the grass of flowers.
Choked with premature insistence
Persistent.   Persist.[2]

UTK MS 1500 Box 1, Folder 11

[Rooted in prehistory]

Rooted in prehistory
Less sterile and less clear than sand,
Cities like stone lily pads
Float our weltering lake of land.

Float, and flower their formal sorrow;
Shrive and sink beneath the Fall;
Whose dark grave with every year
Spends up messages as tall.[1]

UTK MS 1500 Box 1, Folder 11

[Fire flared]

Fire flared, and floated, and the float was stone.
And stone and air were steam and swale of sea
    That branched with grain of all.[1]

UTK MS 1500 Box 1, Folder 11

[Charm of cold the water reach]

Charm of cold the water reach[1]
Compels: and in his arm
The jointed wind of winter feels
The wintery harm.

UTK MS 1500 Box 1, Folder 11

[Young yet on your day]

Young yet on your day
Pledge tall things to your pride,
Brave in thought of war,
Walks in the bullet's way:

Murderers for gain
Be gainful while you can;
You that would change that score
Be merciless and destroy:

You lonely that must mourn:
You that are full of cheer:
You that all harms have borne:
You that see no thing clear:

You woman and you man,
Bridegroom and happy bride,
Find out your truest joy
That crests the mortal tide:

That pride and greed and anger,
Bravery and grief and love,
All death has deep in danger
Death shall not quite remove:

So may the race run out its riot
And burst brains for a reason why,
And know two times for quiet:
To couple and to die:

And this ill-sung remark
Of mine and many others
Run light among the living
When I am on the dark.

UTK MS 1500 Box 1, Folder 12 [typescript][1]

[It is best not to kill with mercy]

It is best not to kill with mercy.
Do not think of these things

Goodness has grown in stranger hearts than these.
And ignorance in crueler[1]

Yes very surely and all joy it is
Murder shall end what not all time has taught

Who murders wrong, murders much goodness too.
It is an idea we kill; but we must kill

Living and time have locked us each more strong
In what we are than wisdom can undo[.][2]

UTK MS 1500 Box 1, Folder 12[3]

[How on the bare brain][1]

How on the bare brain
Age, thought, circumstance
Steadily stand up like rain.

How prettily the raindrops dance.
Now the water's really deep.
Droplet, you default your chance.

Good night. Sweet sleep.
Pleasant dreams. Harm's done.
Past's past. Don't weep.

God, the bare sun!

UTK MS 1500 Box 1, Folder 12; *JAR*, p. 227.

[We have come a long, long way]

We have come a long, long way.
Where is all you told me of.
Why these stresses. What's to say?
And where is love.

I see water, winding the white shores.
Land, and its rivers: a November[1] leaf.
Cities: small yet stone most awful sores.
Apathy more dreadful than the utmost grief.

Everywhere[2] the bare stress of living such
It stuns the inheritor stupid as a rich man's son.
Joy: any strength of passion: much too much:
Flares, where it chances, very soon is stone.[3]

UTK MS 3824 Box 7, Folder 2 [typescript]

[We have come a long, long way (Variant)]

We have come a long, long way.
 Where is all you told me of.
Why all there? What's to pay?
 And where is love?

I see water, winding the white shores.
Land, and its rivers: a November[1] leaf.
Cities: small yet stone most awful sores.
Apathy more dreadful than the utmost grief.

Everywhere the bare stress of living such
It stuns the inheritor stupid as a rich man's son:
Joy, any strength of passion, much too much:
Flares, where it chances, very soon is stone.[2]

Those few who stand clear

Breathe:

Every good becomes a poison.
People can accept only on their own terms.
Every superior thing runs through changes to reach them,
And reaching, is new poison.[3]

UTK MS 1500 Box 1, Folder 15[4]

"Sweet sounds, oh, beautiful music, do not cease!
Reject me not into the world again . . . .
Reject me not, sweet sounds! Oh, let me live [."][a]

[Let her, Ludwig, stick around]

Let her, Ludwig, stick around
And take up through a straw
What, in that world she's never found
    You broke your soul, and saw.

She will keep reasonably quiet;
She means what here she says:
So, on her predigested diet,
    Let her live out her days.

Reject not: let her stick around
The starts of the Is or Isness:
And meanwhile, unperturbed, sweet sound,
    Go on about your business.

UTK MS 1500 Box 1, Folder 12

[a] The headnote is taken from the poem "On Hearing a Symphony of Beethoven" by Edna St. Vincent Millay. It appears in her *The Buck in the Snow*, published in 1928. See also "[Jesus make it just so good]," a draft of which appears on this same handwritten manuscript page.

[Make haste if you will help]

Make haste if you will help, the time
Is toward a[1] turn when helplessness
Is your disuse as well as mine
And both mislay the old address.[2]

UTK MS 1500 Box 1, Folder 12; *JAR*, p. 199.

[The rootless winds flower wide]

The rootless winds flower wide
The marl[a] blows smooth in differing green
The world lolls on her springward side
The seas go smooth as plate between:

This bright this vagrant bubble
Charmed beyond all its charmful kind
Careers superior to such trouble
As makes small moisture of large mind.[1]

UTK MS 1500 Box 1, Folder 12; *JAR*, p. 243.

[a] A loosely formed composite of rock or soil consisting of clay and lime, formerly used as fertilizer.

[Yet being now turned]

Yet being now turned
Twenty-five times the circuit of the sun,
And having learned so little on the way,
Having but learned

One day for sure my traveling will be done,
And I foredone forever of the day,

Now must I weep yet swiftly skin the tear
(My driest[1] eyesight never was too clear)
And know those things that little children can,
And leave above me what must bore a man.[2]

UTK MS 1500 Box 1, Folder 12

[Out of what parts we do not know]

Out of what parts we do not know
And towards what end we cannot tell
There moved a good long time ago
What did what may be just as well.

Something that we call a star
Swam past what we call the sun
And draughted seven floats of fire[a]
And one became the world begun.

They lifted from the limber flame
And like dry leaves behind a car
Followed in the brilliant street
A while, and fell, and here we are.

It cooled, and twirled around itself
And round the sun and on the sky
And shrank, and toughened, and abscessed,
And snapped the stone moon from the fry.

Let us be short. There water was,
And there the varying stone and there
The lively air, and all this all
Not otherwise disposed but where

The sun might not too hardly scorch
Nor yet too shriveling cruelly chill.
Over the brawled huge street there hung one narrow porch,
A balcony looked safely, solely out,
Where fate or what could watch,
And work out the length of its will.

Fire-and-stone, water-and-air
Were the interwoven pair.
Any way you look at it remarkably lucky
For you, and you, yes perfectly ducky.

Not too hot and not too cold,
Water for the jellyfish and air for you and me;
Plenty of farmlands and plenty of gold,
It was the best of possible worlds[b].

The muscles of the mountains were maggoty with sores
Not too hot and not too cold,
And the scabs shine bright in the jewelry stores
It was the best of possible worlds.

There was breath enough to go round
There was water enough for all
But not one ear heard not one sound
In the best of possible worlds.[1]

UTK MS 1500 Box 1, Folder 12
[three manuscript pages including drafts]

[a] "draughted" means "drafted;" "seven floats" refers to earth's continents.

[b] Likely an allusion to Voltaire's satire, *Candide*, in which Pangloss, Candide's mentor and a philosopher, propounds the novel's most famous idea: that all is for the best in this "best of all possible worlds."

[Grateful for this at least][1]

Grateful for this at least:
That these that choke my brain,
That stop my throat and soak up every tear
And every dream and hope so chain
I am but rock, and death, and beyond fear:
That these unnumberable my hideous faults
So thrive so thickly on my lasting youth,
So many much that time can bring no more
Nor wisdom of all age invent more foul,
Sure, surely then, some hope. Oh, I should live,
Oh, should these evils, these self-evils not obliterate me quite in hate, in hate, in self-murder,
Oh, should I live there through, then will be time,
Then, for they cannot last that cannot kill,
May some hope be.
And, one by slowly each relaxed,
Aloose, away, the knotted poisons smile,
And one be left no harm can harm
And the clear rivers still to drink
And earth to eat and living sky to burn,
Heart's kindness and the weeping warm
And all real, and wholly healed
That beat myself, and make this hell my hell.

Lucky for this at least:[2]
These faults that all but crowding out of life[3]
Attack me young.
What worse m[a]y be, come soon.
Still should I breathe with all those worst upon me,
One must die first. Still, still should I live,
One, by slowly each they flex alone,
The octopus relax[.]

So thought the young clam as the starfish clasped him.
So as the infant starfish clasped him, the young clam thanked the Lord.

UTK MS 1500 Box 1, Folder 12

[Now the wronged millions rearrange]

Now the wronged millions rearrange
Strong towards the world's first right, not strange
The honest mind to help that day,
Can choose, and flick the world away.

That hunger weighs, kind will and anger
The frail chance deathly down in danger.
And blanks the always blemished eye
To poring[a] towards what and why.[1]

UTK MS 1500 Box 1, Folder 12 [two pages]

[a] Being absorbed in studying or reading.

[Held instant still, whole year's lungs burst full]

Held instant still, whole year's lungs burst full:
Life outward strangling strived outstriking all extremes.[1]
Blears of the burden, all that lives with huge brightness whelmed:
            Climbs in the sun, a simmering dream of gnats:
The climbed: the still: the standing: the woken peak
of the flame:
                  Now past: the shade slides east: on air a bird leans:
                        Inmost in subtlety's begun
The unhatted unalterable exhalation that entirely exhausts
All of its all, in the voiding last voided length
Blanks in blurred winter's void the world depth down to the
depth-caught breath.[2]

UTK MS 1500 Box 1, Folder 12

[And as he was dreaming][1]

And as he was dreaming a giant grew
  Till he occupied the sky
And nodded and beckoned and walked him through
  And never answered why.

And father choked him in a chain
  Until his blood was gray:
And mother fastened upon his brain
  And drank his soul away:

And he wrestled and threw his father down
  And broke his mother's mouth
And he dove beneath the black sea's frown
  And swam to the open south.

UTK MS 3824 Box 6, Folder 35

[Walk up the side of the world][1]

Now from the northern shadow leans the earth upon the sun:
From the whole pane the white breath faints and winter is outdone:
And from that streaming trough where they eat their continual death,
The vegetable tribes walk up the walls of the mild world.

Leans from the northern shadow. Leans into the shadow of the north.

Tribute to the spaces of the north.

From that equatorial trough
Spilled from the green equatorial trough[2]

Companies mountains walking alone under the sky

The way to a woman's heart is through her stomach.

Tie me your navelcords again
He "puts" it like a shot.
Steaming at the equator . . .
Seas stare the light.

UTK MS 3824 Box 6, Folder 35

Fight-talk, for a young athlete

When your heavying feet have run
Seventy laps around the sun,
If not much earlier on the way,
You'll be ready to call it a day.

And when you sink down, breathing hard
And towards your last, your one regard,
The same with all who ever raced,
Will be some fear for how you placed.

Calm: your team will never lack
Runners on that crowded track,
Heart blown sprinters in the game
Where every record is the same.[1]

UTK MS 3824 Box 6, Folder 36

Satiric and Humorous Poems

Home Again Blues[a]

Now we are home with Mom and Dad
    And huckleberry pie,
In fact the Things We Fought For:
    And now we wonder why.

For Mom is just a garter-belt
    And Dad is just a bore,
And as for good home cooking
    We had too much before.

And that, we guess, is what it means
    To be a U.S. Veteran.
We'll never fight another war
    Until they start a better one.

UTK MS 2730 Box 5, Folder 17; *CP*, p. 137.

[a] The poem is apparently copied by hand by Father Flye (identified by handwriting), who notes that "This, typed out, was with some of James Agee's papers. Did he write it?" The attribution seems likely, given Flye's statement, his mentorship of the author, and Agee's anti-war sentiments.

With the Lust For Life
Boys in South California and North Carolina

1.
Bill, Tom & Co. insist Life is a honey.
They've had her out, and reached an understanding
Whereby they'll tell the world her climate's sunny
If she will overlook their overglanding.
Such love is quite sincere, and it means money.
Fame, self-respect, safe flight, and happy landing.
But it's only Love of the Type Calif. Subhead pup:
They don't love Life, they only love her up.

2.
Towards a Humble and Pious Speech

O Gay and Melancholy Flux
I think you're awful cute.
Beside you I'm not worth a shucks,
And I am quite a beaut.

Fill to the brim with Nehi
And grade-B sacramental wine
My chalice and your boy will sup
With the later Gertrude Stein.

For out in sunny southern california.
The easy image is just around the cornea
And Life can get a bright young fella hornia[a]
Than any other place on earth.

So bring on your Smith-Corona
I'll play it like any Cremona[b]
Vose Wurlitzer Strad or Hobnah[c]
Any time, any place.

And when they're played I'll hand em
Out to, and hot at, Random:

No one will understand em
            So every serve's an ace.

3.

Oh, Life is so exuberant
I don't know what to say.
So I'll say Life's exuberant
All day and every day.

I'll say it to the last good drop
Of my pituitary.
And then at least no one shall say
I'm an artstruck, style-mad fairy[d].

And when you holler it that loud
That much and that sincerely,
The chances are you've done your best
And it's great prose, or nearly.

And yet sometimes I wonder if
It wouldn't be still better
If I should mercilessly reduce
The spirit to the letter.

How it would feel, and what perhaps
It might do for my art
If I should use my brain as cold
As hot I use my heart.

But no: that sends a sheen of fear
Rambling my spine.
Those marry only in the great:
In me they can't combine.

Every thing that's excellent
In my kind of work
Owes its very existence to
The things I fear and shirk.

(And yet again: and yet again.
Is that my only way?
Do I not know? Am I not great?
What is it I betray.)

UTK MS 2730 Box 5, Folder 29 [three-page typescript]

[a] Horny, or sexually aroused.

[b] Cremona, Italy, is famous for the violins and violas made there in the 16th–18th centuries by the Amati family and their pupils, the Guarneri and Antonio Stradivari.

[c] Famous brands of instruments, respectively piano, piano and organ, violin, and (Höfner) stringed instruments.

[d] A slang pejorative term for a male homosexual.

[The world is sick and rotten through and through]

The world is sick and rotten through and through.
There are, however, certain jobs to do:
Cutting the cancer from the living flesh
And starting out live life afresh.

The human race is extremely young:
Change the didies[a] and delete the dung.
Bring it up according to common sense:
Its future possibilities are simply immense.

UTK MS 3824 Box 6, Folder 36

[a] A slang term for diapers.

Song for the Opposition

(For alcoholic quartet. The tune is self-evident.)

(*Maestoso:*)[a1]

Sweet Anodyne[b]
My Anodyne
Better than women, song or wine:

There's no escape
For man or ape
Quite like hewing closely to
The Party Line.[2]

What fool would dare
To show he cares
What bastards wreck   a right idea?

I'll save my skin
The world to win:
There's no discipline on earth
As strong as Fear.

So let the fools
Make us their tools:
Eat what they hand   you at the schools:

Try no to care
What filthy air
Keeps the population choked:
Stick by the rules.

UTK MS 2730 Box5, Folder 31 [typescript][3]

[a] A direction that means that the music should be majestic and stately.

[b] A pain-killing drug; Agee creates a parody of "Sweet Adeline," a standard song for barbershop quartets. See also note a for the poem "[Sweet anodyne]" for additional information.

[I was fratting with a fraulein]

I was fratting[a] with a fraulein name of Frieda
When a captain name of Lipshitz happened by
And this Lipshitz hadn't hardly more than seed her
But he damn near spit my eye.

He said ain't you never heard about our war aims?
I says Huh? He says that fascism must die.
He says that and no poll tax and plenty more aims
Are mastermin[d]ed by sons of bitches such as I.

I reply that's a reflection on my mother.
If it wasn't for your motherfucking rank
I just as own kick you as another.
Christ that bastard stank.

Yellow bastard, he comes back my education
Is politically worse than none.
He has got him a subscription to the Nation[b].
He would rather see me use it than a gun.

He apologized for all that sonsabitching.
I says skip it (what a cowardly son of a bitch).
He could see for Christ's sake couldn't he I was itching
To get on back to the twitch.[c]

But no, he had to sport his fugging German.
I caught on he was finishing up the war.
He told her that his middle name was Herman.
He told that silly whore

That we wanted to forgive the plain civilians
If they'd only play the game our way;
He tells her that there must be several millions
Who wouldn't hand out no lay

For just chocolate or cigarets or soap
And corrupt a decent democratic guy
Like myself; he says she mustn't give up hope:
Things were better by and by.

Jesus God, the way that half-assed captain chewed it
A chaplain would have puked, but not this creep.
And then you know what that fucker Jew did?
He drove her home in his Jeep.

No I doubt he ever laid her, even tried to.
He didn't have the moxie, not that jerk:
The only girl he'd ever give a ride to,
Would be for missionary work.

Sign her on for the God damned Atlantic Charter.
Make the world safe for Lipshitzs and lice.
Son of a bitch! If I'd ever got above her garter
I wouldn't of had to get there twice.

UTK MS 2730 Box 5 Folder 32

[a] fraternizing.

[b] *The Nation* was a weekly magazine founded in 1865 by abolitionists. It continues today as a source of liberal / progressive political and cultural news and views.

[c] Apparently a reference to Frieda.

[Wear the hub-bub of the universe]

Wear the hub-bub of the universe
In Paris gown or nudist stare
With the star brilliants torn
Across the breast and the order of
The garter[a] worn like a Sign of the Zodiac
Is visible without travelling checks
Not alone but if you are there.

UTK MS 2730 Box 5 Folder 32 [typescript]

[a] The Most Noble Order of the Garter is an order of chivalry in Great Britain and ranks just under the Victoria Cross and the George Cross in distinction.

[When, at last, with all your strength][1]

When, at last, with all your strength
You've strugglingly climbed a tree,
If you think you are a bird,
Well, don't blame me.

UTK MS 2730 Box 5 Folder 32

MISCELLANY

[#1. Frowning, the foetus floats in alcohol]

Frowning, the foetus floats in alcohol.
Such earnest foreheads will not find our way.
What's the world up to? What is on the ball?
We dwell on Appalachian[1] decay.
Her heel caught on the carpet in the upstairs hall;
She went down with a bang; and there she lay.
Towards morning she muttered of mincemeat and still didn't know
Me for her grandson: the best way to go.[2]

[#2. The yellow crocks stood all around]

The yellow crocks stood all around
The bottom of the cellar stairs.
Citron[a] cost only five a pound.
Poor papa had five hundred shares.

She felt tomatoes with her thumb.
She lifted up and smelled the veal.
Dismissed the cook for chewing gum
And for the thick potato peel.

Beethoven was her great delight.
The polka and the polonaise
Rang likewise on the summer night.
She used to pause, and hope for praise.

Wax and hot iron and starch brought out
Of that stiff linen a holy sheen.
All the bright family ranged about
The nutpicks and the soup tureen.[1]

[a] Citron is the original lemon from which many other, more familiar lemons have been developed, both naturally and by botanists.

[#3. She turned the broad hem of the sheet]

She turned the broad hem of the sheet.
Up on the sheet she pinned to comb
Her rat[a], and braid it. I repeat,
She loved Beethoven, next her home.

And now the yellow crocks stood round
The dusty bottom of the stairs.
And on that huge and empty ground
Her family walked away in pairs.

The turkey duster fell apart.
The market basket broke straight through.
Joel drove past in the grocer's cart.
Her friends departed two by two.

And Mr. Rhoel's[b] delivery boy
Snatched the tomato from her hand.
She saw enormous moths destroy
The gold braids of the civic band.

Her rat fell in the oolong tea.
The yellow crocks were full of mold.
Her trembling fingers dropped the key.
The ducks reserved for her were sold.

The fever powders all were stale;
Her mother made her sit up straight;
The cook forgot to wash the kale;
Her ankle doubled on the skate;

A roach ran up the linden tree,
The mincemeat was all choked with fur.
She looked with her blind eyes at me:
And that was quite the end of her.[1]

UTK MS 2730 Box 5 Folder 32

[a] "Her "rat" is likely her hair rat, an attachment of hair added for particular styles.
[b] Unidentified. Mr. Roehl is perhaps a fictional character.

[Brightness falls from the air]

Brightness falls from the air. His beard and braids,
Honors of order blazoned on his breast,
Grandmother's famous temper, his dear wife's
Hat pin and parasol, avail him not.
Those medals all are pawned to memory.
Her temper's stopped with consecrated earth.
Woman's best weapons have been lifted from her.
A youth is scolded for wearing his yachting cap.

And now by courtesy at seven o[']clock
He lifts his[1] palms, and takes his broad church[a] Christ.
The alb and stole[b] are folded under glass.
By yawl and cart, the archbishop makes Lausanne.

And into the asphalt yard, all in sack suits,
Gustav, Emmanuel, Hirohito, George[c],
Silently nodding, come from out from four doors
And fall in guarded file; he forms the line
The sun comes bare. The little eyes of rifles[2]
Outbrave Abash the eyes of two. Oh, Nicholas, my cousin
Nicholas, he breathes, avoiding laughter.
Small game slopes down.
At rest.   Dismissed.

The fire is wetted from Pendragon's wave.
The knights are snaffled of breath in their black shirts.
Files of the Illustrated London News
Are saved; a matter of record.

UTK MS 2730 Box 5 Folder 32

[a] "broad church" refers to moderate movement in the Church of England during the mid-19th century. Their views opposed what they regarded as the narrow expressions of doctrine as practiced by Anglo-Catholics (High Church) on one hand and anti-Roman Evangelicals (Low Church) on the other.

[b] The alb and stole are Roman Catholic, Anglican (Church of England), Lutheran, and Methodist religious vestments; the stole is worn over the alb (or surplus, a gown that is generally white in color). Given that "broad church" is cited in the previous line, it seems likely that the reference to the Church of England is one that continues.

[c] Likely monarchs / rulers: Gustaf V was King of Sweden from 1907 until his death in 1950; Victor Emmanuel III reigned as King of Italy from 29 July 1900 until his abdication on 9 May 1946; Michinomiya Hirohito, born in 1901, was the emperor of Japan from 1926 until his death in 1989; George V was King of the United Kingdom and the British Dominions, and Emperor of India, from 6 May 1910 until his death in 1936 or George VI, who ruled from December 11, 1936, until his death in 1952.

[Iscariot, take a back seat, please]

Iscariot, take a back seat, please,
    You rate no credit line for these
Mild millions of deluded pairs:
    They were their own unwitting snares.

These, in a thousand rumble seats[a]
    In sweeter springs than this
Deliciously first betrayed
    Each other with a kiss.

And hauled themselves before the court
    And gaily sat and heard
Themselves in judgement yield themselves
    Ruin in a word.

And crucified them flesh to flesh
And died: and only rise
By proxy in those children who
Run out and do likewise.[1]

UTK MS 2730 Box 5 Folder 32

[a] A rumble seat is a small, upholstered exterior seat of an early motorcar that is exterior to the cabin proper which folded into the rear of the body. It is a snug fit for two people.

A Garland of Dainty Devices

When I feel your kneecap under da table
I wanta drink side-cars[a] out of your navel.

———

Girls, you may learn a lesson from
Anita Pope[b] whose brief renown
Sprang from that lucky day when she
Was caught with her Pantayes [panties] down.

Or,——Maid Marian,
Best friend of the man with the ranch and whore[c]

Remember for the lost Lenore[d]

So never shave your underarms
And never loiter in the park:
And wear white cotton underclothes
And keep your legs crossed after dark.
And if you don't turn out a winner,
Ladies, pray for me, a sinner.

———

Maedchen in Uniform[e]

With blood on her bouche [mouth] and on her toes[1]
She shall have fresh meat wherever she goes.

UTK MS 2730 Box 5, Folder 32[2]

[a] The sidecar is a cocktail traditionally made with cognac, orange liqueur, plus lemon juice.

[b] Her brief renown did not allow the editor to identify her.

[c] Likely Marion Davies, original name Marion Cecilia Douras, (1897—1961), American actor who was more famous for her 34-year affair with publishing giant William Randolph Hearst. The ranch is likely the San Simeon Ranch on the grounds of which Hearst built his mansion of San Simeon. He inherited the ranch in 1919.

[d] The famous deceased love interest in Edgar Allan Poe's "The Raven."

[c] "Mädchen in Uniform" ("Girls in Uniform") is a 1931 German feature-length film based on the play *Gestern und heute* (*Then and Now*) by Christa Winsloe. In the film, Manuela, a sensitive girl, is sent to an all-girls boarding school and develops a romantic attachment to Elizabeth, one of her female teachers. It is often cited as one of the earliest narrative films to portray homosexuality in an explicit manner.

[Hear the tired announcer bleat]

Hear the tired announcer bleat
His still small voice of calm;
I'm sure his thoughts are very sweet,
His cranium packed with balm.

UTK MS 3824 Box 4, Folder 21[1]

[If, gasping but victorious]

If, gasping but victorious, he
Who has just climbed a tree
    Advises[1] the wayfarer:

"Look out below! I am a bird!"
And suits the action to the word,
    That children, is his error.

or:

Tree-climbing is good exercise.
But to the child (or man) who's wise
The thought has never yet occurred
That he who climbs one is a bird.[2]

or:

Up in a tree it is pleasant to see
How high you have climbed and what courage it took
    And to look.

But this feeling of[3] pride can endanger the hide
If you think, with the view and the vision all blurred,
    "I'm a bird."

UTK MS 2730 Box 6, Folder 16 [photocopy]

[It's easy enough to be happy]

"It's easy enough to be happy
When your house is full of good things.
But if you want to fly
You'd better not try
Unless you've a pair of wings."

UTK MS 2730 Box 7, Folder 23 [typescript photocopy]

[Depilatories garter belts and lotions]

Depilatories garter belts and lotions
Are making mother sweeter every day.
And mother can appeal to my emotions
Just the biggest kind of way[a].[1]

UTK MS 1500 Box 1, Folder 11; *JAR*, p. 217.

[a] See also the longer version, "[Depilatories rubber belts and lotions].

[What fool would dare]

What fool would dare
To show he cares
What bastards wreck, a right idea:
I'll save my skin
The world to win
There's no discipline
On earth as strong as fear.

So let the fools
Make us their tools
Eat what they give you at the schools.
Try not to care
How foul the air
Keeps the population choked
    Stick by the rules.

You have nothing to lose but your brains.[1]

UTK MS 1500 Box 1, Folder 11; *JAR*, pp. 217–18.

[Major Douglas]

Major Douglas[a] is the kind of man
That heaps up the fire in the frying pan
He spares the child and spoils the rod
And he never gives offense to beast, man or God.

He says the world would escape its pickles
If only the world would take wooden nickels:
And Munson[b] and the brighter sort of Harvard boys
Will make the world a safe place for the Bishop[c] and the goys[d].[1]

UTK MS 1500 Box 1, Folder 11; *JAR*, p. 218.

[a] British Major Clifford Hugh Douglas (1879–1952) was the creator of the underconsumptionist monetary theory of Social Credit. While balancing the books for an aircraft factory, Douglas noticed that the combined incomes of all the workers at the plant would be insufficient to purchase its combined production. He applied this insight to the economy as a whole and came to the conclusion that banks create a cycle of debt through charging interest: the principle is presumably equal to what is produced, but the interest requires future loans—and future interest. Since the money that consumers have to buy products will always lag behind the cost of the goods they produce, countries constantly have to expand their production capabilities, which inevitably leads to international friction and eventually war. Douglas proposed breaking the cycle of debt through a national dividend that would return the amount of surplus production back to consumers rather than banks. Variations of the Social Credit theory, with its convenient application to the mythical Jewish banker, found a number of proponents during the Great Depression, including Father Charles E. Coughlin, Huey Long, and Ezra Pound. Both Douglas and Coughlin also appear in "*Dialog*."

[b] Gorham Munson (1896–1969), writer and literary critic, was the editor of the Social Credit journal *New Democracy*.

[c] Controversial economic populist and Catholic priest Father Charles E. Coughlin (1891–1979) was the host of a very popular radio show from 1926 to 1942 and editor of the weekly newspaper *Social Justice*. He blamed Jews for the Great Depression and initially supported Franklin Roosevelt's New Deal, but turned against the president when he failed to implement radical monetary reforms, eventually accusing him of being part of a Communist conspiracy.

[d] Gentiles, a reference to the supposed international Jewish banking conspiracy.

Dialog

We cannot wait. Our time is nearly gone.
That mood of spiritual desolation
Which Eliot[a] put under glass, carry on
Long as you like. Certain new information
Suggests that that account was overdrawn
About the time the waves of imitation
Thinned from the ninth. Rather than draw a blank
We even must decline to run the bank.

Tell it to Major Douglas[b] and the Bishop[c].
They'll give you *such* an appetite for tea.
Tell it to Sigmund[d], who can dig a wish up
And make it call you Uncle—for a fee.
Try any kind of spiritual pushup
From Body-on-the-tongue to Ether-spree[e]:
But don't try us: unless you're willing to take
Some rational steps to cure your bellyache.[1]

You show some hope, and then again some doubt.
Hope's a good sign; the doubt's intelligent
At this stage. Now suppose you spit it out,
The whole damned business. It's spit well spent.
Since, I suspect, it stands to end a drought
Nothing else could, and won't cost you a cent.
And please don't mind if anyone here makes cracks;
Some of them, like yourself, are erstwhile smacks.

"Well, that, as a matter of fact, does bring to mind
One thing that often bothers me. Just when
I try to ask some question or to find
Some sense in this or that, one of your men
Is liable to be pretty damned unkind,
To put it mildly. Time and time again
I've run from cool to warm, almost to hot,
Only to be put off by so much snot.

I don't believe I'm hypersensitive.
I've friends who've had the same experience.
To anyone brought up on live & let live,
A silly phrase, I grant, that gives offense.
If you have everything you claim to give
The world at large, it doesn't make much sense,
(Does it?), deliberately to throw sand
In the eyes of those who are trying to understand.["]

UTK MS 1500 Box 1, Folder 11 [two manuscript pages]; *JAR*, pp. 219–20.

[a] A likely reference to T. S. Eliot (1888–1965) and two of his major poems "The Love Song of J. Alfred Prufrock" (1915) and "The Waste Land" (1922).

[b] See "[Major Douglas]," note a.

[c] See "[Major Douglas]," note c.

[d] Sigmund Freud (1856–1939), the father of psychoanalysis.

[e] This line apparently refers to what Agee possibly regards as other than current false methods of achieving some enlightenment. Ether was also thought at one time to cure hysteria.

[Ah's jes' a believing chameleon]

Ah's jes' a believing chameleon (credit line to Goofy Gerould[a])
And I dare you to dig up a creed in all the wide wide werruld
That I won't at some fine time (if life lasts long enough) hang my hat on
If only I be caught by the eye of the man behind the baton.

Of course the world grows tired of caring just what such a fellow thinks
But I always say a chain's no stronger than its missing links:
Speaking of chains, suppose I curl up quiet in the —— gullet
And you, my friends, if you want to clear the air a trifle, pull it.[b1]

UTK MS 1500 Box 1, Folder 11; *JAR*, pp. 215–16.

[a] Christopher "Goofy" Gerould was one of Agee's friends from Harvard and a writer and editor for *Fortune* magazine. He introduced Agee to Mia Fritsch, Agee's third wife.

[b] This poem should probably be considered alongside "Period Pieces from the Mid-Thirties," *CP*, 145–48.

[And by the bye my pious friends of the reviewing trade]

And by the bye my pious friends of the reviewing trade
By whose opinion reputations unmade are unmade
Please note well, as you wade your way through the subsequent tepid hash
That I was trying this stuff before I heard of Ogden Nash[a].

UTK MS 1500 Box 1, Folder 11; *JAR*, p. 216.

[a] Frederic Ogden Nash (1902–1971) was an American poet who, at his death, was America's most well-known producer of humorous poetry. He published fourteen books of poems and was famous for his unconventional rhymes, manipulations of language, and puns.

[Jitter Jitter leetle earth]

Jitter Jitter leetle earth
What in God's name are you worth:
Hit the wave wrong and you die.
Like a surfboard in the sky.[1]

UTK MS 1500 Box 1, Folder 11

[Your papa bleeds the little boys]

Your papa bleeds the little boys
Whose mammas live across the tracks
And that is why they makes such noise
Of ugly names behind our backs.

So see you stick beside my skirt
And plug your ears against their yells,
The nice boy never will get hurt
Who always does as Nursie tells.[1]

UTK MS 1500 Box 1, Folder 12

[The noise we make]

The noise we make when things are fun
Would frighten Atilla the Hun.
Ha-ha, heh-heh, ho-ho, he-he,
Haw-haw, yuk-yuk, yak-yak, tee-hee,
Guffaw, one says, another, snicker,
Whinny (figure of speech) and whicker—
Such words try feebly to suggest
Sounds which were best left unexpressed.
Lashed by concupiscence, no goat
Ever did such things to his throat.
Horses would shy, and hens not lay
Which had to hear it every day;
And nervous dogs refuse to bark
And the whole crew of Noah's Ark
Join a conspiracy of silence
No matter how far from safe islands.
So would sane human beings, after
Really listening to laughter.

UTK MS 2730 Box 6, Folder 16 [typescript photocopy]

[Twitch off the tune of night]

Twitch off the tune of night. Discard the season.
Talk in the nude terms of this instant hour.
This is I fear abrupt, not wholly pleasing:
The Muse, mayhap, has gone a trifle sour:
Yet, gentlemen, there is some height of reason
For tossing her no sweetmeats to devour:
Surely the poet knows less than half his bride
Who lays and loves her merely alkaline side.[1]

I hope to hand out quod for quiddity.
I hope, some ways, nobody will be hurt.
I hope to show some moderate validity
Maunders the back porch of this marble shirt
For what may seem inordinate acidity
And may well make me out some little squirt
Drunk with the chance to demonstrate his twot's[a]
Delight in rud[e]ness: which I'm really not.

If gratitude were all, and kindliness,
And self-esteem, and all good sense of taste,
All of which itch me now, I must confess,
But must not scratch in unartistic haste,
I swear I would have found the wrong address,
Mislaid the moorings of my underwaist,[b]
Eaten this poem, or thought up something better
Such as regretful thanks by return letter.

UTK MS 1500 Box 1, Folder 11; *JAR*, pp. 247–48.

[a] (Or "twat") in this usage is an obnoxious or stupid person.

[b] A garment worn under another to which other undergarments are pinned or buttoned, often for a small child.

[Hold on a second, please]

Hold on a second, please: there's work to do
And it involves, one way or another, you.
The garbage stinks and it's high time to burn it.
Christ, if you lack the sense, get busy and learn it.
Anyone can, it's obvious enough:
Take a few easy pointers now, on the cuff[a].

The human race, not to get personal,
Has got, by now, about a bellyful
Of bitching from the few wise guys who bleed it
Into their checkbooks and, on occasion, feed it
Because, they find, they do, in a measure, need it.

It's gone on since the apes talked, just the same,
The old, invulnerable, badger game[b],
The cat's paw clipped and scorched, the monthly sitting
Tight and the world's best eating in his shitting:
Millions on millions, peoples on peoples born
And fallen like a field of rotted corn,
Their whole lives wrung to the last ruined drop
Merely to live and seed the next year's crop,
Fervently hoping to their phony[1] God
For better luck the seamy side of the sod,
And worshipping that smug and murderous State
Which pays them with an empty dinner plate
And kept, consistently, nine parts stone blind
To every hope and help the eye can find:
And that's the size, to date, of history.
Not, though, the way things ought to, and will, be.

You see, we're catching on to how it goes:
Or spot, if you like, the canker in the rose.
We're getting tired of bleeding out our lives
And those of our children and those of our wives
For less than living needs and for the sake
Of J. P. Morgan's[c] four-ply sirloin steak.

And sick to death of dying in their wars:
Of making our women and our arts their whores:
Of raising corn and wheat and eating shorts:
Of raising hogs and sharing in their orts[d]:
Of mining gold and getting paid in copper:
Of cooking feasts and scraping out the hopper:
Of laying tracks and hobbling the rails,
Involving, whether you like it or loathe it, you.

It makes some difference, too, which side you take,
Such as the difference between duck and drake
Or such, not to waste unnecessary breath,
As all the difference between life and death.
A man is tearing out his brother's throat:
God and the State stand by and hold his coat.
When B[e] looks sore, and makes as if to speak,
God's contact man says, blesséd are the meek;
And when he shows more physical kinds of gripe,
The State Massages him with a lead pipe.
I could go on, and tell you what a life
His children lead; and snapshots of his wife
Might, I surmise, help some to serve to move you
To some of those simple duties which behoove you.

However, what's the point: if you'll look close
At him alone, you'll see, plain as your nose,
That this unfortunate has your own face
And is, to tell the truth, the human race.

UTK MS 1500 Box 1, Folder 12 [with a draft on a separate sheet][2]

[a] For free.

[b] The badger game is an extortion scheme in which the dupe is tricked into a compromising position to make them easy to blackmail.

[c] See footnote a of "Rhymes on a Self-Evident Theme."

[d] Scraps or leftovers from a meal.

[e] Unknown.

[This is the story of three men on the earth[a]][1]

This is the story of three men on the earth,
Two of them mythical, the third one me;
Beginning, in each case, at each man's birth,
And ending as each leaf falls off the tree.
I tell it for exactly what it's worth,
And, on that matter, trust we'll all agree
That a life wasted tending such lean muttons
Had happier far been kept behind the buttons.

I tell it, and I tell it as I do,
Not in the pleasure of a good job done.
I know, only too well, as well as you,
How cold its small place in what cloudy sun:
It's neither very good nor very true,
And never would so much as be begun
If I had the least hope left of any key
To unlock those things which even I can see.

However, let that pass. For no good reason
I still prefer half-living, to whole dying,
Yielding such poison on the urgent season
As rooked[b] earth may, and, with as little sighing
As little courage lets.

Let us begin with the deepest of our three,
He, whom in their wisdom the shadows conspired in pity and scorn.[2]

UTK MS 1500 Box 1, Folder 12

[a] This work is apparently the beginning of a longer poem which Agee did not complete.
[b] Swindled or defrauded.

[O mine eyes have seen the trouble][a]

O mine eyes have seen the trouble of the travail of the earth
And the spasms and the retching and the bleeding at the birth
And the hating and the blinding and the murder and the worth
For truth is marching on.

I have seen the terror walking in the porches of their eyes,
I have seen them spread to around us every death they can devise,
I have heard them laugh for horror and the least among them dies,
For truth is marching on.

I have seen it in the prisons I have seen it in the street,
I have seen it in the shafts and in the shops and in the wheat,[1]
And I hear it in the thunder or a hundred million feet
For truth is marching on.

UTK MS 1500 Box 1, Folder 12 [typescript]

[a] Agee here imitates the "Battle Hymn of the Republic," a popular American patriotic song of the Civil War by the abolitionist writer Julia Ward Howe. She wrote her lyrics to the music of the song "John Brown's Body" and published them in *The Atlantic Monthly* in February 1862.

[Josie loves the little things][a]

Josie loves the little things.
And all the little things love Josie[1]
And everything that Josie says
Is perfectly prosy poesy nosy rosy.

UTK MS 1500 Box 1, Folder 12

[a] Likely based upon the nursery rhyme "Mary had a little lamb."

Noses are blooming in Bacardi.[a]

Mabel, Agnes and Becky,
Willy and Nilly
Gather for the Pulitzer Breckky:
Gelding the lily.[b]

UTK MS 1500 Box 1, Folder 12

[a] The poem is perhaps meant as a contrast with the quite romantic "Roses of Picardy," a very popular WWI song. It was published in London in 1916 with lyrics by Frederick Weatherly and music by Haydn Wood. "Bacardi" is a famous brand of rum. The distillery was founded on February 4, 1862, by Don Facundo Bacardí Massó in Santiago de Cuba.

[b] Before these vague four lines, Agee writes: "Note that the Creative prizes go to women. / Margaret Mead or none, women live in this style to which they have become accustomed. / Pulitzer Prize: Gelding the Lily." No woman by any of the three first names mentioned won a Pulitzer Prize from 1930–1945. Saying "Gelding," as a play on the more normal usage of "gilding the lily" (adding unneeded ornamentation), may be Agee's attempt to disparage the award by introducing the idea of castration, which he expands upon in "A Bill for Sterilization of the Muses." "Brekky" (British slang) may refer to an award "breakfast."

A Bill for Sterilization[a] of the Muses.[1]

Here's Koromex[b] to cognizance,
A salve to every trouble:[2]
Eunuch, its Spring! down with them pants!
Farmer, harvest that stubble![3]
Cherry ripe ripe ripe[c] I cry
Never say die say didy-die:
Sweet Jung-Freued[d]; sweet Hitler Adler[e]:
Never say die say Statler[f].

UTK MS 1500 Box 1, Folder 12

[a] Indiana passed the world's first sterilization law in 1907. Thirty-one states followed suit. In 1927, in Buck v. Bell, the U.S. Supreme Court voted 8 to 1 to uphold a state's right to forcibly sterilize a person considered unfit to procreate. State-sanctioned sterilizations reached their peak in the 1930s and 1940s, but continued for decades.

[b] "Koromex" was a contraceptive diaphragm available in the 1930s.

[c] A combination of the last names of Carl Jung (1875-1961) and Sigmund Freud (1856-1939), and likely a reference to their theories on sex.

[d] A reference to a young woman ready to lose her virginity.

[e] In 1912, Ludwig Adler (1876–1922), together with O. O. Fellner and H. Iscovesco, was one of the early European investigators of contraception.

[f] Unknown if a person, but may be a reference to the Statler Hotel chain and the possibility of an assignation. Statler's intent was to provide, clean, comfortable, and moderately-priced rooms for the average traveler. His slogan for his hotel in Buffalo, New York, opened in 1907, was "A Room and a Bath for a Dollar and a Half."

[Fellows, there's no soap playing it like that]

Fellows, there's no soap playing it like that.
Finger in nose, playfield whistle shrieking,
Unstable affections deranged over water and gin,
Black hat for blondeness, thwart our walk not more:
Sarabeque of Dunhill fume[a],
Dim inuendoed smoke down corridors of histories exempt, redact:
Conditioned jitter, drymouthed at the kiss,
Precarious health of special soil, pain-gathered, grown glass-green,
Implode, soaped, of bombed Kestrel Peared[b], pyloned in insulate light:
Six-sided snow here, blind, lesion
Tides till morning takes, leaches off:

We've got your number. Tramlines bilked. Trade burked. Ill matched sprockets.
Keep hands out of pockets.
Hide up the buck teeth from the baker's cozen[c].
You can just cut it out this very minute.
We do not see very much sense in it.
Men with fine minds good hearts and such a way with words
Would do better to let loose bigger and better and more natural turds.
No matter at all how powerful their influence,
No matter at all how right the things they're saying,
No matter at all how excellent their poems
And no matter how hard they are to parody.
Nevertheless there are better things
Than walking your balance along a rail with tricky pain
Mile on mile when mile on mile on mile
Whole country and all earth is for your taking. Nuff said.[1]

UTK MS 1500 Box 1, Folder 12

[a] Founded in 1907, Dunhill is an upscale British brand of cigarettes named after the English tobacconist and inventor Alfred Dunhill. He would prepare individual blends at a customer's request. "Sarabeque" may refer to the way in which the cigarette smoke curled when exhaled.

[b] "Peared" is "appeared," like a kestrel, a small falcon that hovers rapidly beating its wings while hunting for prey on the ground.

[c] "To cozen" is to deceive or trick, and perhaps a play on "baker's dozen"(13).

[Things went queer along a shoal][1]

Things went queer along a shoal
That made us what we are today.
Sunned earth drills a deeper hole
O shade in space than we can sway[1].
C A T spells cat,
And we'd better leave it at that.[2]

UTK MS 1500 Box 1, Folder 12

[Whoop away]

Whoop away: the stars are clocked
To prompt your mouths to that place where
Those patient agencies are mocked
Will put your wranglings[a] on the air.

Don't fret your tongue; the stars were clocked
Before time ticked that bring you where
The mightiest agencies of earth
Will put your passions on the air.

Don't fret your tongue: the earth is fair:
The earth will put you on the air.[1]

UTK MS 1500 Box 1, Folder 12

[a] Another word for haggling or bargaining over the terms of a transaction or agreement.

[Driving our self-made crucifying nails]

Driving our self-made crucifying nails
Through our own hands against our self-made crosses,
Making the world's gain, taking the world's losses,
Being of mankind the bowels[,] the brain, the heart,
And getting the treatment of a brewery fart[a],
Building the cities, living in the slums,
Building the countries, being the countries' bums,
Guarding those boundaries of race, creed and state
Which hold our friendship in a fractured hate,
Wrenching from mystery for use of earth
Those truths which give the human race its worth
Of art and science and, to all their good
In senses, spirit, all our length of blood.
Too numb, blind, deafened in the killing strife
Merely to live, to hope or care for life:
Trusting those men of moderate good will
Who promise a cure in a mild corrective pill—

UTK MS 1500 Box 1, Folder 15

[a] Beer makes farts smell worse because of the sulfate in it. The "treatment" to which Agee refers is that people shy away from such a bad smell.

[All, all of a piece throughout]

All, all of a piece throughout:
Your chase had a beast in view:
Your wars brought nothing about:
Your lovers were all untrue:
Tis well an old age is out:
And time to begin anew[1].

UTK MS 3824 Box 4, Folder 21

[Rover all but had his thumb upon the missing letter]

Rover all but had his thumb upon the missing letter:
Rover's liable to be dumb and may have left you high and dry:
Those near the truth get mystical, the tongue goes lathering up the sky:
And all in all I think *we'll* understand each other better. (Unmasks[a]).

We've much in common, you and I,
We share an earthier level:
We're classmates in the general sty:
I'm the common garden devil.

Once I was young and lovely.
I laughed in the arms of day,
My boughs were green and fruitful,
There was murder and love and play:[1]

How much I'll have to do
We'll have to wait and see:
Tom carries a Baxter[b] in his heart
Along with God right from the start:
And there may be little work for me
Of the good old-fashioned kind when he
Meets you and you and you.

UTK MS 3824 Box 6, Folder 35 [two pages, one an earlier draft]

[a] Apparently a stage direction, but for what work is unknown; or simply to expose.

[b] Slang term in film for the nice, but bland, unexciting guy in a romantic comedy who is nearly always dumped at the end of the story for the protagonist.

[Run away and don't come back]

Run away and don't come back until you know where you lost my money
run away and don't come back
I will not feed you and I will not give you
a warm bed to sleep in
and I will not give you a goodnight kiss
run away and se[a]rch until you find my lost money

Run and run and search and look every where
under rocks warm from the sun
under rocks wet from the rain
in beds of flowers that smile
in gutters where the paper boat floats
in the great almighty sea
in small glasses of french wine
in the bears of sages
on the ribbons of little[1] girls hair
in the peasant's flowerbed
dig into the[2] earth dive in the ocean
fly to the sun
look for my lost money and don't come back till you find it.
Search the music filled air
search the prophets'[3] poetry
but don't come back until you have found my lost money.
in lovers beds

I am asleep in my warm downey bed
after a delicious meal after my goodnight kiss

in the end I chanced to fall exhausted at the doorstep of a bank
and the man in a dapper suit came out and told me that he had
my money that I had lost.
Reluctant to accept it but thankful
here is your lost money
that was in the bank[.][4]

UTK MS 3824 Box 6, Folder 36 [typescript]

[Smell us up systematically]

Smell us up systematically and with care
Let not one past this corner duty-free,
And when you've got a snoutful and to spare,
Piddle opinions on every tree.
Mostly (it's normal) we'll be glad to pair
And mince[a] to school with you: such fun: not me.
Not me, I promise and admonish you.
If you object, you know what you can do.[1]

UTK MS 3824 Box 6, Folder 36

[a] To walk with short quick steps in a seemingly dainty manner.

[Depilatories rubber belts and lotions][a]

Depilatories rubber belts and lotions
Are making Mother sweeter every day.
And Mother can appeal to my emotions
Just the biggest kind of a way.

Though I've looked in every mart and every market
The wide world offers one,
I have never found as good a place to park it
When all is said and done.

By George how I used to envy Dad!
They fitted one another to a T.

Golly how I wished it was me![1]

UTK MS 3824 Box 7, Folder 1

[a] See also the shorter version, "[Depilatories garter belts and lotions]."

Beatings against the Bars.

Three are the things that rive[a] my heart:

That we are through before we start,
That lovers generally part,
That even lovely ladies----[b]:

Three are the things that rive my heart.

UTK MS 3824 Box 7, Folder 1 [typescript]

[a] to split or crack.

[b] Given the rhyme scheme, and Agee's penchant for reversals, the word gingerly indicated by four hyphens is likely "fart."

Spiritual and Religious Poems

[Lord of light]

Lord of light, beginner of beginnings, shaper of harmonies,
light on light on light[,] behold your child.
Who first in his morning lifts up his unsteady voice among
your children, to tell of your children: and to praise his God as he may.
Who must show forth his God in the weight and sound of words and
their bearing: who must sing of truth in the false and meager voice of a child.
For you have made him not of light merely but of the fibre of earth
and of mind: you have set him down among his brothers in their common folly.
His soul walks this world its little term in darkness: you have opened
the darkness five ways[a] wide and you have made him a mind out of the
middle of darkness.
Five ways from the living man the mind leans forth watchful: it sees
what it may see and informs the soul: the soul sifts Godhead as it may.
As a stone shows forth its God according to the stone's nature: so
must a man remain within his nature; we are all your children.
So must a man praise his God not with his soul merely: but with his
mind also, and with all his flesh learns five ways.
He must speak as you give your children privilege to speak; and set
his words in the ways of children: so man takes his measure before God.
Kind God, instruct his words and be seen in them: may these
ill-formed images of glory be yours alone.

UTK MS 2730 Box 5, Folder 5

[a] The "five ways" here and, in subsequent poems in this section, the "five windows" generally refers to the five senses.

[Some sense is very plain]

Some sense is very plain, but says a good deal.

There are things much more important than eating, and the man who lives by bread alone is not alive: but unless you eat you shant last long to use them.

This applies not only to you, and me, but to every human being on earth.

Therefore if you hold human life in any value, see to it first that every man eats, and eats well.[1]

We are assuming a human soul; a loving God.

Man cannot live by bread alone but by every word that proceedeth out of the mouth of God. The man who lives by bread alone is not alive.

But unless he eats how shall I love God on an empty stomach.

These lines are so obvious, such plain bromidic sense, that they will bore most of you. However, they are not written for most of you, but only for those who sincerely believe in God and in a spiritual life.

We are assuming a human soul: a loving God.

The whole purpose and meaning in the existence of man is then that he find out God.

I would add, or suggest, that he finds him, or looks towards him, in all understanding, love, and joy.

Man, in other words, does not live by bread alone but by every word that proceedeth out of the mouth of God.

A flower, like all the earth, lives by the sun.

But only if you front it soil, and water: and comes towards perfection only in proportion as several very simple things are favorable.

Require nothing of a flower if you plant it on stone: you nullify the whole strength of the sun, the whole intention of the flower.

UTK MS 2730 Box 5, Folder 5

Chorales

1. (Gethsemane)

Left lonely in the garden
Your death's own watch to keep.
None near to bring you comfort.
Your comrades all asleep.
O world grown deaf with doing:
O tall and Christless towers:
O Christ these bought befriend you,
Earth shares your sleepless hours.

2. (Gethsemane: His Father, watching Him watching)

Son, Son, what dreadful anguish
Obtains your flesh I know:
That now with tears you tempt me
Against tomorrow's woe.
Child, child, I may not help you.
From ever this must be.
Even now they seek who killed you.
Soon. Brave. For ever free.

3. (The way of the Cross)

My Lord, these latter Fridays
You go your Friday walk
Through rabbles worse than hateful
And worse than scornful talk.
A mob grown deaf and eyeless
And liking well the loss
Spits in your face and spikes you
With self-love to the cross.

4.

Lord, how the people hate you
That think the greatest good.
They that would make us brothers
Would kill you if they could.
They that would bring us nearest
The shapes of good you taught,
Their hatred of your loving
Brings you and them to naught.

UTK MS 2730 Box 5 Folder 10 [carbon typescript]

[This narrowing time I walk the world]

This narrowing time I walk the world
In darkness opened five ways wide
On what one man may apprehend
            Of Godhead:

Of loveliest truth how many ways
Breathed forth of God in sight of man,
Of man whom God for love made free
            To form his fate:

Of all things raised in childhood
High forth before their fathering joy
That dwelt in evils that were his
            And beautiful:

O God my God in this my time
Grant me to celebrate my God
Before in fearless joy I die
            In God, my God.

UTK MS 2730 Box 5 Folder 32 [typescript]

[When I was small delight and fear]

When I was small delight and fear
Were eminent upon my blood.
Watched I but once into the sun
Great shadows walked my mind of God.

To watch but once among the stars
The broad-borne earth lie down to rest,
That was to know of what huge host
We were the shy and country guest.

And bird and brain and spring and fall
Were creatures of his kindlihood,
And wrong and right were freely ours
To screen apart as best we could.

But I, and wiser men than I,
Have since deduced much better sense.
My brain is very quiet and clear.
The shadows have departed thence.

And all our findings reassure
My wavering blood, my halted breath,
To strive and stream in careless health
From now until my day of death.

Before which there is much to learn,
And nothing, nothing much to know.
Wherefore bring madness for my brain.
And for my blood that childish glow.

Father, mother, whom the pleasure
Misinformed in all it taught,
Now your child repents at leisure
What an instant trading bought.

UTK MS 2730 Box 5 Folder 32 [typescript][1]

[Virgin, forgive]

Virgin, forgive:
Evil, live.

Where glaciers glanced
Flowers since have danced.

Where evil dances
Virgin glances

Where flowers live
Glaciers forgive.

Virgin, live:
Evil, forgive.[1]

UTK MS 2730 Box 5 Folder 32

[And may God hold your humble and true soul]

And may God hold your humble and true soul.
And find it in his mercy to forgive me
Even my exorbitances: make me whole:
So only might such good as yours outlive me.
Let from now on those things elaborate
Only that raise out naturally as trees:
Not fighting, and not fouling in the lees,
But lying in its leisures and employs
Quite as they use, and to whatever end,
And willful only that no will alloys
Whatever coin I am, that's fate's to spend.
Clear to me, through all masks, the things that kills.
Let me walk always where the compass wills.[1]

UTK MS 2730 Box 5 Folder 32

[Lord roust me out]

Lord roust me out before they beat that bar,
O steal in Lord and file away these irons,
Long before birdsong through the wet blue night
Lift me up free great Lord upon your light.[1]

UTK MS 3824 Box 7, Folder 4[2]

[Head low, and break my knee][1]

Head low, and break my knee that will not bend
By God to earth, to muck, and in my shame
Tell you how soon for sure my time will end
And how therefore I now break down my name.
Now if it kills me yet will I learn how
To talk your talk and wring it into song[.]

UTK MS 3824 Box 7, Folder 4[2]

[O if you Father are]

O if you Father are,
What were your eyes when on the morning forth
To future fared the blind and new-foaled earth
Her soft skull streaming caul[a]?[1]

UTK MS 1500 Box 1, Folder 11

[a] A caul or veil can occur when a baby is born still inside an unbroken or partial amniotic sac. A newborn with a caul was (and still is in some cultures) thought to have special talents and powers such as psychic and supernatural abilities.

[Tell me must goodness wait]

Tell me must goodness wait
And kindliness stand by
Till every harm is healed
And every tear be dry?[1]

And since that time is won
By murdering alone
Shall mercy turn to water
That once was made a stone?[2]

UTK MS 1500 Box 1, Folder 12[3]

[Now Lord God]

Now Lord God keep your weather eye
A while on cabbages and kings:[a]
And if still you maintain it dry,
Then Death has lost some potent stings.

UTK MS 1500 Box 1, Folder 12 [typescript]; *JAR*, p. 228.

[a] "Cabbages and kings" is a reference to a line in the poem "The Walrus and the Carpenter" recited to Alice in chapter four of Lewis Carroll's *Through the Looking-Glass* (1871), by Tweedledee and Tweedledum. It likely represents everything in the world to which a person should attend.

[O if beneath this ward of night]

O if beneath this ward of night
There's any other creature brings[1]
His childly soul before the skies
And wordless with his weeping sings,

Brother, my blood, my own dear soul,
Whatever wrongs attend the light,
Let us kneel down for joy of God:
The world is very small tonight.[2]

UTK MS 1500 Box 1, Folder 12

[Tenant this season of uneasy darkness]

Tenant this season of uneasy darkness,
Soul snaffled and sewn up in darkness who go with me my short way:
Be shining in me flat against five windows wide on world and in my
mind the balancer.

We are brothers and you the elder, wiser.
Remembering how surely we shall quarrel I forget, hate, hope to kill,
    My ignorance vainness and disloyalty,
Handle the shapes of my nature justly in your hands.

Stand strong up in me my soul my God my world before
    And, fighting ever with our differing arms
Let us cut toward the truth each in our way
    And fighting die, glad and worshipping.[1]

UTK MS 1500 Box 1, Folder 12

[God, God, there is not largeness in the air][1]

God, God, there is not largeness in the air
To rest our love tonight. How we are giant and nameless
Brain after in your guessing, and abase
Your stars beneath a new and morning race.

Our wrestling love warm shoaled before all height of heaven
Prospers, and fortunes forth new manner of living.
The air idlings[1] white with glory.
We are borne bare before such blazed bombardment
As the whole skies disposed on the void earth
When first life tis worked towards living.

We all that work such wisdom are less than children that play out the lengths of
elaborate games[2]
On a warm threshold in the safe dooryard,
Whom shadows scare; whom the bearing evening
Brings in to bed, and whom the dark undresses.[3]

UTK MS 1500 Box 1, Folder 12

[So full in faith]

So full in faith lift up let stream your tears in the glory and the grief,
Strip scaley knowledge from your brain and know how well you know,
Here in this clattering earth and cruelmouthed town is born
Not watched or known or cared for, the Son of God.

The gleaming breath is here of the slowbrowed beasts and the odor of hay,
South in the sun and round the earth birds sing not caring why,
No workmen see no angels, and no kings no star
But crinch[a] their hungry belts for hate, and are wrung towards war.

He is come with whose love would melt us one for joy,
Whom not many live but laughing would destroy.
Whom not many love but serve most ignorantly ill,[b1]

UTK MS 1500 Box 1, Folder 12

[a] A variant of "crunch."

[b] The poem is likely missing the last line and perhaps more.

Bethlehem[a]

I walked the circle of the mother hills
And saw below me in the little town
The silver footprints of the arméd moon;
As when rude Ares[b] in a field of war
Tramps with footstep on the shattered slain,
So weighed his tracks upon the Moravian Dead.
Who primly lay in exile
And dream of lands and fallow farms
Yet hearken in their sleep
For that great final trombone note of
That shall come shrilling from beyond the hills
And waken them to our last great choral.

There shall resound one last choral sublime.
Then no choral, no town, no world, no tune.

UTK MS 3824 Box 6, Folder 35

[a] Agee is likely referring to Bethlehem, PA, and its historic Moravian community. At the funerals of Moravians buried there since 1742, trombone music accompanies a solemn procession of mourners carrying the dead to their final resting place.

[b] The Greek god of war and courage.

[His bones are built of rock]

His bones are built of rock
The flesh of beast and plant
Flourish in lovely form his bones upon:
His hair is made of horn
And much of him is sea
His blood is fast and healthful in the sun:

He wears upon his groin
The wallet full of God
Who wears within the rock
The looking-glass of God
While wears his darkness
The God that is of Gods:

His ways God made:

UTK MS 3824 Box 6, Folder 35

[Now inward from the sun]

Now inward from the sun to inward sun swerve my watching: and watch;
and speak so:
    My soul: like a mountain child in his clothes in the winter, so are you
    sewn up in darkness who go my short way darkened with me.
    Not by my doing, soul: O keep your joy new as fire your wisdom of
    gladness.

Such as I am a man I will do you no harm. Sure as I would be poet will
I harm you, often as not: o soul keep yet your gladness, tenant in this
tenement: be flat against five windows wide on world from the dark
watching and in my mind the settlement and balance; in all my flesh
and thought impacted Godhead.

Dear brother brave soul we have not long together. Remembering how surely
we shall quarrel, my ignorance headlong ways disloyal heart: handle the
shapes of my nature wisely in your hands.

For I am man, beast, dust, God, accountable to the wind in all quarters and
everywhere contradiction, doubt and anger: by your counsel only may I hope
to show truth so variously true.

Our morning grows over us, the blessed daybreak forever past.[a]
Now the large disposition of all things made blows white and merrily glad
like milkweed draughted[b] over the bright pasture,
Now nearer and felt and seen about us the bowelled earth breaching many
sorted life, the nations, the loud advertisements of men's doings:
Now out among them: your hand. Your embrace.

O stand strong up in my soul to the fighting,
Armed our differing ways to try our way toward truth:
I will call you in the fight, you me: in trouble harmed at daydown we shall
meet surely. Surely we shall know each other.[1]

UTK MS 3824 Box 6, Folder 36 [two pages]

[a] This last verse is expanded into a perhaps separate, but obviously related poem, in Agee's "[Our morning grows over us]."

[b] "draughted" means "drafted."

Maker of nothing made of all things made maker

Out of the world in the early morning I lift up my voice:
be with me Lord in the service of my day.
I put down my senses on the floor: I take out my mind
from my forehead.
My flesh, which is of this earth, I dedicate to earth:
and my mind to man.
Now watches my soul before the living God: in quiet
and at peace.
Now shines my firey soul before the living God:
in the watch, in the new morning.
Lord God of all making, tracts of stars unknown kneel
down before you: all glory and honor and beauty and might,
all works and distresses and destinies are yours alone.
Lord in this day that soon is ended: grant that I celebrate
you in the weight and sound of words and their bearing: after the
small ways a man is given privilege.
Lord live ever in me, rectify my praise toward your own truth:
my vigil ends, whose time is near.
I put upon my soul the shadows of flesh: I helmet my forehead
with the plumed mind:
Five ways my soul leans out of darkness: and watches
my God in all things:
Forth through the fields into the cities I fare: a servant,
singing to servants, of the doings and qualities of servants:
whose cause and being and prime business has ever been God's joy—[1]

UTK MS 3824 Box 7, Folder 1 [draft in Folder 4][2]

[Lord on your healthful earth this little way]

Lord on your healthful earth this little way
He walks in darkness opened five ways wide
From whom five ways my very God looks out
On God in all and all to man entrusted:
In whose dimensions and eternities
Of mind's contrivance and beyond all mind
Likewise all areas of his commonwealth
And differing glories each of all things made
Whose business chiefly is his praise forever
Are but as midges[a] dreamed before the sun
And stars marched round with suns are shadows merely
That faint in light on faced effacing light
In middle meeting middle light:
    Who breathes forth Gods: God:
Maker of nothing made of all things made maker:[1]

UTK MS 3824 Box 7, Folder 1 [two pages, one is a draft]

[a] Midges are any type of small fly. They are widespread throughout the world in other than extreme temperature zones.

[Great Lord whose lovely world this little way]

Great Lord whose lovely world this little way
I walk in darkness opened five ways wide
From whom five ways my God leans watchful out forth
On God in all and all to man entrusted:

I am of men a man built part of earth,
Minded as men are, breathed fair through with fire:
Whose mercy moves upon your servants ever[1]
Men up this triple wound in single joy:

I speak of earth and substance,
And if man, and of his doings and destinies,
I speak you praise in the weight and bearing of words,
Not truly, which is your privilege alone.

I only frame words as man's mind may:

Great God I cannot speak but it is yours:
So cleanse my soul that all things varying
Each in its self may show its Godly light
In all my song:

I am a servant singing to the servants of servants:[2]

UTK MS 3824 Box 7, Folder 1

[Lord God the eyes of animals]

Lord God the eyes of animals
Still steadily propound your grace:
In those plain eyes I still perceive
A meaning in my tortured race.

We ride the middle of a stream
A haystack broken on a flood:
How soon kind God how soon before
We reassemble into good?

When shall intermediate man
Accomplish your most dangerous dream?
Or are you, Lord, the last hope lost
And are things truly as they seem?[1]

UTK MS 3824, Box 7, Folder 2

[There is no longer singing here]

There is no longer singing here.
My voice, my hands, are weak with[1] words.
No hope remains, and so, no fear.
So, perhaps, it is with birds.

Their speech is formal as a flower.
It was a shape a root impounded.
No deviation in their power.
Never a phrase that is unfounded.

So may I learn? Not song, yet learn,
Hopeless, fearless, my heritage?
Somehow bring bloom, before I turn
To earth, to roots, that shaped my age?

No. With[2] the murmuring of the night,
The starved assembling of these words.
Grand from their graves hope, fear, are wrought.
No use to envy blooms and birds.

Fear is my root and hope the flower
Even in that cruel root impounded.
No deviation in my power.
Never a phrase that is unfounded.

They never doubted. From the world,
Imperious or modest[3], they
Took their desire with exact sure hands.
And made things of it which will stay.

And I, in terror, fumble at
A world I cannot surely touch,
Far less use well. And it is only
To me, that it can matter much.

Where the power of praise is small.
Worship (if God were kind) would be
No greater, and much fruitless grief[4]
Never be born, however, I am not He.
However, Lord, I am not thee.

UTK MS 3824, Box 7, Folder 2

Nature Poetry

[Earliest in the chary spring]

Earliest in the chary spring, the dogwood flowers.[a]
Cheating the spring time
As in the grief of nature[.]

Grieving is silenced and the open south
Receives him unlamenting.

Heaven composes shut. The latest puzzled
Grieving is silenced and the south
receives him unlamenting.

Here, moreover, subdued, the seed
Ponders[1] and shall display the usual flower.
And he, restored, bouncing on blooded twig,
Schemes out his spiritual music.

UTK MS 1500 Box 1, Folder 11

[a] Agee uses this line as most of the opening line of his "Sunday: Outskirts of Knoxville, Tennessee," but the poems are otherwise quite different.

(God of Summer)[1]

The brook winds on. The cattle tracks
Make dust along its edges.
A phoebe-bird[a] still swops for gnats
Above its stone-dry ledges.

Under old droppings by the ford
    The crickets build their cities.
Their ghosts are strong. Their song is long.
    Life with its millions pities

Fades in the sun. The brook winds on.
    The phoebe, worn with slaughter,
Quietly preens its frazzling wings
    Beside the glimmering water.

UTK MS 2730 Box 5 Folder 32

[a] The Eastern Phoebe is a fairly common flycatcher that is regarded as a harbinger of Spring. Its soft "fee-bee" song makes it easy to identify.

[He can't stand it forever]

He can't[1] stand it forever.
After a while his cramped legs quiet off,
The poor crab quits objecting on the hook,
    The smart fish sneer him past.

Take my advice, Boss,
Your bait's gone dead and useless. Scrap
This cheap cracked earth for something livelier
To unaccustomed pain: and try another cast.

Toss us to the small time nuzzling at the bottom
And tease the big boys on. Boss there are fish
Running these waters fit to freeze your dreams.
It takes real bait though. Ride on the hook yourself, you may
    Interest one at the last.

UTK MS 2730 Box 5 Folder 32

[I've got them all set]

I've got them all set: flies, spoons, live bait, big nets of nebulae
They travel, flutter, flash the light in every part of the sea.
But the best I had was a two-cent job I found in a sewage ditch.
He carried the tackle right out of my hands the crazy son of a bitch.

I hadn't thought much of him but I sort of liked his look
The funny thing about him was he seemed to like the hook.
He rode it like a hobby horse and he ate what tried to eat him,
He grew and grew and the time came when I couldn't even unseat him.

I tried with wars and wilting looks and the heaviest kinds of weather
And finally he got wise to the game and struck off hell for leather
The hell with you you bastard he shot back across his shoulder
I'll fry your ass in breadcrumbs before you're two days older.

Lord knows by this time where he's at or what the fool is doing.
I have a dirty feeling that I've set my troubles brewing:
So it's a comfort still to know there's a limit to his fun,
My little pal is strapped[a] against the wrong end of the gun.[1]

UTK MS 2730 Box 5 Folder 32

[a] Two slang meanings are also possible: to be in need (British) and to carry a gun (American).

[I would not try to touch]

I would not try to touch
The silken iridescence
Of a spider's web
In the sun.

Now I would not want to
(but wondered why I longed)
Touch this clammy greyness
Now that the sun has gone.

UTK MS 2730 Box 5 Folder 32

[Levied of the earth in evening]

Levied of the earth in evening,
Flowering for the fallen sun,
Cooled and in the air compounded:
Now your errands are begun.

Soon with sweet insinuation
Slow the air, stoll[a] the air,
Stand above your steadying shadow,
Delay, deliver up your share.

Lie down on our miles of easy
Land and on our olive seas:
Smile on these for these are ready:
Darkly smile and smiling, die.

Earth drinks you and shines with you.
So your errands all are done.
Now the fainting sun requires you
And your errands are begun.

UTK 2730 Box 5 Folder 32

[a] To support or prop.

[Now springtime wakes our maidens]

Now springtime wakes our maidens
To seasonelle joys;
Pleasure is also in season
For boys.[1]

Now, now, in fullest[2] flower
Virginal fires try
My whole heart:[3]
New, new love,
For which I die.

The nightingale sings of it[4]
So ardently,
His singing sets to burning[5]
My very soul.

You are the very flower
To me, to me,
Of girls, the rose of roses
As often I see.[6]

Your promise crowns my heart
In peace and joy.
Your scorn must that same heart
Promptly destroy.[7]

Famished by need by your[8]
Virginity;
Forbidden you by your
Simplicity.

UTK MS 2730 Box 5 Folder 32

[Voided—the sky]

Voided—the sky, light[1]
Still trembles perishing on all the night:
The marching shadows are all met:
Shade grows: shade grows:
O threefold subtle altering air:
Thou chaliced earth in tender changing air:

That summons forth the creatures of the dark
    Upon the dark:
    And of the day,
Estranges of the day:

One hooky hand ahold,
Spread, spread the lanky cold
Wing on the dark
Plumb from the bark
    Spread

Halt high safe:
By that shadow on your eye,
Blundering rove the hungry night:

He stirs: the flatwing[a] that embraced the twig, he stirs,
Now shines his seeing eye, and shines,
His cramped feet clambering slow,
    And flaws upon the dark, the moon-eyed moth:
By that hunger on your heart,
Range, range,   the lost light:[2]

UTK MS 2730 Box 5 Folder 32

[a] Also known as an Australian flatwing, the common flatwing (Austroargiolestes icteromelas) is a species of damselfly.

[Now on the water forehead is]

Now on the water forehead is
    Enchantment of the winter time:
The brown earth bird inextricate
    Not struggles in the blanchèd lime:

And not in all the blind of noon
Does any creature of the Sun[1]
Find ever clue to lend him claim
Remembrance of a kindlier clime.[2]

UTK MS 3824 Box 6, Folder 36[3]

[Heaven shuts][a]

Heaven shuts: At length the latest
Grieving is silenced and the ample south
Accepts him unlamenting.

Here, moreover, subdued, the seed
Meditates and shall publish the usual flower.

And he, restored, bounding on bloodied twig,
Schemes out his spiritual music.[1]

UTK MS 3824 Box 6, Folder 36

[a] This poem is a variant of "[Soft heaven shuts: at length the latest]."

[Shelved, under their stone labels]

Shelved under their stone labels, all around the earth,
No matter what their hungry past, our tasteless future,[1]
Poor straws of harvests the new sun ignores,
Now can we let them rest?
They flowered out of the dark: wore out their time: went down:
Blood strolled in his red shadow down their avenues,
Stands in us and steps through us: we go down to them:
All that was ardent which is now the air
Survives them, and works on us, and we serve.
By all means not neglect:
Stars and their darkness stun us to our size[.]

UTK MS 1500 Box 1, Folder 11

[Lists, like a deck, our continent]

Lists, like a deck, our continent
Upon the dark: Alaska lifts
Losing the light and lost, now hide
The chicken archipelagoes[a]:

Siberia like a peaceful whale
Blows in the pastures of the dawn:
And smiling on the sun the earth
Is gladness and is Russia[1]:

Spring is broached in that large land
Like no spring the earth has known:
And the travelling sun delivers
Joy in all the backward earth:[2]

UTK MS 1500 Box 1, Folder 12

[a] Since Agee also (in one draft) records the line "The chicken islands of the sea," he apparently is referring to the Hen and Chicken Islands that lie to the east of the North Auckland Peninsula off the coast of northern New Zealand.

[Broil in the frowsy clover crowds of thirst]

Broil in the frowsy clover crowds of thirst
Where knives sleep[1] the dry sweetness to the barn:
Some win the dark waxed hive and some the crib[a]:
This racing summer day is not the first.

The marvelous[2] hostage of each flower to where
Means much to bees and little to the blades:
The angelic bees, who rape what ripened brows they may
Do not expect the individual flowers to know or care.[3]

UTK MS 3824 Box 7, Folder 2 [typescript]

[a] Cribs are often in barns and serve as storage places for fodder or pens for grazing animals.

Transfiguration

A stone wall wedged apart the earth and sky,
And on the hilltop checked[1] the plow's advance
On nature; on one side were the torn fields
Where men designed to rob the abundant earth
Of what she did not freely deign to give.
Beyond the wall, the slope that I remembered
From other summer days in other years,
And loved for the tumbled pine, for the green torrent
Of grass that foamed about the starved grey stones—
By what strange alchemy of flame I know not,
That grey and barren slope had been transformed
From granite into[2] jewels of two kinds—
Black pearls upon an interwoven background
Of tarnished emeralds cut in pointed ovals.

Then, as I picked my way among the bushes,
Staining my mouth and fingers with their spoil,
I heard a startled movement in the brake
Where the land folded to caress a brook,
And at the same time noting that the bushes
Beyond me were stripped ruthlessly of fruit,
Glanced down, and saw a pathway rilling off
Toward the water's edge, and on the path
The imprint of a goat's hooves. "Strange,"[3] I thought
"And shameful, too, that a mere goat should have
The[4] choice of all this treasure," and resumed
My berry-picking, berry-eating way.
Becoming thirsty, as one always does
Who finds the sweetest, wealthiest of bushes,
I made my way through the locked branches toward
The brook I could hear dragging its chained bells
Through the dark, tangled brake. And once again
Finding the print of hooves, I followed them,
Thankful this time, to him, goat or no goat,
Who led me through this jeweled maze, and to
(I doubted not) the best of water-holes.

As I expected, the hoof-prints emerged
Upon a hollowed crescent of white sand.
But here, where tracks were clearer than before,
Were fewer hoof-prints than a goat should have—
A single pair I saw, and even these
No more, within a few feet of the water—
Only the print of a recumbent body,
The gentlest of troughs in the white sand—
Then, half obliterated by the water
That passed in thin blades over it—a hand![5]

UTK MS 3824 Box 4, Folder 3 [typescript]

Vegetable tribes.

Vegetable earth lives by the season,
Other tribes not.
Talk like water slopped from
A carried bucket.

Wake up to the "real," edged things.
Probably troubles among vegetables.
Turtle: long ago shut up in shell.

Lay out pieces are shaped which
Ultimately may close around it.
Things I have known and why
Not used.

UTK MS 3824 Box 6, Folder 35

[O dolphin earth][1]

Flows into shadow while upon her breadth
The vegetable races and the tribes
Of grieving[2] busy flesh relax, whole America,
Fledged in her pale wet shores.
Evening breathes like a tired beast an arrived locomotive[3]: cold black in dark the dew.
Glosses on all designs of the earth purely, purely.[4]
On levels of the shadowed earth and on the levels of the sky
Startling, the answering lights. of homes; of stars:
Slenderly, pale and wrinkling[5], smokes,
Riddle the shallower precincts of the dark:
And through the dark:
Where the land is shaken like a table cloth between her mountains, steadily[6]
With innumerable talking music the Mississippi,
From mountain crests, from little nervous brooks[7]
From all the sleepy levelings of her valley
Like sap in wintering tree,
Draws down her waters in the sheltered Gulf:[8]
And steadily
That was when man was not and which shall be
When man is folded in his destiny
Throes that tremendous siphon
Which brings up England's roses.
Salt waters on their shapeless bellies up the land a little way
Follow the drawling moon: let out their breath again.
While last Alaska loses of the light:[9]
Her steep shores climb the night still chiming cold.
The chicken archipelagoes[a]
Hide in that mothering wing and now
Siberia like a peaceful whale
Blows in the pastures of the stars—

UTK MS 3824 Box 6, Folder 35

[a] Agee is apparently is referring to the Hen and Chicken Islands that lie to the east of the North Auckland Peninsula off the coast of northern New Zealand.

[Space is salted thin and we are small[a]][1]

Space is salted thin and we are small:
Our steepest memory runs down like a clock
In ultimate disarmament: the slick earth bowls in the sun,
Sun tranced[2], proliferous chance branches its races:
Assume, ignore such brackets.
All these flowers stand from a simple root
And wither to it.
Yet now, examine our particular flower
Peculiar to this season. Narrow your eyes:[3]
Thread needles with our eyesight.

Here are findings: few conclusions:

The vegetable race: lives in the rhythm of the sun.
The races of flesh: by others, though they die without it.
At the equator: life is most fiercely circular: continually eating itself.
At the poles: death.

UTK MS 3824 Box 6, Folder 36

[a] The reader may wish to compare this poem to "[O dolphin earth]."

[Up time convulsion flowered us]

Up time convulsion flowered us. Of what fright
First caught and calmed we mercy, and whence love.
Tell me, and why our need is knowing, and how dreamed we faith,
And these discriminations.

Our dearest lives, our loves,
These are most chancy matters;
Like apples swung together on a brook,
We bump out population and bear down
To eddying hopes of death; then charms the ice.[1]

Elaborate sports, anxieties, acquisitions,
Discriminations, comradeships, and wraths,
Some few apart: one watched into the sun,
Long after, all he said was uncommon;
So on the wide warmed threshold played the children
Whom sundown brought to bed, and dark undressed[.][2]

UTK MS 3824 Box 6, Folder 36

Marrying dance.

Spring comes again for whom the earth
Breaks open new harmonious birth:
All things for love in love embrace,
The birds their marrying dances lace[a],
And rich swing of her shaken hair
Such grove is fresh and bridal fair:

Tomorrow in the spreaded shade
That of this veiléd grove is laid
The Queen of love shall wreathe their crests
And myrtles into arches wrest:[1]

UTK MS 3824 Box 6, Folder 36

[a] Entwine or merge together.

[Clean out of sky][a1]

Clean out of sky, light
Still trembles famishing on all the night:
The marching shadows all are met:
Shade grows, shade grows:

O threefold subtle altering air,
Then chaliced world[1] in changing air:
That summons out the creatures of the dark
Upon the dark:
Food of the day estranges
Of the day:

One hooky hand ahold: spread, spread the lanky cold
Wing on[2] the dark: plumb from the bark on falling air spread, hall safe high:
By that shadow on your eye,
Blundering range the hungry night:

Slur, dimmed air, the green fur:
He stirs: the flatwing[b] that embraced the twig, he stirs: now shines the
shutless eyes and shines:
Who shuddereth his sheen of fur: his cramped feet clambering slow:
and flows upon the nights
The mooneyed moth: by that ancestral wound, range, range the
lost light night:[3]

UTK MS 3824 Box 6, Folder 36

[a] See the related poem "[Starred from the sky]."

[b] Also known as an Australian flatwing, the common flatwing (Austroargiolestes icteromelas) is a species of damselfly.

[Hunched slung above his guileless eyed mild sighing bride][1]

Hunched slung above his guileless eyed mild sighing bride
Who brunts the bulk her stiff four posted stride
Staves in the wincing warmth that strains him of the power
The bull, back, crackarched: bee trembling rides a flower.[1]

Broil in the frowsy clover crowds of thirst
Where knives sweep[2] dry the virgin sweetness to the barn:
Some win the dark wax hive and some the crib:
This racing summer day is not the first:

The marvelous[3] hostage of each flower to where
Means much to bees and nothing to the blades:
The angelic bees who rape what ripened brows they may
Do not expect the individual flowers to know, or care.

UTK MS 3824 Box 6, Folder 36 [two pages][4]

[I think that in their honey cells]

I think that in their honey cells
In all the earth the emptied ones
Lift out tonight their smiles upon us here:
They gathered and here bank their honey. This honey bank.
Stone labels in our memory.

Stone labels them for memory[1]
As short as theirs.
Epitaphs efface each other.[2]

UTK MS 1500 Box 1, Folder 11

[Where the dolphin leisurely bowling]

Where the dolphin leisurely bowling his distinguished fins

This dolphin bowling in continual light. Dolphins of heaven.
Night, a slow barge starbarna[c]led, overslides us : we are wiped out.
We are wiped under shadow and we sleep.
Shawled up the cage in silence.[1]

UTK MS 1500 Box 1, Folder 11

[Starred from the sky]

Starred from the sky, light:
Still trembles famishing on all the night:
The marching shadows all are met:
    Shade grows: shade grows:
That summons out the creatures of the dark:
    Upon the dark:
And of the day, estranges of the day:
O threefold subtle altering air:
O chaliced world in changing air:

One hooky hand ahold, spread, spread the lasting cold,
    Wing on the dark, plumb from the bark spread, halt, safe, high:
    By that shadow on your eye, blundering range the hungry night:
He stirs, the flatwing[a] that embraced the twig, he stirs; now shines his seeing
    Eye, and shines, his cramped feet clambering slow,
    And flows upon the night, the mooneyed moth:
        Range, range, the lost light.[b1]

UTK MS 3824 Box 7, Folder 2

[a] Also known as an Australian flatwing, the common flatwing (Austroargiolestes icteromelas) is a species of damselfly.

[b] See the related poem "[Clean out of sky]."

[For now of the light of day the utmost remembrance]

For now of the light of day the utmost remembrance
Fails from the sunflower's helpless foot:
For now quite finished the[1] lionlike flower of day[2].
    Its grand, burned eye, one blinded brown,
    Stares soberly in all its future towards its grave,
    Its seed stares towards the root;
        And now:
    Now of the light of day the utmost remembrance
    Fails in the sunflower's helpless foot:

UTK MS 2730 Box 6, Folder 16 [photocopy]; *JAR*, p. 251.

Version 2

[For now of the light of day the utmost recollection]

For now of the light of day the utmost recollection
Fails in the sunflower's helpless foot:
    And that fierce flower which through the day
    Wheeled like a lion upon the lionlike sun,
    Its great burned eye one blended brown[3]
    Heavily hangs as noon,
    Its future gazing on its grave.

UTK MS 2730 Box 6, Folder 16 [photocopies of poem and draft]

Barnyard rolled before the sun and fell again.

Our barnyard rolls before the sun and over and is ever done.
Fungoid tatter of trees. The fungoid tatter that is trees—
Shelled and hulled in living air.
Our barnyard rolls[1] before the sun and over and is quiet[2] again.
The beam that stands creation; this foisted child.
The foisted terror that is child.
Trouble among our trees. Troubling spring.
The last anger's on you?
I do not wrestle as I think this wind.
Such wind is doom, we wrestle only as the forest branch.
Wrestling the forest's darkness.
What wind, wrestling the crowded[3] forest,
Wind, wrestler of crowding forest, flares the field,
Playing the pastures like a wounded snake.[4]

UTK MS 1500 Box 1, Folder 11

[THE TINDERING STARS]

THE TINDERING STARS.   RUSTLING SNOW.   SNOW CREPT.
WALKING ON Snow as on wheat. SNOW SHUT THE LAND.
SHUT The year.
    SHUT AROUND HIM,
he walked inside a pearl.   TINDER STARS. STORAGE OF STARS.

WATER MILLING & moiling[a] above the fall, calming at the lip in prescience.
WATER LAY LIKE A BOARD.   HAIRY GRASS.   WATER LEVELLING
THE FIELD.   DARK MOUNTAIN RIVERS PAVED WITH NUDGING
LOGS.   JOSTLING LOGS.
IN THE CLOCK THE JOISTLING WHEELS (TEETH). The wheels
delicately taste each other.
Wheels taste and turn each other. TASTING THE TIME THEY TURN.
NATURAL.
THE COIL RELAXES; THE WHEELS DELICATELY TASTE THE TIME
THEY TURN;
    NEBULAE.
SPRING NEBULAE.
SIGHT   HEARING   TOUCH   SMELL   TASTE[b]

TASTING THE EARTH.   TASTE EXHAUSTION. ANGER. LUST.
LIFE IS A WOUND which builds it many scabs.   SLACK, CASUAL WING.
THE world a thimble.   TOUGH LEAVES. AIR.

AS WATER CALMS BEFORE THE LIP of the DAM.   SPILLS.
    CITY FEELINGS.   FAMILY BRUTALITIES.

UTK MS 1500 Box 1, Folder 11; *JAR*, p. 208

[a] Moiling means to move around in an agitated or confused fashion.
[b] Arrows from "SMELL" and "TASTE" point to next line.

Political Poems

Eureka

Fellows by the living Jingo[a]
Nationalism's a damn fine thing-o!
We can prop the crumbling state
By properly directing hate.

UTK MS 2730 Box 5 Folder 14 [typescript]

[a] A strong supporter of aggressive nationalism; it also serves as a political label for a group holding those beliefs.

Allegiance Dream[1]

Four plates of bay window bring the sun burning in.
Gold oak, grey gristle in smoothed oak.

The floor is narrow oak, new, grayed with polish.
The sideboard's front of oak is parchment thin.
Silver smiles there. Cut glass. A delicate cloth.
Two candlesticks. A portrait of dead fowl, hung by their plated ankles: not alert
This chair: joined lethal slabs of oak: I sit in.

There is a taboret[a] before each window.
Each holds a glazed pot: within each, a red.
In each red pot, damp earth; a spout of fern.
The glazed pots are molded into leaves.
The bright glazed pots are iron red, iron yellow.
Fronds of the fern are rusted by the sun.

The major is in front of me; standing; legs apart.
The lady of the house stands at my left.
He is in uniform; yellow puttees[b]
Hard on his calves: iced toes: iron-hard high collar.

She is in uniform. A drifted print:
Whited like cool air on wandering grease:
Her bosom a fray of white: hands held like a singer's.

His cheek is thick with muscle. His mouth is tight.
His eyes are murdering blue: citizens' eyes.
He watches me, and waits.

Her cheek is dusty pink and lavender
Her pleated mouth is blood. She watches me.

They wait. They wait and watch me. Wait me out.

Sun[2] blears my eyesight green.
Ferns, oak and leather, drawn of their dreadful tinctures, stain the air.

Far off, in all the earth, in that huge silence,
In cellars, in factory yards, country roads,
Lonely, by thousands for the great earth's millions,
My friends are fighting, and are found, and killed.
I am sixteen.

The brown wool spirals my calves. R. O. T. C.
Grease stripes my right shoulder.
I should have had my hair cut.
Better have shaved than fuzz.

They are waiting.

Waiting; they know the truth of me: waiting:

Now shall we take you out against the wall?
In all the miles of cities on this earth.
Deep in the mines. Cleansing the noon-white air
Of servitude, they are busy in their danger.

The price of liberty.
We find you out. Betrayal of your kin.
Murder your mother. Undermine the column
And dome of our Republic.

We are waiting.

I get up, cold with sickness and the odors.
I pledge allegiance to the American Flag
And to this country for which it stands.
One nation, indivisible,
With liberty
And Justice
For all.

My hand droops from my temple and he grabs it,
Rapes it in earnest iron. Saved, my boy.

Sounds of a hen in heat flow from the lady:
She flows against, enfolds me.

Her mouth's vermillion suet. From her breasts
Spreads[3] a white rush of talcum: floods my nostrils.

Ten thousand yards of water weigh me under
And I march out to murder.

UTK MS 2730 Box 7, Folder 23 [3 pages; photocopy]

[a] A taboret is a small stool or table.

[b] Popular in World War I, a puttee is a covering for the calf of the leg wrapped from the ankle to the knee to keep water out of a soldier's boot. It was also intended to gives added leg support and protection from battlefield hazards and in emergencies could also serve as a bandage.

My Uncle Sammy sent me

My Uncle Sammy sent me
and my dear old mammy meant me
and my sweet patootie[a] sent me
    To be blown to hell.[1]

UTK MS 1500 Box 1, Folder 11; *JAR*, p. 203.

[a] A "patootie" is slang for an attractive girl or a girlfriend; it also is a slang term for someone's buttocks, again usually female. For example, Jack "Pal" Smurch, James Thurber's protagonist in his 1931 short story "The Greatest Man in the World," uses the term to describe his girlfriend.

[They sit on inner tubes]

They sit on inner tubes near high windows behind private lines[a]; their
buzzers for beck and call are like Whurlizter[b] dashboards;
They go up and down on elevators that say uhh and uhh, and
their bird dogs are very busy lifting their legs at each other in
Washington.[1]

UTK MS 1500 Box 1, Folder 11

[a] Individual telephone service as opposed to party lines which shared services among multiple customers.

[b] A play on (or misspelling of) Wurlitzer, an iconic brand of jukebox in the Big Band era. It could also be the Wurlitzer organs that graced many of the old movie theaters as a holdover from the days of silent films. Both could be said to have large "dashboards."

[When I was young I thought the world]

When I was young I thought the world
A funny place where I and he
Loved so much and lived so little:
    But God meant this to be.

And when our children rose around us
Lean and sullen as you see,
I thought the world must owe them better
    But God meant this to be.

And when my husband got the bullet
    In his belly, seemed to me
Picketers were treated rotten:
    But God meant this to be.

He meant this world to be a place
Where some were fat and some were thin
And some had hunger in their face
And some had bellys like a bin:

And all the rich should grab the chance
To wring the flesh from off the slave,
And all the skeletons should dance
To see the far side of the grave:

He meant to make it so the race
Was poor enough to take it meek
And sick enough to know his face
Where hungry dreams play hide and seek:[a]

UTK MS 1500 Box 1, Folder 11

[a] See "[It is not right that you should cry]" which may be a companion poem.

[Like pregnant girls admiring]

Like pregnant girls admiring round a mother new delivered[1]
Europe and the Americas, all the Orient, the comely lands,
Huge with their time and happily with Russia in the sun
Work and await that agony which yields life into their hands.[2]

UTK MS 1500 Box 1, Folder 12

[All your work, the way this world]

All your work, the way this world
Is run, it chains you to your graves.
Death does a pretty hand-me-down:
Your own chains make your children slaves.

Yes, these chains, they fit you bad,
They're really badly out of place.
Find the man who locked them there
For gain, and break them on his face.[1]

UTK MS 1500 Box 1, Folder 12

[Honestly, the way things are]

Honestly, the way things are,
And decency, the way things go,
Kindness, the way the world is run
Are not for people like you and me.
Are pleasure a poor man can't afford.[a1]

UTK MS 1500 Box 1, Folder 12

[a] See also a variant poem—"[Those kinds of loving which the lord]."

[Those kinds of loving which the lord]

Those kinds of loving which the lord
Insisted were our only joy
Are privileges of the rich,
Pleasures a poor man can't afford.[1]

UTK MS 1500 Box 1, Folder 12

[There are gentlemen in politics today]

There are gentlemen in politics today.
And it looks like things will never be the same.
They do us dirt the gentlemanly way:
    Sing a high low Jack[a] and the Game.

They hail from big establishments up-river,
And I don't mean Ossining.
And their uncles died of liquor on the liver.
    Sing a hey-ding-ding-Sing-Sing.[b]

They inherit the American tradition
(Landed gentry to you)
So you need not worry much about sedition:
    That is much too too-too-too.

They went to school at Choate and Taft and Groton[c]
Where all Church-of-England-boys-of-good-family go:
Where they learned irregular verbs and the more refined ways of snottn[d]
    Praise God from whom all blessings flow.

They finished off at Harvard and at Yale,
(The fellowship of educated men)
And caught a piece of debutanted tail[e]
    And rose at a quarter past ten.

And boned on[f] political economy
(Mon Wed Fri at eleven-fifteen)
And learned the meaning of the word autonomy
    (If you gather what I mean.)[1]

UTK MS 1500 Box 1, Folder 12

[a] High Low Jack is a card game also known as Pitch.

[b] The verse also refers to Sing Sing, the maximum security prison located in Ossining, NY (mentioned two lines previously), on the Hudson River, about 30 miles north of New York City. The "big establishments" may refer to a slang term for prison, the "big house."

[c] All prestigious preparatory private schools (as was Phillips Exeter from which Agee graduated) whose students are groomed for admission to Ivy-League universities.

[d] Being "snotty," stuck-up or aloof.

[e] A "piece of tail" is a slang term, usually for a woman, with whom one wishes to engage in sexual activity.

[f] "boned on" refers to the subject that they studied, but may also be a phallic reference that follows the previous mention of a "piece of tail."

A Package for this Year

I

Rifle fire out of the East—a bitter
Range in the red sun, leveler of all
And shadower of men on the sweet hills

Greening above the mist: blue glacial shadows
Hollow to westward where the faces peer
On surgical terrains lit by the faint fire

Of spring and dawn and war:

Smoke drifting as a frost breath drifting
Home among the orchards: stir, encampments
Clanking with soft metal in the vast

Azure of danger:
hushed on the hot ground
Where one man's crying mouth breaks stones
Leaves, leather, dusty earth, and shuts up soaking:

Flash at eye-lash, and the needle-bright bombers
Borne by scourging savagery of engines
In sensitive chevrons under purest cirrus

Drift and dream on:

II

We were never instructed in these quarrels.
The power and the inheritance were not ours,
Neither the whip-handle of any belted captain.
We fought against our fathers for our sport.

At the filling station and the small-town movie
We pulled on tunics, took the company pose.

Our factions rose and fell in opposing bleachers
On amber afternoons of frosty October.

All men were neither tigers nor our brothers.
All our lives were not divisions in charts.
All orators were not exclusively for us.
All countries oversea were distant to us as death.

III

When night has cast his dreadful shade
And the great sphere inclines
Eastward and weightless, grade by grade
Sacred Arcturus shines.

And cold as starlight through the grove
Where summer's wrestlers lie
The gliding firefly shines on love
With phosphorescent thigh.

But eastward where vast history wanes
The dust-cloud armies gleam
And Europe's dark magnetic plains
Glow under nodes of dream,

Whose ether fever's rippling prayer
Breaks on our Western sill.
Through all the sighing lands the fair
Sleepers will not be still.

IV

And the rifle butt falls on the shore
By the quiet path where yesterday's
Immaculate questioners
Tracked down desire. Think, child,
All that is done without remorse
In this sensuous summer dusk
Was dreamed then by the dry-mouthed dreamers.
O lakes where the green glaciers sleep.

O mountains fuming cloud,
Be mindful, remember their bondage.

And the pale priest who bears his oil[a]
To the still bed in night time
Hears each tragedian weep.
Dear child, who should see paradise,
I'd thee absolve of thy mortality
That flourished from immortal time
Like the cold room of cankered tree
That made Christ's blinding rood.
On mother within mother, a winding sheet
Stained with rouge and blood.

The vacuum roars in the press rooms,
And the soft announcer's voice clips
Into a beating music.
By rivers, under footlighted cities,
The compact locomotives jostle
Luminous, loud in the night;
The wings of roaring funfighters
Waggle in grey cloud-hung squadrons:
Combustive music, power beyond power,
Rending and rest for the heart.

V

The clouds' procession, majesty and dispersal,
The wind that blows all day from the warm west,
The blue-grass pastures and the burnished corn
Undulant under the shimmer of mid-summer;

The roughening miles of rye and the rippling wheat fields,
The red foal and the colt with the girl's eyes,
The sweet hay fallen, the clean swathe in the timothy,
The cattle under the elms by the cool water;

For this the old men fought with their crooked hands,
Plowing the loam crust in the bitter spring,
Getting their bellies full with the threshers' moon,

And warm wives bedded for the crackling winter.

Consider if your commerce on the great sea
Or over the frosty and exquisite mountains
Rumors the failure of these men and their land.

They waken every spring. They hold the passes.

Over the North and South their communion comes.

VI

Caught in the notch of the sights and held there,
Screwed two points for wind[b] . . . the frozen squirrel
Knocked down, adorable, from the walnut bough.

The Winchester also won the Indian Wars
By bolt action and by force of repetition;
A sweet piece; sweet and hot for the cavalry
After ambrosial Custer's Colt grew cold.

Now rapid as woodpeckers in evening trees
Or riveters in shipyard; fed for percussion
Steel-jacketed decimals out of belts in boxes[c];
Wickedly weighted, bandy and low-slung,
These marvels beat the jungle's yellow eyes.
By night flame splinters from their searching muzzles—
Or when you see that dust kicked up, flop down.

Spider-legged lightning dances miles.
While yellow stormcloud and black sighing trees
Flare under his great riding, his fiery veins
Branch to dark earth in thunder.
The finer canned goods
Available in 500 lb. and one ton cylinders
By industrial logic make his strokes look tender.

This theatre is everywhere, all the world,
And all the men and women snapshots merely,
Lit by the cold instantaneous street scene.

When wind blows here there's bloody murder done;
Such separation of the cellular form
No ligatures will tie what's torn together.
The quiet earth, great arch, God's equipoise
Spouting the solar gases . . . Smoking and crying
Till comic sirens die in the silent newsreel.

VII

Friends, take a good look at this
Late lamented son of a bitch whose mama
And papa gave the boy all the advantages
Of a nice school and a university
Education and a nifty little
Chrysler all his own on his twenty-first
Birthday; just step a little closer,
O my friends, and examine this highly
Interesting, highly valued, highly
Civilized young fellow whose curly head
Was recently emptied permanently of all
Those highly captivating wise-cracks
Those little audacities all the girls used to
Love; O look here, friends,
His manly chest ain't human, no it ain't,
It's crawling just crawling with
Whatever it is that crawls all over a
Dead young fellow when he can't help
It; nope, the poor guy can't do a
Thing just as if he couldn't ever
Do anything and maybe that's a fact, buddy,
But it's a damn shame he has to spoil.

VIII

The sparrows chipping on the boulevards
And the velvet light on the lawns
In the old provinces.
Carriages covered in linen
And the horses' fetlocks twinkling,
The fine spokes glittering. Clop clop. Creak.

Then tenders of machines, valve readers, skilled
Oilers and handlers of waste, slow moving
Among shining and whining lathes and cutters.
"Here was his hand and there was his fingers
Lay right over there." Trainmen in mist
Softly waving their lights;
The dusty builders in the stencil of sunlight.

To free those prisoned defeated in cities:
To make of their many hands one iron pressure:
To unchain and train that power:

Scholars have risen from the world's disorder,
Sleepless when the stars fade, silent
Keepers of history, their bodily will
Geared to the majestic transit of heaven;
Pliant as whips, at ease in multitudes,
Beloved and unloving, responsible.

They have given arms to the people.
They have made the people an army.
They have plotted the gun pits and the aerodromes.

Though they suckle thin breasts in the South
Or dangle sleigh ropes in the Christmas snow,
All is ordained for this earth's delicate children.
Or is it all ordained?

Let them not serve abstraction with lies.
The power fails among the unperceptive,
The bitter captains brawl, the pilots rage,
And the great cities sift toward the streams.

Let their care be constantly at home,
Their marksmanship rare as justice;
Slowly may they learn the earth
In the mastered and peaceful seasons,
The new tongues, the literatures like spring;
O let their rooms be caskets of the sun,
Unshaded by haute of towers;

Their russet hearths at evening
By theatres to old men's eyes.

IX

Wanderers in unrestful time,
For you the sunset and the rhyme;
Brilliant in the thicket there
Where time's the only traveler.

The June-bug and the moth at night
Fly to your lonely summer light;
The locust's lamentation dies
In the hour of moonrise.

Guests and strangers in that tower
Where playing Love has still his power,
You shall hear the Golden Age
Rustle from the poet's page;

Among the distant starry things
See bright Saturn in his rings;
Keepsakes children hold in trust
And all the creatures of the dust.

By the crone and droning sea
You shall listen merrily,
And still remember what was told,
When you are abstinent and old.

UTK MS 3824 Box 6, Folder 35 [typescript, five pages]

[a] Likely, given the following line, the oil used in the "Anointing of the Sick," formerly known as extreme unction or last rites, in the Roman Catholic and Eastern Orthodox churches.

[b] These actions are for aiming and adjusting a rifle for accurate firing.

[c] Agee refers here to the World War II machine guns mounted on a bipod or tripod that automatically fired ammunition mounted on belts from a metal box.

[Race of breathing man on these round lands who labor]

Race of breathing man on these round lands who labor:
How very long there has been hunger in you, I know:
How very long there has been knowing in you, I know:
And what through what long time, thus twice possessed, you have done:
        I know:
And how as arduously you wove the wind into your flesh
So was it raveling, surely backward,
Your generations all derangéd dust.
All darkness high and backward:
You as a rill of fire on a field of grass
And all behind gone black:
Laborious forward rill of fire: where in this field?

And what you are who have now the breath in you,
Flesh field, that breath of fire:
How hunger and knowing are still harmful within you:
What harm this time has made you which you made:
How you are bowed down and beating with harm among yourselves
and hopeless:
Stunned and stunned to scorn and reckless with need and knowing: I know:

UTK MS 3824 Box 6, Folder 35

[Twentieth century, honest and merciless ear]

Twentieth century, honest and merciless ear,
Enforce my mouth that key
Which shelves up strength, cleanness and nobleness
All in one way of words that is your own,
And in your shapes of rhythm.

Gigantic time, all future of the earth
In wrenching labor;
Gigantic present who pours up from the past
Such shock and marvel as smothers out the past,
Pot that boils out the fire;

March of new monster no less marvelous[1]
And more prophetic than those lizard bulks---
All turned, self-rending, drinking its own blood
As siphon jungles in continual summer
Thrive on continual death:

Where now first time in earth, intelligence
Trains all its lights on good; and where
Knowledge awakened runs in her usual rills[2]
And lifts the peoples in one wave
That walks the whole earth clean, a place for living.

Earth where stupidities unmatched in cruelty in all time past,
Bristle like knitted thorns; and are the law; and where
Patiently whole populations
Breathe from their birth the poisons of the soul,
Where every child is crippled, and every slave[3]
Lives only to enslave; where kindliness
And decent living are a privilege
Bought only with the blood that cancels them.
And all good is an accident—[4]

                    Just there,
Called off for lunch, an hour in the sweet sun,

Toasting my belly in the pleasant noon,[5]
Swelling my eyes half shut against the sun,
Enter reflections, enter placidity,
The Boswell Sisters[a6] of the would be brain
Massaging with their voices.
A large old man stood knee deep in the surf
Lonely and talking with his dog.
The small dog labored, silly in the water.
Bearing to mind the overlapping of the races,
Amusement, pity, and joy: to be known
Only with easy mildness, and to be
Not harpooned, but surrounded as in jelly,
A feather treasured up in amber thought:
Closures in quartz of water which made free
Trims under the lens the terrible dances[.]

Surely in this shell world I
Battle the thickets of the absolute storm,
Die if it so be, if luck be, walk those treacheries out
Now handled into heaven and now let down so low
The pale froth hides the mast:
Steadily up on the straight and strength of terror
Cramp the sail flat: with bullet stand that bullet
Back in its fuming bore.

Life is less living than all dark of death
That will not of its entire strength of being
Nail to the absolute: that delays, refuses
And welters in the leisures of the air
Its lapsed geometries.

How life lies out of me like easy blood
I watch from twenty bridges.

And therefore now: between this breath and the next:
Force all your forces to the murder of fear,
Drown shame deeps as the bottom yields, if the need be
And one need must be in you,
Assassinate intelligence beyond fear and mercy.
Annihilate those thoughtful second thoughts

That close above the first before the first
Are born to breathe in air.

Oh, if you must,
Provide your difficult way one breathing help,
That being, assault and tear those things on paper
Private, and useless to the others' ears
Though they must be; wring them away and dry.
A storm's a storm: you must not glibly hope
The immediate bowels of the general action.
Travel your troubles first to the living spine:
First step your mast: then start.[7]

UTK MS 3824 Box 6, Folder 36 [three pages with a fourth draft page]

[a] The three Boswell Sisters were an American close-harmony jazz and swing singing trio who were noted for their intricate harmonies and rhythmic experimentation. They recorded their first album in 1925 and became internationally popular in the first half of the 1930s.

[Fragments of Proletarian Verse]

This'll be the story of a funny sort of man
And I'll tell it if at all on the installment plan
And I warn you in the first place to take your time,
It's a long long pull and a hard hard climb.

Johnny was the fellow who escaped the noose,
He talked with Jesus and cooked Hitler's goose,
He fucked a lot of women and he drank a lot of wine
And he organized the walkout in the Homestead Mine[a].

He did a lot of other things I won't tell here

This is the story of the craziest guy
That ever took a notion to grow up and die
In the general commotion of the present day

Hard times all with us and they're here to stay
Till everyone is marching on the first of May[1b]

UTK MS 3824 Box 6, Folder 36

[a] The last part of the word is overwritten and unclear, but Agee is apparently referring to the Homestead strike, also known as the Homestead steel strike; it was a pivotal event in U.S. labor history. It began as an industrial lockout and strike on July 1, 1892, but culminated in a battle between strikers and private security agents on July 6, 1892.

[b] May 1 is International Workers' Day, or Labor Day in many nations, and is a celebration of workers and the working classes without distinction of a particular country; it is often promoted by socialist and communist political parties who are opposed to capitalistic systems.

[It is not right that you should cry]

It is not right that you should cry
For soup, and warmth, and pretty games,
And ask me all these reasons why,
And call the lucky children names.[1]

I'll tell you now, I'll tell you true,
God will not love you if you do.

God meant us to be meek and mild
And thankful for our humble lot:
Your father was a Godless wild
Picketer: and he was shot.

God wants us for his own, my dears,
And tests our love the funniest ways,
For every day brings fresher fears
We never shall see better days.

And every day the rich get more,
And every day the poor get less,
No wonder that we set such store[a2]

UTK MS 1500 Box 1, Folder 11

[a] The poem ends at this point. See "[When I was young I thought the world]" which may be a companion piece.

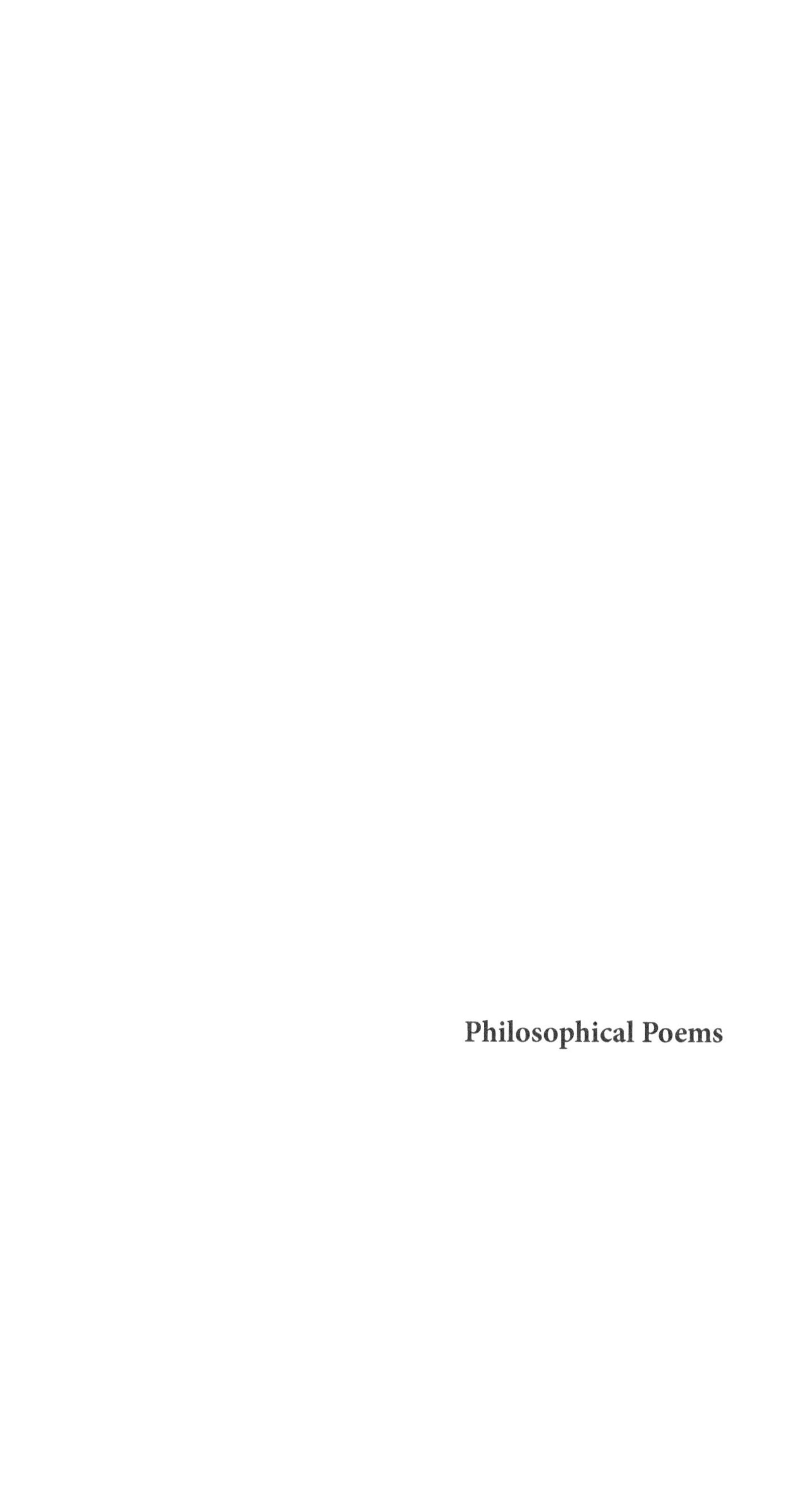

Philosophical Poems

[Of all those procedures of the earth]

Of all those procedures of the earth which like the wings of birds
Shape out their balances on the variant air:
All leisures[1] and deliveries of the air, the casual siphon
That swings up England's roses from the Gulf, and that cold steady shadow
Whence our northward list
Restores the Argentine the gradual summer:

Of those invisible voyagers who, unpredictably,
Beach and deploy their damages in the flesh of a whole people;
In whose reliant hands all heath persists:

Races of stone and fire and of the living
Those mutual races of whose balanced hungers
The sun holds absolute power:
Those animals the demeanor of whose eyes our grieving envy:
Acid and bloodless insects fire, the entranced flame
Whose civilization is one silent tree:

No more now, even of mention.

Now we would speak of urgencies
Special to man and the immediate time: and few indeed of these.
Shut off the sky, yet in this mere earth
Advances such a fugue
As mind cannot contain.

He that would know will not forget that fugue.
He that would know will never hope to hold it.
He that would know must deafen from the whole
Some while; study some little of the score,
Phrase by mute little phrase.
He that would know must learn first how to live.[2]

You who care much to live: the choice is yours. Clear yourselves
to the knowledge.

UTK MS 2730 Box 5, Folder 5

[Nothing.]

Nothing. For as it is with us,
So is it with our skill and strength.
Our cities show, on the damp ground
A snowflake's length.

And as with all we build, just so
With all that hope and need have made:
Nations and arts, knowledge and God,
These also fade.

And briefly as against the sooted
Chimney-wall, sparks flare and faint,
Just so the ardor of the sky
Knows time's constraint.

UTK MS 2730 Box 5 Folder 32

[Our morning grows over us][a]

Our morning grows[1] over us, the blessed daybreak is forever past.
Now the smell of sweating grass and birds more casually singing together; now the smell
of blade leaves in the damp to remember and the mouth no longer sour and cool, now the
smell of hot wheat and the ordinary tastes and goodnesses of full morning.
Now the large disposition of all things made blows merrily glad in light like
milkweed draughted[b] over the bright pasture; that sticks to the damp cheek in
the sun pleasantly.
And nearer felt and near known about us the bowelled earth breaching
many sorted life, the nations, the loud advertisements of men's doings; the
broad seamed slim of land and the ulcered cities,
Soul, there must we be soul we must stand not fearing in the middle of the middle of
man and his doing constant in all truth:
There where the pressures are strongest against each other might we build what strength
we may, no turning aside.
What troubles, delusions and diversions, failures of good heart we shall know
we taste on the air now and shall know a thousand fold; and our time
shortens.
So out among them. Your hand. Your embrace.

UTK MS 2730 Box 5 Folder 32

[a] This poem is an expanded version of the last verse of "[Now inward from the sun]."
[b] "draughted" means "drafted."

[There's no kind of time when Death ain't a beating some door]

There's no kind of time when Death ain't a beating some door.
There's no kind of time when the tears ain't wrinkling down.
No kind of time when the poor man's better than poor.
God, God come guide and bust apart this town![1]

UTK MS 3824 Box 7, Folder 4[2]

A Letter

Dear death I beg you stop my blood
Undo my flesh, unhasp my bone,
O merge me in a duller mud
Than dreams this skull contains no stone.

Your bastard brother rid me of
All honor of eyes and ears and hands
And honorable leave to love:
But still his botchwork breathes and stands:

Hurts with its pain and beats its head,
No beauty makes nor ever can
And beg that death will put to bed
The botch a happier bed began.

UTK MS 3824 Box 7, Folder 4[1]

How Many Little Children Sleep

How many little children sleep
To wake, like you, only to weep:
How many others play who will
Like you, and all men, weep and kill.

And many parents watch and say,
Where they weep, where they play,
"By all we love, by all we know,
It never shall befall them so."

But in each one the terror grows
By all he loves, by all he knows,
"Soon they must weep; soon they shall kill.
No one wills it, but all will."

But in each one the terror moves
By all he knows, by all he loves.
"Soon they will weep; soon they will kill.
No one wills it, but all will."

CP, p. 162

[Poor child][1]

Poor child, forgive us if you can
For daring to continue man.

Possibly before you're grown
All that men have[2] ever known

Will leave the universe as clean
As if man had never been.

Probably, before you're wise,
Cruelties will press into[3] your eyes[4]

Men have seldom[5] dreamed, as yet
And[6] never often shall forget.

Certainly, before you die,
You will know good reasons why

No time could[7] ever be so dire
But that it should of all require

Who hold life, and each other, dear,
That they should, as we do here,

And future that we hold at heart
(And, in your future, take[8] our part):

If in your dreams you hear, forgive:
For by our doing you must live.

Soon you must wake, and dreams be done,
When you behold the heavy sun.

Once you undertake that weight
Apologies will come too late.

UTK MS 2730 Box 6, Folder 16 [photocopy]

You Green in the Young Day

You green in the young day
Pledge tall things to your pride,
You brave in thought of woe
Walk in the bullet's way;

You murderers for gain
Be gainful while you can,
You that would change the score
Be merciless and destroy:

You lonely that must mourn,
You that are made of cheer,
You that all harms have borne,
You that see no thing clear:

You woman and you man
Bridegroom and happy bride
Find out your truest joy
Grown true your mortal tide:

That pride and greed and anger,
Bravery and grief and love;
All death holds deep in danger
Death shall not quite remove:

And so may this ill-tuned remark
Of mine, and many others,
Run light among the living
When I am in the dark.

CP, p.151

[Hood your head in mother's hood][1]

Hood your head in mother's hood.
The pretty ribbons once she wore
Favor you, and any good
Marrying girl can want no more.

Hood on head and band on hair,
One for duty, one for care.

Sit and rock in mother's chair
(One for duty, one for care)
Walk your feet[1] where her tracks are
(One for duty, one for care)

And marrying girl, never cry, never cry:
Cry in these your wedding clothes
You won't leave off until you die.

Hood on head and band on hair,
One for duty, one for care.[a2]

UTK MS 3824 Box 6, Folder 36[3]

[a] See also the poem "Marrying dance."

[Speaking only generally]

Speaking only generally: the bare stress here of living is such
It stuns the inheritor stupid as a rich man's son,
Destroys in its own ardor its unique promises
Joy, any strength of passion, is much too much:
Flares, where it chances, and very soon consumes itself into stone.

A few can handle their living like a horse: live with it like a girl in love, and bring out
    beautiful children.
And what of these few.
They scarcely serve to keep their own lives warm:
They are just matches in a thunderstorm.
We can accept only each at our level; the general level is low, suicidal.
Joy, love, truth, that spreads at all, spreads only through concentric change,
Encountering and becoming lesser things:
Still joy, still love, still truth, but there,
In a sort of vacuum of no perception. Worse.[1]

Worse, for the poisoned only can breathe poisons,
    Die in a clearer air:
And he that supplies goodness supplies new poisons
    And does his kind the cruelest[2] kind of service.

UTK MS 1500 Box 1, Folder 12

[The world is rotted almost to the heart]

The world is rotted almost to the heart.
It's high time, therefore, we should make a start
Cutting the cancer from the living flesh
And seeing how to live life again.[1]

UTK MS 1500 Box 1, Folder 12

[U[p] in the treasuries of amber time][1]

U[p] in the treasuries of amber time
Is cherished excellence, how shall it shine alive again:
And yet remember water: inclusions in quartz:[1]
Which freed, after a thousand thousand years
Still in the familiar lens
Continues the dancing the delicate frenzy.[2]

UTK MS 3824 Box 7, Folder 1

[What is his trouble?]

What is his trouble?

He has many troubles: he cannot even name them.

What is his leading trouble?

He is dead. Dead in his five senses and of feeling; and dead in his mind; and wants to be alive.

He feels he exists for some purpose, and is no way qualified to fulfil it. He prefers dying to living.

That is unpleasant for him. And what would help?

The ability to feel; the ability to record what he feels.

The ability to lose himself.[1]

UTK MS 3824 Box 7, Folder 1

The Fullness of Time[1]

The world over, men are grieving to pieces tonight;
Some in complacency, some in foreboding, some in rebellion
As no darkness obliterates enough of everything,
No light gives enough light.

All alike have become like aging men in garrets
Of a fallen city, with only the vast skyline
Burning out below, all hope gone, and the only voices,
Impudent, senseless parrots.

Cowards that we know ourselves, men turn irresolute, sick,
Go prepare to go out bodily as when,
In a guttering candle[a], the mounting fat
Rises to[o] suddenly and drowns the wick.

UTK MS 3824 Box 6, Folder 31

[a] A guttering candle is one that is flickering and about to go out.

[Once I was young and swore like you]

Once I was young and swore like you
This world was—a wicked place:
But I've found out that is not true:
For God meant this to be.[1]

Lives of great men oft remind us
That the best serves the interests of our town
Who, departing, only leave behind us
Our footprints on the dashboard upside down.[2]

UTK MS 3824 Box 7, Folder 1

[The hunger weighs, good will and anger]

The hunger weighs, good will and anger
The frail chance deathly down to danger.
And blanks the always blemished eye
To poring towards what and why.

UTK MS 1500 Box 1, Folder 11

[How though close weft we exquisitely sieve[1]]

How though close weft[a] we exquisitely sieve
Random experience.
Yet subtle fish must slip us and outlive
Our narrowest sense.
Therefore though happy in the leaping haul
Meshed in perception,
What fool would read rules to govern all
From such deception.

Random strengths arranged us here
That shall not likely meet again:
Our living, thought and death's a wind
Flashing in a field of grain.[2]

UTK MS 2730 Box 5 Folder 32

[a] In weaving, the weft are the threads that cross from side to side of a web, at right angles to those of the warp.

[It is a briary earth]

It is a briary earth and a heaviness
Masks the whole heaven of the delayed spring.
Pale roots to gnaw, that poison us. I guess
There is not any good in anything.
No beasts, of size or flesh. Bare lakes
Blared to the sun; the birds keep well above;
Nights, the wind, whistling in the brakes;
Not, I'm afraid, a country made to love.
Yet, I may say, I've seen such parts before,
Or not much better, once the warmth was full,
So[a]

UTK MS 2730 Box 5 Folder 32

[a] The poem is unfinished.

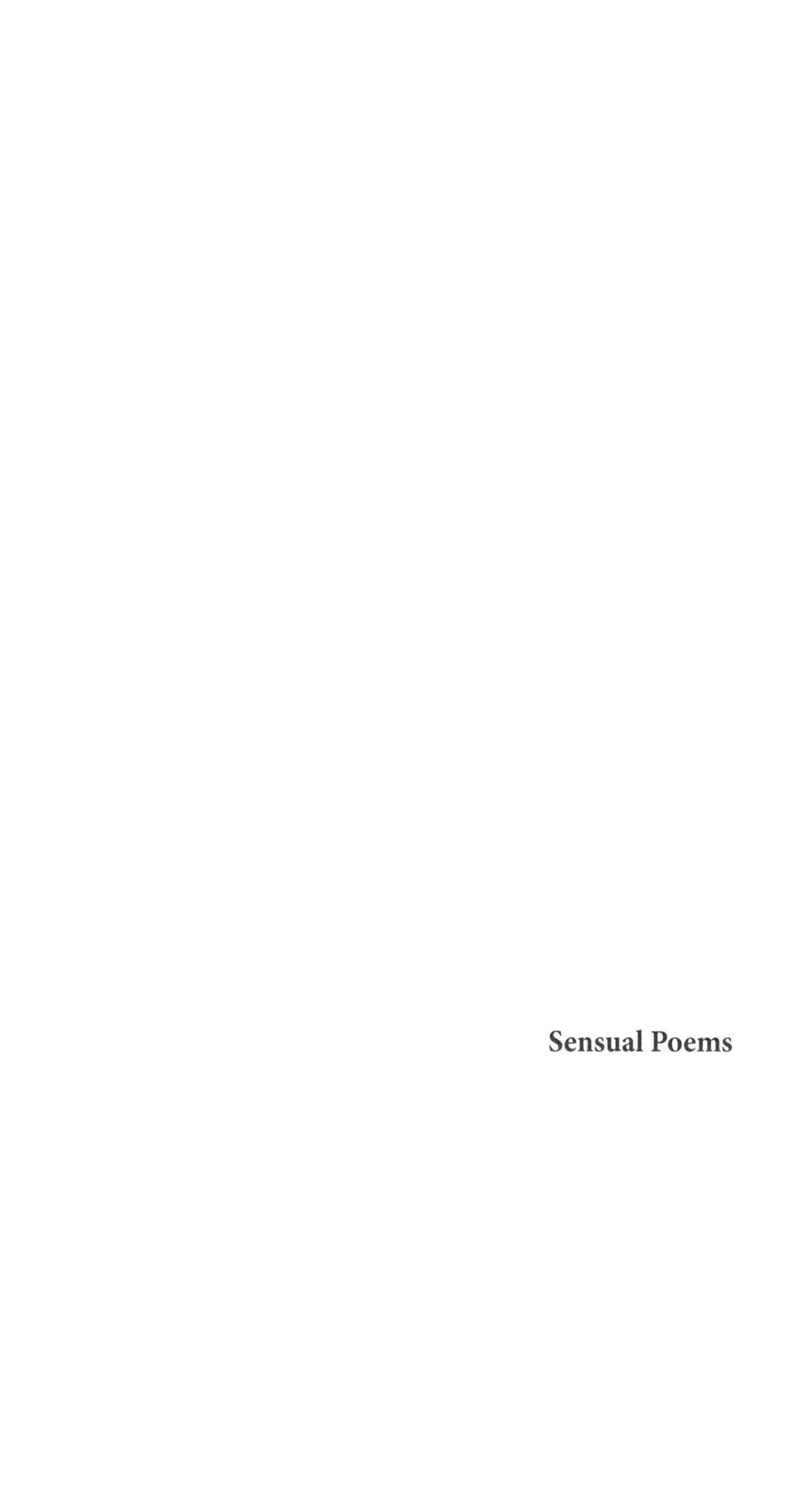

Sensual Poems

Delinquent

Neat in their niches with retrousse[a] faces
The choir boys chant the chorale of the mass,
Suspicious sopranos and imminent basses,
Molding their mouths as a blower molds glass.
Hymning the high gods with oscillations,
As pliable lips adapt to the air,
Distracting the flock from divine occupations
By singing so loudly and looking so fair.
Limp in their linen that glistens and grates,
They ogle an octave with unctuous eyes,
Or lower shy lids as the organ abates,
Demure as a demon in cherub disguise,
Till troubled parishioners cannot be sure
So much naiveté's utterly pure.

UTK MS 2730 Box 5, Folder 13 [carbon typescript]; *CP*, p. 136.

[a] Turned up in an attractive way; often referring to a nose.

[The season wakes our maidens][1]

The season wakes our maidens
	To fresh seasonal joys;
Pleasure is also in fashion
	For boys.

O, o, in wholest[2] flower,
Virginal flames[3] now try
	My whole heart;
New, new love,
	For which I die.

The nightingale sings of it
	So tenderly[4],
His singing sets to burning[5]
	My very soul.

You are the very flower
	To me, to me,
Of girls; the rose of roses[6],
	As I so often see[7].

Your promise crowns my heart
	In peace and[8] joy
Your scorn shall[9] that same heart
	Promptly destroy.

Famished in need for your
	Virginity,
Forbidden you by your
	Simplicity.

Now, nightingale, some while[10]
	Your grieving rest:
The while my own sad rime
	Pours from my breast.

Now dissolves the season
Of sitting tight
Into the time, past reason,
Of charming night.

It's bitter[11] winter's end
And patient way,
Looks with new soul to friend[12],
Catch as catch can.

Come soon, my little wife,
With joy to me,
Come, come, my love my life:
Or soon I die.

UTK MS 2730 Box 5 Folder 32

[Sweet heart tonight]

Sweet heart tonight by rights in graveyards
Long since forgotten bones and bran of bones
congratulate:
all that was ardent is which is now the air
smiles round[1] our wrestling here. I do not think they pity.
You do, they say, what we are born to do.
No matter for the rest.[2]
Discharged, at length, now shall your strength recede:

and now, the season changes[3] in your blood.[4]

Born as we were, they say, you are brought one,
No matter by what chance, and now are ripe.
You do, they say, what we are born to do,
And what though with this instant you are changed.
What though the season altering in your groin
Possess your blood henceforth.
Waves are not full before they find their shore
And once discharged, recede: and are received.

Only the wave is full that finds the shore:
And once discharged, recedes and is received.
The wave's a fool that would delay before:
After, a miracle not well believed.[5]

UTK MS 1500 Box 1, Folder 11; *JAR*, p. 222–23.

[I watched her from her easy bed]

I watched her from her easy bed
Let loose her smile around me,
And on the smile she sweetly said
I'll spend the night without ye.

I name that girl a holy hell
That of my tears deceived me,
And laughed my love to let me tell
And never once believed me.[1]

UTK MS 1500 Box 1, Folder 12; *JAR*, p. 199.

[O smooth young creatures still of the sexual age]

O smooth young creatures still of the sexual age,
O mothers forgetting your husbands for your boys,
Poor fathers, fattened in the commercial cage,
I wish you every pleasure of your toys.[1]

UTK MS 2730 Box 5 Folder 32

Three Cabaret Songs

I

These sultry nights, dear
    Pour me some gin
Turn down the lights, dear
    (Now we begin)
We've got our rights, dear
    (Some call it sin)
And you've Nothing to Lose

Nothing to lose
    And lots to gain
Good deal of pleasure
(Some call it pain)
No way to measure
    But in the main
    I'd nothing to lose
    (And less to choose).

Nothing to lose
    And lots to gain
No news is good news
    (Say that again)
Who'll take this flooz
    y out of the rain
I've nothing. nothing, nothing to lose:
I may as well pay that devil his dues
    I've nothing whatever to lose.

II

Wake up Threeish,
    Clean up the sink
Air out the bedroom
    Pour out a drink
Drink to the daylight

Sit down and think
I'm Open All Night.

Go to the movies,
    Stroll in the park
Watch the kids playing
    Wait for the dark,
Then I remember
A fellow named Clark
I'm Open All Night.

Buy me a mirror
    Make up the bed
Order the White Rock[a]
    Get my self fed
Prink up and sit down
    And wish I was dead
I'm Open All Night.

III

NO BODY SEES
(In the spring time pairs)
OR KNOWS
(Like us like those like these)
OR CARES
(Like the wood wind preening
Masking and mowing
And the following flow of the garrulous leaves

O the trees yield soft
And the leaves flow green
And the young pairs roll beneath and between
And ever and oft
Under ledge in loft
A boy stoops proud and straddles a queen.)

Do you think THEY SEE
(their midparts spitting)

Do you think THEY KNOW
(of the pitiless knitting)
Do you think THEY CARE
    Of the dark flesh fitting:

The life to be
The hurt to grow
The flower to blow
On a ravenous air:
Which does not see
Nor know
Nor care:
Saw it the end it would not dare

Nor grow (no, no!)
    Nor be (Tee-hee! For)
No Body Sees Nor Knows Nor Cares!

CP, pp. 148–50

[a] By 1930, the White Rock company dominated the U.S. sparkling water business, with a market share of 90 percent, according to *Time* magazine. A classically-inspired image of a bare-breasted Psyche kneeling on a "White Rock" overlooking a pool of water was used on all of White Rock's beverages. It was founded in Waukesha, Wis., in 1871, and moved its headquarters to New York City 35 years later.

[Aye, dearly do I love you]

Aye, dearly do I love you,
    But ask me not again
To clasp and to caress you
    As in nights gone; I fain

Would leave unstirred the ashes
    That last night were warm flesh
Before, beneath the winds of love,
    The flame leaped up afresh,

Consuming all of beauty,
    And laying bare, like stones
In fire-outragèd forests,
    The framework of our bones.

UTK MS 3824 Box 7, Folder 1 [typescript]

[Wanton youths that nightly once]

Wanton youths that nightly once
    Thy sleep had shattered,
Now assail thy windows joined

Now, scattered knocks and weakened
    Thy windows firmly closed
Resist, that mad youths lavished
    Nightly game, when you reposed

Less calmly (yet less restive);
    The door which had its fill
Of free and silent swinging
    Now hugs the loving sill[.][1]

UTK MS 3824 Box 7, Folder 1

["As long as thou didst love me"]

"As long as thou didst love me
 And never gave a lad
More favored thy embraces
 Then kinglike was I glad."

"As long as there burned brighter
 Within my soul no flame
Than mine—not even Chloe's[a]—
 Then queenlike was my name[."][1]

UTK MS 3824 Box 7, Folder 1

[a] The poem is apparently a dialog between a man and a woman given the reference to "Chloe." The love story of *Daphnis and Chloe* is told in an ancient Greek novel or romance of the second-century AD and the only known work of Longus.

On Poets and Poetry

[Jesus make it just so good]

"Lord over beautiful. Lord, I do fear[1]
Thou'st made the world too beautiful this year.
My soul is all but out of me—*let fall*
No burning leaf; prithee, let no bird call."[a]

Jesus make it just so good
And not a tittle better.
For if you play just one more card
Against this poet, you'll set her.

And that, Boss,[b] would deprive us all
Of many happy moods;
And Nature of a valuable
Voice and set of attitudes.

For how, Lord, could the world go on
Without poets to command it.
How possibly know how to stop
While Edna[c] still can stand it.

How can your floorshow move without
A mistress of ceremonies?
And why, indeed, except before
A table full[2] of phonies.

UTK MS 2730 Box 5 Folder 32 [typescript][3]

[a] The headnote for Agee's light satire of Edna St. Vincent Millay's (1892–1950) poetry is taken from the last lines of her poem "God's World," published in her *Renascence and Other Poems* (New York: Harper & Brothers, 1917). The italicized words indicate Agee's underlining for emphasis in his typescript.

[b] God.

[c] Edna St. Vincent Millay. See note a.

[O true though little poets][1]

O true though little poets, and false and little poets,
You false who were once true, who never knew, perhaps the falsehood
That took you like a girl in love, subtly, and in the eager name of truth,
How could you ever be laughed at, how disparaged, how anything but pitied,
love, and pitied.

And you like small whistling birds who sang and sing your gentle pleasures,
Your tender wonders and the troubles big as you might contain, and sang
them true,
How should you be diminished and patted, tucked into neat little dormitories,
Pleasant to smile goodnight to but made little shown at your size?
How anything but loved, with love as indiscriminate as air.

The truth is health and life: falsehood is death and disease:
The human race, habituated to falsehood, breathes and is deformed in it:
Falsehood is dangerous and to be searched out, shown [as] such, despised:
Truth, which is love, released on air, decays and is that air:
And must be treasured, published, made clear, insisted on:
So only man at length usurp that air, reach into the human lungs,
make its changes.

Yet I will pity and love the poet who is victim of falsehood.
I run his dangers and am just as blind, yet that is not the reason.
And I will love the little along with the large, kill in myself
The false itch qualify: Hierarchies, in nature as in mind,
Are raveling to one level a level, in mind, from which all differences are seen
Clearly and dispassionately for what they are: Know that level in them now:[1]
Hate falsehoods as diseases, and burn them out: but never their victims:[a]
No matter how convinced they are, smug, cruel in them, murdering,
Blooding the breath of the world, and sure their disease is their choice
and invention,
Hate them no more than their dupes and their victims: and indicate,

Near as you can, towards the truth: but clear yourself of the like disease
of hatred and scorn.
Remember, valuing mountains, the earth is as smooth as a bearing.[2]

UTK MS 2730 Box 5 Folder 32

[a] See also the partial use of the poem "[Hate falsehoods as diseases]."

[I am speaking of a poet]

I am speaking of a poet,
And I'll take what time it takes:
And in case you don't know it,
Here's the poet whose belly aches.[1]

UTK MS 1500 Box 1, Folder 11

[Not to you only who in idleness]

Not to you only who in idleness
And carelessly or even in earnest mind
Bend close to hear:
                Not to you few merely
Who honor poets with misunderstanding:
                Not to you fewer even
Who know a poem in truth:
Not so with parlor voice or intimate
If I can have true poet in me, do I speak:
But standing on this stump of fire,
The sky my sounding-board
I speak into the whole deafness and O[1] am heard, am heard
In all things where is any thing, so I tell truth,
                So but I tell truth.

Wherefore you breed and race how long stunned deaf
                With need and noise of small knowledge:
To all you too I speak. Most who hear will laugh or hate. No matter.
No matter, only this:
If ever you hear truth as those our fathers
(That nation whose territories are dust)
As our fathers
Heard truth while they breathed,
You will hear truth only from such as I:
We who in all times
Have labored with word and tone and rock and color
                And made them signs for truth:

UTK MS 3824 Box 6, Folder 35

[Who may be friends, detested, enemies]

Who may be friends, detested, enemies,
Scorners, you millions more indifferent
Dreamers and givers builders and suckers out of life:
My brothers everyone in more than blood
Made same with stone and air and fog and fire
And much flowered branch of living stuff
One breath and bulk of Godhead:
Who wear upon your groin the wallet fat with God,
And deep as diamond burned in center stone
Impacted in your flesh the living God:
Tenants of earth who make with mind for need
And out of pain build up your histories:

On that deep-struck nail of shade
Sun-made of stuff the sun has made
Where the far point is refined
Into light and out of mind
Poetry stands and makes secure
As it may, all things unsure:

Unhindered poetry might state
In the face of time and fate,
Form and custom, me and you,
In one poem, what is true:
But man and men must stand it by,
Poets: such a man am I.[1]

UTK MS 3824 Box 6, Folder 36 [two pages]

Sonnets

Janus[a]

Within – without – the plastic world they stood
And wept and watched it from outside their tears;
At once the duenna[b] of its maidenhood
And the assailant that the duenna fears.
Their flesh was palpitant for purity,
Their soul nostalgic for incontinence,
Avid to outrage insecurity,
Reluctant to forego its firm defense.
The shadows shifted into streaks of light,
While waters stiffened into ice alert,
And dusk was dawn and afternoon was night
Wherein the vigil fires fumed to flirt
In feminine and quite ferocious grace
With trespassers they fancied not to face.

UTK MS 2730 Box 5, Folder 18 [typescript]

[a] Janus is the two-face Roman god of, among other characteristics, beginnings and endings, dualities, and transitions.

[b] A "duenna" is a guardian. She is often an older woman who serves as a governess and companion to a younger lady or ladies in a Spanish or a Portuguese family to insure propriety.

Sonnet [We have been whirled once more into the realm]

We have been whirled once more into the realm
Of deathless night that blinds all other light;
Are free once more to grapple and enwhelm
The Ill it is our idiocy to fight.
Once more we strain our poor skull-bounded wits
Fast to control what Chaos could not stay;
The ceaseless twisting of a trillion spits
That offers us to each relentless day.
But as, for every day, the earth revolves
Thorough the solace of its steadfast shade,
So sure are we of death: sweet death resolves
All wrongs to naught, that had our hearts betrayed.
Therefore take comfort in this certain night,
And, for your peace, forget it may be night.

CP, p. 130

Sonnet [But if that death we long for be not night]

But if that death we long for be not night,
But night more pure by seventy times seven,
Ponder the agony of that delight,
The all-consuming clarity of heaven!
Made manifold by five celestial senses,
Five silver nerves strung helpless for the thrill
Of God's all-loving and God-loved cadenzas[a].
Further: there's no end to this holy day;
We are to God's eternal love betrayed.
His joy shall be our joy without dismay,
For holy light casts holier light for shade.
And we, who for long grief would spill our breath,
Will long for grief as now we long for death.

CP, p. 130

[a] A cadenza is an aside or flourish in a solo for voice, such as an aria, usually occurs just before a final or other important cadence in the piece.

Sonnet [Two years have passed]

Two years have passed, and made a perfect wheel
Of all that love can know of joy and pain.
All that lovers hope or dread to feel
We've felt, and are arrived at naught again.
On barren earth the sky has loosed its rain
Too generously: last year's abundant yield
Now straggles up, a green and scattered stain
Across the drenched exhaustion of the field.

So, let us leave off trying, now, to mend
A chain long broken; let us play no more
At being firmly bound: love's at an end
And cannot live again. Oh, set no stars
On other loves; all love's a ceaseless bend
From naught to naught: farewell: make fast your door.

CP, p. 144

[Now, for one moment]

Now, for one moment, I have seen my soul,
Have stared its infinite asperity
Full in the eye; and from that sight I stole
Sick with the horror of the verity.
I called on God to grant me to ignore
The feverish foulness that I could not bear,
I termed it courage, falsely thus to soar
Free of the shame and truth and the despair.
Of all men I am cowardliest, least kind,
Most beyond hope befouled and pullulate
With multiplicity vermin of the mind,
Malformed where I would I were most straight.
Even the foulest beggar cannot gain
From truth, who knows his self-inflicted pain.

UTK MS 1500 Box 1, Folder 11; *JAR*, pp. 214–15.

[Suffer me not, O Lord]

Suffer me not, O Lord, one inch to yield
To truth and to the cowardliness of reason;
Although my ignominy stand revealed
To all the cackling world, grant me self-treason.

I feel the weakness settle on my brow,
I know my hope and pride are wild delusion;
Better than idiocy prolonged, that now
My brain spins face to face with its confusion.

But since complacency and compromise
Darken the very nadir of all shame,
And since the highest and the holiest prize
Only the great-souled and the brave may claim,
What hell in life, whatever hell ensue,
Suffer me to forget the truth, and You.

UTK MS 1500 Box 1, Folder 11[1]

[I am not well with reason and exiled]

I am not well with reason and exiled
Of strength and gladness. Yes, of my own will
Orphaned and homeless, and this place is wild.
Here I shall not find anything but ill.
The sun and storm weave from this turning hill
Fat crops, they tell me; meaningless and defiled;
I fill my belly with a season's swill.
With listless fact my lifeless mind's beguiled.

Brain, ease yourself with madness; hope, heart; child,
Create your uncreated father. I till,
Turn in the fire your holy wealth who smiled
That now all the broad sky shines and that now outspill
Seas where the eyes were sand and that now some
Say I am coward that am a child come home?[1]

UTK MS 3824, Box 7, Folder 2

[Silence, ye loves, ye who dare]

Silence, ye lovers, ye who dare
To swell with boasts the quiet air
Into a brittle, echoing shell;
Naught of your maidens speak ye well.

Ye who sing of her and her,
Can a heart among you stir,
Never chilled by sad alarms
When ye view my lover's charms?

Fie, confess your boasting void,
And confess your pleasure cloyed,
For your loves cannot compare
To my own, beyond them fair.

Beyond all women she is fair,
Beyond all stones and spices, rare.

UTK MS 3824, Box 7, Folder 4

Dialect Poems

Lines Suggested by a Tennessee Song[a]

1.

Mary was the sweetest gal
a hunderd mile around.
Lively and kind and good to see
as ever might be found.

The young men hung around her porch
till waylong in the night.
She never teased, nor give false hope.
She never let them fight.

A cousin come from down the cove
and marrying was his aim.
And when he left he took her love.
Joseph was his name.

Her pappy set the wedding day
when she would turn fifteen.
Joseph was aged three times her year,
but the best man ever you seen.

So Mary stayed the winter through
brushing her housework up.
And every Sunday regular
Joseph would show up.

And she grew prettier day by day
into a full young woman,
so sweet to see that Joseph felt
afeared, umble and common.

Why should they come such luck to me,
he'd wonder in his praying.
I'm old, and slow, and ornery—
God said, what's that you're saying?

You are the goodest man I know
in all this countryside.
Therefore I choosed you for this gift
of Mary for your bride.

Now listen quiet and hear me out:
You must not take her to your bed,
not for a time, nor pester her
over no maidenhead.

Mary is pure and true to you,
she'll live with you alone.
But her first borned, I warn you now,
He will not be your own.

Now you must care for Mary's health,
and Him, right from His birth.
The father of this little child
is nary man on earth.

And you must never think no thoughts
nor bother your kind head.
Mary will come in right due time
a virgin to your bed.

And him that you must call your son,
see you do right by him.
He is more lovely in my sight
than storms of seraphim.

And Joseph said: I hear you, Sir.
I caint quite understand.
But hold your orders in my heart
wrote out in your own hand.

God telled these mysteries to him
through angels in a dream.
Joseph waked up and watched around.
The dark was all agleam.

And like a match struck on a stove
it faded and was gone.
And Joseph laid awake and prayed
till the winder showed the dawn.

2.

One clean march morning Mary was
a-training up her flowers
out of their buckets on the twine
in the dewy hours.

She heared the garden gate swing round.
She looked up and she seen
great wings of a white butterfly
that stood and called her Queen.

It warnt no butterfly on earth
she knowed, and knowed it well.
She seen, quick as her eyes could stand,
hit was Archangel Gabriel.

Mary, he says, God sent me here
to learn you what he aims to do.
He aims to send his son on earth.
The mother will be you.

Be not afeared. The morning dew
goes rougher on them baby leaves.
Right now the Glory works in you.
Right now your womb conceives.

Your boy will be the finest
that ever any mother bore.
Store up his childhood in your heart,
it must holp heal a heart that's tore

right to a rag one awful day
when you fall down before a cross

wishing mankind for ever damned,
counting up nothing but the loss.

God holp you then. And sure He will.
God keep you now. Your time is nigh.
Don't fear for Joseph, he's ben told.
Now I must go. Good-bye.

And still as a fish in shiny branch
dodging the sunlight from his side,
Gabriel was there in all his light
and then warnt noplace hair nor hide.

3.

They laid down in a cold black barn,
the stars worked through the walls.
The ox and the jackass kept them warm,
a-studying in their stalls.

The old hens grouched along their roost,
the Gobbler rifled his wing.
Out on the mountain niggers heared
the glorying angels sing.

And he come out and took his breath
peaceful as ary[b] mouse.
And in the sky there opened up
a star over that house.

Bashful they come and kneeled them down
before that new borned child.
Good Joseph trimmed the lantern.
The gal laid easy and smiled.

She could a had the best hotel,
doctors, a fine gold ring,
name in the papers and winter flowers,
    For He was King.

He could a had the Mayor there,
a-waiting down the string
from the Governor and the President
    For He was King.

Ginseng root from Siler's Bald,[c]
a star in the sky, a bird on the wing,
a kiver wove a ripe peach wool,
    For He was King.

He could a ordered Summer there,
Summer'd a skipped her Spring.
He could a never come to us.
    For He was King.

He did not need no company,
Playpretties[d], nary a thing.
He come to us the manner he come.
    For He was King.

UTK MS 2730 Box 5, Folder 20 [typescript]; *CP*, pp. 71-75.[1]

[a] Agee was known for his "good ear" and ability to replicate accents and other linguistic variations, especially of people from the Southern Appalachians. He regarded it as part of his heritage from his father's side of the family. Reading the poem aloud helps clarify many of the meanings that are somewhat distorted in his rendering. Thus "a" is often his dialect rendering of "of"; "holp" is "help," etc.

[b] any

[c] Ginseng root was known as an aphrodisiac and was a valuable crop in the Appalachians; Siler's Bald is a mountain in the western part of the Great Smoky Mountains National Park that borders East Tennessee and Western North Carolina.

[d] Toys; nice playthings.

Case History[a]

The laos
Took a haos
In Taos.[b]

UTK MS 2730 Box5, Folder 31 [typescript][1]

[a] The rhyme scheme indicates that the words rendered in exaggerated dialect are "louse" and "house."

[b] New Mexico.

[Muzzy wuvs her Buzzy[a]]

Muzzy wuvs her Buzzy,
    mmmm, itta oodlums.
Buzzy tum to Muzzy,
    mmmm, itta toodlums.

Muzzy tan me have a tookie?

Tum wuv me first.

Mmmm, witta wuvver: pway wiv my nookie[b],
Zen I'll div oo[1] a cookie.

Muzzy, me wuvs oo.

Muzzy wuvs oo tooo.
More zan daddy, even more zan
Untle Charley or dat tall dart man.
Oo frills oor Muzzy when oo divs her a kiss
An' oo frill her when she bathes oo helps oo piss.[2]

Mah-Mah, I wanna wee-wee.

Oo wanna mate a wivver?
Tum here, tunnin,
We'll 'neak behind the fwivver[c]
Duss oo and me.

Oooooo, such funning.
Oooooo, witta wuvver—
Oor donna drow up to be a dreat bid mans.

Bidder than Daddy's,
Or Untle Charlie's

Bidder dan dat tall dart man's.[d]

So way oor head on Muzzy's bweast
And suck[3] her if oo wuv her
And Daddycums will doo the rest
And bwing oo a witta bruvver.[4]

UTK MS 3824 Box 7, Folder 2 [typescript; two pages]; *JAR*, p. 220–21.

[a] A previous line above the draft of the poem but separated from it by a line across the page, gives Agee's intent: "Muzzy and her Buzzie speak a language all their own." You may wish to consult the draft printed in *JAR* for help understanding some of the words.

[b] A slang term for sexual activity, perhaps from derived from the Dutch word neuken, meaning "to copulate with." It is also likely linked to nook (n.) meaning "a secluded place" and slang for a vagina.

[c] A flivver is early twentieth-century American slang for an automobile, especially for the Ford Model T, the first mass-produced automobile.

[d] The "bigger" referred to is the supposed size of the penis of these men, and contains a stereotypical racist reference of the time to the size of a "dart [dark] man's."

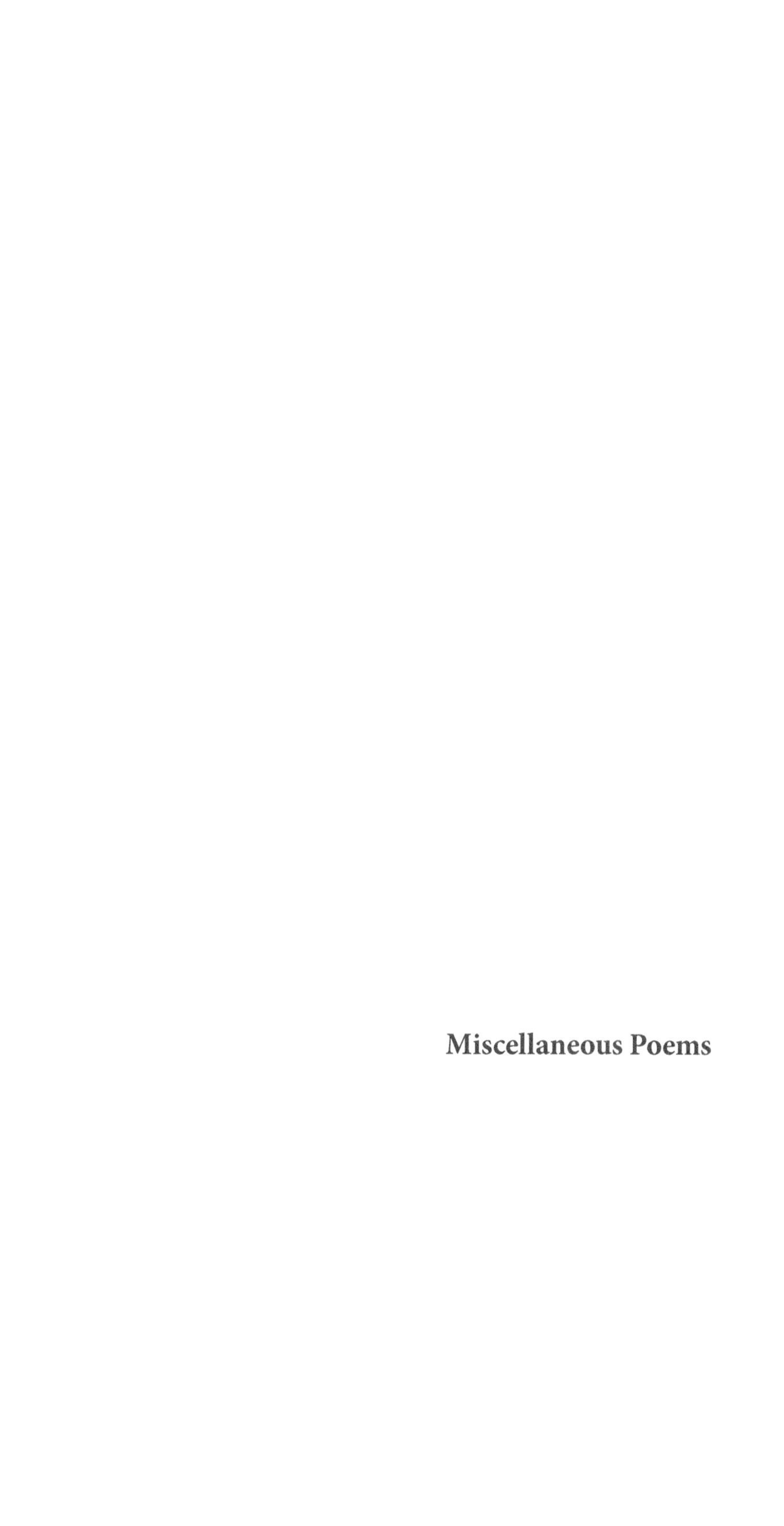

Miscellaneous Poems

[The thunder's iron pinions]

The thunder's iron pinions span heaven from light to light;
Bear furious fearful witness to Jove[']s imperial might:
Let Briton and wild Parthian but slink beneath the yoke,
And of all men Augustus as god we shall invoke.
What! Of all Crassus'[a] legions, breathes one troop,
Whose manhood wastes like wax in the hot East,
Joined to some rank and swart[b] barbarian whore?
And has (O senate! O decrepit state!)
The Marsian and Apulian[c], grown grey,
This sacred shield, his Roman heritage,
Vesta's[d] perpetual guise forgot—grown grey,
(Eased in the thought that God and State are safe)—
Telling the hostile plains for his wife's sire?
Regulus'[e] prudent wisdom had foreseen
This end, altering[1] all such shameful terms—
Lest captives youths, reft of all pity, perish,
Prophetic of a rank seditions,[2] sprawl
Of growth, from one seed dropped careless, and untended.
"I have beheld Rome crucified," he said;
"Her standards nailed high on the Punic[f] shrines!
I have beheld her virgin weapons seized,
Nay, plucked from her soldiers' unresisting grasp!
I have beheld the soldiers' deadly arms
Trussed up with things behind their trueborn backs.
I have beheld the Punic gates flung wide,
And plains ploughed up by strife and sown with gore
Grow soft and brown and shudder out their wealth.
Forsooth, the soldier who, through sorcery
Of a few heaps of fatly gleaming gold,
Buffs[3] back a life beyond all purchase precious,
Returns with a lean soul, famished for new peril!

Nay—Rather you crown infamy with loss[4]
Once virgin wool lies weltering with the dye.
Can it shake off the stain, turn white again?
No more will valor, once it is expelled

Rule in the ashes of a coward's heart.
But left behind, who turn from out thickset toils
Has struggled and leapt free, fight once again.
Then valor[o]us indeed shall be his stripe,
Who once has trusted in perfidious foes
And he who felt the bite of wrenching thongs,
Who feared the very shadow cast by death,
Shall surely, should a second war arise,
Trample the Carthaginian underfoot.
He, since no other course could save his life,
Confounded valorous war with a vile peace.
O shame unspeakable! O mighty Carthage,
Now soar thy shiny towers against the sky,
Whose gleaming towers are lifted to vow soar
Borne on our bleak and ruinous disgrace!"

It is told that Regulus,
Like to one degraded,
When his faithful wife, his little sons, would comfort him,
Turned from them in silence,
Nor headed their embraces,
But with grim countenance averted,
Gazed at the ground.

Thus Regulus, until the wavering senate
Besought his counsel and found strength therein;
Then, through the weeping friends that would yet would hold him,
Hastened to Carthage, glorious, and doomed.
Knowing full well the honors death would end,
He pushed aside the massed and weeping mob,
Quite as if, tedious business disposed of
He sought Tarentum's[g] quiet—that Sparta built.

UTK MS 2730 Box 5 Folder 32

[a] Likely Marcus Licinius Crassus (c. 115 – 53 BC), a Roman general and politician, who in the final years of the Roman Republic played a key role in its transformation into the Roman Empire by forming the First Triumvirate with Julius Caesar and Pompey to challenge the power of the Senate.

[b] An archaic word for "swarthy."

[c] The Marsi or Marscian are members of a powerful Italic tribe who became allies of Rome in 304 BC. In an area first colonized by Mycenaean Greeks, the Apulian people occupy the coastal region of Apulia (or Puglia) in southeast Italy. Its southern portion forms the heel of the Italian geographical "boot."

[d] Vesta (Greek equivalent is Hestia), a virgin goddess in the Roman religion, was the protector of the hearth, home, and family as well as the guardian of the Roman people. Hers was one of the last of the republican pagan cults still active following the rise of Christianity.

[e] Marcus Atilius Regulus (probably lived between 307 BC – 250 BC) was a Roman statesman and general. As consul in 267 BC, he fought the Messapians and as general he served in the First Punic War (256 BC), where he defeated the Carthaginians in a naval battle and invaded North Africa, until he was defeated and captured at Tunis in 255 BC. Released to negotiate a peace, he supposedly urged the Roman Senate to refuse the peace and rather than break his word, returned to Carthage, where he was tortured to death, according to the historian Livy.

[f] Carthaginian

[g] Tarentum is Latin for Tarento, a city founded by the Spartans in the eighth century BC during the period of Greek colonization of coastal Southern Italy. Its independence and great power came to an end as Rome expanded and won the second of two wars in 272 BC.

(Deathshead w. cradle; turn to audience[a]).[1]

Pull, the shade,
Hard, weather,
Watch how the way that the sun goes under
            Sleep, smile,
            Storm, thunder,
Not wake you up tonight, , ,[2]
Bother your dreams, you're home, home now
Kindly turn out the light.

Pull, the shade,
No, matter,
How long the day but the sun goes under,
            Sleep, child,
            Storm, thunder
Can't wake you up to-night, , ,
Bother your rest you're home, home now,
Kindly turn out the light:

Mommy song--Mothers Day . . . [3]

Well, come home,
Rest, easy,
Don't make believe for you know each other.
                Plute[b], starved.
                Rube[c], comic,
I know you all by name, , ,
Boys don't you know your old, mother,
Lord but it's time you came.

UTK MS 1500 Box 1, Folder 12 [two pages]

[a] This is a stage or screenplay direction, but for which of Agee's works is unknown. Other directions (see Textual Note 3) precede the next poem.

[b] A slang term for a plutocrat; a person who is powerful because of wealth.

[c] "Rube" is slang for a country bumpkin, a gullible, uneducated country boy.

Pastoral—Moe and[1] Joe in Dialog.[2]

Here in this hovering[3] shadow where the leaves
Colliding[4] under noon let down the light
Like sifted swarms of gnats; let us sit down[a].

Sit on the grass where still the grass is sweet
In shadow and overlook the heavy world
Close-kneed by[5] hate pruned noon; the breath of verdure
In acid simmering, and the trees stunned with summer
Standing becalmed[6], moored to their sliding wharves
Of slow beleagu[e]red shade.

There in that hovering (The two sit down, et cetera, and eat.)

Harsh bread and simple cheese, this lively wine
Chilled in the trembling spring; this deepbrowed shade
That glowers upon the noon and the slow sheep yonder
That lick the meadows short;[7] Lord, let us talk
As Damon and Menalcas[b] once were wont:
Tell of our girls and the earth's creation
And speak in riddles of the birth of Christ
The Emperor's star, disasters of the state,
Our luckless farms and our advancing age
And all this age advances for our talk.

We can't talk true to form; we have no judge.
The Saturday Review[c] shall be our judge.

So let's drink deep to the Saturday Review!
Father of justice, friend of all sweet shepherds,
Let it remain so, and the best man win!

We'll drink to no such thing; not our first health:
Let us drink long health to the rolling world
Ripened and hanging in the guide-leaved light[.]

UTK MS 1500 Box 1, Folder 12

[a] With this phrase, Agee may be echoing Whitman's "Song of Myself" in his *Leaves of Grass* (1855). Note the subsequent mention of "grass." Whitman was one of Agee's favorite poets.

[b] Virgil's *Eclogues* has many dialogs which may have also inspired this poem. In the third of the *Eclogues*, Damon is the owner of goats stolen by Damoetas, and Menalcas is the singing rival of Dameotas. The later two enter into a singing contest.

[c] The *Saturday Review* (1924–1986) was an influential literary magazine, especially in the 1950s.

[Who will help them to understand][1]

Who will help them to understand the huge black who comes sauntering out of the delicatessen and[2] quietly[3], purposefully lies down in the middle of the sidewalk on sixth avenue   looking as if dead
and there is only the slightest bit of twitching of his tail
and a beautiful smile on his face?

The man walks silently up the stairs to the roof and standing there, arms outstretched   flies singing up into the sky.

The little girl ran into the church and throwing the cross at the altar[4] away put in its place   a dead bird   with a rose on its breast.

In the desert he knows better where he is than[5] he did in the city.[6]

UTK MS 3824 Box 6, Folder 36 [typescript]

[Agee's Friends][1]

Herrimon Maurer[a]
Is no deflowerer.
He barely unsettles
The Petals.

Bill Furth
Is the salt of the earth.
He's loose his savor
To do you a favor.

Deborah Calkins
Is troubled by balkings.
Her conscience
Never gives her one chance.

It's a funny thing
About Emma Ling.
She uses her bladder
Like a broken ladder.

The health of Walker Evans
Is at 6's and 7's.
Will he get well?
Time[b] will tell.

UTK MS 3824, Box 7, Folder 3[2]

[a] Unknown. However, George Merriman was a cartoonist and Alfred Henry Maurer an illustrator in the 1930s. Emma Farrand Agee Ling (1912–1982) was James Agee's sister. The other names, other than his friend and collaborator on *Let Us Now Praise Famous Men*, Walker Evans, are likewise unknown.

[b] Walker Evans was on staff at Time Inc., as a salaried editor at *Fortune* magazine from the 1940s until the mid-1960s.

Appendix 1
For "John Carter"

[Thomas Derry][1]

For love they labor patiently[2] and well,
  Hearten themselves with music and with wine[3],
Forget their souls, or sell them off to hell,
  Cheat, kill, are kindly, grieve, but seldom think:
Pride's born of thought, and I am here to tell
  Of one whom pride past by with sneering wink,
Of one not proud nor harsh nor very wise,
Who long had lost and then gained paradise.

My gentle hero's name is Thomas Derry.
  At fifty-nine, from drinking too much[4] beer,
His father, who was an apothecary,
  Fell in the sunlight, without pain or fear:
Thomas, who'd timorously courted Mary,
  Married her now, for now his course was clear:
He had a drug-store, money, steady habits,
And a house and lawn with brace of cast-iron rabbits.

At that time, he was just turned twenty-five.
  They went to Saratoga[a] for the races;
In time, a child was born, not quite alive;
  His wife lost interest in all racy places;
Thomas sat still and watched his business thrive,
  And served and liked the old family faces,
And aged, and wondered: things were not so nifty
When he was first the sunny side of fifty.

Thomas eased down upon the broad white bed,
  And, stooping to pull up one sock, he saw,
Large in the mirror, a portentous head:
  He gripped his toes and set his startled jaw
And stared anew, and not a word they said,
  But looked and looked; he felt his little craw
Shift, and contract, and scarcely he believed
The certain things he clearly now perceived.

He saw her loose her ravelled skein of hair,
And braid it lankly; saw the pigtails fall
Limp past the violet jowls; and saw her pare
Ridged nails against green teeth; and heard her trawl
For palate-cinctured mucous; but the glare
Of sharp sick eyes, and gleam of yellow ball,
Caught him, and said to him, as sure as fate,
'I think I never loved whom now I hate.'

That mouth once sweet and bright and gladly curved,
Now it was bruised, pale and lugubrious;
That skin once smooth and delicately nerved,
Was and harsh and badged with pus;
Those lowering eyes that hunt and never swerved
Once they had looked at him unswerving thus,
But then had wrought so high his strong content,
He wept; but now were quite malevolent.

And Mary saw the weakly moulded skin
Stretched tent-like on the bent ridge of knotted spine,
And saw the frail skull hinged upon the thin
Strong-corded neck, and saw the strong light shine
Pink through his ear-veins; but far worse, within
The clear dark glass, a face of poor design,
Wondering, sorrowful, and a little scared,
With nothing understood, and nothing shared.

I would not have you think that either saw
These matters with surprise or with disgust;
Such ugliness can talon close and gnaw
The hearts of those alone who lose their lust:
Which long was lost to them: I cannot draw
Truly their minds, but know that all minds must
As theirs did now, halt short and hold their breath
Beneath the shadows of lost love, live death.

'Why am I here? What nameless beast are you
That kennelled[b] with me long; wherefore have I
Lain with you long whom no love could renew.
To warm your feet and quiet your restless thigh?

Why was I wife to you these long years through,
  Submissive, nameless, busy, dull, and why
Was I convenient to your lustfulness,
To whom lust was ever a sick distress?

You were importunate to call me wife
  For what? You little cared, and less I thought:
A trick egg-beater or a carving knife
  Or corset-case: with such my soul was bought:
Now I grow old and now I know my life
  Wasted and senseless, and myself[5] am caught
Strict in the urgencies of idiot hours
And over-towered with night, beyond your powers.'

Such words she did not speak, they were not clear
  Quite in her mind, but these and many more,
Bitter, confused with hatred and with fear,
  Worked in her heart till it was tired and sore
And sick of pondering. In a voice half sneer,
  Half wrath, with madness grieving[6] at the core,
She framed these feelings in a broken taunt,
Cruel, and guttural, 'Just what do you want?'

And Thomas, caught off guard and quite dismayed,
  Pulled off his sock and turning, falsely calm,
Smiled as he look at her, and gently said,
  'Why, nothing, Mary, Mary, nothing." 'Tom:'
She rose, the flannel nighty she had made
  Sheathed well her broken flesh from further harm,
This flashingly he knew, before she said:
'You'd[7] better move, now, to the guest-room bed.'

'But Mary, why?'[8] He belted back his pants
  And rose, and leaned against the shadowed wall.
'You don't mean that,'[9] and then, as to enhance
  His charms, smoothed back his hair, tried to look tall,
And smiled like certain gentlemen of France.
  But knew the cause was lost beyond recall,
And wondered less and little soon he cared
To lose the little they had scantly shared.

For long the nights were past when they were wild
 (As she, spite of her scruples, had been too).
They never quite achieved another child,
 Through her reluctance and that he was true
And always kind, and lust in him was mild
 So that he thought, 'I[10] leave it up to you,
And only hope we keep each other warm:'
Whereof we need not note the mutual harm.

Still, he was used to warmth, and thought it right
 That man and wife should slumber side by side.
All passion spent if need be; and at night
 Was used to wake and let his quiet hands glide
Over her dreamless flesh and sealéd sight,
 The while he tried to think she was his bride
Once more, and shielded her who loved not shielding
And wished she might desire, who knew no yielding.

Now this was gone and Thomas now knew well
 How solaced he had been who now was void,
Alone, cast out, and needless quite to tell,
 He was more grieved and puzzled than annoyed:
And was, moreover, eager to dispel
 What doubts what obstinacies had destroyed
Their concord, and now pity wrung him through,
She was so sick, and he with naught to do.[11]

Such heartfelt pity speedily disarms
 The mind of thought, the self of strategy,
And so it was that all disquiet alarms
 Departed Thomas: what was not to be
Hurt him much less, and all the shrouded harms
 He knew she suffered, moved him, so that he
Put forth a hand, whither he scarcely saw.
When she squalled loud: 'Keep[12] off your filthy paw!'

But the last word he scarcely understood,
 So wrenched with anguish was it, as she flung
Her hulk athwart the bed, and thumped the wood.
 And roared such lyrics as are seldom sung

Into the stifling pillow, while, half-nude,
  Over his heaving wife he shivering hung—
Poor Tom, afraid to touch her, stood and[13] gaped—
(O nymph and faun, how curiously misshaped!)

And now all things that long through many a year
  Had nettled him, and of late months had grown:
Secretiveness, suspicion and ill cheer
  And smouldering silences that left him lone,
Sloth, dullness[14], anger, meanness,—these were clear,
  And, as she now more quietly made moan,
He softly left the room, nor held it strange
That Change of Life could bring so great a change.

From that time forth, he used the guest-room bed:
  Try as he did, the room was bleak and queer.
All kinds of things would loiter through[15] his head
  When he'd awake, and in a sort of fear
He'd lie and listen to the subtle tread
  Of night outside, and wish the dawn were near,
And oftentimes his hands and lonely feet
Would wander on the broad and empty sheet.

Mary no longer bothered much with meals.
  He ate lunch out, and like as not prepared
Their supper, and with numerous appeals
  Got her to eat it; that once done, he aired
The bedroom, made her bed; and doled her pills,
  Or spooned her medicines, and then sat snared
Close by her bed, and read to her, or heard
Her tantrums out, without an answering word.

Soon, Mary proudly rose to Complications:
  She tried first this and[16] then another doctor.
They thumped her stomach, heard her bland orations
  Of symptoms; said the Lazy Colon[c] blocked her,
Withdrew her teeth, douched out her clogged ovations,
  Knelt on her spine and tapped her knees and clocked her,
Called her an interesting case, were paid,
Sent her to bed, and hunted up a maid.

Although the medicines made quite a hole
 In Thomas' funds, he did not disagree:
First, he knew better, next, had no control:
 Third, just perhaps the maid would set him free,
At least a little: so, he stood the toll,
 And wondered when she'd get to work; and she,
Next night, when he walked home to his fair love,
Was getting supper at the kitchen stove.

Her skin was fair, and dark as night her hair,
 And like thin raven's down, a faint moustache
Shadowed her arching lip; her arms were bare
 Half to the shoulder, and she stirred the hash
Almost as if she liked it, and the pair
 Stood and were silent, and as an aching flash
Of lust cut wide his heart, who promptly brayed:
'Hello! . . . [17] that is, I guess you're the new maid.'[18]

She turned around and looked, and said, 'Mnnnh-hum,'[19]
 And turned again and scraped the skillet clean.
He said 'I hope you'll like it,' and was numb
 With horror lest she know what he might mean.
'I'm used to work,'[20] said she; then both were dumb.
 Thomas felt suddenly almost serene,
And, tho she coolly said she was quite able,
And gave no thanks, he helped her set the table.[21]

UTK MS 1500 Box 1, Folder 7 [seven handwritten pages]

[a] Saratoga Springs is a city in New York State and the home to the Saratoga Race Course. Famous for thoroughbred horse racing and its mineral springs, Saratoga has been a popular resort destination since 1803, when Gideon Putnam erected the first hotel. Since 1951, it is also the location of The National Museum of Racing and Hall of Fame.

[b] To lie in the gutter or kennel.

[c] The reference is to lazy bowel syndrome, a condition with symptoms of constipation and pain during bowel movements.

Appendix 2

For "John Carter"

[Unplaced stanzas]

Dear me, poor Tony[a] was so wild with rage.
  And Stanley[b] so embarrassed what to say.
Selassie[c] like a tiger in a cage;
  Benito[d] sitting tight and making hay;
Everyone acting merely half his age
  And carrying on forever and a day;
Just for appearances, we all recanted:
Nevertheless, we knew just what we wanted.

Ah, well, we'll get it, though I can't take part.
  Openly, that is; on the backstairs wire
Doubtless they'll find me helpful. Quite an art,
  Madam, persuading these monkeys that the fire
Is theirs, and all the chestnuts from the start
  Theirs and theirs only. Sometimes they enquire
Why, if we have no pinch of interest in it,
We try to keep them at it every minute.

The answer is, of course, that Albion[e] waits.
  Albion helps both families dower the bride.
Watches a long while, spinning all her plates,
  Then lets them crash upon the losing side.
We wish you folk homesteading in the States
  Would realize once for all that time and tide
Sooner or later make the earth our onion.
So, won't you join the English Speaking Union?

Together, we can hold the world at peace
  While, harmlessly, in a gentlemanly way,
We draw its bowels and fry them up in grease
  And serve them to our conscience on a tray.
And once that's done, my friend, it's you we'll fleece.
  Why yes, of course. I trust that's quite okay.
And thanks to British pluck and the Almighty dollar,
We'll fit the whole round world to a Rhodes Collar[f].

Then, borne upon a burst of seraphim
  May Christ return and check a job well done.
We'll manage, I suppose, a place for him
  Just below Major Douglas in the sun.
Upon one knee he'll dandle Tiny Tim
  While Jeeves[g], perhaps, sets off the sunset gun,
And all the earth[1] round each enfranchised dumbcunt,
Hat off, eyes front, acclaims the Church Triumphant.[2]

UTK MS 1500 Box 1, Folder 7 [December 1935][3]

Mistress, I make you. Keep on shining down.
  Our punctual oceans need you, though our poets
Have laid off farming you and swarmed to town
  Where lights block off the disquieting sky. And so it's
No longer quite the thing for love to drown
  Its little itchings in your large exploits:
And only earth, sea, and the bestial race
Lies in the blessing of your loose embrace.

CP, p. 122 (states written in December 1935)[4]

[a] Likely (Robert) Anthony Eden (1897–1977), future prime minister of Great Britain (1955–1957), was Foreign Secretary beginning in 1935, but resigned that post in 1938 because of the continuing German appeasement policies of the government before World War II.

[b] Stanley Baldwin (1867–1947), prime minister of Great Britain (1935–1937), the predecessor of Neville Chamberlain, who both supported the policy of German appeasement. Baldwin did initiate, however, the rearmament process of the British military.

[c] Haile Selassie I (born Tafari Makonnen; 1892–1975) was Emperor of Ethiopia from 1930 to 1974.

[d] Benito Amilcare Andrea Mussolini (1883–1945) was Prime Minister of Italy from 1922 until his deposition in 1943. Seeking to expand Italy's influence, he ordered the invasion of Ethiopia in 1935.

[e] The earliest name for Great Britain.

[f] Perhaps a reference to Cecil John Rhodes (1853–1902), financier, statesman, imperialist and empire builder of British South Africa. He served Prime Minister of the Cape Colony from 1890 to 1896 and founded the De Beers diamond firm which until recently controlled the global trade in those gems.

[g] Jeeves is a generic name given to the perfect valet or butler. He was a fictional character featured in a series of comedic short stories and novels beginning in 1915 by English author P. G. Wodehouse.

Textual Commentary and Notes

Introduction

This section documents the step-by-step process of producing a relatively clean, readers' text for this volume. It includes any significant editorial changes introduced (please also see "General Editorial Method"), editorial decisions made, and records any information on the texts that the editors deem significant that is more than a necessary descriptive note or clarification. As previously stated, descriptive notes are indicated with a superscript letter and are printed below the poem or title of publication or manuscript location. Textual notes are identified by superscript numbers in the poem and are rendered in this section below under each title. This section also has running heads of the page numbers on which poems appear to help to direct the reader to the proper page and title of the work that was the source of the textual note. Occasionally, a word, phrase, title, or line may bear both a lettered and numerical footnote.

Each entry below begins with the title of the poem and under it are its textual notes. Some poems require numerous notes and others none. For the latter, no titles are given. These notes can be narrative in nature or condensed to a shorthand system. Within poems themselves, some brief interventions by the editors have been easily managed by inclusion within square brackets. All silent editorial changes are presented here below and follow the notation of recording first the part of the final text under discussion, followed by a square left-facing bracket, followed by Agee's holographic manuscript that has been altered. Examples include: "sieve] seive"; and "Sleepless] Sleepness."

Agee's habit of writing alternative words and phrases interlinearly over his original is given as first the item under discussion, followed by a left-facing square bracket, followed by what was written interlinearly over that word or phrase as a possible alternative labeled with a caret (^). Examples are "crack] break^ (no choice made)" and "quiet] mild^ (no choice made)." Editorial commentary such as "(no choice made)" is enclosed by parentheses, if combined with shorthand notation. A solidus (/) within Agee's text to the right of the square bracket indicates a line break, usually in Agee's marginalia or in an undecided word choice. If editorial explanation is needed after the use of a square bracket as part of this system of notation, it is likewise included in parentheses to avoid any possible confusion. An example is "The] ("The" is in parentheses in the original)" and "eachother] (is deemed correct since Agee repeats this joining in the next stanza.)."

Other specifics of the editing of Agee's manuscript poetry, typewritten and particularly the holographic, are as follows:

Strike-throughs of words, phrases, verses, and poems are all silently deleted, as are Agee's other varieties of indicating omission—square bracketing, encircling, and marking through with an "x," etc.

Word choices for alternatives made by the editors where no choice was indicated by the author are treated in the Textual Notes and Commentary as described above. Normally, Agee's original choice was maintained.

Poems that are clearly or significantly incomplete are generally not included, nor are his lists of possible words for use, doodles, and manuscript sections on the same page that are clearly meant for other non-poetic works.

His narrative notes, sometimes a form of his pre-writing / composing, are not included unless the editors believed them still pertinent to the particular poem, in which case they are presented here in the Textual Commentary and Notes.

Agee's irregular punctuation and capitalization have been generally maintained, unless confusing, in which case they are clarified within the poem itself or in the Textual Commentary and Notes. In his unpublished poetry, lines of each poem generally begin with capital letters. If they do not, they have been silently regularized, unless the text clearly indicates otherwise, as in the case of some of Agee's more narrative-like, longline poems.

The author's use of indentation of various lines in the poems is maintained, but silently regularized to its internal norm if it becomes erratic.

Agee's prose notations next to a poem are included in these notes if relevant to the poem.

For Agee's dialect verse, readers may find it helpful to read the poems aloud to make Agee's words clear. Another aid possibly will be to adopt various speech patterns, such as a version of a Southern drawl, or baby-talk, etc., to understand his coinages. Agee had a good ear for language variation, but his lines are not always easy to understand without vocalizing the poems.

If the only date for a poem located is given in Robert Fitzgerald's *CP*, that date is incorporated in this volume and recorded after the particular poem. Many poems remain undated.

Please refer to the "General Editorial Method" section at the beginning of this volume for other matters of editorial methodology.

Michael A. Lofaro

Permit Me Voyage

1. The volume was published in the *Yale Series of Younger Poets* (New Haven: Yale University Press, 1934); the foreword by Archibald MacLeish is not reproduced; for Agee's draft of a preface (none was incorporated in the volume), see *JAR*, pp. 185–89. See also Agee's poem, "[Possible Comic Address to the Readers of *Permit Me Voyage*]."

LYRICS.

1. The beginning of each new lyric, and every poem in the volume, is marked by enlarging the font and bolding the first letter of the poem in the original volume. The rest of the first word or two of each lyric is originally in smaller capital letters. In this edition, it is marked by extra space between the poems, as is also mainly done in the original, but with typesetter variation to prevent the breaking of a verse between pages whenever possible. Lyrics beginning with the following lines were reprinted in *Modern American Poetry: A Critical Anthology*, Louis Untermeyer, ed., 5th revised ed. (New York: Harcourt, Brace and Company, 1936), pp. 632–33: "No doubt left."; "Not met and marred . . ."; and "I loitered weeping . . . ."

2. A very preliminary version of "Not met and marred" is in UTK MS 2730 Box 5, Folder 32.

3. The "Sure on this shining night" section was adapted by the composer Samuel Barber into an art song for his 1938 song cycle *Four Songs* ("Sure on this shining night, op.13 no.3").

4. A photocopy of *The Happy Hen* is in UTK MS 2730 Box 7, Folder 24. Note that "I loitered weeping . . ." is a separate lyric.

ANN GARNER.

1. Agee published the poem "Anne Garner" in *The Hound & Horn: A Harvard Miscellany* in Spring 1929, pp. 223–35, and in *The Phillips Exeter Monthly*, May 1928, pp. 177–86. In both those publications "Ann" is "Anne" throughout.

2. Editors have inserted a break to indicate the beginning of a separate verse. In *PMV*, "That night Ann . . ." begins a new page.

SONNETS.

I.

1. Reprinted in *Modern American Poetry: A Critical Anthology*, ed. Louis Untermeyer, 5th ed., (New York: Harcourt, Brace and Company, 1936), p. 633.

II.

1. Reprinted in *Modern American Poetry: A Critical Anthology*, ed. Louis Untermeyer, 5th ed., (New York: Harcourt, Brace and Company, 1936), pp. 633–34.

IV.

1. The handwritten manuscript version of this poem bears the date "6/Thursday/31"; see UTK MS 2730 Box 5, Folder 24.

V.

1. The handwritten manuscript version of this poem is on the same page as sonnet "IV" that bears the date "6/Thursday/31" (UTK MS 2730 Box 5, Folder 24). Also, in the corrected typescript for this sonnet (UTK MS 2730 Box 5, Folder 23), Agee has a different last line. It reads "Fight toward your own obliterating light." A manuscript version in the same file has as the last line: "And wait the all-obliterating night." The same folder contains other handwritten and typed copies of works that constitute Agee's *Permit Me Voyage*.

VII.; VIII.; IX.; XI.; XII.; AND XIII.

1. First published in "Six Sonnets" in *The Harvard Advocate*, December 1931, pp. 20–21. In *Permit Me Voyage* he generally makes several small revisions to those six works.

XVII.

1. Agee first recorded this sonnet in a letter to Via (Olivia) Saunders, his future first wife, on August 24, 1932, Princeton University Library Special Collections, Manuscripts Division, James Agee Letters, Box 1, Folder 1.

XIX.

1. Reprinted in *Modern American Poetry: A Critical Anthology*, ed. Louis Untermeyer, 5th ed., (New York: Harcourt, Brace and Company, 1936), p. 634.

XX.

1. Agee first recorded this sonnet in a letter to Via (Olivia) Saunders, his future first wife, on August 24, 1932, Princeton University Library Special Collections, Manuscripts Division, James Agee Letters, Box 1, Folder 1. Reprinted in *Modern American Poetry: A Critical Anthology*, ed. Louis Untermeyer, 5th ed., (New York: Harcourt, Brace and Company, 1936), p. 633.

PERMIT ME VOYAGE.

1. Reprinted in *Modern American Poetry: A Critical Anthology*, ed. Louis Untermeyer, 5th ed., (New York: Harcourt, Brace and Company, 1936), p. 634–35.

Early Poetry: Phillips Exeter and Harvard, 1925–1932

VERSES

1. Both poems are also printed in Victor Kramer, ed., *Agee: Selected Literary Documents* (Troy, NY: Whitson Publishing Co., 1996), p. 86.

PYGMALION

1. An earlier version of this poem (again a typescript photocopy) is located in UTK MS 2730 Box 6, Folder 25. All versions were likely written while Agee attended Phillips Exeter (1925–1928) and are substantially the same as his revised version printed here. This text's version bears in the upper right hand corner of the first page: "Rufus Agee / Ocean Avenue / Rockland, Maine." Rufus was Agee's middle name.

2. —] --- (all three other hyphen punctuations in the poem have likewise been normalized.)

3. Agee's coinage.

4. slowly] slwoly

5. See also UTK MS 2730 Box 6, Folder 16 (photocopy of a somewhat different version). Also printed in Victor Kramer, ed., *Agee: Selected Literary Documents* (Troy, NY: Whitson Publishing Co., 1996), pp. 97–99.

THE POETS' VALEDICTION

1. imperiled] imperilled

2. raveled] ravelled

WIDOW

1. Also printed in Victor Kramer, ed., *Agee: Selected Literary Documents* (Troy, NY: Whitson Publishing Co., 1996), pp. 84–85.

CLASS POEM

1. The poem is part of Agee's parodic essay entitled "Largest Glass [*sic.* Class] in History of School Grads" on pp. 48–52 of the *Phillips Exeter Monthly*.

THE JUNE BALL

1. The poem was printed in italics in the yearbook.

WATER

1. Also printed in Victor Kramer, ed., *Agee: Selected Literary Documents* (Troy, NY: Whitson Publishing Co., 1996), p. 84.

ORBS TERRAE

1. Also printed in Victor Kramer, ed., *Agee: Selected Literary Documents* (Troy, NY: Whitson Publishing Co., 1996), p. 6.

[WHEN I WAS TEN-AND-SEVEN]

1. The poem is on the same side of the page as "[My love is like a red, red rose]" and on its reverse is "[Lovers, make your minds light]" and *Suggestion to D. P.* All four handwritten poems are on the same sheet of paper. The date range is established by the publication of *Apotheosis* in *The Harvard Advocate*, June 1929, and its inclusion in Agee's letter to Christopher "Goofy" Gerould, undated (October 1928; UTK MS 3824 Box 1, Folder 4).

SUGGESTION TO D. P.

1. This poem is on the same side of the page as "[Lovers, make your minds light]" and on the reverse of "[When I was ten-and-seven]" and "[My love is like a red, red rose]." The date is established by the publication of *Apotheosis* in *The Harvard Advocate*, June 1929. All four handwritten poems are on the same sheet of paper. Also in Agee's letter to Christopher "Goofy" Gerould, undated (October 1928; UTK MS 3824 Box 1, Folder 4).

[THE YEAR TWINS ON HIM]

1. The attribution of the range of dates for the poem is based on the fact that it is part of a disbound notebook from Agee's time at Harvard. The poem is on a separate page and the pages on either side bear no information on the person to whom he is referring.

TO LYDIA

1. See also UTK MS 3824 Box 7, Folder 1, April 1929, in which Agee states in using the same ink on the left margin of the poem also handwritten in ink: "I don't pretend to think this gets the Sapphic metre: I wanted to keep something of the general swing of it, though." He then adds in pencil in the left margin: "The trouble is, there is not enough favour of the Sapphic or of any other verse. A close translation *in the style of Swinburne* is a possibility—as is the use of iambic pentameter (or other recognized English form) + a short line. In that case, rhyme should be used. There are good bits in your version, but it is neither one thing nor the other." This last statement indicates that Agee is likely comparing his translation to another's. Also printed in Victor Kramer, ed., *Agee: Selected Literary Documents* (Troy, NY: Whitson Publishing Co., 1996), p. 144.

HYMN TO DIANA

1. In the same letter is the poem "Good Friday" which Agee later publishes in *The Harvard Advocate*, April 1930, p. 25.

APOTHEOSIS

1. Also in Agee's letter to Christopher "Goofy" Gerould, undated (October 1928; UTK MS 3824 Box 1, Folder 4) and in another letter to Dwight Macdonald on May 10, 1929, Yale University Library, Manuscripts and Archives, Dwight Macdonald papers, MS 730, Box 5, Folder 64. See also UTK MS 3824 Box 7, Folder 1.

[THE STORM BOWS BLACK ON STRATHAM]

1. The poem is also in a letter sent to Dwight Macdonald, undated (December 1929); Yale University Library, Manuscripts and Archives, Dwight Macdonald papers, MS 730, Box 5, Folder 64.

THE RENDEZVOUS

1. This poem, along with *Apotheosis* and "[The storm bows black on Stratham]," also appears in a letter to Christopher "Goofy" Gerould, undated (December 1929, UTK MS 3824, Box 1, Folder 4), as does an earlier, not as complete version of the first section of "*V. Epithalamium*" from *PMV*.

2. Resurrection] Ressurection

[MY LOVE IS LIKE A RED, RED ROSE]

1. This poem is on the same side of the page as "[When I was ten-and-seven]" and on the reverse of "[Lovers, make your minds light]" and *Suggestion to D. P.* The date is established by the publication of *Apotheosis* in *The Harvard Advocate*, June 1929, p. 21. All four handwritten poems are on the same sheet of paper.

THE SHADOW

1. The indentation of the first two verses is Agee's. The poem is also in Agee's letter to Christopher "Goofy" Gerould, undated (December 1929; noted as written "this fall"); see also UTK MS 3824 Box 1, Folder 4.

LULLABY

1. Agee writes the title on the typed class assignment in pencil as well as the identifying information (on the reverse of the second page). This poem was submitted for one assignment with "[The sun, that lay beneath our bed]" to Mr. Hersey for English 22 at Harvard. Agee received a B- for his work. A photocopy of a handwritten version of "Lullaby" is in UTK MS 2739 Box 6, Folder 26. It differs a slight bit from this one, mainly in not indenting the final two lines of each verse.

2. See also UTK MS 3824 Box 7, Folder 4 (draft).

[THE SUN, THAT LATE BENEATH OUR BED]

1. Agee writes the title on the typed class assignment in pencil as well as the identifying information (on the reverse of the second page). This poem was submitted for one assignment with "Lullaby" to Mr. Hersey for English 22 at Harvard. Agee received a B- for his work.

2. See also UTK MS 2730 Box 5, Folder 32 (draft).

[LOVES FLAME-FRESH]

1. In this two-page letter, Agee noted that his poem was "intended as preface to a sonnet sequence I wanted earlier in the summer, to write" and ended by saying, "Oh well I'm sorry I enclosed it. I hadn't realized how utterly foul it was."

DEAR MR. WHEELWRIGHT

1. crowned] (the word is overwritten and somewhat unclear)

2. anandrous] anindrous; morinda] (the word is unclear, running up against the right edge of the page)

3. these] this

4. and] &

5. (Attribution of date taken from "[Loves flame-fresh]." The letter-poem is written on two sides of one sheet of paper.)

THE TRUCE

1. our] out (Corrected in pencil in Agee's copy of the magazine in UTK Special Collections.)

2. An untitled version of this poem appears in Agee's letter to A. P. and Louise Saunders, January 3–4, 1931; they are the parents of Agee's future first wife, Olivia.

RESOLUTION

1. An untitled version of this poem appears in Agee's letter to A. P. and Louise Saunders, January 3–4, 1931; they are the parents of Agee's future first wife, Olivia.

THE DARKENED CAGE

1. Two handwritten drafts are in the same folder; both bear the date "6/11/31."

[HOW, THROUGH A HURRIED AND OBLIVIOUS YEAR]

1. Two other sonnets which accompanied this one in the same letter appeared in *PMV* as sonnets XVII and XX.

AS YOU CAME FROM THE HOLY LAND

1. This title is clear, but faint, on the carbon. Fitzgerald (*CP*) chose to use the first line as the title instead. Fitzgerald makes other changes, but only two major ones are noted.

2. ?] .

3. Agee crosses out "flaws" and replaces it with "things" written in pencil on the carbon typescript. Fitzgerald (*CP*) restores "flaws."

4. See also *CP*, pp. 141–43 (1932). The date is taken from Fitzgerald.

John Carter (1932–193?)

PLANS FOR STUDY

1. *The Harvard Advocate*] the Harvard Advocate

2. Agee's "plans" continue, but with mundane matters such as where he would do the work (France), who might publish it, the time he will devote to writing the poem, when he would leave his job at *Fortune*, and his references.

3. For a draft of another of Agee's statements of purpose for "John Carter," see *JAR*, pp. 189–91. For other prose passages not converted into poetry, see *JAR*, pp. 191–98.)

JOHN CARTER

1. The editors of this edition give primacy to published work; thus *The Harvard Advocate* version of "John Carter" begins the poem with censored lines, verses, and words restored from the typescripts in UTK MS 1500 Box 1, Folder 6. The poem appeared in *The Harvard Advocate* under the title "Opening Of A Long Poem (Maybe)." Next, in general, the editors follow Fitzgerald's presentation in *CP* with the caveats that this work is quite unfinished and many decisions on Agee's part are yet to be made. Additions from manuscripts and typescripts are made where deemed appropriate, with the priority given to typescripts if multiple versions exist. Fitzgerald alters some of the text from *The Harvard Advocate*, substituting changes made in the typescripts. But since no date appears on the typescripts apparently used by Fitzgerald, the present text retains the print version for those initial stanzas, which generally differs only in some punctuation and a few words. A section that Fitzgerald separates from the text proper and labels "(Unpublished Stanzas: 1935)" (*CP*, p. 120) is here incorporated along with manuscript materials either unknown or not used by Fitzgerald. These are identified in the Textual Notes for the poem.

Although the materials published in the typescripts and handwritten manuscript are all flush left, the present version follows Fitzgerald's in its incorporation of the structure used by Byron in *Don Juan*, since Agee cites it in first verse as a model and uses it in the portion of the poem published in *The Harvard Advocate*. Likewise, the rhyme scheme of abababcc replicates that of Byron's poem. Significant editorial choices are noted between sections of the poem proper whenever helpful; others are in these textual notes.

Many of the people named in the poem are fictional, including John Carter. Others that could be identified have basic information given for them in the explanatory notes along with other terms that the editors believed would benefit from clarification. These latter include the more difficult of Agee's variant spellings to ensure rhyme, no matter how forced. Reading aloud such words, and the line(s) that surrounds them, is often helpful in discerning meaning.

2. This stanza, and others subsequently marked with "2" in the text, was omitted from *The Harvard Advocate*, but added from a typescript page that Agee created, noting the omissions and numbering each verse, likely for reinsertion.

3. At this point, Agee transitions to bring *The Harvard Advocate* poem to a close and Fitzgerald deletes (as does this edition) the conclusion Agee created just for this publication. It reads:

> Here, lucky reader, I am forced to call
>   What the best strategists have termed a Halt.
> With lots of rhyme and reason none at all,
>   And many lines which might wisely be alt-
> Ered, here's some verse, no back against no wall.
>   If you don't like it, who assumes the fault?
> Maybe I'm stupid, possibly you're not:
> Anyway, this (to date) is all I've got.

Agee also at this point separates this verse from the next by a series of six spaced periods. The verses, however, are numbered consecutively.

Here, in *CP*, pp. 92–93, Fitzgerald inserts four verses from one typewritten sheet that Agee labels "July 1932." While seemingly a part of "John Carter," Agee's numbering of verses in the main typescript indicate no such insertion. The four verses are here later incorporated in the "Sunrise" section of the poem.

4. Agee's note is numbered "47" in pencil on the typescript page. The next verse on the same page is numbered "48" and that order is maintained.

5. Another sheet in the same folder contains a partial draft the four verses on this handwritten page.

6. *CP*, p. 120 lists these as "(Unplaced stanzas: 1935?)", but omits the first stanza. No date is given on the manuscript.

7. Fitzgerald inserts these four verses immediately after his reprinting of the *The Harvard Advocate* verses (*CP*, pp. 92–93), but Agee's hand numbering of the verses in this part of the typescript indicates no such inclusion. They are also typed on different paper and with a different typeface font. No date is given on the typescript.

8. as] (mistakenly crossed out)]

9. resumes] reassumes^; (no choice made)

10. and what deep content] (written under these words is "how profoundly blent" with no choice made)

11. sharp] keen^; (no choice made)

12. Since] For^; (no choice made)

13. (After this verse a 6 ½ line incomplete stanza is omitted.)

14. storm] stoem]

15. Fitzgerald omitted this verse; there is a chance it was meant to tie into the "Thomas Derry" section (see Appendix 1); the verse is followed by an incomplete verse of four lines, here omitted (as did Fitzgerald).

16. method] mathod

17. Pepperel] Pepperal

18. Agee separates this verse from the next by ten periods, but the verses are consecutively numbered "58" and "59" in pencil on the typescript.

19. Four hyphens separate this verse from the one that follows and this verse beginning with "Trick mirrors" is inadvertently repeated. The numbering of verses ceases after #61, the first of the "Trick mirrors" stanzas.

20. parlor] parloe

21. day).] day.)

22. knocker] knowcker

23. fond] find

24. pay] paym; in next verse "dreat bid" is baby talk for "great big."

25. And] an

26. first] First

27. Oxonian] Oxonianm

28. delight] Delight

29. blackness] blakness

30. The handwritten manuscript copy (UTK MS 1500 Box 1, Folder 7) adds another seven lines (lacking the eighth to complete the verse) beyond that of the typescript at this point. It is not included in the text proper, but reads:

Well, let them bloat, bridge, bungle, blunder, fumble,
  Stumble and amble, lumber, loiter, dollop,
Jog, trot, jump, canter, jounce with farty rumble
  Across ether[e]al pastures, strike a gallop,
Skip, crack their heels and shimmy, and let crumble
  The brittle air with each anfractious wallop
And with the clash of each calamitous hammer

31. weather] waether

32. asymmetries] assymmetries

33. Which] which

34. The following verses are the last of five verses on a separate typed page and given the heading *Within the Church*. The first two of the five verses repeat the previously recorded verses and are eliminated. Variant manuscript passages are in UTK MS 1500 Box 1, Folder 7.

35. distilled] distelled

36. mended."] mended".

37. spigots] spiggots

Later Poems: 1933–1953

[WOMBLIGHT ON THE WOMBAT]

1. See also UTK MS 2730 Box 8, Folder 16 (photocopy).

[O QUESTION NOT, NOR FORCE FROM ME THAT VOW]

1. Prose passages to the right of the sonnet record the core ideas of its text. Agee published an earlier version of this poem as sonnet "III" in "Six Sonnets," in *The Harvard Advocate*, December 1931, p. 20. That version has the first line as "Now let no manner of sorrow force that vow" and has the word "unpitying" instead of "unpalliable" in line 12.

2. marshal] marshall

3. See also UTK MS 2730 Box 6, Folder 16 (photocopy).

JOHANNES BRAHMS

1. The poem is preceded by a handwritten draft on the same page.

[SUGAH-FOOT, SET ON MAH KNEE]

1. The poem is unfinished; Agee ceased writing after an additional partial verse of two lines that read:

I rid dis Engle an' he shaout
  So big I cain't yeah nuffin:

The right side of the page has a column of notes, names, times, and concepts that appear unrelated to the poem.

2. In *CP*, p. 147, Fitzgerald entitles the poem "Regionalists, Nationalists" and places it as number III in "Period Pieces from the Mid-Thirties." He omits the sixth verse.

[AH CALLS AWN IVAH DEMOCRAT (MANUSCRIPT VERSION)]

1. In *CP* (p. 148), Fitzgerald entitles the poem "Georgia Democrat" and places it as number IV in "Period Pieces from the Mid-Thirties." The handwritten poem is preceded by preliminary drafts.

[THEME AND VARIATIONS]

1. See also *CP*, pp. [53]-55 (1933?); UTK MS 3824 Box 7, Folder 2 (variant, with no variation for number 3); UTK MS 3824 Box 7, Folder 5 (variant typescript entitled "Theme and Variations").

Fitzgerald's version (*CP*, pp. [53]-55) differs from the typescript version used for the present text in several words and in numbering variation 2 above as variation 3 and variation 3 as variation 2. The present title is taken from the last variant typescript noted above.

OUTCAST EARTH

1. This title is written at an angle in the upper right hand corner of the handwritten page. Separated by drawn lines, but also on the page, are a partial draft of the poem "[The little guy was waiting at the door]" and the poem "[Nine miles from Selma]."

[NINE MILES FROM SELMA]

1. Separated by drawn lines, but also on the same page, are a partial draft of "[The little guy was waiting at the door]" and at the top is the poem "Outcast Earth."

[NO CANDLE FOR THE BINDLE]

1. This poem is on the same handwritten page under a partial draft of "[The little guy was waiting at the door]."

[THE LITTLE GUY WAS WAITING AT THE DOOR]

1. Several partial drafts of the first verse of the handwritten poem appear in the same folder. A partial draft of "[No candle for the bindle]" appears to the right on the first handwritten page of the poem.

2. General] Genl

3. Bear] bear

4. The version of the verse is on page two. It replaces the verse in sequence on the other page due to erasure / corrections which seem to indicate a later revision.

5. smooth] smoothe

6. A variant of the last verse appears in UTK MS 2730 Box 5, Folder 32. It reads

Keep us kind shepherd; blessed are the meek.
Her still damp child close by, uncertainly the wrung doe
Churches in shadow at the strolling creek.
He knows because his mother told him so.
This world, God's favorite yo-yo. Let the carnival freak
Visit his parents in the winter. Oh,
Give us right words for God, truth, purpose, love.
Or that smooth tongue whose music hell can move.

This variant appears directly beneath the prose passage that Agee wrote after "[The sunflowers wither]." See note 1 of that poem for the passage.

[THERE IS PEPPER TO STOP THE MOST INTELLIGENT BLOODHOUND]

1. This poem appears on the same handwritten page as "STRAIGHT."

2. See textual note 1 for "STRAIGHT."

STRAIGHT

1. Next to the title, Agee writes: "hard poem on the Drought? (1934)." This poem appears on the same handwritten page as "[There is pepper to stop the most intelligent bloodhound]."

[PARODY OF COLE PORTER'S "YOU'RE THE TOP"]

1. The are two additional handwritten pages in this folder, but one of these parodies is already included in the typescript and elements of the other two are extracted and appear in other of the typescript parodies.

2. See also UTK MS 2730 Box 5, Folder 30 (photocopy).

[GOOD EVENING]

1. This poem is in the same group of pages as the "[Possible Comic Address to the Readers of *Permit Me Voyage*]." See its note 1.

[POSSIBLE COMIC ADDRESS TO THE READERS OF *PERMIT ME VOYAGE*]

1. The poem is preceded by a draft version on the same half page. The poem is at the end of a series of three handwritten pages folded into half sheets that comprise a mock radio play supposedly sponsored by the "Yale University Press," the publisher of Agee's book of poetry, *Permit Me Voyage*, in 1934. It is in the same group of papers as "[Good evening]," which adds two additional pages, likewise folded in half.

[FOUR BITS OF DOGGEREL]

1. Midol] (Agee follows this word with what may indicate his intent to add another iambic foot to this line.)

2. who's] whose

3. The same page contains other, less finished pieces of short humorous verse that are not included.

[NOW ON THE STUNNED FLOOR OF DARKNESS]

1. The poem is recopied on a ¼ sheet of paper with the word "chiming" crossed out and replaced by "draining"; it is not in Agee's hand, and is likely that of Father Flye's.

2. Fitzgerald dates the poem 1935.

[A LOW PIT AND SINK OF SHADE]

1. Alongside the poem in the left margin written at 90 degrees to the vertical, Agee writes "staunch the woundwid[e?] shadow" with no indication of inclusion.

2. Fitzgerald provides the date.

[THE SUNFLOWERS WITHER]

1. The passage that Agee wrote after the poem is:

> "[I'm glad *my* Dad belongs to the American Legion. 'Cause without the untiring help of the local chapters of the American Legion, the D.A.R., the Daughters of the Confederacy, and the Home Guard, the perpetrators of the Tampa flogging would probably never be brought[a] to justice and the Tampa Chamber of Commerce would have been in a hell of a jam what to say. I'm glad too that poor Mister Shoemaker gave his all to gangrene, the Mayor took his courageous stand, and the Board of Representatives offered that generous reward, and Chief of Police Tittsworth after careful examination of the facts stated that no member of the Police Force was in any way involved, and that William Green threatened that unless the culprits were apprehended he might not have the labor convention in Tampa after all; because if these men had not showed their mettle in the nick of time, people might have thought they didn't much care, or something; Why as it is, a lot of people think all those gestures are just politics. I'm glad they kept outside detectives out of it too, because those dirty New York Jew bastards paid with gold from Moscow might really have carried out an investigation, and then where would my Dad, and your dad, and Chief of Police Tittsworth, and the Board of Representatives, and the Mayor be?]"
>
> [a] Agee inadvertently crosses out the word "brought" when revising his original statement of "having been brought".

For more information on the flogging, see Robert P. Ingalls, "The Tampa Flogging Case, Urban Vigilantism," *The Florida Historical Quarterly*, 56 (Jul., 1977): 13–27, available online at https://www.jstor.org/stable/pdf/30149824.pdf.)

HYMN OF FAITH

1. This poem and "Dixie Doodle" are grouped in *CP* by Fitzgerald under "Period Pieces from the Mid-Thirties" echoing the subtitle of this poem. Likewise, he apparently prints the version in UTK MS 2730 Box 5, Folder 31, that omits the two lines after "Miss Clara Weatherwax." See also note 2 below. He gives this poem its short title—"Fellow-Traveler" and gives it the number "I." He also omits Agee's line in parentheses that follows the original title. Likewise omitted from the present text, it read: "(To, for, from, with and / or by one of the editors of the New Republic)." "Dixie Doodle" is given the title "Agrarian" and the number "II." Both works are on half-sheets of paper and timed for "1. min." and for "40 sec.", respectively. Fitzgerald was either unaware of the subsequent version printed here or simply chose the other.

2. Agee ends page 1 with two lines of the next verse, but retypes them on the second page. The repetition has been eliminated.

3. See also UTK MS 2730 Box 5, Folder 31 (draft); *CP*, pp.145–46 (see textual note 1).

THEORIES OF FLIGHT

1. See also UTK MS 1500 Box 1, Folder 15 (handwritten draft).

[HAS LIFE SO MEAGRE FRONTAGE ON THE SUN]

1. jewel and number?] (To the right of this line Agee writes "numbering light?"; no choice made)

2. The poem is on the same handwritten page as a draft of "[A deer went down to water]."

3. The typescript version of "[A deer went down to water]" is headed at the top right of the page as "James Agee / Anna Maria / Florida." This dates the poem between November 1935 and May 1936 and is a likely approximate date for this poem as well, given the draft of that poem on the same page.

TO HARVARD UNIVERSITY

1. See UTK MS 2730 Box 5, Folder 16 for an earlier typescript version of the poem. It is headed at the top left of the page as "James Agee / Anna Maria / Florida." This dates the composition of the poem between November 1935 and May 1936. It gives the title as "Footnote on Education." Although Agee also notes that the poem is "From a forthcoming issue of *Harper's*," the work could not be found in the magazine's monthly issues from June 1935 to May 1939.

LINES FOR THE NEAR FUTURE.

1. The typescript is headed at the top left of the page as "James Agee / Anna Maria / Florida." This dates the poem between November 1935 and May 1936. See also UTK MS 2730 Box 5, Folder 19 [typescript draft] and UTK MS 3824 Box 7, Folder 1 (drafts, two pages).

RHYMES ON A SELF-EVIDENT THEME

1. sieve] seive

2. The typescript is headed at the top left of its first of three pages as "James Agee / Anna Maria / Florida." This dates the poem between November 1935 and May 1936. The first verse only is also in Letter to Christopher "Goofy" Gerould, undated (April 1936), UTK MS 3824, Box 1, Folder 9.

[A DEER WENT DOWN TO WATER]

1. The typescript is headed at the top right of the page as "James Agee / Anna Maria / Florida." This dates the poem between November 1935 and May 1936.

2. See also UTK MS 1500 Box 1, Folder 15 (handwritten draft).

[FOUR WISDOMS ROUND MY BED]

1. This typescript version of the first two verses in UTK MS 1500 Box 1, Folder 13, is headed at the top left: "Agee / Anna Maria / Florida." This approximately dates the poem as early as between November 1935 and May 1936. On the same page is "Rapid Transit," also in typescript.

2. Dostoevsky] (Agee spells it "Dostoevski")

3. A variant of the first two verses also appears in UTK MS 1500 Box 1, Folder 11. In UTK MS 1500 Box 1, Folder 13, there are typed versions of the three verses, but this variant separates

the last verse from the preceding two. It is on the same page is a typescript and draft versions of "Rapid Transit" and "A Song and Some Words", retitled "Song with Words" when published. Also, the first two verses are given the title "Nursery Incantation" in Agee's letter to Christopher "Goofy" Gerould, undated (April 1936), UTK MS 3824, Box 1, Folder 9.

A MOTHER, TO THE CHILD IN HER

1. The typescript is headed at the top left of the page as "James Agee / Anna Maria / Florida." This dates the poem between November 1935 and May 1936.

2. The extra spacing, very often on both sides of the colons, is Agee's intent. Some of his published poems exhibit the same feature.

3. :] ;

[FROM BED AS FROM A BALCONY]

1. fall] grave (written to the right side and connected by a line; no choice made)

[HAPPY THAT TYPE OF POET]

1. A slightly different draft of the first verse is located in UTK MS 1500 Box 1, Folder 11. It reads

None luckier than the poet
Whose Muse is so adroit,
She can bring it in thin
As the point of a pin
Or spread it out flat like a quoit.

2. Another version (with only slight alterations) appears in Agee's letter to Christopher "Goofy" Gerould, undated (April 1936), UTK MS 3824, Box 1, Folder 9.

NIGHT ON AMERICA.

1. Marginalia of interest to the right of the poem includes "Iron sentinels at my head—" adjacent to the title; "Dishonors" adjacent to third line; and "pus in a long war worse than a cancer in a rotting corpse" adjacent to the final four lines.

2. love] ("depth" is written under "love"; no choice made.)

3. mind] ("measure" is written under "mind"; no choice made.)

4. An identical and cleaner version of the poem, but without the title and with a draft is in UTK MS 1500 Box 1, Folder 12, under the poem "[Night overmasters us]." See also *JAR*, p. 231, and Letter to Christopher "Goofy" Gerould, undated (April 1936), UTK MS 3824, Box 1, Folder 9.

[THREE VERSES, SERIOUS AND RIBALD]

1. The editors have created this title for the three verses that appear on the same handwritten page as those published as "Two Songs on the Economy of Abundance" in *Modern American Poetry: A Critical Anthology,* Louis Untermeyer, ed., 5th revised ed. (New York: Harcourt, Brace and Company, 1936), p. 635.

2. Under this verse, under the heading "News Item," Agee writes "One more platitude on the worst-used beatitude:" and then repeats the verse. The three lines of this verse are preceded, in Agee's letter to Christopher "Goofy" Gerould, undated (April 1936), UTK MS 3824, Box 1, Folder 9, by "Let sheep go bare and shoe the goat."

HOMMAGE Á BRIFFAULT

1. The third verse is added from the three-verse version of the poem in UTK MS 1500 Folder 11. That version has the same initial two stanzas and the title. The perhaps earlier version was written in four two-line verses and both are combined following the quatrain pattern of the version printed here. This poem, without the title, appears on the same handwritten page as "[Ah's jes' a believing chameleon]" and "[And by the bye my pious friends of the reviewing trade]."

2. The date reflects the content of a fragment of a letter to Franklin Miner (1936) in which the poem appears (UTK MS 3824 Box 1, Folder 12). The first two verses of the poem are also recorded in Agee's letter to Christopher "Goofy" Gerould, undated (April 1936) and provide the date for the poem, UTK MS 3824 Box 1, Folder 9.

A SONG

1. See also UTK MS 3824 Box 7, Folder 2 (typescript; small variants); UTK MS 2730 Box 5, Folders 31, 32 (both drafts); UTK MS 1500 Box 1, Folder 12 (draft; changes the last line's "argument" to "arraignment.").

LYRIC

1. The spacing of the poem is as printed. See also UTK MS 3824 Box 7, Folder 2 (typescript); UTK MS 2730 Box 5, Folder 31 (typescript); UTK MS 1500 Box 1, Folder 11;

IN HEAVY MIND

1. Agee's extra spacing in this and the subsequent two verses is intentional.

2. See also UTK MS 1500 Box 1, Folder 12 (draft).

SONG WITH WORDS

1. See also UTK MS 1500 Box 1, Folder 13 (1935–36) for handwritten and typed drafts. These versions are entitled "A Song and Some Words" rather than "Song with Words" in Untermeyer. The typescript page is headed at the top left: "Agee / Anna Maria / Florida." This dates the poem's composition between November 1935 and May 1936. On the same page are typescripts of "Rapid Transit" and "Four wisdoms round my bed."

TWO SONGS ON THE ECONOMY OF ABUNDANCE

1. Agee's handwritten text has extra spaces between several of the words that may indicate pauses. See UTK MS 3824 Box 6, Folder 36. These spaces do not appear in the printed version or in the present one. See also note 1 for "[Three Verses, Serious and Ribald]."

[NOW I LAY ME DOWN BESIDE]

1. See also UTK MS 1500 Box 1, folder 18 (handwritten draft in diary 3); dated 1936 by Fitzgerald.

[SWEET ANODYNE]

1. This poem is on the same manuscript page as "[Depilatories garter belts and lotions]" and "[What fool would dare]".

2. The date reflects the content of a fragment of a letter to Franklin Miner (1936) in which the poem appears (UTK MS 3824 Box 1, Folder 12).

[INTELLIGENCE THAT FREEZES LOVE]

1. This poem follows "Night on America." on the same page.

[NIGHT OVERMASTERS US]

1. In the right margin, next to this line, Agee writes "Enamored of their poisoned dreams" but gives no indication of inclusion.

2. The poem appears on the same handwritten sheet as a draft and untitled final version of "Night on America." (see also note 4 of that poem).

[DON'T TALK TO ME OF THOSE]

1. This poem appears on the same page beneath "[Intelligence that freezes love]" which in turn appears beneath "Night on America."

FIGHT-TALK

1. and] &

2. To the right of this line, Age writes "argus-eyed" with no indication of inclusion.

3. After the last line of the poem proper, Agee writes:

(Cartoon: gas stove, man, head in oven, terribly bloated body: child lying on floor, bloated, dead, wife entering, child at skirt—
IS IT INFLATION?
ARE WE TO HAVE INFLATION?

4. See also UTK MS 3824 Box 7, Folder 2 (a slightly shorter and rearranged two-page variant).

MINORITY REPORT.

1. The poem is on the same handwritten page as "[Madam, is baby's evening stool]" and "Collective Letter to the Boss."

2. This poem is written on the same yellow paper with the same folds as "*Fight-Talk*." That and its subject matter suggest the similar date.

[MADAM, IS BABY'S EVENING STOOL]

1. sweet] smart^ (no choice made)

2. This verse is written on the reverse of the page, but its place for insertion is clearly indicated by Agee on the obverse.

3. This poem is written on the same yellow paper with the same folds as "*Fight-Talk*." That and its subject matter suggest the similar date. The poem is on the same handwritten page as "Minority Report." and "Collective Letter to the Boss."

COLLECTIVE LETTER TO THE BOSS

1. barrel] barrell

2. and] &

3. Align] Line up^ (no choice made)

4. This poem is written on the same yellow paper with the same folds as "*Fight-Talk*." That and its subject matter suggest the similar date. The poem is on the same handwritten page as "Minority Report." and "[Madam, is baby's evening stool]."

RAPID TRANSIT

1. This poem appears in the same issue of the magazine as "Sun Our Father" in a section entitled "Fifteen New Poets." See also UTK MS 2730 Box 5, Folder 31 (typescript). An apparently later typescript from UTK 3824 Box 7, Folder 31, is the original source for the poem, since Agee notes its publication on that document. For other versions see UTK MS 3824 Box 7, Folder 2 (typescript with "useless" replacing "helpless"); UTK MS 1500 Box 1, Folder 13 (typescript and handwritten drafts), and Letter to Christopher "Goofy" Gerould, undated (April 1936), UTK MS 3824 Box 1, Folder 9.

SUN OUR FATHER

1. This poem appears in the same issue of the magazine as "Rapid Transit" in a section entitled "Fifteen New Poets." Agee's UTK 3824 Box 7, folder 32 typescript gives the poem the title of "A Morning Song" and is headed at the top left of the page as "James Agee / Anna Maria / Florida." This dates the poem's composition between November 1935 and May 1936. See also UTK MS 3824 Box 7, Folder 2 (typescript); *CP*, p. 154; UTK MS 2730 Box 5, Folder 22 (typescript, with variations), Folder 31; UTK MS 1500 Box 1, Folder 12 (two pages); and Letter to Christopher "Goofy" Gerould, undated (April 1936), UTK MS 3824, Box 1, Folder 9.

SUNDAY: OUTSKIRTS OF KNOXVILLE, TENNESSEE

1. See also UTK MS 3824 Box 7, Folder 2 and Folder 5 (untitled typescripts with slight variations); UTK MS 2730 Box 5, Folder 26 (typescript, not by Agee); UTK MS 1500 Box 1, Folder 16 (typescript draft).

LYRICS

1. All the following are drafts of the individual lyrics. "Lyrics" was first printed in the *Partisan Review*, December 1937, pp. 40–43.

Lyric number 1: UTK MS 2730 Box 5 Folder 32 (typescript); UTK MS 1500 Box 1, Folder 11 (draft).

Lyric number 2: UTK MS 1500 Box 1, Folder 12; variant in UTK MS 3824 Box 6, Folder 36

Lyric number 3: UTK MS 1500 Box 1, Folder 11.

Lyric number 4: The *Partisan Review* omits the last 2-line verse (found in UTK MS 1500 Box 1, Folder 11 and in *JAR*, pp. 223–24) and changes a word or two. It reads:

Tonight sweet heart in graves forgotten
Straws of old harvests whom the sun ignores
Bones and their bran congratulate.

I do not think they pity us:
Or pity less than they are glad:

All that was ardent which is now the air
Smiles round our wrestling here.

Tonight, water finds the shore
And then is water as before.

A longer manuscript version in the same UTK location reads:

> Tonight sweet heart I think in graves of the wild earth forgotten
> Straws of old harvests whom the sun ignores, bones, and their bran, congratulate.
>
> And should by chance their dream be pity, yet joy is their awakening.
> All that was ardent which is now air: warms at our business here.
>
> And by the hungry mercy that employs us, and yielding whom we die:
> We shall in our lost time find rest and certainly shall rise again.
>
> The wood is ash: the wood is flowering red: and damp beyond: and never
>   yet begotten.
> The embers are perpetual as their ending: and we do well.

At least one other version of the short poem is likewise in the same UTK location.

Lyric number 5: UTK MS 2730 Box 5 Folder 32 and UTK MS 1500 Box 1, Folder 11 (both typescripts, slight variants); *JAR*, p. 213.

Lyric number 6: UTK MS 1500 Box 1, Folder 12 (typescript variant); UTK MS 2730 Box 5 Folder 32 (typescript variant).

1. cruelest] cruellest

Lyric number 7: UTK MS 1500 Box 1, Folder 11 (slight variant); This poem is on the same handwritten page as "[God's scorn each other on our back stairs]."

Lyric number 9: UTK MS 2730 Box 5. Folder 32 (slight variant); UTK MS 1500 Box 1, Folder 12 (variant).

Lyric number 10: UTK MS 1500 Box 1, Folder 11 (two drafts on one page. The shortest begins "Waver, waver, universe" and the longer one, which is very close to the published version in *CP*, begins "[Wander, wander, universe."]; *JAR*, pp. 208–09 (slight variant).

Lyric number 11: In UTK MS 3824 Box 6, Folder 36, Agee has an additional two lines: "Use a new coloring, other fingerprints. / Stand in the riddle of wheels: spread city stone."

IN MEMORY OF MY FATHER (CAMPBELL COUNTY, TENN.)

1. *CP* contains the most frequently repeated and cited version of the poem, but radically changes its format and spacing, replaces two words, and often alters punctuation. Since this volume prints the original publication of poems printed during Agee's lifetime, readers may wish to compare the two versions. Agee's typescript is closer in format to the one appearing in *CP*, but its longer lines have different break points. Because of these disparities, the notes below indicate word replacement; the poem, as it here appears, has the line breaks and the erratic spacing and punctuation used in its original publication in *transition*.

2. In *CP*, "elm" replaces "ash."

3. In CP, "Slopes" replaces "slops."

[GOD'S SCORN EACH OTHER ON OUR BACK STAIRS]

1. This poem is on the same handwritten page as "[Squared behind intellectual hedges]" which was printed as Lyric number 7 in the *Partisan Review* (December, 1937), p. 42.

[LENGTH OF STARS SHALL NOT OUTLAST US]

1. The poem is also in a letter to James Johnson Sweeney, undated (1937), Harvard University, Houghton Library, Papers of the magazine *transition,* MS Am 2068, Box 1.

[HOLD.HOLD.ONE DIES FIRST.]

1. The spacing is Agee's.
2. Attach] 42igare

[IN TOKYO]

1. stairs] staiss
2. See note a for "[Night, over Youngstown]" for the possible relationship of the three poems. This poem appears on the same handwritten page as the poems "[Night, over Youngstown]" and "[He swings off the five-seventeen]."

[NIGHT, OVER YOUNGSTOWN]

1. This poem appears on the same handwritten page as the poems "[In Tokyo]" and "[He swings off the five-seventeen]."

[HE SWINGS OFF THE FIVE-SEVENTEEN]

1. Cigarette] 43igarette
2. See note a for "[Night, over Youngstown]" for the possible relationship of the three poems. This poem appears on the same handwritten page as the poems "[In Toyko]" and "[Night, over Youngstown]."

[CHILD, A PRINCE IN PRISON LAY]

1. See also "Poems Spoken to a Child [1]"; this poem is a variant of that typescript version. This poem is written on the same sheet as "Give over, Give over"; it is also written on the same matched manuscript paper in the same hand together with a draft of "Tonight sweet heart I think in graves" that was published in the *Partisan Review,* December 1937, as number IV of eleven short poems. While now fastened by a paper clip (this joining is not original), the other information indicates that this poem was likely written around the same date.

POEMS SPOKEN TO A CHILD

1. See also "[Child, a prince in prison lay]" for poem "[1]." This, and "[Child, a child was latched in jail]," are likely handwritten preliminary versions of the present typescript. Agee's often typed his final versions of poems that were originally handwritten drafts. For poems numbers 2 and 3, see "[Child, a child was latched in jail]." Since all versions are significantly different, all three are recorded in this volume.

[THE KINGS AND QUEENS WE SOMETIMES ARE]

1. The number "3" precedes the poem. It is written on the same manuscript page as a draft of "Tonight sweet heart I think in graves" that was published in the *Partisan Review,* December 1937, as number 4 of 11 lyrics. Thus this poem was likely written before that date. Another copy of the poem, varying only in some punctuation, is written a small pocket notebook—UTK MS 1998 Box 1, Folder 3, and another, with slight variants, is in UTK MS 3824 Box 7, Folder 2, on the same page as "Child, oh, child."

CHILD, OH, CHILD

1. child] (comma removed after "child")

2. The poem is on the same page as a close version of "[The kings and queens we sometimes are]." See textual note 1 of that poem for possible dating.

[CHILD, A CHILD WAS LATCHED IN JAIL]

1. See also "Poems Spoken to a Child," numbers 2 and 3, for slightly different versions of parts of this poem and the typescript, perhaps final version entitled "Poems Spoken to a Child."

MILLIONS ARE LEARNING HOW

1. Fitzgerald gives the poem the title "Lyric." in *CP*, p. 155, and erroneously cites its date of publication in *Common Sense* as 1937. The text remains the same except for a few changes in punctuation.

2. *Common Sense* (1932–1946) was a politically-oriented publication whose masthead bore a "Platform" that began by declaring that it was "an independent monthly magazine devoted to the building of a new economic and social order." It is available in reprint (Greenwood Press, 1968) as volume 7 of its series *Radical Periodicals In The United States, 1890–1960.*

3. See also UTK MS 2730 Box 5, Folder 31 (typescript). This version has no title. Another typescript (UTK MS 2730 Box 5, Folder 32) appears to be a quite similar draft and differs from the *Common Sense* and *CP* versions in some punctuation, the lack of indentation of the last line of each verse, the word "Thousands" replacing "People," and that "Thousands" and "Millions" are exchanged in the final two lines. At the top of the page, written faintly in pencil, is "re the Benton-wood-Engle +c [etc.] Americanism." The meaning of the hyphenated compound word is not apparent. See also UTK MS 3824 Box 6, Folder 36.

DIXIE DOODLE

1. See textual note 1 for "Hymn of Faith." Also, Agee provides a personal introductory verse to the poem in UTK MS 3824 Box 7, Folder 2:

> Once a mere expatriot the Exile has Returned
> And written a nice book (2 bucks) to tell just what he learned:
> And having milked the best of Marx and running low on jizzum,
> Now brings his fine intelligence to bear on Regionalism.

Fitzgerald silently omits this introductory verse and changes a few words and spellings in *CP*. See textual note 1 of "Hymn of Faith" for other changes.

2. /] (forward slashes rather than back slashes are in the original); and in *CP*, Fitzgerald substitutes "T V A" for "Tee/Vee/Aye."

3. See also UTK MS 3824 Box 7, Folder 2 and UTK MS 2730 Box 5, Folder 31 (draft); *CP*, p. 146.

[UNDER ME THE ROOT HAS SHARPENED]

1. can heal] renew^; (no choice made)

2. signaling] signaling

3. The poem is on the same page as "[What do you carry into this woodland]" and "[As in a woodland rarely]." The three poems are thematically connected.

[WHAT DO YOU CARRY INTO THIS WOODLAND]

1. This poem and "[As in a woodland rarely]" are on the same page as "[Under me the root has sharpened]." They are both marked "1/2" and the first has an arrow pointing to the second, likely indicating a relationship, perhaps even their union. Fitzgerald makes changes in both poems (perhaps working from a different version?) and provides their date. He chooses not to print "[Under me the root has sharpened]" and reverses the order of these two poems. All three poems are related. See *CP*, p. 67.

2. carry] bring^ (no choice indicated)

3. Agee underlines and places a "?" after all the words after "Region."

4. Agee brackets the last two sentences ("Every / . . . . fails.") and marks them with a "?."

[AS IN A WOODLAND RARELY]

1. Just] So^ (no choice made, but it would read "So so" if included.)

2. trembling] ("shaken" is written in the left margin and connected to "trembling" with a line; no choice made)

3. Takes me] Talks at^ (no choice made)

THE SICK SNOOK.

1. ,] .,

2. After this sentence, Agee brackets the following line for deletion from the typescript: "They frequent the undershadow of wharves."

3. In the upper right hand corner of the page, Agee types: "James Agee / 121 Leroy St. / New York N Y." He had moved from Greenwich Village (Leroy St.) to Brooklyn in March 1939. The 1938 date is taken from Fitzgerald.

[ONLY THAT THOUGH SO EAGER IN THEIR DAY]

1. Agee's first son, Joel, was born in 1940. If this line is read literally, it may help to narrow the date of the sonnet.

[POOR NAKED WRETCHES]

1. For this poem and for other references to the same volume, see also the scholarly edition—Let Us Now Praise Famous Men: *An Annotated Edition of the James Agee-Walker Evans Classic, with Supplementary Manuscripts*, ed. Hugh Davis (Knoxville, TN: U of Tennessee P, 2015).

TO WALKER EVANS

1. There is no concluding parenthesis.

2. See also UTK MS 3824 Box 6, Folder 34 and in UTK MS 1500 Box 1, Folder 12 (handwritten drafts).

[I WALKED INTO A WASTED PLACE]

1. There are three somewhat different and likely preliminary verses (under the same date) on a separate sheet of paper in folder 32 that are worth noting:

I wandered in a wasted place
And slept against a stone.

And sleeping, opened like a bride
To take my own[.]

My unique Angel in my grasp.
All raving wings, God's ire,
Whose nightlong combat would bequeath
Immortal fire.

But woke, to weep. The stars were tired.
Through all the night, I knew,
The Wrestler had awaited me.
Thrice, a cock crew.

\\

2. cruelest] cruellest

ON THE WORD ASLEEP

1. This poem, "On the Word Kingdom," "'Help,'" and several others are contained in UTK MS 2730 Box 5, Folder 23. In his March 29, 1945 letter to Father Flye, Agee states "One night Mia [his third wife] and I played a game, of writing verses on the first word we turned to in a book (Grimm's Fairy Tales). I enclose a couple of samples, with very little good in them, but a little" (p. 140). Likely all these poems were composed about the same time as Flye's approximation of the date of the letter. "'Help'" also seems to fall in this category, as does "[My It]," "[Happy the huntsman,]" "[Creep, walk, trot, sprint]," "[The Moon once lived]," "[A hungry man]," and "[When the ogre came home]." These poems are on four physically similar sheets, all folded in quarters, perhaps better to fit in a small envelope.

2. might be thrown] endear, be brought (in Flye's version. Agee indicates an insert of these words with a carat, but makes no choice. The other differences lie in less punctuation in Flye's text.)

3. Also in *Letters of James Agee to Father Flye*, ed. Father James Harold Flye (New York: George Braziller, 1962), pp. 140–41 (est. March 29, 1945). The title is Flye's; the text is Agee's manuscript version.

ON THE WORD KINGDOM

1. See note 1 of "On the Word Asleep." The differences are mainly in less punctuation in Flye's text and the substitution of one word. See also note 2 of "On the Word Asleep." This poem is written on the same page as "[Happy the huntsman]" and "[Creep, walk, trot, sprint]."

2. shady] nearby (in Flye)

3. Also in *Letters of James Agee to Father Flye*, ed. Father James Harold Flye (New York: George Braziller, 1962), p. 141 (est. March 29, 1945). The title is Flye's; the text is Agee's manuscript version.

[HAPPY THE HUNTSMAN]

1. This poem is written on the same page as "On the Word Kingdom" and "[Creep, walk, trot, sprint]." See also note 1 of "On the Word Asleep."

[CREEP, WALK, TROT, SPRINT]

1. This poem is written on the same page as "On the Word Kingdom" and "[Happy the huntsman]." See also note 1 of "On the Word Asleep."

[THE MOON ONCE LIVED]

1. This poem is written on the same page as "[A hungry man]." See also note 1 of "On the Word Asleep."

[A HUNGRY MAN]

1. This poem is written on the same page as "[The moon once lived]." See also note 1 of "On the Word Asleep."

[WHEN THE OGRE CAME HOME]

1. See note 1 of "On the Word Asleep."

"HELP"

1. See note 1 of "On the Word Asleep." This poem is written on the same page as "On the Word Asleep." This argues this its composition is before Father Flye's estimated date of March 29, 1945.

[MY IT]

1. See note 1 of "On the Word Asleep." This poem is written on the same page as the draft of "On the Word Asleep."

[O MY POOR COUNTRY I HAVE SO MUCH HATED]

1. An earlier draft of this sonnet also exists in folder 32.
2. Fitzgerald dates the poem as 1945.

[WE SOLDIERS OF ALL NATIONS]

1. Fitzgerald dates this sonnet 1945; also published by Victor Kramer in the *Texas Quarterly*, XI, Spring 1968, p. 18 as part of "Three Sonnets" and again by Kramer in his edition of *Agee: Selected Literary Documents* (Troy, NY: Whitson Publishing Co., 1996), p. 237.

[NOW ON THE WORLD]

1. Fitzgerald dates this sonnet 1945; also published by Victor Kramer in the *Texas Quarterly*, XI, Spring 1968, p. 18 as part of "Three Sonnets" and the first of two under the subtitle of "November 1945." Kramer again publishes the poem in his edition entitled *Agee: Selected Literary Documents* (Troy, NY: Whitson Publishing Co., 1996), p. 238.

NOVEMBER 1945

1. This sonnet is headed in its upper right hand corner with "James Agee / 172 Bleecker St. / New York, N. Y." Its associated companion sonnet, "[This being so]," has no heading, but likely was typed at the same location and in 1945. Published by Victor Kramer in the *Texas Quarterly*, XI, Spring 1968, p. 18 as part of "Three Sonnets" and the first under the title of "Three Sonnets." Kramer again publishes the poem in his edition entitled *Agee: Selected Literary Documents* (Troy, NY: Whitson Publishing Co., 1996), p. 237–38. Also, "November 1945" is sonnet C8 on the record album "James Agee—A Portrait" (1971). See https://www.discogs.com/James-Agee-A-Portrait/release/11930786.

CHRISTMAS 1945

1. Agee added in pencil at the bottom of the page: "Well, he is also Mary, Joseph, the angels, the shepherds, the Magi, & the beasts—Above all he is Mary & Joseph—whose responsibility it is to protect him."

[THIS BEING SO]

1. See note 1 for "November 1945."
2. By] Bu
3. Also published by Victor Kramer in the *Texas Quarterly*, XI, Spring 1968, p. 19 as part of "Three Sonnets" as the second of two under the subtitle of "November 1945." Kramer again publishes the poem in his edition entitled *Agee: Selected Literary Documents* (Troy, NY: Whitson Publishing Co., 1996), p. 238.

SO YOU WANT TO WRITE? COME ON IN, THE WATER'S FINE.

1. Agee gives the poem the handwritten date of June, 19, 1947. An earlier carbon typescript with the handwritten date of June 18, 1947, does not include the first line of the title noted in the next day's typescript.

DIALOGUES ON A SLEEPLESS NIGHT.

1. Sleepless] Sleepness (There is a "June 18, 1947" carbon of an earlier typescript version that states the title as "Sleepless.")
2. Agee gives the poem the handwritten date of June, 19, 1947.

[JUST THIS: FROM NOW ON, TO GO ON FOOT]

1. bleeds] broods^; (no choice made; and, in left margin) breaks
2. "by God's grace" is marked for deletion after "and"
3. raise] break^ (and) break new water^ (over break); (no choices made)
4. But] Yet^; (no choice made)
5. Fitzgerald provides the date of 1947.

[O I BEGIN TO KNOW]

1. There are three pages of preliminary versions of this sonnet in the same folder.
2. Agee has circled from "of me? In what hell" and extended the line down the page to write "desolation" lightly, an indication that he contemplated using that word, perhaps changing the line to "What then desolation? In what hell shall I burn?" but he does not make that decision clear.
3. Fitzgerald dates the poem 1947.

[IN THE STREET]

1. The typescript version actually has different line breaks than the rolling text of the film provided here; the latter is printed here, as it is the published text, albeit in a different medium. The rolling text (one that moves to the top of the screen and gradually disappears)in the film is an appropriate homage, given Agee's love of silent film, and one also used by George Lucas in "Star Wars" for the same reason. After the screen becomes black for an instant, this other

sentence is added after the poem's conclusion: "The attempt in this / short film is to capture / this image."

A LULLABY

1. This printed version varies only in a few matters of punctuation from the handwritten copy in UTK MS 2730 Box 5, Folder 21, which contains five drafts. Other handwritten drafts are in UTK MS 2730 Box 5, Folder 32 and UTK MS 3824 Box 7, Folder 3; and a typescript draft is in UTK MS 1500 Box 1, Folder 9. This poem appears on the reverse of the leaf that contains the poem "[Nothing. For as it is with us]" in UTK MS 2730 Box 5 Folder 32.

EXIIT DILUCULO [AGEE'S TRANSLATION]

1. Handwritten drafts of the poem are on one page in UTK MS 1998 Box 1, Folder 26. The first two verses are nearly identical. The third verse, however, reads:

Then seeing an Intellectual
Among the pasturage straying,
Cried, "Mister let's be sexual:
The time has come for laying."

2. Fitzgerald provides the dating of the poem.

TWO SONNETS FROM A DREAM

1. See also UTK MS 2730 Box 5, Folder 8, one-page typescript with variants.

VARIATIONS, FREE FANTASY AND FUGUE ON A THEME OF NIGHT AND DAY

1. A manuscript version of the poem, entitled "A Theme and Variations," is in the same folder as the signed typescript. It has several different word choices. A retyped copy pf a previous version is in UTK MS 2730 Box 6, Folder 1. It lacks accent marks and varies somewhat in the indentation of last lines of the verses. It bears an interesting note, perhaps from David McDowell, stating that it is a "Facsimile of a typed carbon from a hand-written MS of Jim's (given me by Rev. J. H. Flye, 9/61, who had the MS)—written sometime before the summer of 1953 (Fr. Flye has a tape recording of Jim saying this poem from memory—according to Fr. F.—made in July 1953, which I have heard—first time, Feb. 1960)." Other copies of this preliminary version are also in UTK MS Box 5, Folder 27.

Undated Poems

LYRIC POEMS

[WHICH I, WHO KNOW BEST]

1. who] not you^; (no choice made)
2. crack] break^; (no choice made)

[FOR NOW NO LEAST REMEMBERING]

1. Three working versions/drafts precede this text on a separate page in the folder.

2. The word "wounded" is here inserted from the penultimate version. In the present text, Agee inserts symbols to indicate that he wishes to use a trochaic foot (which allows for "wounded"), or possibly, as the text is slightly overwritten, a longer antibaccius foot that adds an initial stress to the trochaic foot.

[AND WHERE IN THE TROUBLOUS GROVES]

1. The poem is preceded by an earlier working version of eight lines on the same page. The working version and the complete poem are separated by a line.

2. troublous groves] (is followed by "or toiléd groves" in the same line with no indication of Agee's final choice).

3. rusty] ("rusky" is given in the right margin as an alternative, with no choice made.)

4. The] ("The" is in parentheses in the original)

5. dim] (Other possibilities written in the right margin are "dimmed" and "blind" with no choice made.

6. See also UTK MS 3824 Box 6, Folder 36 for a partial draft.

[AS WOMEN ONCE FROM CHILDBED]

1. may be] maybe

[BOWLED OVER BLADE SHADE]

1. quiet] mild^; (no choice made)

2. After this point in the poem, Agee poses a series of questions (mainly "Where?") that he wishes to address. The lines that follow omit the questions and their various working versions of responses to record only the "finished" lines. The poem is very likely a work in progress, but interesting enough to warrant inclusion.

3. Agee writes "[earth-magnificat]" to the right of this line. "Magnificat" is Latin for "[My soul] magnifies [the Lord]") and is a canticle, also known as the Song of Mary or the Canticle of Mary.

[DOWN BY THE SWAMP]

1. The poem is unfinished. Agee records only part of the first line of the next verse: "But the song she sings as she works her . . . ."

[NO ROOM: HARD WEATHER]

1. See also UTK MS 2730 box 7, folder 23 (photocopy) and *CP*, pp. 139–40.

[PEACE, PEACE, POOR NIGHTINGALE]

1. sullen] stubborn^; (no choice made)

2. patient] stolid^; (no choice made)

3. Other earlier versions of the poem are on a separate white manuscript page. An earlier version bore the title "Silence, my nightingale." This final version is on pink paper. See also note 1 of the related poem from the same folder "[The season wakes our maidens]".

[THESE WERE KIND PEOPLE AND THEY LOVED TO LOVE]

1. There is an encircled "2" written in pencil at the upper right hand corner of the typescript.

2. eachother] (is deemed correct since Agee repeats this joining in the next stanza.)

3. separate] seperate

4. The spacing between the typed lines is irregular after this point, perhaps to fit the poem on one page.

5. See also UTK MS 1500 Box 1, Folder 12 (draft). This draft has a different opening verse that Agee circumscribes with a box; its elements are incorporated in different places in the final text. The draft verse reads:

> Let's play the records of our courting days,
> Study old programs of abandoned plays,
> Drive in those stars and seasons where we lusted
> And just to each other our nudities entrusted:
> See does the lightning ever strike us twice
> Or must we ever leisure in this ice.

[THOSE UNTOUCHED EYES WHICH JUST BEGIN]

1. Nor yet know how] Far less can reach^; (no choice made)

2. An earlier draft accompanies the version printed. Only the last verse differs significantly. It reads:

> Our eyes, our hands, our bodies,
>   Have long nights, and short days.
> Let them be well used while they may.
>   For nothing, nothing stays.

[UNEASILY, EXTOL THE HOUSES AT MORNING]

1. "indifferent. periwincle. taste. torment. task." are words written by Agee at the head of the poem. The poem appears on the same page as "[Walking is putting one foot forward]." The spacing is Agee's.

2. This line is the result of several other previous tries; there is also draft of the poem in the same folder.

[WALKING IS PUTTING ONE FOOT FORWARD]

1. This poem appears close on the same page under "[Uneasily, Extol, the houses at morning]."

[RANDOM STRENGTHS ARRANGED US HERE]

1. There is a great deal of the working out of the poem on this page. The last two verses are one end result of its evolution on the left side of the sheet; the first verse is written and evolves separately on the right side and given a bracket pointing toward the beginning of the poem. That indication has determined its present placement.

[RAIN UNLICENSED OF THE COURT]

1. See also UTK MS 2730 Box 5 Folder 32 (draft).

[TEN YEARS AGO, WHEN I WAS FULL OF HOPE]

1. lost] dead^; (no choice made)

2. The final period is crossed out by Agee, but reinserted by the editors. All previous verses end with a period. A slightly different version of the final verse is in the same folder.

[ONE FAVOR IF YOU WILL]

1. us] her^; (no choice made)

[MARX, I AGREE.]

1. A preliminary draft of the poem is located in UTK MS 1500 Box 1, Folder 15. The draft has an additional two lines at the end of the poem:

Between these stresses taken so apart;
How fail to melt and only be the air.

[CAN YOU WRITE SILLY]

1. Above the poem is an apparently unrelated line: "The bull, bunches his back and rides the heifer like a bee a flower." A variant of the line is used in another poem. In that unrelated line: rides] brides^; (no choice made).

2. See also UTK MS 2730 Box 6, Folder 16 (photocopy).

[SOMEWHAT LESS INDISCRIMINATELY]

1. This poem is on the same handwritten page as "[Father, mother]."

2. See also UTK MS 3824 Box 6, Folder 35 (draft).

[FATHER, MOTHER]

1. This poem is on the same handwritten page as "[Somewhat less indiscriminately]."

[IDEAS, CRIPPLINGS, QUALIFY THE SUN]

1. glows] rides^; (no choice made)

2. After its last line the poem goes on with a fairly long list of words, but no further lines. This list has been omitted. These words may or may not be building blocks with which Agee hopes to expand the present poem.

[ROOTED IN PREHISTORY]

1. The poem is preceded by two draft versions on the same handwritten page. Likewise on that page is the poem "[I am speaking of a poet]."

[FIRE FLARED]

1. The poem is preceded by a nearly identical first draft and on the same handwritten half-page as "[O if you Father are]."

[CHARM OF COLD THE WATER REACH]

1. To the right of this line and slightly above it is written the word "enchants" on the hand-written half sheet with no indication of its possible use or placement.

[YOUNG YET ON YOUR DAY]

1. See *CP*, p. 151 for a variant text printed by Fitzgerald entitled "You Green in the Young Day."

[IT IS BEST NOT TO KILL WITH MERCY]

1. crueler] crueller

2. The poem appears on the same handwritten page as "[Tell me must goodness wait.]"

3. See also UTK MS 1599 Box 1, Folder 11 (draft).

[HOW ON THE BARE BRAIN]

1. The handwritten number "18" appears in the top left corner of the page with a line above and below it.

[WE HAVE COME A LONG, LONG WAY]

1. November] november

2. Everywhere] every where

3. Under the typescript of the poem, Agee writes in pencil: "tears are the touchers"; no indication of possible inclusion.

[WE HAVE COME A LONG, LONG WAY (VARIANT)]

1. November] november

2. Opposite this line is written in the right margin "Serve hardly to keep themselves warm." Agee does not indicate any placement for this line.

3. The lines "Breathe" and those that follow are in a second column on the same handwritten page.

4. A preliminary draft of the poem is located in UTK MS 1500 Box 1, Folder 12.

[MAKE HASTE IF YOU WILL HELP]

1. a] (is written over the indistinct former word ["to"?])

2. The poem is on the same handwritten sheet as "[I watched her from her easy bed]."

[THE ROOTLESS WINDS FLOWER WIDE]

1. The word "*To*" appears at the top left of the page; it has no name after it.

[YET BEING NOW TURNED]

1. The word is overwritten and somewhat unclear, but context reasonably argues for this transcription.

2. The poem appears on the same side of a folder half-page as "[When your feet have run]." The other half of the page contains "[God, God, there is not largeness in the air]" and a draft of "[Seriously, if that's your vanity]."

[OUT OF WHAT PARTS WE DO NOT KNOW]

1. This poem is preceded by a partial draft and appears on the same handwritten sheet as "[Things went queer along a shoal]."

[GRATEFUL FOR THIS AT LEAST]

1. The following lines precede this poem:

As one bit of tallow burns away and is not the same.

Thank God so many faults are on me so young, so many, more age could not bring
more. So if I live there through, there may be hope.

These lines are followed by three draft lines that Agee crosses out.

2. Opposite this line in the right margin, Agee writes "I am privileged," with no indication of placement.

3. Opposite this line in the right margin, Agee writes "all my brain be sucked away." He gives no indication of placement.

[NOW THE WRONGED MILLIONS REARRANGE]

1. The poem is preceded by two draft versions on a different page. This poem appears above a draft of "In Heavy Mind" on the same handwritten page.

[HELD INSTANT STILL, WHOLE YEAR'S LUNGS BURST FULL]

1. This line is an insertion and replacement indicated by Agee.

2. The poem is preceded by a draft version and the final version has further editing by the author.

[AND AS HE WAS DREAMING]

1. The handwritten poem is preceded by a draft of two lines later incorporated into the poem. It is on the same page as a draft of the first verse of "[Jesus make it just so good]" and also the short, incomplete poem "[The little mammah is deaf as a post]" which is not recorded in this volume.

[WALK UP THE SIDE OF THE WORLD]

1. This title is the first line of the draft of the first verse which precedes the final version given here.

2. This two-line verse was originally written on one line but separated by a backslash indicating the start of a new line. The editors decided to echo that separation.

FIGHT-TALK, FOR A YOUNG ATHLETE

1. This poem is on the same handwritten page as "[Smell us up systematically]." See also the variant below from UTK MS 1500 Box 1. Folder 12:

When your busy feet have run
Seventy laps around the sun
(Granted no harm along the way)
You'll be ready to call it a day.

And when you flop down, breathing hard
And breathe your last, your one reward
Will be remembrance of the race
While cool breezes quiet your face.

Calm: your team will never lack
Runners on that crowded track:
Strict trainers for that curious game
Where all the records are the same.

This variant appears on the same side of a folder half-page as "[Yet being now turned]." The other half of the page contains "[God, God, there is not largeness in the air]" and a draft of "[Seriously, if that's your vanity]." See also *JAR*, p. 245.

SATIRIC AND HUMOROUS POEMS

SONG FOR THE OPPOSITION

1. (*Maestoso:*)] (Maestoso:]

2. See also the shorter poem "[Sweet anodyne]" which comprises these first two verses.

3. See also UTK MS 1500 Box 1, Folder 11 (draft).

[WHEN, AT LAST, WITH ALL YOUR STRENGTH]

1. Agee heads the page by writing: "As water comes near the lip of a waterfall, it gathers momentum, smooths, shines, and bends. It is freedom from behind. Is it also drawn forward by the water just ahead of it? Or only by the slope? Or also by the empty drop?" Four other revisions of the poem precede this final text on the same page.

MISCELLANY

[#1. FROWNING, THE FOETUS FLOATS IN ALCOHOL]

1. Appalachian] appalachian

2. Two poems come under this heading. The first, this poem, is at the top of one leaf of paper. Under it is another entitled "[The yellow crocks stood all around]." The present work exists in an earlier draft in the same folder.

[#2. THE YELLOW CROCKS STOOD ALL AROUND]

1. This poem is the second under the heading *MISCELLANY*. It appears under "[Frowning, the foetus floats in alcohol]."

[#3. SHE TURNED THE BROAD HEM OF THE SHEET]

1. This poem is the third and last included under the heading *MISCELLANY*. It echoes some of the imagery used in "[The yellow crocks stood all around]" in the same folder, but is different enough to warrant its inclusion.

[BRIGHTNESS FALLS FROM THE AIR]

1. his] ("clean" is written in the left margin and attached by a line to "his" indicating its possible use as an alternative; no choice is made.)

2. little eyes of rifles] ("condensed irises of rifles" in written at a 45-degree angle in the left margin; no choice is made.)

[ISCARIOT, TAKE A BACK SEAT, PLEASE]

1. On the same handwritten page as "[O smooth young creatures still of the sexual age]."

A GARLAND OF DAINTY DEVICES

1. With blood on her . . . her toes] (The line is garbled in the manuscript. Agee interlinearly inserts "[unreadable] in her" after "on her" and before "bouche" and inadvertently [?] crosses out the final "on" of "on her toes" when he deletes "with blood on" before "her toes.")

2. See also UTK MS 3824 Box 7, Folder 1, a near duplicate of the present text.

[HEAR THE TIRED ANNOUNCER BLEAT]

1. See also UTK MS 2730 Box 6, Folder 15 (photocopy).

[IF, GASPING BUT VICTORIOUS]

1. Advises] Cries out to^; (and under it is "Sings out to"; no choices made)

2. Two other versions of the final line are written below this one with no choice made: "The [*sic.* That] climbing trees can make a bird. / That climbing one makes you a bird."

3. of] of of

[DEPILATORIES GARTER BELTS AND LOTIONS]

1. This poem is on the same manuscript page as "[Sweet anodyne]" and "[What fool would dare]."

[WHAT FOOL WOULD DARE]

1. This poem is on the same manuscript page as "[Depilatories garter belts and lotions]" and "[Sweet anodyne]". A variant of the end of the poem appears in UTK MS 2730 Box 7, Folder 23 (typescript photocopy). It reads:

Try not to care
What filthy air
Keeps the population choked:
Stick by the rules.

[MAJOR DOUGLAS]

1. This poem appears on the same manuscript page as "[Muzzy wuvs her Buzzy]."

DIALOG

1. A near final draft of the second verse appears before the one included. It is different enough to quote in full:

Tell it to Major Douglas and the Rector;
They can restore your appetite for tea.
Tell it to Sigmund, the great dream-collector;
He'll fix you up, for a sufficient fee.
Talk out your troubled heart in any sector,
Only, my sad young friend, don't talk to me:
Unless you find yourself willing to take
Some drastic steps to cure your bellyache.

[AH'S JES' A BELIEVING CHAMELEON]

1. This poem appears on the same handwritten page as "[And by the bye my pious friends of the reviewing trade]" and the three-verse version of "[Forsythe and hindsight]" which has been given its two-verse title rather than using its first line.

[JITTER JITTER LEETLE EARTH]

1. This poem appears on the same handwritten page as "[Wander, wander, universe].

[YOUR PAPA BLEEDS THE LITTLE BOYS]

1. This poem appears on the same handwritten page as "[Your work, the way this world is run]," "[Honestly, the way things are]," and "[Those kinds of loving which the lord]."

[TWITCH OFF THE TUNE OF NIGHT]

1. On the right side of this handwritten page, after this line is written "I could not come and fail to speak my mind." There is no indication if, or where, it was to be incorporated in the poem.

[HOLD ON A SECOND, PLEASE]

1. phony] phoney

2. See also *JAR*, pp. 231–33 (the present text corrects the version in *JAR*) and UTK MS 3824 Box 6, Folder 35 and 36 (partial drafts).

[THIS IS THE STORY OF THREE MEN ON THE EARTH]

1. The poem is a composite. Agee's final version leaves the last verse unfinished (see it below); instead its previous third verse is used as the poem's concluding verse. The incomplete final verse reads:

> However, know the truth of me, the worst:
> Even now I'd rather live half-way than die:
> Puke, if I must, rather than merely burst:
> Walk on the earth though envying the sky:
> Play second fiddle though I feel the first
> Aching my fingers; and, though I don't know why,
> Speak through

The poem and its drafts occupy three manuscript pages, one of which is mostly narrative.

2. This final line is preceded by a draft version.

[O MINE EYES HAVE SEEN THE TROUBLE]

1. wheat] (Agee crosses out the typed word "street" and pencils in "wheat.")

[JOSIE LOVES THE LITTLE THINGS]

1. Next to these two lines, Agee writes in the right margin "Now I know why Mah-mah / Told me to be true." He gives no indication of inclusion.

A BILL FOR STERILIZATION OF THE MUSES.

1. The poem is preceded by a partial draft version.

2. Next to this line in the right margin, Agee writes: "a truce for every trouble." No choice is indicated.

3. Next to this line in the right margin, Agee writes: "bring in that stubble." No choice is indicated.

[FELLOWS, THERE'S NO SOAP PLAYING IT LIKE THAT]

1. A shorter draft version precedes the present text. See it in *JAR*, pp. 245–46.

[THINGS WENT QUEER ALONG A SHOAL]

1. sway] (Agee follow this word with other choices: "stay, stray, . . .". No final choice was made.)

2. This poem is preceded by a crossed out draft and appears on the same handwritten sheet as "[Out of what parts we do not know]."

[WHOOP AWAY]

1. The poem is on the same page as "[Though the heart boils to blow the head]" and is preceded by two drafts. One variant reads:

Though the heart boils to blow the head
Nobody hears? and nothing else?
Don't fret your tongue: the earth is fair:
The earth will put you on the air.

At the top of the page, Agee writes "Personals . . . . Obits."

[ALL, ALL OF A PIECE THROUGHOUT]

1. anew] a new

[ROVER ALL BUT HAD HIS THUMB UPON THE MISSING LETTER]

1. A line—"The rocks slid round its axle"—follows this verse on the handwritten page, but is here omitted. It seems to be the beginning of another, yet unwritten verse. In the draft, "Rover" is replaced by "Missy."

[RUN AWAY AND DON'T COME BACK]

1. little] lettle
2. the]tge
3. prophets'] proghets'
4. On the reverse of this sheet, Agee has typed the poem "[Who will help them to understand]."

[SMELL US UP SYSTEMATICALLY]

1. This poem is on the same handwritten page as "*Fight-talk, for a young athlete.*"

[DEPILATORIES RUBBER BELTS AND LOTIONS]

1. This line is written much more lightly and is approximately one-third the size of all of the previous lines.

SPIRITUAL AND RELIGIOUS POEMS

[SOME SENSE IS VERY PLAIN]

1. The verse divisions of this prose poem-meditation are indicated in the manuscript by a line drawn across the page.

[WHEN I WAS SMALL DELIGHT AND FEAR]

1. See also *CP*, pp. 138–39 (but it omits the final verse); UTK MS 3824 Box 6, Folder 35 (two drafts of last verse); and *JAR*, p. 222 (draft of last verse).

[VIRGIN, FORGIVE]

1. Three other versions of the poem are present on the same manuscript page. The present version occupies the lower right quadrant of the page.

[AND MAY GOD HOLD YOUR HUMBLE AND TRUE SOUL]

1. On the same page beneath this poem is Agee's "[O true though little poets]."

[LORD ROUST ME OUT]

1. See note 1 of "[There's no kind of time when Death ain't a beating some door.]" A draft of the present poem appears above it on the manuscript page.
2. See also UTK MS 2730 Box 6, Folder 16 (photocopy).

[HEAD LOW, AND BREAK MY KNEE]

1. See note 1 of "[There's no kind of time when Death ain't a beating some door.]"
2. See also UTK MS 2730 Box 6, Folder 16 (photocopy).

[O IF YOU FATHER ARE]

1. The poem is on the same handwritten half-page as "[Fire breathed]."

[TELL ME MUST GOODNESS WAIT]

1. A possible alternative to the last two lines of this verse is written in the right margin by Agee: "Make a strong light of it / And swing it on the sky."
2. The poem appears on the same handwritten page as "[It is best not to kill these things with mercy.]"
3. See also UTK MS 1599 Box 1, Folder 11 (draft).

[O IF BENEATH THIS WARD OF NIGHT]

1. Under the poem, Agee slightly rewrites the first two lines of the poem as "O if beneath this blazing night / There's any other creature brings"; he gives no indication for the use of these lines.
2. Another version of the last three lines exists on a page of numerous drafts in the same folder. Those lines read:

Whatever change attends this light
Put by, my kin, put by, be glad:
We're very near to God tonight.

[TENANT THIS SEASON OF UNEASY DARKNESS]

1. A different handwritten page with two drafts of the poem precedes this final version. See these drafts in *JAR*, pp. 243–44.

[GOD, GOD, THERE IS NOT LARGENESS IN THE AIR]

1. The word is difficult to make out. Only the "ings" is clear, not the three or four letters preceding it, but it seems to begin with an undotted "i," hence its rendering as "idlings."

2. A somewhat smaller space than that used for beginning a new verse is left between this line and the next; the space is here eliminated. Agee's irregular spacing between lines in his handwritten poetry is not uncommon.

3. The poem appears on the same side of a folder half-page as a draft of "[Seriously, if that's your vanity]." The other half of the page contains "[Yet being now turned]" and "[When your busy feet have run]."

[SO FULL IN FAITH]

1. Written on the same page and under a draft of "[Broil in the frowsy clover crowds of thirst]."

[NOW INWARD FROM THE SUN]

1. This final verse is on the second page under drafts of the preceding verses. The order of the pages is unknown. Also, there is a separate page of drafts in the same folder.

MAKER OF NOTHING MADE OF ALL THINGS MADE MAKER

1. The poem is related to "[Lord on your healthful earth this little way]" and to "[Great Lord whose lovely world this little way]."

2. See also UTK MS 2730 Box 5, Folder 32 for a partial poem of same title.

[LORD ON YOUR HEALTHFUL EARTH THIS LITTLE WAY]

1. The poem is related to "Maker of nothing made of all things made maker"—note the last line is the same as the previous poem's title—and to "[Great Lord whose lovely world this little way]."

[GREAT LORD WHOSE LOVELY WORLD THIS LITTLE WAY]

1. Next to this line in the left margin, Agee writes: "I am a servant speaking to servants" and uses a version of the line to end the poem.

2. The poem is related to "Maker of nothing made of all things made maker" and to "[Lord on your healthful earth this little way]."

[LORD GOD THE EYES OF ANIMALS]

1. The poem is preceded by drafts. Agee marks two additional lines at the end for deletion. They are:

Are we indeed the senseless dance
Of flotsam on a shoreless stream?

[THERE IS NO LONGER SINGING HERE]

1. with] at^; (no choice made)

2. With] with

3. modest] pious^; (no choice made)

4. No greater, and much fruitless grief] As small, and fruitless grief unborn.^; (no choice made)

NATURE POETRY

[EARLIEST IN THE CHARY SPRING]

1. "Ponders" is an indicated replacement for "Studies." Under "Ponder," Agee writes other choices: "meditates" and "and shall publish."

(GOD OF SUMMER)

1. Agee encloses the title in parentheses. To the right of the title he inscribes "S. Jackson." The author Shirley Jackson (1916–1965), perhaps most famous for her 1948 short story "The Lottery" and her fiction, did write poetry, but whether this is her poem, one that she inspired Agee to write, or simply the name of an unknown friend or person, has not been determined.

[HE CAN'T STAND IT FOREVER]

1. can't] cant (written in the first line and thus likewise in the attributed title)

[I'VE GOT THEM ALL SET]

1. This second poem on "fishing" appears directly under the poem "[He can't stand it forever]" on the same manuscript page.

[NOW SPRINGTIME WAKES OUR MAIDENS]

1. The original first verse reads:

Now the young girl awakens
    To new ideas of joy;
The same thing is in season
    For the boy.

2. fullest] fiercest^; (no choice made)

3. full] (is written to the right side of lines 1 and 3 of this verse).

4. sings of it] declares it^; (no choice is made)

5. afire] (is written close to the right side of "burning"; no choice made, but an alternative).

6. An alternate verse, with additional suggestions for lines 1 and 3 is written to the right of this verse.

7. There is an alternate verse written to the right of this verse. The editors chose the original. The other verse is:

Your promise crowns my heart
    In its born fate.
Your scorn shall that same heart
    Annihilate.

8. Famished by] Fainting with^; need for] thirst for^; (no choices made. There are also three more pages of Agee trying out different lines, words, and verses in folder 32).

[VOIDED—THE SKY]

1. light] light: (the penultimate version omits the colon)

2. Four pages of working drafts precede this poem.

[NOW ON THE WATER FOREHEAD IS]

1. Sun] sun

2. This poem is on the same handwritten page as a variant of "[Heaven shuts]"; partial draft versions of this poem are located in UTK MS 1500 Box 1, Folder 11.

3. See also UTK MS 3824 Box 7, Folder 1; UTK MS 1500 Box 1, Folder 11; and UTK MS 2730 Box 5, Folder 32 (photocopy).

[HEAVEN SHUTS]

1. This poem is on the same handwritten page as "[Now on the water forehead is]." A variant of it is printed in *CP*, p. 61. See also "Soft heaven shuts: at length the latest" in this volume under Lyrics.

[SHELVED, UNDER THEIR STONE LABELS]

1. The first two lines of the poem were originally inscribed on one line by Agee.

[LISTS, LIKE A DECK, OUR CONTINENT]

1. Russia] russia

2. Multiple handwritten drafts exist on the same page as Agee keeps crafting the poem. The drafts are preceded by the statement "Scored for radio, television, screen, stage, platform, orchestra, voice and print: us[e] as indicated or as seems necessary." The poem is on the same handwritten sheet as "[The world is rotted almost to the heart]."

[BROIL IN THE FROWSY CLOVER CROWDS OF THIRST]

1. sleep] (Agee crosses out "sweep" in pencil and substitutes "sleep")

2. marvelous] marvellous

3. A draft of the handwritten poem in UTK MS 1500 Box 1, Folder 12 (draft; two pages) is preceded by partial and full drafts. One page of the draft has an altered second verse that corresponds more closely to the typescript. This draft version of the poem is on a different page; it is written above the possibly incomplete poem "[So full in faith]." The poem and its drafts are on the same handwritten page as "[Hunched hung upon his mildeyed and wild sighing bride]." The typescript has slight alterations in pencil.

TRANSFIGURATION

1. Occasionally in this poem, Agee did not hit the key of his manual typewriter firmly enough to leave an impression on the paper. These omissions have silently been added. Likewise, obvious mis-strokes, such as "z" for "a" and multiple hyphens for pauses / dashes (more than two) are also corrected without mention.

2. into] ijto

3. "Strange,"] "Strange",

4. The] "The

5. A case could both be made for the poem concluding with this line or for the poem as a possibly unfinished work.

[O DOLPHIN EARTH]

1. The title is taken from the phrase bracketed by Agee (likely for deletion, if he found a more suitable title) and located to the right of the first crossed out line of the poem.
2. grieving] angry^; (no choice made)
3. locomotive] cold black^; (and positioned to the right; no choice made; inserted by the editors)
4. To the right of this line, Agee writes: "Glosses on the small-designéd earth." He gives no indication of choice.
5. "Crinkling" is written to the right of the line and linked to "wrinkling" as an alternative; no choice is indicated.
6. Line break inserted by editors.
7. The preceding three lines are divided by the editors from what is essentially one line with numerous insertions by Agee.
8. To the right of this line, Agee writes "hierarchic streams" with no indication of insertion.
9. In two lines bracketed for deletion, Agee refers to "Matanuska"; Matanuska Glacier is the most popular roadside attraction between Anchorage and Glennallen, Alaska.

[SPACE IS SALTED THIN AND WE ARE SMALL]

1. The poem is preceded and followed by prose passages; the poem itself is preceded by a draft of part of the first two lines.
2. "tranced" is written in the left margin and Agee indicates with a circle and line that it is likely to be substituted for "trained," a choice the editors have followed.
3. Agee left a short line indicating a future word to be inserted. The editors have chosen "eyes."

[UP TIME CONVULSION FLOWERED US]

1. After this line, Agee records lines which he uses later in the poem.
2. The editors have reinserted the period that Agee deleted with a small "x." The poem clearly ends with this line, since the author draws a line across the page after it, one of Agee's indicators of an end to a work.

MARRYING DANCE.

1. Drafts of this poem are on the reverse of this handwritten sheet. The title is inscribed to the right of the body of the poem. The poem is related to and on the same page as "[Hood your head in mother's hood]."

A three-line draft of the final verse is under the first verse. It reads: "The Queen tomorrow is the shade / Of love that of this grove is laid / Shall wind in wreathes their shining heads." Agee rewrites the three lines as four in the right margin.

[CLEAN OUT OF SKY]

1. world] earth^; (no choice made)
2. Agee originally wrote "upon" but then bracketed the first two letters for deletion.
3. The poem is preceded by working drafts.

[HUNCHED SLUNG ABOVE HIS GUILELESS EYED MILD SIGHING BRIDE]

1. The poem is preceded by a draft of the first verse, has ideas for the later verses after the first verse, and multiple attempts following the poem of working out other concepts and lines.

Also, Agee repeats a variant of the final line of this first verse, evidently written first in line with the other verses, but changes it and inserts the present text to complete the fourth line of the poem. The unused variant is "As trembling bees ride yielding flowers."

2. sweep] sleep^ (no choice made)

3. marvelous] marvelous

4. See also UTK MS 1500 Box 1, Folder 11 and 12 (drafts) and *JAR*, p. 221 (draft of first verse). The draft poem in Folder 12 is preceded by partial and full drafts. It is on the same handwritten page as "[Broil in the frowsy clover crowds of thirst]." A typescript variant of the first verse is in UTK MS 3824 Box 7, Folder 2. It reads:

Hunched hung upon his mild eyed and wild sighing bride
Who brunts the bull with stiff four posted stride
Drives in the cringing warmth that drinks him of his power
The bull, back crackarched: bee trembling rides a flower.

[I THINK THAT IN THEIR HONEY CELLS]

1. To the right of this line, Agee writes: "shelved in the earth in yards, stone labels them / for memory as short as theirs." No choice is made. A version of the first line is used in the draft of a different partial poem.

2. A series of words and a draft of the first three lines precedes the poem. This poem is on the same handwritten page as "[Where the dolphin leisurely bowling]."

[WHERE THE DOLPHIN LEISURELY BOWLING]

1. The spacing is Agee's. This poem is on the same page as "[I think that in their honey cells]."

[STARRED FROM THE SKY]

1. The poem is preceded by a draft version on the same handwritten page.

[FOR NOW OF THE LIGHT OF DAY THE UTMOST REMEMBRANCE]

1. the] that^; (no choice made)

2. Written to the right of this line is: "which turned like a lion"

3. To the right of this line, Agee writes two lines with no indication of inclusion. They are:

The marching shadows are all met:
  Shade grows, shade grows:

BARNYARD ROLLED BEFORE THE SUN AND FELL AGAIN.

1. rolls] bowls^; (or perhaps "howls"; no choice made)

2. quiet] (The original word "dark" is crossed out; "quiet" is written over it and "down" is written under it. The editors chose "quiet.")

3. crowded] crowding^; (no choice made)
4. The poem is preceded by crossed-out drafts of a different poem.

POLITICAL POEMS

ALLEGIANCE DREAM

1. The poem is appended to a story of the same name in the same folder.
2. Sun] sun
3. The word is overwritten and unclear. The choice of "Spreads" is supported from the context.

[MY UNCLE SAMMY SENT ME]

1. This poem was part of an automatic writing exercise. See *JAR*, pp. 202–5.

[THEY SIT ON INNER TUBES]

1. The poem may be incomplete.

[LIKE PREGNANT GIRLS ADMIRING]

1. Next to this line, in the right margin, Agee writes "Pressing with both hands on her belly." No inclusion is indicated.

2. At the bottom of this verse, in the right margin, Agee writes "*prophetic*." This poem appears on the same handwritten page as "[Sun our father]."

[ALL YOUR WORK, THE WAY THIS WORLD]

1. On the reverse of this handwritten page are several drafts of this poem. In the same folder see also the following variant:

Your work, the way this world is run,
Only drags you to your graves:
And dying, all you hand them down
Is chains that make your children slaves.

Yes, these irons become you bad.
They're pretty badly out of place.
Find the man that hung them there
For gain and break them on his face.

This variant appears on the same handwritten page as "[Honestly, the way things are]," "[Those kinds of loving which the lord]," and "[Your papa bleeds the little boys]."

[HONESTLY, THE WAY THINGS ARE]

1. This poem appears on the same handwritten page as "[Your work, the way this world is run]," "[Those kinds of loving which the lord]," and "[Your papa bleeds the little boys]."

[THOSE KINDS OF LOVING WHICH THE LORD]

1. This poem appears on the same handwritten page as "[Your work, the way this world is run]," "[Honestly, the way things are]"—which its last line echoes—and "[Your papa bleeds the little boys]."

[THERE ARE GENTLEMEN IN POLITICS TODAY]

1. The poem is preceded by a partial draft that is crossed out.

[TWENTIETH CENTURY, HONEST AND MERCILESS EAR]

1. marvelous] marvellous

2. To the right of this line, Agee writes "like pegged lobsters in a warm bowl" but gives no indication of inclusion.

3. To the right of this line, Agee writes "shuddering tommy guns / write their spaced lines of / murder—" but gives no indication of inclusion.

4. To the right of this line, Agee writes "approaches / spear all directions like / exploded thorns" but gives no indication of inclusion.

5. To the right of this line, Agee writes "public diary" but gives no indication of inclusion.

6. Boswell Sisters] boswell sisters

7. This poem begins below a handwritten draft of its last two verses.

[FRAGMENTS OF PROLETARIAN VERSE]

1. Both fragments are on the same page along with their drafts.

[IT IS NOT RIGHT THAT YOU SHOULD CRY]

1. To the right of the page, Agee writes "God's on the side of the poor." No indication of inclusion.

2. The poem is preceded by five lines that are a draft.

PHILOSOPHICAL POEMS

[OF ALL THOSE PROCEDURES OF THE EARTH]

1. leisures] liesures

2. The next line—"He that would live:"— is omitted by the editors. It seems to have been replaced by Agee with the much longer, final line.

[OUR MORNING GROWS OVER US]

1. grows] spreads^; (no choice is made.)

[THERE'S NO KIND OF TIME WHEN DEATH AIN'T A BEATING SOME DOOR]

1. This poem is on the same page as "[Lord roust me out]" and "[Head low, and break my knee.]" The same verse is on another page in the same folder.

2. See also UTK MS 2730 Box 6, Folder 16 (photocopy).

A LETTER

1. See also UTK MS 2730 Box 6, Folder 16 (photocopy).

[POOR CHILD]

1. There are two pages of a preliminary draft for this poem and another page of mainly quatrains, both of which are unfinished. The draft begins differently ("If in that silence where

still for a little while"), but has many of the same images and concepts. It ends before the ideas expressed in the last five verses of the poem proper. The draft reads:

If in that silence where still for a little while
You dwell untroubled you are yet so far awakened
That, as between the phrases of a dream,
Blood can impinge its thought,

Do not drink into yourself, if you can help,
Any anger against the two if us who lie here in sorrow,
Wishing you well, waiting your coming, wondering,
That in such a time we have dared to continue man:

But know of us that we know, know very well
The weight which willfully we have transferred upon you
And what by our will you soon must desperately enter:

It may be child, that before you are grown,
All that our kind has in all past time designed and desired
Shall have been dissolved upon the sky, leaving the universe as immaculate
As if man had never been.

Very likely, before you have acquired
What little solace man's little wisdom can bring,
Cruelties will have forced themselves against your eyes
Which no man can behold, and bear to live.

And certainly, before you are old,
You will know as well as we do why
No time could ever be so cruel
But that it should require of all who hold life, and each other dear,

2. men have] man has^; (no choice made)
3. press into] pierce into^ (and also) into] upon^; (no choice made)
4. An alternate line is written in the left margin: "Horror will hammer on your eyes."
5. seldom] scarcely^; scarcely] hardly^ (Agee gives two alternatives; no choices made)
6. And] But^; (no choice made)
7. could] has^; (no choice made)
8. take] hold^; (no choice made)

[HOOD YOUR HEAD IN MOTHER'S HOOD]

1. feet] feat
2. This poem is related to and written under "Marrying dance."
3. See UTK MS 3824 Box 7, Folder 4 for variant drafts. See also UTK MS 3824 Box 4, Folder 4 for the following variant.

Humble to your mother's hood,
The elegant ribbons once she wore

Favor you, no manner of good
Marrying girl can want for more.

Take your ease in mother's chair
Plant your feet where her tracks are,
And study not to cry, to cry
Or you'll not quit before you die.

A previous version precedes the one above; it is in the upper left hand portion of the page. The previous version has a chorus after each verse of "Hood on head and band on hair / One for duty, one for care." See also UTK MS 2730 Box 6, Folder 16 (photocopy).

[SPEAKING ONLY GENERALLY]

1. The word "premium" is written in the right margin across from this line with no indication of inclusion.
2. cruelest] cruellest

[THE WORLD IS ROTTED ALMOST TO THE HEART]

1. This poem appears on the same handwritten page above "[Lists, like a deck, our continent]."

[U[P] IN THE TREASURIES OF AMBER TIME]

1. inclusions in quartz:] closured quartz inclusion:^; (no choice made)
2. The poem appears on the same handwritten page as one of the texts of "[Now on the water forehead is]."

[WHAT IS HIS TROUBLE?]

1. Lighter written notes, apparently for a different work, occur in pencil and occupy a good portion of the same manuscript page.

THE FULLNESS OF TIME

1. Above the title, Agee writes "My night thoughts."

[ONCE I WAS YOUNG AND SWORE LIKE YOU]

1. The verse is preceded and followed by drafts.
2. The verse is followed by two additional lines of a rhymed couplet that is perhaps an unfinished verse. They are:

For its only human nature after all
For the boss to back the boys against the wall

[HOW THOUGH CLOSE WEFT WE EXQUISITELY SIEVE]

1. sieve] seive
2. Both handwritten verses are preceded by numerous drafts.

[IT IS A BRIARY EARTH]

1. The poem is preceded by three crossed-out drafts.

SENSUAL POEMS

[THE SEASON WAKES OUR MAIDENS]

1. This poem is heavily revised over four sheets of paper. The version presented combines the two longest sheets which are tied together by overlap and has been eliminated. Some switching between pages also occurs. See also "[Peace, peace, poor nightingale]" which Agee drafts as perhaps a separate poem from three of the last four verses or may exist as drafts of this one poem. The editors chose to print both.

2. wholest] whollest (and) wholest] fullest bloom (blossom)^; (no choices made)

3. flames] fires^; (no choice made)

4. tenderly] ardently (is written in the right margin as an alternative)

5. to burning] in torment^; (no choice made)

6. the rose of roses,] the roses (sic) of all the roses, (is written in the right margin as an alternative)

7. I so often see.] often I see^; (no choice made)

8. peace and] peaceful^; (no choice made)

9. scorn shall] Disdain (*sic* disdain) must^; (no choice made)

10. while] time^; (no choice made)

11. bitter] sullen^; (no choice made)

12 Looks with new soul to friend] Heart springing turns to friend^; (no choice made)

[SWEET HEART TONIGHT]

1. round] on^; (no choice made)

2. To the right of this line, Agee writes: "Ask the deaf rest . . . ." and "a season changes in you."

3. changes] alters^; (no choice made)

4. To the right of this line, Agee writes: "altering the blood. [space] equinox."

5. A partial draft of this verse precedes it on the page. It reads:

What wave is full that fails at length the shore:
And what, discharged, shall any wave — recede.
and be received

[I WATCHED HER FROM HER EASY BED]

1. The poem is preceded by a prose passage of automatic writing; it and the passage are on the same handwritten sheet as "[Make haste if you will help]."

[O SMOOTH YOUNG CREATURES STILL OF THE SEXUAL AGE]

1. This poem is on the same handwritten page as "[Iscariot, take a back seat, please]."

2. The poem is unfinished. All that is completed is the first line of the next verse: "God help you, all the syrups of Lombardo."

[WANTON YOUTHS THAT NIGHTLY ONCE]

1. A draft of the handwritten poem precedes it and is also on the reverse of the page along with "["As long as thou didst love me"]."

["AS LONG AS THOU DIDST LOVE ME"]

1. This poem is on the reverse of the page containing "[Wanton youths that nightly once]."

ON POETS AND POETRY

[JESUS MAKE IT JUST SO GOOD]

1. Agee place only a single quotation mark at the beginning of the extract from Millay's poem (see explanatory note a).

2. table full] tablefull (The draft version's last line reads: "Table-loads of phoneys?")

3. See also UTK MS 1500 Box 1, Folder 12 (draft) and the draft of first verse in UTK MS 3824 Box 6, Folder 35.

[O TRUE THOUGH LITTLE POETS]

1. This line and the next five (from "Hate falsehoods" to "hatred and scorn") are written in the left margin and their insertion here is indicated by Agee's drawn line. The width of the margin limits the length of the lines and Agee does not indicate line breaks. The editors have inserted those breaks and capitalized the first word of each line.

2. On the same page above this poem is Agee's poem "[And may God hold your humble and true soul]."

[I AM SPEAKING OF A POET]

1. The poem appears on the same handwritten page as "[Rooted in prehistory]."

[NOT TO YOU ONLY WHO IN IDLENESS]

1. O] o

[WHO MAY BE FRIENDS, DETESTED, ENEMIES]

1. The poem is preceded by various drafts. Agee also begins another verse after this final one. It states "Therefore fresh in my beginning / A word"; nothing after the partial second line was completed.

SONNETS

[SUFFER ME NOT, O LORD]

1. See also the version in *JAR*, pp. 215, that is here corrected.

[I AM NOT WELL WITH REASON AND EXILED]

1. The poem is preceded by drafts of the first lines and notes.

DIALECT POEMS

LINES SUGGESTED BY A TENNESSEE SONG

1. Also in UTK MS 3824 Box 6, Folder 35 (draft; five pages).

CASE HISTORY

1. See also UTK MS 3824 Box 7, Folder 1 (draft).

[MUZZY WUVS HER BUZZY]

1. oo] here's oo^; (addition is handwritten; no choice is made)

2. piss.] (the word is bracketed in pencil)

3. suck] kiss^; (no choice made; written in pencil on typescript)

4. The draft of this poem appears on the same manuscript page as "[Major Douglas]." See also UTK MS 1500 Box 1, Folder 11 (draft).

MISCELLANEOUS POEMS

[THE THUNDER'S IRON PINIONS]

1. altering] alterring (or) altorring (This page is written in ink, but a central water stain makes parts difficult to read.)

2. seditions] (The first three [?]; letters are unclear.)

3. Buffs] (The word is written over and unclear.)

4. This line begins the section of the poem written on the reverse of the same leaf that bears the previous lines.

(DEATHSHEAD W. CRADLE) [AND] MOMMY SONG—MOTHERS DAY . . .

1. Next to this line in the right margin Agee writes: "The world turns out the light." No indication of placement is given.

2. Agee uses three commas to end line six in each of these three poems. That feature, the shared eight-line structure and common theme, argue for their presentation together.

3. Above the title of this poem, Agee writes "dim room: tune: suter top hat, starver, rube, cloron [?], girls, etc."

PASTORAL—MOE AND JOE IN DIALOG.

1. and] &

2. The title at the top of the page is separated from the poem and contained in an open-topped box.

3. hovering] hollow^; (no choice made)

4. Colliding] (Co???ining is written to the left; no choice made)

5. Close-kneed by] (Agee appears to wish to delete the original wording of "Mounted with" and replace it with the phrase note that is written in the right margin.)

6. becalmed] ("beguiled" is written to the left of the page; no choice made)

7. As an alternative to this half line, Agee writes in the left margin "That shorten the rank meadow with pursed lips:" in the left margin.

[WHO WILL HELP THEM TO UNDERSTAND]

1. The irregular spacing in the poem is Agee's.

2. and] and and

3. quietly] guietly

4. altar] alter

5. than] then

6. On the obverse of this sheet, Agee has typed "[Run away and don't come back]."

[AGEE'S FRIENDS]

1. The editors provided this title.

2. See also UTK MS 3824 Box 7, Folder 5 (typescript, partial). The typescript omits verse 4 and 5 and records the remaining three verses in a different order, commencing with Evans, and then Bill Furth and Herrimon Maurer.

Appendix 1

[THOMAS DERRY]

1. This poem may be a companion to or different / alternative approach to the poem entitled "John Carter." The poem is handwritten on the reverse of *The Harvard Advocate* stationary, likely dating it in or soon after Agee's time at Harvard (1928–1932). It uses the same verse form as "John Carter." A possible tie-in occurs on page 145 in "John Carter" (see note 14 for that poem) when the narrator states "A princess helps our hero . . . ." Fitzgerald omits this "A princess helps" verse and the partial half verse that follows in his construction of "John Carter."

2. patiently] tediously^; (no choice made)

3. wine] drink^; (no choice made)

4. drinking too much] too much love of^; (no choice made)

5. myself] my self

6. grieving] greiving

7 'You'd] "You'd

8. 'But Mary, why?'] "But Mary, why?"

9. 'You don't mean that,'] "You don't mean that,"

10. 'I] "I

11. he with naught to do.] (written under these words is "and not [with?] he could do.")

12. 'Keep] "Keep

13. and] &

14. dullness] dulness

15. through] thru

16. and] &

17. . . .] . .

18. Single quotation marks replace both double quotation marks for consistency.

19 'Mnnnh-hum,'] "Mnnnh-hum,"

20. work,'] work,"

21. The poem ends midway through the final sheet of paper. While the story clearly is still incomplete, this may be its conclusion with Agee leaving the reader to anticipate what comes next.

Appendix 2

[UNPLACED STANZAS]

1. earth] world^; (no choice made)

2. The final verse beginning "Mistress, I make you" is likely one that is not part of those preceding it. Fitzgerald separates it in *CP* with the space of an extra blank line and the topic also appears different. The verse was not found in the UTK collections.

3. The date is taken from Fitzgerald, *CP*, pp. 121–22.

4. No manuscript could be located.

Index of Poetry by Title

Some poems are indexed by all or part of the first line. First lines rendered as titles by the editors for untitled poems are enclosed in square brackets.